THIERS AND THE FRENCH MONARCHY

ADOLPHE THIERS ABOUT 1848.

THIERS AND THE FRENCH MONARCHY

By JOHN M. S. ALLISON

ARCHON BOOKS
1968

FIRST PUBLISHED 1926
REPRINTED 1968 WITH PERMISSION
CONSTABLE & CO., LTD.
IN AN UNALTERED AND UNABRIDGED EDITION

LIBRARY OF CONGRESS CATALOG CARD NUMBER: 68-21684
PRINTED IN THE UNITED STATES OF AMERICA

TO
M. L M. AND R. S. M.

PREFACE

IN an obscure grave in one of the large cemeteries of Paris rests the body of the man who for sixty-one years played an important part in the affairs of France. Gambetta, Hugo, Zola, and others have been honoured by their country and their ashes have been borne in triumph to the Panthéon, but Thiers was so strong and so daring that even to-day he has many enemies in France—else, why has not he received a similar honour? It is in a humble way to render justice to him and to try to explain to the friends of France the nature of one of the greatest men that France has produced, that this first book has been written. The years 1797–1848 that are covered by this book are only the preparation for the great career and the glory that he achieved in 1870. *Adolphe Thiers and the French Monarchy* will be followed in due time by *Adolphe Thiers and the Second Empire*.

It would be almost impossible to express adequately my gratitude to those who have been of assistance and invaluable service to me. In France I am indebted first of all to the late Émile Boutroux, Director of the *Fondation Thiers*. Only a few months before his lamented death he opened the way for my researches in Paris. To Monsieur Henri Malo, Director of the *Bibliothèque Thiers* at Paris, I owe my deepest thanks. Without his kindly assistance and criticism it would not have been possible to complete this book. I am also indebted to Monsieur Raimbault, Director of the Musée Arbaud at Aix-en-Provence, to the Directors of the Bibliothèque Nationale, the Archives Nationales, the Archives of the Ministry of Foreign Affairs and the Public Record Office, for their courtesy and consideration. To Professors Allen Johnson

PREFACE

and Charles Seymour of Yale University I wish to express my gratitude for their helpful criticism and suggestions. To Mr. Gilbert Troxell of the Yale Library I am indebted for assistance in the matter of proof-reading and correction.

J. M. S. A.

New Haven, Conn., 1925.

CONTENTS

CHAP.		PAGE
	PREFACE	vii
I.	THE GENERATION OF THE 'NINETIES	1
II.	MARSEILLES AND AIX. 1797–1821	4
III.	AT PARIS. 1821–1823	20
IV.	THE RESTORATION AND THE *HISTORY OF THE FRENCH REVOLUTION*	48
V.	THE CRITICAL YEARS. 1824–1829	69
VI.	THE *NATIONAL*. 1830	86
VII.	EXIT CHARLES X. JULY, 1830	103
VIII.	ENTER LOUIS PHILIPPE. 1830–1832	126
IX.	MINISTER OF THE INTERIOR. 1832–1835	163
X.	THIERS AND HIS RELATIONS	196
XI.	PRESIDENT OF THE COUNCIL. FEBRUARY–AUGUST, 1836	208
XII.	CLASSICIST AND COALITIONIST. 1836–1840	243
XIII.	THE SECOND MINISTRY. 1840	271
XIV.	LEADER OF THE DYNASTIC OPPOSITION. 1840–1846	292
XV.	THIERS, PALMERSTON AND BANQUETS. 1846–1848	324
XVI.	EXEUNT LOUIS PHILIPPE AND THIERS	346
	EPILOGUE	361
	BIBLIOGRAPHY	362
	INDEX	373

LIST OF ILLUSTRATIONS

	FACING PAGE
ADOLPHE THIERS ABOUT 1848	*Frontispiece*
THE YOUNG THIERS	24
THIERS: WRITER AND HISTORIAN	64
THIERS: DAUMIER'S CARTOON, 1834	145
MADAME THIERS, THE MOTHER	198
MADAME ADOLPHE THIERS	200
MADAME DOSNE	202
THIERS' RESIDENCE AT THE PLACE SAINT-GEORGES	204
THIERS: PRESIDENT OF THE COUNCIL	212
THIERS: DAUMIER'S CARTOON, 1840	273
THE STUDY OF THIERS AT THE PLACE SAINT-GEORGES	305

THIERS AND THE FRENCH MONARCHY

CHAPTER I

THE GENERATION OF THE 'NINETIES

FRANCE had had great men in literature and in the arts previous to the year 1789, but between the outbreak of the Revolution and the year 1815 there is a gap in French genius. Some few names occur that stand out from the black and red background of those terrible years: Fabre d'Eglantine, the idealistic creator of the Revolutionary Calendar, Rouget de Lisle, the author of the *Marseillaise*, Joseph Chénier, whose greater song, the *Chant du Départ*, thrilled the hearts of those eager young men who went forward towards the frontiers in the vain hope that they would spread the gospel of Liberty over Europe, and André Chénier, who celebrated the great events of the early days of the Revolution, are mere exceptions to the general rule of the commonplace and the crude. With these and the great orators and the painters like David, who depicted in all their terrible realism the ravages of suffering on their poor subjects, the list is closed. There is a gap, a dark age, in French production that is not spanned until Napoleon has made his last journey to exile. It is only with the year 1815 that this revival comes, but even then it is to quite a degree a result of the Revolution, for the men who were to revive the glories of France were mostly the children of the Directory, and the years of the Directory were the birth years of a new France. Writing of this period, one of the new generation has said:

THIERS AND THE FRENCH MONARCHY

"At what period was the *patrie* the fairest and the grandest? The horrors of revolution seemed to be calmed; the murmurs of party sounded far off as the distant rumblings of thunder. Men regarded the few remaining agitations as the normal life of a free State. Commerce and finance emerged from a frightful crisis; the soil, restored to industrious hands, was about to become fertile again. A government of bourgeois, our equals, ruled the Republic; the best were called to succeed them. All ways were open. France, at the height of her power, was mistress of all the land that extends from the Rhine to the Pyrenees, from the sea to the Alps. Holland and Spain were to join their fleets to hers and together to attack the Maritime despotism. Admirable armies flaunted their tricolours in the faces of those kings who had wished to destroy them. Twenty heroes, varied as to character and talent, the same only in age and courage, were leading our soldiers to victory. Hoche, Kléber, Desaix, Moreau, Joubert, Masséna, Bonaparte, and a host of others were advancing together. Men weighed their different merits, but no eye, however piercing, saw yet, in this generation of heroes, evil or guilty men; no eye beheld him who would die at the flower of his age, attacked by an unknown ill; him who would die by a Mussulman's dagger, or, under enemy fire, who would betray the *patrie*, who would oppress liberty. All seemed pure, happy, and full of promise. All that was but for a moment. But such times are only moments in the life of a people, just as in the case of the lives of individuals. With repose we were going to find opulence; as to liberty and glory, there they were in the hollow of our hands. 'The *patrie* must be not only happy but sufficiently glorious,' an old man had said. This wish was accomplished. Frenchmen, you who have seen since then our liberty stifled, our *patrie* invaded, our heroes shot, or unfaithful to our glory, never forget those immortal days of liberty, of grandeur, and of hope."[1]

THE GENERATION OF THE 'NINETIES

This is a highly idealized conception of the Directory, but it was written by one of its children who was a patriot, young, and oppressed by the dull, inglorious days of Charles X. The phrases are pompous, the descriptions only too untrue to the facts, but they are symbols of the new France that was born in that time, and that came into active power twenty-one years later. Intellectually, France could never be the same; the mark of the Revolution was left ineradicably upon her brow. There was a new mind born of the Philosophers, the Terror, and the suffering that was brought and nurtured by the Napoleonic régime that followed. The artistic, literary, and philosophical genius of France became different. A new school of thought became paramount among Frenchmen, the freedom of art, the brotherhood of literature, the democracy of the mind; in other words, the school of the Natural and Romantic.

One is very apt to forget that these new elements appeared in France at the very height of the Revolution, and that in great part they were impressed upon a generation that came into being while the Revolution was nearing its crisis and its end. This is the importance of the Generation of the 'Nineties; it gave to France the finer things of the Revolution; in art, Horace Vernet, Scheffer, Corot, and Delacroix; in literature, Lamartine, Scribe, de Vigny, and Balzac; in the schools, Villemain, Victor Cousin, Augustin Thierry, Mignet, Auguste Comte, and Michelet; in the tribune of the Government and in the Press, de Rémusat, Carrel, Duvergier de Hauranne, and Adolphe Thiers. These were the heirs of the Directory and these were the men who were to continue the Revolution. To them, in great part, France owes her Nineteenth-century renaissance.

NOTE TO CHAPTER I

Thiers: *Histoire de la Révolution*, VIII. 431–33.

CHAPTER II

THIERS—MARSEILLES AND AIX (1797–1821)

THE Directory was in power; the evil days of the Terror were no more, and for a time Marseilles could enjoy a respite from tumult and from riot. Very likely the spring of 1797 was an idle time in the south of France. The country breathed again, but was not yet able to resume its normal existence. Over the frontiers the guns of the army were booming; there was activity in the seaports as well, for the British fleets still roamed over the Mediterranean. But Toulon interested them more than Marseilles, and it is not unreasonable to suppose that the latter city lay tranquil and comparatively idle in the bright sunshine of the Midi, on a particular April day of the year 1797, when two men and a woman were seen to approach a dusty and shabby bureau of the Civil Registry in the Cours d'Isle. With them was an infant three days old who must, according to the new laws, be brought before the municipal authorities for registration. They entered the bureau and the usual slouchy and indifferent *fonctionnaires* drew up, in front of the little waif of humanity who was presented to them, the following formidable document:

> "In the year V of the French Republic one and indivisible, on the 29 Germinal, at five o'clock, citizen Marie Simeon Rostan, officer of public health and *accoucheur*, living in the rue laterale du Cours, number 154, house 6, appeared before us, clerk of the municipality of the Midi, canton of Marseilles, and in the office of the town clerk, and presented to us a boy at whose birth he said he

had presided, and whom he declared to have been born on the 26 of this present month at 2.30 o'clock, parents the citizeness Marie Madeleine Amic and the citizen Pierre Louis Marie Thiers, proprietor, at present absent, in the house of the mother, rue des Petits-Pères, number 15, Isle Cinq, to which (infant) he gave the *prénoms* Marie Joseph Louis Adolphe. Record of which performed in the presence of citizens Pierre Roussel, proprietor of the rue des Petits-Pères and Jeanne Imbert, hairdresser, living on the same street, being major witnesses, of which the second has declared that she cannot write, we have signed with the first witness and the witness appearing with him.

   (Signed) Rostan, officier de santé,
P. Roussel. J. Jourdan, officier public adj'nt." [1]

According to this act, Louis Adolphe Thiers, journalist, historian, twice President of the Council under Louis Philippe, and Chief of the Executive Power 1870–73, was born on April 16, 1797. A child of the Revolution he was, and as a man he was destined to witness and to participate in three other Revolutions. His mother, Marie Madeleine Amic, was the daughter of Claude Amic and of Marie de Santi-L'homaca. His father was Pierre Louis Marie Thiers, son of Louis Charles Thiers and of Marguerite Bronde.[2] Of the family of Amic little is known. They were of meridional extraction and came originally from the little town of Bouc, in the Department of the Bouches-du-Rhône. Claude Amic's marriage, however, brings in a rather curious element, for his wife, Marie de Santi-L'homaca, was a Greek, and through her the young Adolphe Thiers was related to André and Joseph Chénier, the poets of the Revolution. Much more is known of his paternal ancestors. Through his father, Louis Adolphe Thiers was descended from a line of respectable and capable bourgeois. His paternal grandfather, Louis Charles

THIERS AND THE FRENCH MONARCHY

Thiers, born in Aix-en-Provence in 1714, came to Marseilles in 1762, and shortly after his arrival was appointed by royal patent the custodian of the Archives. In virtue of that office he assumed an important position as secretary-general and comptroller of the finances of the Commune of Marseilles.[3] It was in this capacity that he undertook the rebuilding of the streets and the sanitary reorganization of the city, only to be deprived of his functions after the outbreak of the Revolution.[4] During the early years of the Revolution, both the Thiers and the Amics appear to have lost comfortable fortunes.

Adolphe Thiers, then, was born into a material poverty. But this unhappy condition was accentuated by the fact that he was born out of wedlock. At the time of his birth his father, a worthless son of a very worthy parent, was married to Marie Fougasse. Fortunately for his latest offspring, Pierre Louis Marie's first wife died in May 1797, and the bereaved husband, influenced perhaps by what must have been for him an unusual attack of conscience, legitimatized his son by a tardy marriage with Mademoiselle Amic. This accomplished, he deserted his wife and infant son, not to reappear until a later and more inconvenient time, when Adolphe had become a prominent figure in Parisian society.

Within two months of his birth, the young Thiers was left to his fate by the desertion of his unworthy parent. The prospect was not promising, but there was better fortune in store for him. Though impoverished by the Revolution, his mother's parents and a sister of his father's, Madame Victoire Pretty, undertook his care and his schooling. His early religious and secular education was the particular interest of his Aunt Victoire. It was in the cellar of her house in the Allées des Capucines, 25, that her nephew received the sacrament of baptism, for the parish of Saint Vincent de Paul was still closed by the order of the State.

It was, as well, through her generosity that he received

THIERS—MARSEILLES AND AIX

his first schooling as a day-pupil in a school at Marseilles, where he studied Latin and French.[5] We are told that he was a small child, and at first sickly. When he was seven he resembled a child of five years, but his indefatigable energy and his strong will were soon noticed. These early years witnessed the fall of the Directory and the establishment of the Consulate. In 1802 came the Empire, and Louis Adolphe became the young subject of Napoleon Bonaparte.

In the seventh year of the Empire his real schooling began. At that time he was entered at the Lycée of Marseilles, where he began his first serious studies. These studies are not without their significance.

When the young Thiers entered the Lycée, the Napoleonic régime was at its height and the schools of France, like all other French institutions, were completely under Imperial control, and a totally new system of education prevailed. France had girded herself for world-dominion, and all aspects of French life were directed towards this end. Like all other French youths of his time, this child, born of a Revolution that was to free all men, entered into a great pitiless machine that resulted in a more complete enslavement for them. The curriculum prescribed at the Lycée of Marseilles was that which Napoleon dictated from Paris. It was not classical, as in the old days, nor economic and social as is so often the case to-day. The end and aim was the attainment of a practical, scientific, and military education. Consequently, Adolphe Thiers was trained in Latin, Mathematics, Topography, Geography, and History. Speaking of his experiences in the school and of their effect upon his later life, he has said: "The government took possession of me, as it did of all the youths whom their parents could be induced to part with, and put me into a military school, from which the seniors were drafted off every year; the few who had distinguished themselves to be made officers, the rest to be spent in the next campaign. The life was very hard, but its hard-

THIERS AND THE FRENCH MONARCHY

ships, instead of killing me, as had been most probable, gave me, in a couple of years, an iron constitution." [6]

To his relatives it soon became evident that their protégé was manifestly unfitted for a military career. He resented the restraints and hated the discipline. Furthermore, at that time a military life did not appeal to him. But Thiers never had occasion to regret that he had begun his education under the auspices of Mars. It gave him what he chose to call " an iron constitution," but more than that, it afforded him a real understanding of military science that was of invaluable benefit to him when, many years later, he undertook to write the *History of the Consulate and the Empire*. Having decided to give up a military career, he appears to have turned his thoughts to the legal profession as early as 1814. In that year his mother wrote to a relative telling of her son's lack of interest in commerce and of a growing desire to study law.[7] Finally the wish that he had expressed was gratified, and in September 1815, he was withdrawn from the school with the intention that he should begin his new studies at once. His Professor of Rhetoric, Monsieur Brunet, had already given him a certificate that declared, in no uncertain terms, his confidence in the brilliant future that lay before his young pupil.[8] Between September and the month of November, Thiers and his mother left Marseilles for Aix-en-Provence, and his adventures in the world were begun.

In spite of the fact that Aix was only about thirty kilometres distant from Marseilles, the change must have been a great one for the young Thiers, for the two cities were so different that they might have been at opposite ends of the earth. Marseilles was on the sea, while Aix was high in the hills. One was a stirring seaport, at times noisy and dirty, but the other was a quiet, dreamy, little town, not given much to commerce. The sea town had become a hotbed of Revolutionary interests, but the little hill-top community lived in the past, a past that extended far back into the glorious Middle Ages. To-day, Aix is a charming little spot, but a village dead, and far removed from the bustle and whirl of the modern world. The scene of Thiers' student days must have been much the same in 1815. For what use had many of its good citizens for the Revolution? Then, as now, it was a seat of the old aristocracy. Elegant, conservative, proud, it lived in the past, and most of the citizens who passed along its quiet, majestic, old avenue, lined with plane trees, thought little of the Revolution and less of Revolutionists. To them, the fall of Napoleon and the Restoration of the Bourbons in the person of Louis XVIII had been a satisfactory event. There was a gentle dignity about the little town—a staid and dreamy romance that made it an ideal setting for the youth of the man whom it would one day proclaim their own. It was there that Thiers made his first efforts, dreamed his first dreams, and met his first love. It was there, too, that Thiers received his first inspirations, but these came not so much from the law school as from the environment in which he found himself, and where he communed with his first friends.

Situated on a plateau above the coast line that runs from Marseilles to Toulon, Aix affords occasion for interesting walks, and in his idle hours the young law-student would ramble over the hills and about the narrow streets of the little town. These rambles he delighted in, and even as an old man he loved to recall them. It was during them that he thought out his philosophy, solved his problems, and made his resolutions. During one of these he met his lifelong friend.[9] Thiers had not been in Aix many months when he encountered that strange, quiet, faithful Mignet who never left him, who even lived near him during the great days at Paris, and who was always accessible to him by means of a small communicating door built into the great wall that surrounded the house of Thiers

THIERS AND THE FRENCH MONARCHY

the statesman in the Place St. Georges. Wandering over the hills, he and Mignet, the son of a *maître-serrurier*, discussed their dreams of France, dreams that they dared not mention often in the conservative town, and entered, as youth is wont to do, into heated arguments on the existence and nature of God. To these walks and to the discussions that accompanied them, Thiers, the old man of the 1870's, often referred, and to some of them may be due his last and unfinished work, the *Plan d'un ouvrage de Philosophie*.[10]

The young Thiers must have been a dreamer in those days, and though he himself never admitted it, and often declared that he despised dreamers, there is ample evidence of the fact in a letter quoted by the "Bourgeois de Paris," who claims to have seen the original. The style resembles so much that of his other letters that its authenticity can hardly be questioned. In style it is the Thiers of later days, but in sentiment it betrays a Thiers not well enough known to the world at large.

"My dear Cousin,
Our mutual silence has lasted too long. The ties of blood and of friendship unite us, but our friendship is too silent. We ought to know each other better. People love each other more only when they are better acquainted. In any case it is the first step that costs. I wish to be the braver of the two, although that rôle suits me less well than you. Timidity is a very bad counsellor; I put it aside for ever, and we shall soon be, I trust, old friends. Our only regret, perhaps, will be not to have begun sooner, but we still have time, and there remains all our life to be friends.
Our friendship, though not very old, will have the advantage of new-born babes, who are always the most cherished members of the family. Frankness, good-nature, gaiety—that is what two friends of our age need. With that we shall have much to say to

each other, and there will be no empty spaces in our letters. For my own part, I wish to set you a good example, and if I do not fill my pages with ideas, I shall at least give you words. I shall talk to you of cases, politics, moral philosophy, and gallantry. I shall be sincere about the faults of others. In a word, I shall not spare you any of the follies that indicate the wisdom of our hemisphere. And you—will you not tell me what goes on in yours? Is there nothing to talk over concerning your lovely country? They tell me that adventures happen there as elsewhere. Do not fear to be too long. In the correspondence of two friends the lengthiest is not always the one who loves the least.

In fine, the first step has been taken. We were like two persons, who, ready to pass through a door, persisted in conceding the privilege to each other. Why waste time? I have passed through first. I embrace you, my dear cousin, and I am your friend for life.

A. THIERS." [11]

The recipient of this letter is unknown and the world is ignorant as to whether this friendship continued.

The letter is evidence of one salient fact about Thiers, his tremendous wealth of friendship, and a trait that he never lost, to which his lifelong friendship with Mignet and Rouchon-Guigés is a fair monument. In youth, as in later years, he hungered for friendship, and yet in 1816, as in 1850, it was not an easy thing for Thiers to obtain, for he was opinionated and determined, and his political views were so often at variance with the sentiments of men otherwise sympathetically inclined to him. This was always true, but it was particularly the case in 1816. Into conservative Aix he had come, and because of that very characteristic of the little town, Thiers found at first but very few comrades. In fact, quite early in his student days he became an object of suspicion to the rigid Aixois. He was known as an admirer of the Roman Republic. It was rumoured, and rightly, that he did not admire the restored Bourbons. He wrote a tragedy entitled *Tiberius Gracchus*, in which he set forth his liberal opinions, and he began the preparation of a work on Kosciusko. Certain people even credited the report that he had joined the Carbonari and had taken an oath to kill the King![12] Thiers never learned the art of controlling his tongue. He found many hearers but few sympathizers, and among the latter his professors and the prosperous men of the town were not to be numbered. Mignet adored him, but Mignet was almost his own age, and does not appear ever to have been the mentor. One imagines, in the intimacy that developed between them, Thiers the leader and never Mignet, strong and determined as he could be on occasion. Older men, more experienced friends, were needed to guide the young Liberal and to assist, consciously or unconsciously, in the development of his opinions. And these were not lacking. He and his mother had relatives and acquaintances in Aix, the Thiers having been themselves natives of the town. When, therefore, the removal was made, the two were not unknown to at least two families who aided them, and among whom the son found sympathetic friends ready to listen to him and even to advance him in the paths of Liberalism. A letter to Monsieur d'Arlatan de Lauris gained him admittance to the home of a brilliant magistrate of the city, who was not a Conservative, and an introduction to a Dr. Arnaud found him another friend, likewise a Liberal. At the houses of these two men he could give expression to his youthful admiration for Danton and for the Conventionists. His words did not shock them, though they were anathema to his associates, his superiors at the law school, and even his mother, who had expressed regrets for "our good and unfortunate King Louis Sixteenth."[13] Monsieur d'Arlatan and Dr. Arnaud became his firm friends, and it was through them that he established his first relations with the notorious Liberals, Manuel and Étienne, when he went to Paris five years later.

During the first years of his sojourn at Aix, Thiers was occupied by his studies, by his discussions with Mignet, and by his relations with the quiet little circle of Liberals with whom he became identified. It is likely that he found Mignet and the Liberals far more profitable than the dull routine of the class-room. Youth is ever thus! It does not appear that he was much concerned with his scholastic studies, and within a short time he had turned his attention to writing, in the hope that from that he might gain recognition and a few additional coppers to augment the small income on which he and his mother must eke out a living. As an outgrowth of his work at Marseilles he wrote, in 1817, a treatise on Spherical Trigonometry. The same year he gave evidence of a decided variety of interests by composing an essay treating characters of Romantic Literature entitled *Sur l'Éloquence Judiciaire*. This effort was awarded the prize by the Academy at Aix.[14] But it was not until the latter part of the year that his writings attracted any marked attention.

In that year an event of great importance to him occurred. The Academy of Aix announced a prize for the best study of a local moralist of the early eighteenth century named Vauvenargues, who was one of the great figures of Provence. His work, the *Maximes*, had been very widely read during the pre-Revolutionary period, and was especially remarkable because it contained less of the pessimism with which so much of the work of that century was permeated. The optimism and calm dignity of Vauvenargues appealed to the youthful spirits and hopes of Thiers and he decided to enter the competition. He set to work with eagerness, and to judge by the style of the essay he must have enjoyed himself thoroughly. One phrase occurs in the essay which is worth repeating. It might almost be said to be the motto of the later Thiers, so typical is it of his later life.

> "Avoid those men who are a burden to themselves and to others, who rail at that which they cannot do and pass across the earth unperceived and despised. Be active, that is the great maxim; act, but act according to your nature. Let everyone take stock of himself, and if he finds that he has nothing, then let him stay where Nature has placed him. But if he feels himself a warrior, let him run to arms; a poet, let him sing; an orator, let him speak; a philosopher, let him meditate. It is God who commands him and who will punish him with enemies, ennui, and unhappiness if he fails to act according to his inspirations." [15]

To him, even from the early days at Aix, this law of action became a rule of life.

Thiers had been induced to enter the competition by Monsieur d'Arlatan, who himself was a member of the Academy.[16] But when the august body met to consider the matter of award, that over-zealous gentleman so warmly supported one particular essay that his more conservative colleagues became suspicious, and decided that the unknown author must be the young Liberal who was known to frequent the d'Arlatan house. Unwilling to countenance in any way the radical opinions with which Thiers was credited, the Academy voted to postpone the competition until the following year. Nothing daunted, Thiers withdrew his composition, but let it be known that he would compete when the contest was reopened, and that, in the meantime, he would rewrite his essay. When the prize was again announced, Thiers deposited his essay at the office of the Secretary. At the same time it became known that a new contestant had sent an essay from Paris. The

THIERS—MARSEILLES AND AIX

Academy met and debated on the merits of the two. Finally, delighted to be able to discountenance Thiers, they awarded the prize to the contestant from Paris and bestowed a simple *accessit* upon the essay which they supposed had been written by the violent young radical in their midst. But when they opened the envelopes containing the real names of the authors, they discovered, to their dismay, that Thiers was the author of both essays. Great was the delight of Monsieur d'Arlatan and the Liberal *coterie* of Aix.[17]

The Vauvenargues episode marks the first success of the future historian, but it has yet another significance. It is, in a sense, the first step made towards a literary career. The success of this effort, together with certain other factors, determined his vocation. For some time the latter had been a matter of great concern to him. The Lycée at Marseilles had disgusted him with a military career, and the law school at Aix does not appear to have convinced him that the life of a barrister was for him,[18] but he was poor, and the precarious state of his finances and his reluctance to leave his mother made him hesitate to make such a radical change. For a time, at least, he would be a lawyer. Together with Mignet, he was admitted to the Bar of Aix in 1818, and together they began to practise their profession. Sometimes, even, they worked on the same cases, and they enjoyed a modest success. It is related that previous to Mignet's departure for Paris, they were both called to plead the case of a man accused of incendiarism and murder. The case had acquired a certain notoriety owing to its spectacular nature. With great zeal and labour, the two young practitioners set to work. Both presented remarkable arguments, and expended much eloquence thereon. Thiers, we may be sure, used bombast, for that was a weakness that it took him years to overcome. Thiers had the prisoner acquitted of the first charge, while Mignet had him condemned for murder. The verdict was rendered and the budding young lawyers were given a great ovation. But pride must have a fall. It was then discovered beyond a doubt that Thiers' client was actually guilty of incendiarism and innocent of murder!

At the Bar of Aix Thiers was recognized for his eloquence and for his ability at argument. He was logical and clear. He was frequently successful. Though he lost his case, he established quite a reputation for himself for his prosecution of a charge of kidnapping. But Aix was not to be the scene of great triumphs. There were hard and bitter trials, even failures, that he must experience before he would be able to master the demands of a dull court in a sleepy little town, let alone such an audience as the tumultuous Chamber of Deputies to which he was already aspiring. As a public speaker, the youthful Thiers had obvious handicaps and serious faults. He was of unimposing appearance. Small of stature, he employed quick, short gestures, the actions of a man nervous and uncertain of himself, and this impression was not mitigated by his high-pitched, falsetto voice that frequently amused his hearers and made them lose the trend of his lucid and logical arguments.[19]

These defects, together with other considerations of a more intimate nature, finally decided him to abandon the law and to seek his fortune at Paris, whither Mignet had already gone. The Vauvenargues episode had disclosed to him a new *métier* that appealed to him, but more than all else there was Aix. To him it did not offer the future that he desired. Its glory lay in the past, and the old régime was no more. He must go to the heart and centre of new France, the France of his beloved Revolution. It was Youth calling to Youth.

There was, as well, another consideration that moved him. The sultry climate of the Midi was undermining a constitution that at best was none too vigorous. In September 1821, he wrote to his friend, Émile Benoit: "I leave to-morrow; I am overcome with tears. My two mothers (Madame Thiers and Madame Amic) break

THIERS—MARSEILLES AND AIX

my heart with their grief. I am ill; I am feverish; my breast burns; I breathe with difficulty. I must leave or dry up on the tree. The future is awful but the present is unendurable. It is ground that is withering; I must go, no matter what it costs." [20]

The departure from Aix was not an easy thing for Thiers to accomplish. He dreaded the parting with his mother and with Madame Amic. It was hard to leave his good friends, d'Arlatan and Arnaud. Rouchon-Guiges was a dear friend whose companionship he cherished. In Paris there was only Mignet and the unknown. There remains another name to be added to those grieved by his departure.

During his student days Thiers had met with Émilie Bonnefoux and had fallen in love with her. Evidently the affair had become a serious matter, and the young law-student had promised marriage; this at least must have been the understanding at the moment of his departure, for in the letters of Émilie there is a decidedly proprietary tone. Apparently the father of the young girl mistrusted him, but Felix, her brother, had confidence that Thiers would observe his promises.[21] Of Émilie's feelings in the matter one cannot be certain. Very likely, true to her kind, she feared the unknown influences to which he might be exposed. Upon his departure Émilie wrote to a friend in Paris bidding her care for her lover and watch him.[22] Her injunctions to Madame Huret were quite specific. From Paris in December, Thiers wrote to Benoit again: " Go to see my poor Émilie. How dear she has become to me since I left her! How that charming girl has claimed my heart since our separation; everything is endeared by privation." [23] Well might Adolphe bewail his Émilie! Well might Émilie beseech Madame Huret to watch Adolphe! All was in vain. Within the space of two short years the letters from Paris became less frequent, and the tone of Émilie's epistles to good Madame Huret changed from loving concern to perplexity, from perplexity to despair. Finally, despair gave way to anger.[24] Two more years and Émilie passed from Thiers' life in a most disagreeable manner. An irate father visited the recalcitrant Adolphe in his lodgings at Paris. A duel, harmless, but a duel, followed.[25] Several years later Thiers, a minister of the King, remembered the grief that he had caused and appeased his former adversary by finding, unbeknown to him, a comfortable position in the departmental administration of the Bouches-du-Rhône for Bonnefoux père. He writes to Monsieur Thomas, his friend, the prefect of Aix: "There is an excellent man, very honest, who is going to Marseilles. I had family troubles with him long ago. He was a particular friend of Manuel, who was our witness of a duel which nearly was fatal. I was in the wrong; there were mitigating circumstances, but I was in the wrong. I shall be very glad to undo the evil that I unwittingly did him—without his knowing it, however, for his pride, which is extreme, would make him refuse it." [26]

In this way the accounts were closed and the harmless indiscretions of youth were erased.

But that is looking ahead; we are still in the year 1821, when Thiers, full of regrets for his Émilie, his relatives, and his friends, was making his departure from Aix. In tears he wrote to a friend, on the very eve of his departure: "As to myself, I am going to follow my destiny. Will it be good or bad? I know not. Whatever happens, I am resigned, for they call us philosophers and we must be worthy of the name." [27]

This particular philosopher soon dried his tears in the bright sun of success in Paris.

NOTES TO CHAPTER II

[1] Copy of birth certificate of Adolphe Thiers, Bibliothèque Thiers.
[2] Genealogy of the Thiers family.
[3] Teissier: *L. C. Thiers*, p. 3.

[4] Réglement pour la Perception des droits à Marseilles, p. 54. Teissier: *L. C. Thiers*, p. 8. Gastaldy: *Thiers*, p. 11.
[5] *Ibid.*, pp. 23-25.
[6] Senior: *Conversations—Second Empire*, I. 137. *Thiers: Plan d'un ouvrage*, p. 2.
[7] Madame Thiers: Marseilles, September 12, 1814. Bibliothèque Nationale, 20,601, No. 2.
[8] Monsieur Brunet: Lycée de Marseilles, April 1814. Bibliothèque Nationale, 20,601, No. 2.
[9] *Memoires d'un Bourgeois de Paris*, II. 287.
[10] Thiers: *Plan d'un ouvrage de Philosophie*.
[11] Quoted: *Memoires d'un Bourgeois de Paris*, II. 288-89.
[12] *Le Correspondant*, 1922: F. Benoit, p. 787.
[13] Madame Thiers: Marseilles, September 12, 1814. Bibliothèque Nationale, 20,601 m., No. 2.
[14] Zervort: *Thiers*, pp. 19-21. Thiers: *MSS. of Vauvenargues*, 1821: Bibliothèque Thiers, fol. 543, No. 8.
[15] Thiers: *Vauvenargues*, 1821, pp. 36-37: Bibliothèque Thiers, fol. 543, No. 8.
[16] Martin: *Thiers*, p. 16.
[17] *Le Constitutionnel*, November 30, 1821. Simon: *Thiers*, etc., p. 134. Remusat: *Thiers*, p. 16. Thureau-Dangin: *Histoire du parti liberal*, p. 205. Copies of the two essays may be seen at the Bibliothèque Thiers in Paris. Both essays treat the same subject and have the same point of view, but the style is absolutely different.
[18] Lanzac: *Thiers*, p. 8.
[19] Zervort: *Thiers*, p. 19.
[20] Quoted: *Le Correspondant*, 1922, p. 792, F. Benoit. Thiers, Paris, to F. Benoit, September 17, 1821.
[21] Felix Bonnefoux, Toulouse, to Madame Huret, December 19, 1822. Musée Arbaud, Aix-en-Provence.
[22] *Le Correspondant*, 1922, pp. 791-92, F. Benoit. Émilie Bonnefoux, Aix, to Madame Huret, September 17, 1821.
[23] Quoted: *Le Correspondant*, 1922, p. 795, F. Benoit. Thiers, Liancourt, to F. Benoit, December 6, 1821.
[24] Émilie Bonnefoux, Aix, to Madame Huret, January 26, 1823. Musée Arbaud, Aix-en-Provence.
[25] Felix Bonnefoux, Barcelona, to Madame Huret, January 23, 1824. Musée Arbaud, Aix-en-Provence.
[26] Thiers, Paris, to Monsieur Thomas, 24, *circ.* 1833. Bibliothèque Thiers, Paris, No. 42.
[27] Thiers, Paris, to father of Ambroise at Mirabeau, n.d. 1821. Bibliothèque Nationale, No. 20, 601, No. 3.

CHAPTER III

AT PARIS (1821-23)

THE Revolution had brought the Empire, and during the first twenty-one years of Thiers' life the Empire had reached its greatest glory and gone the way of all great despotisms. Bourbon King in 1814 had succeeded Bonaparte Emperor, and except for the brief interval of Napoleon's spectacular return from Elba, Bourbon had contrived to remain on the throne of France. But it had not been an easy task. " The foreigners gave us the Bourbons, but France gave us the Bonapartes." These words had been in the mouths of many while Thiers laboured at the Bar of Aix, and try as he might, Louis XVIII seemed unable to forget their sad truth; he was even less successful in driving the thought from the minds of his subjects. In fact, it would have required superhuman powers for King Louis to forget the unpleasant circumstances attendant upon his two restorations. If the shade of his martyred predecessor did not return to remind him of the fact, his princely brother whispered it in his ear; and when Charles of Artois had the royal ear to himself, he was likely to add thereto an admonition to ignore further the Charter, that ignominious bargain with Revolution. Or if Charles and his Ultras were absent, the King heard, in the streets of his Paris, the railing songs of the poet Béranger that delighted workmen and bourgeois and offended the ears of monarchy with the revilings of royal police, *émigrés*, and Jesuits, and their praises of the Rights of Man. The Ultras, Monsieur Charles, and Béranger all had one song, but the tune to which they sang it was different. Their song was the Charter.

AT PARIS

The Charter of 1814 was abominated by the Ultras, tolerated by the growing *Doctrinaires*, and accepted by the *Idéologues*, La Fayette and Benjamin Constant, as the sole excuse for having a Bourbon on the throne. By clubman and radical it was despised. In the eyes of the Ultras alone was it a confirmation of the fact that Louis XVIII had succeeded Louis XVI. To them alone it was a charter of continuity. On the other hand, because of it, *Idéologue* and budding *Doctrinaire* regarded the King as the heir of the Revolution, for had not the Charter sanctioned the Revolution? So it seemed, at least, to three-quarters of France, and for proof of their contention they pointed to its high-sounding phrases about the equality of all men before the law, the equal eligibility of all for civil and military positions, the restrictions on arbitrary imprisonment, the freedom of religion, and the freedom of the Press. These phrases might be a consolation to the fervent Liberal, but at the same time there were matters of regret. There was a qualifying phrase, for instance, in regard to the liberty of the Press. Freedom of the Press was declared, but the means for its arbitrary curtailment were provided by the words with which the law concluded, "while conforming to the laws which are necessary to restrain abuses of that Liberty." Then, too, there were other matters of debate; while the Charter gave to France ministers, it did not signify that they should be appointed from the majority. Ministerial responsibility to the Chamber of Deputies was carefully ignored. Again, the Charter provided for an elective chamber that should meet every year. The franchise was 300 francs in direct taxes, but it did not provide an electoral system. Of all these discrepancies the greatest was Article XIV, which allowed the King to promulgate special laws in times of danger. What laws, when, and of what nature? Was the Charter a guarantee of Revolutionary liberties, or a cleverly devised instrument to operate the return of the old régime?

THIERS AND THE FRENCH MONARCHY

These were some of the questions that arose in the minds of Frenchmen while the Bourbons were striving vainly to consolidate themselves.

To these questions neither Louis nor the Government would give answer, and so others attempted to answer for them. In the very first years of the Restoration, certain reactionary members of his court who were grouped around Charles of Artois, made a tremendous effort to commit the King and to establish their control of the Government and the finances, but the " White Terror " subsided, and Louis, too experienced to allow himself to be drawn into such indiscretions, consented to the suppression of the movement. It is even possible that he feared his over-enthusiastic brother Charles and the Ultras, for, immediately after the attempted reaction, Louis appeared to favour a moderate Liberalism. The Decazes Ministry promised much in the way of reform as to Press laws and electoral methods, but this was never carried out, for the assassination of his heir, the Duc de Berry, revived the King's fear of Revolution and drove him back into the arms of more conservative advisers. Consequently Decazes retired, and the Richelieu Ministry made its appearance to inaugurate the practice of a mild but more definite royalism that would establish, it was hoped, a policy more pleasing to the bolder elements of the Restoration. When the young Thiers came to Paris, the well-meaning Richelieu was in power. His Ministry, however, was not destined to be of long duration. Within a short time, Richelieu found himself faced with a European situation which he could not handle to the satisfaction of anyone in France, not even the King himself.

Outside the boundaries of France, Revolution had again raised its head. In Spain, in Italy, and in Greece, Nationalism and Liberalism asserted themselves; the French Liberals resented the reluctance of the Government to align the tricolour with the Constitutional army in Spain, the Carbonari, and the Hetaria

AT PARIS

Philika. On the other hand, Ultras were outraged because Richelieu had not obeyed the dictates of Reaction and declared against the uprisings. On December 2, 1821, the Ministry fell, and the pendulum resumed its slow but steady swing towards the Ultras. The old régime appeared to have gained by the nomination of Villèle as successor to Richelieu.

To the Ultras it may have seemed that at last the day of their power had returned and that they would again dictate from Paris. In reality, however, such could never be the case, for Paris was different and could never return to its old state of society. Commerce and industry had begun to make their impress, and now the coaches of bankers and ironmongers vied in magnificence with the equipages of princes and dukes. Paris, too, had newspapers which Villèle might try to control, but even his laws could not break the bourgeois of his new habits. He had begun to think, to gather and to develop his own opinions. The Ultras might collect in the Faubourg St. Germain at the hotels of the *ancienne noblesse*, but the bourgeois did not envy them. He, too, had his salons, those of the Chaussée d'Antin, where the great bankers, Laffitte, Rothschild, or Perier opened their doors to him, or, if he preferred, he might go to the quarter of the Arsenal where Nodier received, with Hugo and Alfred de Vigny. Bourgeois Liberalism joined with Romanticism and fraternized to the tune piped by Béranger. And while Béranger piped, Bourgeois talked, and while he talked, he conspired. Sometimes, even, he expressed regret for the glories of the Revolution and of the Empire.

In 1821, then, Paris was different, and in 1821, as in 1924, this city of the Seine set the mode. With seven hundred thousand inhabitants, it ruled and dominated the remaining twenty-nine million three hundred thousand souls in France. Consequently there were many small Chaussées d'Antin in the provinces, although, it is true, few Hugos, Nodiers, and de Vignys were to be

THIERS AND THE FRENCH MONARCHY

found beyond the fortifications of the capital. Middle class was slowly coming into its own, but it was making its way not only by means of salons. In other phases of society the famous generation of the seventeen-nineties was beginning to be felt. Villemain, a Liberal, was in the University, and also Cousin, Jouffroy, Guizot the Protestant, and Michelet the Romanticist. In the Chamber, too, there were General Foy, Royer-Collard, Manuel, newly returned from exile at Brussels, and Benjamin Constant. The Press, that weapon dreaded by monarchy, was sharpening its pens. The *Débats*, the *Constitutionnel*, the *Courier Français*, and the *Globe* were all of the new generation. In brief, a whole phalanx was preparing to meet Reaction in the guise of Ultras and Church on their own ground.

They were increasing in numbers, these cohorts of the *Jeunesse Libérale* of France, but there was one weakness that deterred their progress. These youths of France had no common doctrine but only doctrines. They regretted the past glories of France and they hated the foreigner; so much they had in common, but each looked to the future in his own particular way. As regards the future of France they seem to have been in agreement concerning only one matter. With the possible exception of La Fayette and his followers, each of them regarded a silent man, and on him they pinned their hopes; but the hopes of very few were the same. La Fayette may have seen in him a plank to Republicanism; Guizot beheld in him Constitutionalism; Chateaubriand a moderate Bourbonism. What Louis Philippe d'Orléans saw in himself in those days no one knows, and probably we never shall know. Guided by instinct or by experience, this gentleman went everywhere and established himself nowhere.[1] He avoided conspiracies and appeared to have a positive hatred of ovations. He played with Royal Château and with Chaussée d'Antin. He consulted Monarchy about the education of his children, but in spite of his royal cousin's dis-

THE YOUNG THIERS.

AT PARIS

approval, he sent them to public schools. He consorted with Ultras, but he associated, too, with Manuel. He lent money to Benjamin Constant, and Laffitte was his banker.[2] He was friendly with Monsieur Charles, the Comte d'Artois, but he was on terms of intimacy with Talleyrand—Talleyrand first Bonapartist and then Bourbonite, first Bishop and then *Incroyant*. He opened the doors of his Palais Royal to nobles and to bankers.[3] The walls were hung with tapestries of the Revolution and the Empire. He exhibited the paintings of Horace Vernet; he interested himself in revolutionary prints and portraits.[4] These were the evidences of conspiracy, if there was conspiracy, in 1821.

Into such a society Thiers, newly come to Paris, made his début during the later months of the year 1821. Mignet had come to the capital in July, and in September Thiers joined him.[5] Upon the latter's arrival they took a room in a hotel in the Passage Montesquieu. The house was small and mean. The street was dark and dirty and was located in a crowded and noisy section. Their room was on the fourth floor. "A plain bureau and a walnut bed were the principal furnishings, to which should be added white window-curtains, two chairs, and a small table unsteady on its legs. A door communicated with another room, but this door was closed and in its embrasure they placed a book-shelf that held very few books, and on the wall a very poor engraving of Corinne."[6] This was the home of the two young friends from Aix for some time.

The first months were not easy by any means. Thiers was homesick, and this condition was aggravated by an empty purse.[7] He and Mignet took work wherever they could find it. Mignet was on the *Courier*,[8] and for a time Thiers wrote articles on politics, art, the theatre, or any available subject. These articles he placed where he could. His first steady employment came when he was engaged to act as secretary to the Duc de la

THIERS AND THE FRENCH MONARCHY

Rochefoucauld, and for a time he resided at the château at Liancourt.[9] But this relationship, extraordinary in itself, for the Duc and his young secretary must have been in cordial disagreement in regard to politics, was terminated when the Richelieu Ministry fell, and December 23 found him back in Paris.[10]

In the meantime, fortune had begun to smile on him. Upon his departure from Aix, Dr. Arnaud had given him a letter to Manuel, the notorious Liberal. At that time Manuel and Thiers had two things in common that Arnaud hoped would lead to a friendship advantageous to his young friend; they were from the Midi, where Manuel had spent some time as Professor at Aix, and they agreed in regard to political matters. The older man seems to have taken kindly to his youthful compatriot, and through him Thiers was introduced to Étienne, editor of the *Constitutionnel*, and to Laffitte.[11] Due to the efforts of his newly discovered friends, he was taken on the *Constitutionnel* in November 1822.[12] There he began his career as a journalist.

The life of a journalist in the Old World in those days does not seem to have resembled the life of a beginner in that field of writing to-day. Journalism in France then, as now, was an art, and not the hasty task of gathering sensational news for large black or red headlines on the first page of the morning or evening issue. The newspapers of France taught the people; through them the great ones of the nation spoke to the people. Newspaper reading was an institution, not an amusement, or a means to while away a few idle moments by indulging in sensationalism. The most important part of the sheet was the editorial, and on this section journalists of the early nineteenth century spent much care and thought. Consequently, to read that Thiers arose at five o'clock means that it was to study, and six hours of the morning were devoted to this task. At eleven he would join Mignet and some of his young associates to dine at a café near the Palais Royal. The

AT PARIS

afternoons were passed at the *bureaux* of the *Constitutionnel*, and the evenings were devoted to increasing his acquaintance with the Liberal bourgeoisie to whom he had been presented.[13] And yet, in spite of the fact that his time was so occupied, he does not seem to have been happy. "I am condemned to stay in Paris, where I am prey to the eternal ennuies that my fate sends me and that I bring on myself," he writes to Madame Étienne.[14]

Already disillusion had come. Paris was not the golden city of his dreams. Its vastness overpowered him, and he felt lost in the great merciless, ceaseless routine of public life in which his was a small and unimportant part. His craving for friendship was not gratified, and he longed for the more peaceful life of Aix and the quiet understanding sympathy that he had known there. "Well, my noble Rouchon, do you think that I have forgotten you because I have not written you for several months? Do you imagine that I am surrounded with so much genius, truth, and friendship that I have forgotten him who is all these things and more to me? No, I am carried away with things (to do); I am swept on without, however, thinking less of those things that formerly held my attention and that will hold it for ever. We have simply adjourned, but I do not believe that we are separated. For our happiness and our mutual security we must think and live together. I need your whip, so gentle but so stimulating, and more than all else I need your good criticism, which brings me back, without fail, to the simple and the noble. I hope that the milk which you have made me drink will not degenerate, but for my own good and for my own heart I wish that I were with you. There you see the effects of absence and of separation. I talk to you as from afar, as when many things have passed, and I assure you that everything is as it used to be. All that shows me that we are very far away from each other. In spite of this I can tell you that you are never for an instant out of mind. You are in my solitary temple and to it I repair every day."[15] But the die had been cast; a journalist he had become, and journalism could not profit him in Aix, where his readers would be few and his articles less acceptable.

Manuel's patronage set Thiers definitely on the path that he would pursue the following eight years. Manuel too, was a writer for the *Constitutionnel*, and he undertook to initiate his young friend into the customs of the profession. This journal was the paper most hostile to the Bourbon restoration, and represented all phases of the traditional opposition. On its staff were to be found former Bonapartists and former Republicans joined, for the moment, into a group of Golden Mean; Évariste Demoulin, Étienne, Tissot, and Cauchois-Le Maire;[16] but the arrival of this new contributor changed somewhat the character of the paper. Thiers brought new life to their old theories. He redressed their antiquated and banal arguments in a novel form. During the first year he wrote articles on contemporary politics, on literature, on history, and on the Salon of 1822. His broad acquaintance with all subjects made it possible for him to write on many things, and his remarkable facility of mind enabled him to master quickly, after a few hours' study, a subject that had been previously unexplored by him. His thirst for a universal knowledge made this task a pleasure and not a tedium, for the young Thiers was interested in all things. Furthermore, he interested his readers; his style was simple, easy, unaffected, and logical.[17] The same lucidity of argument and precision of phrase that had aided him at the Bar of Aix gave him an early success in the year 1822. At the outset, however, his versatility blinded his superiors to his peculiar aptitude for political discussion and he continued to write on a variety of themes. In all of them he remained true to the colours that he had assumed. He had attached himself to the revolutionary school in politics, and so he was a revolutionary in art and in literature. This fact is plainly indicated in his criticisms of the Salon of 1822.

These articles he regarded as mediocre, even at the moment of their composition.[18] But they had the virtue of being sincere and original, and their interest was further enhanced by the fact that the young critic was personally acquainted with his artists. He had made the acquaintance of Gérard, Girodet and Horace Vernet. He frequented their ateliers and visited them in their villas in the country. He desired to become a sort of Mæcenas and succeeded to quite an extent. Once he had attained power he placed his artistic acquaintances in lucrative positions where they served ably and well.[19] Of all of them he admired Gérard the most, and before long a real intimacy developed between the writer and the artist.[20] He sat with him as he painted the Duchesse du Broglie, whose striking resemblance to her mother, Madame de Staël, impressed him.[21] Gérard's *Corinne* he declared to be " l'ouvrage le plus idéal et le plus vrai de l'art." [22] Through Gérard he discovered the genius of Delacroix and predicted the success of Horace Vernet. He was not a lover of the conventional; he desired the natural in painting as he desired the natural in literature. He hated the *impressif* school, for he abominated and failed to comprehend their subjectivity and their psycho-analysis. As an art critic he was successful, but that is not to say he was a good critic or that he was possessed of a real artistic sense. A hasty glance at the ghastly Thiers collection with which the Louvre has been burdened would be sufficient proof to the contrary! Gigantic bronze and plaster casts of atrocious Renaissance masters, frightful reproductions of Rubens, and minor artists must have lent an air of true Bohemianism to the mansion in which the later Thiers lived. As an art *connoisseur* he is amusing, but there is more than the comical aspect to this interest that he developed. One cannot but

THIERS AND THE FRENCH MONARCHY

admire the efforts of the urchin of the rue des Petits Pères, Marseilles, who tried to understand and to appreciate.

In art he was thoroughly Voltairian,[23] and being an adherent of that revolutionary school, he was, as well, a Classicist. For in those days men were not so foolish as to divorce progress from Classicism. Among his writings of this year there is a series of essays on classical and romantic literature which appeared in a small weekly known as *The Album*.[24] In these articles there is a breadth of view and a cosmopolitanism that is indicative of the real spirit of early nineteenth-century France. They contain in its essence the best of the Revolution and none of its excesses, and betray a freedom of appreciation that eighteenth-century France would never have known. The following is an illustration of that brotherhood of art and democracy of mind that the generation born of the late eighteenth century brought into Western European genius.

> " O France, dear Fatherland, one of thy children rejoices to-day that he was born on thy soil, and he prefers thee to all other mothers. Thou art neither proud nor disdainful, although the first among nations. Thou dost not contest rivals nor foreign glories. Thy children are just, for they have found at thy heart only generous sentiments; they love their native land, but they know that other lands (too) have beauty. Although they have a free and fertile genius, they are not afraid to imitate the works of their neighbours and to perfect their discoveries. They have listened to the wisdom of all the wise and from them they have composed the purest doctrines. They have not admitted of a philosophy without hope; more than all, they have thought on divine power. They have not revolted against the evils of life, but have borne them courageously. More capable and more judicious,

they have the better sung of man, of nature, and of the gods." [25]

The Salon of 1822 and the essays in *The Album* are evidence of the versatility of the young author. But another work of the same period displays Thiers in a different light and in a rather astonishing mood. From the beginning of his residence in Paris he had been a frequent attendant at the theatre. In later life he did not lose his interest, and as Minister he was quite active in the direction of the national theatres at Paris. It was this interest that led him to write, in 1822, a " Notice " to the *Life of Mistress Bellamy*, the famous actress of Covent Garden. In the " Notice " Thiers appears in a new light. He is a moralist and an advocate of the moral laws of society. He takes his work very seriously, almost too seriously, and there is an amusing aspect to his remarks. At this time Thiers himself was known as a *bon vivant*. In his letters he is constantly reproaching himself and he frequently acknowledges his lack of sobriety. When he comes to review the stirring life of Mistress Bellamy, he appears to be shocked into an almost puritanical solemnity. The irregular circumstances that surrounded her entrance into the world and the extraordinary situations in which she found herself made him stop, possibly, and survey his own life, and the unfortunate conditions under which it began. There may be, indeed, a reminiscence of the rue des Petits Pères, Marseilles, and of his father, the roving, rollicking Pierre-Louis-Marie Thiers, in the solemn words with which he begins his concluding remarks :

" So, no matter how brilliant the gifts which Nature has made us, no matter how happy the circumstances that fortune allows us, true and certain happiness can only be found in a regular life. Born of illicit passions, thrown into the midst of disorder, living in chaos, in spite of all talents and the greatest kindness, and all that should conciliate man, Mistress Bellamy was still a unique example of evil chance and of that punishment that Nature always enjoins upon those who infract her laws." [26]

It is difficult to imagine Thiers as the *penseur* and the moral philosopher, and it is impossible not to suspect that there was a twinkle in the bright eyes of the little man as he sat before the desk in his bare room in the hotel of the Passage Montesquieu and penned these words.

But these writings, while they may have pleased and interested his readers, did not make of him a marked man, and he was beginning to find the road to success a very steep one.

"I could be happy if I had my two mothers, my other duties accomplished, my happy friends, and my thoughts to myself and not forced to be turned first one way and then the other. The future is not fair nor happy. It is vast, that one feels and sees everywhere. I have been more circumspect in my conduct than in the past, and this has come without much effort but within the natural progress of things. I am slowly gaining the just minds; I torment the false minds, and what is odd enough, I have not made very many enemies; nevertheless, I have a few; I am preparing to make some and I see them in the offing. How can one avoid knocking down obstacles (in one's path), and where they are men, *there* are enemies. My money affairs are not so bad, and they will continue to mend. To sum it all up, the world is pursuing its destiny; reality pierces through things. I shall have what I am worth, no more, no less, and I can no more hide my evil than my enemies can hide my good. Mignet lives as I do, but less rapidly. His business will succeed, however, and so will mine. Two articles

AT PARIS

of his on the letters of St. James brought him into relations with Talleyrand, who searched for the author everywhere." [27]

The opportunity came sooner than he may have expected. Thiers' letter was written in May 1822, but three months later he was able to announce to Rouchon another project which he seems to have thought of declining at first.[28] It was this project that brought the young writer definitely into the limelight. Oddly enough, it was a foreign power that gave Thiers the opportunity of entering the political arena.

The year 1820 had witnessed revolts against Reaction in the guise of the Metternich system in Naples, Piedmont, and Spain. In the latter country Revolution had made great headway, and finally had driven the would-be absolutist Ferdinand from the throne. The unfortunate King had appealed to Metternich in 1822, and the Congress called at Verona had, in spite of England's protest, committed to France the task of re-enthroning the overthrown Ferdinand. Louis XVIII, now more sympathetically inclined towards the reactionary school, had eagerly assumed the cause of Ferdinand, but parliamentary debates had ensued, and one Ministry, that of Richelieu, had fallen over the question of war or no war. The Ultras, of course, demanded a policy *à outrance*, while Liberals of the La Fayette and Manuel groups had declared that a war to suppress freedom ought to fail and would fail.[29]

The Liberal sections especially were divided on this question, and discussion of the intervention in Spain became quite general throughout France. Here was an opportunity for an able writer, and Thiers was selected by his senior colleagues to make a tour of inspection along the frontier. It can hardly be doubted that there was a double purpose in this journey. For the coterie of Liberals with whom he was associated, Thiers was to make a true report of the state of things. It was even believed that he was to interview the leaders of the Spanish Liberal armies.[30] For the public, however, he was to collect and publish amusing and scandalous data in regard to " the Army of the Faith." He himself acknowledges this in a letter written from Tarbes during the journey : "There will be nothing of what really impressed me, for it is not written for those who quarrel over war and peace." [31] The journey to the Pyrenees began in October 1822. A month was spent *en passant* at Marseilles, in Switzerland, and in Provence. The actual inspection of the Spanish frontier occupied only part of November and December. During this journey Thiers took careful notes, and the account of his observations was compiled in the form of a pamphlet that appeared in the following year. This pamphlet took Paris by storm. It was entitled *Les Pyrénées et le Midi de la France pendant les mois de novembre et de decembre 1822.*

The Pyrenees is itself a remarkable document for those who would know the real Thiers. It is a veritable pantheon of his talents. In it are found all the humour, serenity, minuteness of detail and of observation, and power of description that so characterized his style. He ridicules Paris officials, Italian inspectors, Genevan guards, and the " Army of the Faith " in Spain. He describes with the phrases of a true poet the natural beauties of Provence. His verbal portraits of Tarbes and of the approach to Marseilles became famous, and were often repeated by his readers, and quoted in travellers' guide-books of the time. His comments on the condition and morals of the French troops are valuable and enlightening.

The story of the journey begins with an account of the author's attempt to obtain a passport. The young Thiers calls upon the Commissaire of Police to make his application.

AT PARIS

Thiers: " I declare that I desire to circulate freely and that I wish a passport."

Commissaire: " For what destination ? "

Thiers: " For foreign parts."

Commissaire: " For foreign parts ! And at such a time as this ! Where *are* you going ? "

Thiers: " To Switzerland."

Commissaire: " What business calls you there ? "

Thiers: " None."

Commissaire: " None ! And do you imagine that without reasonable motives Monsieur le Prefet will allow you to leave ? "

Thiers: " If I choose to travel without reasonable motives must Monsieur le Prefet find them for me ? Anyhow, is not the fact that I wish to see the country sufficient ? "

Commissaire: " That is enough ; the authorities will see what they can do for you. Come back in three days."

Thiers: " In three days ! And what if I am in a hurry, all my arrangements made ? "

Commissaire: " In three days."

Thiers: " But, please, has anyone complained to Monsieur le Commissaire about me ? Is there any reason to suspect me ? "

Commissaire: " None whatever."

Thiers: " Monsieur le Commissaire is therefore pleased with me ? For here good citizens must be those with whom he is not acquainted."

Commissaire: " In three days." [32]

Undoubtedly this conversation was highly coloured for the purpose of amusing his readers, and yet it must be true in essentials, for evidence exists that Thiers' passport was only obtained with difficulty and that his movements were carefully followed by the Bourbon Government at Paris. As a matter of fact, from the moment of his departure he was signalled to the various departmental authorities, and most of his actions were reported by the secret police; most, but not all of his actions, however. The Government of the Bourbons suspected that he was an envoy of the Paris Liberals to Mina, the leader of the Spanish Constitutionalists, and while they do not appear to have been able to substantiate the fact, it appears that he managed to escape their vigilant eyes and enter Spanish Cerdagne. Once across the frontier, he learned much from d'Erole and Mina, and when he set out to return, the harebrained young adventurer nearly lost his life during his passage over the mountains.[33]

Meanwhile Paris and provincial officials were at considerable pains about his movements. The Prefects of the Bouches-du-Rhône, of Ariège, and of the Hautes-Pyrénées reported minutely his actions and the names of those with whom he met.[34] Some of them did not credit him with too good a character. The Prefect of the Bouches-du-Rhône, for example, made the following report: "His political opinions are very bad, and his conduct has always been that of a *partisan outré* of liberalism. But," he adds, "le sire Thiers a de l'instruction." [35]

It is not unlikely that Thiers, thoroughly cognizant of these facts, enjoyed himself hugely, and purposely sought to mystify the watch-dogs of the Bourbon Restoration. This may account, in great part, for the raillery at officialdom that he employs so frequently in the book.

The passport at last procured, the author then proceeds to relate his experiences with the functionaries of the countries that he desired to visit. To him Geneva was ideal. Here was true freedom, but a freedom of which he did not fail to make sport. At the frontier he is accosted by the Douaniers: "Who are you?" "A Frenchman." "Your name?" "Adolphe Thiers." "Have you a passport?" "I have not." "Enter." With such freedom the author is delighted, but he adds:

AT PARIS

" Depuis, je n'ai plus su qu'il existât un gouvernement à Genève ! "[36] When, however, he tried to enter Savoy, it was another matter. He was brought before the censor at Chambéry for having in his possession a book on the French Revolution.[37]

It was after his visits to Geneva and Savoy that our young traveller came to Aix and Marseilles. At least this is the itinerary described in the book. At this point the character of the pamphlet changes. Thiers is serious; he describes the industries and agricultural products of the country with the minute and wearisome exactitude of a German student making the *grand tour*. But even at that there are lighter touches. He is writing now of the land of his birth, and from time to time he is carried beyond the consideration of material things. When he describes his own Provence, the poet supersedes the practical man :

> " It is only when arriving at Aix that one can have a true conception of this beautiful country, beautiful in its aridity. It is when reaching the last high hills, partly enveloping Marseilles, that one is suddenly enthralled by a magnificent sight that travellers never forget and that, inspiring Joseph Vernet, revealed to him his true genius. Two great chains of mountain ranges open up, cover a vast area, and, plunging into the sea, disappear finally in the waves. Marseilles is enclosed in this circle. Arriving from the north, one beholds suddenly an immense basin in all its extent; its brilliant colouring overpowers one. Shortly afterwards one is struck by the form of the ground and its peculiar vegetation; the rugged, rounded hills with their rich green apparel, approaching the borders of the Saône and the Garonne." [38]

Chapter V begins the study of the Pyrenees proper. But here Thiers is not at his best; he will not say all that he knows.[39] He visits the "Army of the Faith," which had just been thrown back upon the French frontiers. He confines himself to relating curious and picturesque details. The picture of the leaders, their poverty and their credulity, is amusing as well as pathetic. His descriptions of King Mata-Florida, with his pages, ministers, and monks, is kindly but ironical.[40] In spite of his intention to the contrary, however, the author becomes serious near the end, and attempts to consider some of the questions raised at Paris. Spain would welcome French soldiers, and the French soldier will obey his orders. He will do so because he is well-disciplined and because he has no conception of the meaning of the words "Legitimacy" and "Return to Religion." At this point Thiers makes a bold stroke. He tears aside the veil with which men were trying to becloud the real issue which, he declares, remains the same: Shall we have a return to the old régime? or not? That is the real issue at the bottom of all of the other problems. In this way he launches his own attack on the Restoration. *The Pyrenees* is but the prelude to a later work that was entitled *The History of the French Revolution*. He has grown since the days of Aix, when he was only the object of suspicion to a group of Conservatives in a dreamy little town of the Midi. From the date of the publication of this first pamphlet his movements were carefully guarded by the police. The Government of the restored Bourbons was alarmed by this "avocat qui n'exerce pas sa profession."[41]

This journey completed, Thiers returned to Paris in December. For him the return was difficult. Once more he had been in his beloved Provence, and it was not easy to go back to Paris. His curiosity was satisfied, and the capital seemed to him to have no more to offer. The journey which he had anticipated with such enthusiasm was accomplished, and his heart was heavier than when he had set out upon it. He was entirely disillusioned. But these were only momentary regrets, for the publication of the pamphlet gave him the opportunity that he needed. *The Pyrenees* created for its author a reputation and determined the field in which he would specialize. Political discussions in the *Constitutionnel* and in other papers were now left to him. *Vauvenargues* in 1821 freed him from the law, and in 1823 *The Pyrenees* released him from the worries and annoyances of hack-writing. There was another result of this latest publication, however, the importance of which must not be forgotten. Some of the *Pyrenees* essays first appeared in the *Constitutionnel*, and these articles had much to do in establishing the interest of another great man in him; they brought him to the notice of the most adroit and most experienced statesman of the time. The young Thiers was presented to the veteran Talleyrand.

The relations of these two men are shrouded in mystery. It is a very difficult problem to determine just when they began, and how great was their effect upon the later career of the younger man. Both of them have guarded their secret carefully, and in view of the paucity of personal material on this question, it is not unreasonable to infer that they may have wished to carry the secret with them to the tomb. Nevertheless, certain remarks of Thiers have come to light which make it possible to determine a few facts in regard to their early relationship. His earlier biographers inform us that the acquaintance began previous to the journey to the Pyrenees. Earlier in the year 1822 Monsieur de Montlosier had written a violent pamphlet entitled *De la Monarchie Française*. In this pamphlet the reactionary interpretation of the Charter had been upheld. In March 1822, in the columns of the *Constitutionnel*, a very adequate reply had appeared. This reply had been written by Thiers, and in his article the opinions of the *Doctrinaires* had been supported. It may have been this article that first called Talleyrand's attention to Thiers,[42] or it may have been that Talleyrand's interest in Mignet's reviews of the *Letters of St. James* brought the old man of the Revolution into contact with his young protégé.[43] At any rate, the appearance of *The Pyrenees* settled the matter, and one evening Thiers met Talleyrand at the house of Laffitte. Whenever the encounter took place, and it seems to have occurred at Talleyrand's request, it was a memorable event in Thiers' life. The old diplomat embarked upon a discussion of the Spanish question, during which his memory of events seems to have become a little befogged. "We shall have to fight an insurrection," he said, "the worst sort of war. At another time I tried to dissuade Napoleon from interfering in Spain's affairs. Napoleon did not heed me, and in the trap into which he fell he wasted his armies and gained no glory. Well, if we abstain from interfering now, history will repeat itself." To this Thiers replied: "The Spanish have a very vivid remembrance of what the guerillas cost them, of all the pillage and destruction they cause. They will have no desire to experience again such trials. They will be even less desirous to do so, since it is not a question of national, but only political, independence, and certainly the majority will consider the invader as a liberator rather than an oppressor. 'L'Espagne est une Vendée éteinte.'"[44]

Talleyrand appears to have been impressed by this confident stranger who dared to disagree with him, and he invited him to call at his house. In the words of Thiers, from that hour Talleyrand adopted him,[45] and from this friendship both derived considerable advantage. The younger man found in the experienced old statesman a friend, sympathetic, loyal, and inspiring. Due to the latter's influence and to the assistance of other friends, he was enabled to buy a sufficient amount of stock in the *Constitutionnel* to give him a voice in its direction. Cauchois Lemaire and Thiers bought a share which was to entitle the latter to a vote. The first assistance came from Baron Cotta de Cottendorf, a

AT PARIS

well-known editor of Leipzig with whom Thiers had become acquainted when he moved from the Passage Montesquieu to rue de Choiseul, where Alexander Schubart, a publisher and friend of Cotta, lived. The Baron was an astute man of business who was keenly interested in journalistic enterprises at Paris. It was Cotta and Laffitte who gave him this start.[46]

But out of this association grew other things. Thiers visited Talleyrand frequently. They discussed politics, and Thiers voiced often the opinions of Talleyrand in his articles for the *Constitutionnel* and the *Tablettes*. " He never asked me to do anything, but he had a certain way of looking at me and of addressing me that I soon understood, and when he had something to say to the public, he mentioned it before me."[47] In the same breath the older Thiers recalled that Talleyrand did not at that time conspire with him. " Il ne préparait rien et il prévoyait peu (il était bien trop nonchalant !) il attendait ; mais l'évènement une fois survenu, il l'acceptait san discuter et personne n'avait un coup d'œil aussi prompte et aussi juste pour en tirer parti."[48]

These words may well be taken as a true description of the attitude of Talleyrand, bourgeois, and Louis Philippe in 1823. In spite of the violent statements of writers who favour a more reactionary school of politics, there exists no definite and available material to prove other than an attitude of silent waiting on the part of those who would one day unite to bring Louis Philippe of Orléans to the throne.

The establishment of his own identity in Paris by *The Pyrenees*, the friendship with Talleyrand, and his new relation to the *Constitutionnel*, made living somewhat less of a problem for Thiers, but these more favourable conditions did not permit him to adopt a less strenuous method of working, or to take his ease. " J'ai deux diners à servir tous les jours à Paris et à Aix," he wrote.[49] The duty of keeping his mother and other relatives he had already assumed, and he was determined not to forget these obligations now that better times had come to him. Nevertheless, of necessity his life became less monotonous and more varied. There were more demands on him. There were the conventions of society to be observed. He must frequent the salons of the bourgeois hostesses and maintain the welcome that he had already established there. In the circle of the Liberals and of the *Doctrinaires* he became a frequent visitor; a short, little man, with eyes singularly bright, so bright, in fact, that they seemed to illuminate the large glasses which covered them; his mouth twisted into that dry little smile that became so familiar to France, and that was so dreaded by his enemies, talking with an unparalleled vivacity and *esprit* on all subjects, from finance and astronomy to religion. There was more confidence, more certainty, than had appeared in the eager and nervous barrister of Aix. Paris must have changed him, but the change was not only in manner, there was also an alteration in appearance. He had learned to care for himself, and he must have had a more vigorous bearing. The portraits of him at this period of his life are sufficient evidence of this fact. Then, too, he had learned the manners of society. Though born in the provinces, he did not long retain the outward characteristics of a provincial. To succeed, he must do as the young Parisians of his age were wont to do, and in following them Thiers frequently ran into debt. Like them, he must indulge in some form of recreation, and he selected the one that was probably least suited to him when he attempted to master the equestrian art. This was an effort for which he was manifestly unfitted because of his small stature and his quick, nervous temperament. But Thiers was not to be outdone. He frequented the *ménage* of Carréga, a former officer of the Empire, noted and admired by Parisians for his skill as a horseman. Under that veteran's direction the young provincial set himself to his task, and in this instance, as in many others, went to extremes. He wished to be a second Alexander. So great was his enthusiasm that the delightful Bourgeois de Paris, who had observed him, remarks: " I am almost surprised that in his ardour to become a cavalier he did not attempt to become a jockey in a steeplechase, as did so many youths of good family." [50]

The social metamorphosis of Adolphe Thiers was not the only development of the year 1823. Another change, perfectly logical at his age, occurred; his political opinions began to crystallize and to become more definite. He had always been an admirer of the Revolution; he had always adhered to the Liberal side. Even his attitude to Spanish affairs was not in line with that of the Ultras. What sort of Liberal was he?

It seems unlikely that this question could have been answered before the year 1823. With that year, however, he had begun to evolve a political doctrine. In October 1823 he wrote these lines:

" Two things are beginning to be accepted in regard to our political situation. The first is the present triumph of the aristocratic party and the powerlessness of the Opposition; the second is the necessity of waiting until this party has completed its destiny and its life. For the one, life consists first in forming and in growing, then in dominating exclusively. Finally it will fall to pieces by its very victory and dissolve into its last elements. The accomplishment of this process is more or less rapid according to the times, places, and political circumstances. In a democracy where one party recognizes nothing as above it, where it involves the sovereignty of the people, and where, in fact, it exercises the same; where nothing moderates its passions, it lives with greater brilliancy, *éclat*, and rapidity, and in two or three years its time of decrepitude will come. It is different in the case of an aristocracy that,

THIERS AND THE FRENCH MONARCHY

invoking monarchical authority, is forced to submit to it and endure moderation." [51]

What is this, after all, but Talleyrand's practice of waiting? But while waiting, Thiers would formulate a new political philosophy.

Unlike La Fayette, d'Argenson, and Manuel, he did not feel that the apparent conspiracy of monarchy against the charter justified conspiracy against monarchy. He had passed beyond those Liberals who felt that Monarchy was at best a concession that had to be made temporarily for the peace of the country. If not, then, a Liberal of the type of Manuel, what was Thiers? Was he *Doctrinaire?* Even here a distinction should be made between him and the Royer-Collard–de Broglie–Duchatel–de Rémusat school. These men were far more theoretical and far more scholastic than he was. Sincere in their belief in a moderate liberalism of philosophy, literature, art, and politics, they were willing, nevertheless, to accept Monarchy if Monarchy, or Republic for that matter, would apply these principles. But Thiers was different, and this difference was due, in great part, to his history. Born in 1797 of the Revolution, educated under the Empire, hating both clergy and aristocracy, admiring only the strength of France under the Empire, he had witnessed the terrific fact of humiliation at the hands of foreigners, when the Reaction of 1814 had set in. Living in the south, he had experienced, undoubtedly, much of the more vicious Reaction of 1815. And when, in 1821, he came to Paris, he brought his love of France and of her grandeur, his admiration for Revolution and Empire. These he put in the Liberal Press of Paris, and these appear in his earliest writings. Yet it should be remembered, as de Rémusat points out, that never for a moment was he anarchical.[52] His advocacy of liberty was always restrained by his love of system and order. From these sentiments Thiers finally evolved a middle conclusion

AT PARIS

that was not in accord with Manuel's satellites nor yet truly *doctrinaire*. This middle policy was nothing less than Constitutional Monarchy. While admiration of England was then a common thing, it had not yet been advocated as a platform.

In theory Thiers was unique, but he was also unique in method. To bring about such a change he did not advocate revolution, but reconstruction. It was not necessary to uproot the Monarchy, to destroy the Charter, to decentralize France. Only one principle must be driven from France, and that was " Legitimacy," the doctrine of the Ultras that declared the right of the restored Bourbons, the successors of Louis XVI, to rule as Louis XVI had ruled. It is wrong to regard Thiers as the exponent of Republic or the enemy of Monarchy; " Legitimacy " was his only political hatred, and to accomplish its overthrow he devoted all his energies during the seven succeeding years. For this campaign the little author of the *Journey to the Pyrenees* was already sharpening his weapons in 1823. His weapons were *crayons*, and the field for the conflict was the field of history!

NOTES TO CHAPTER III

[1] de Gerainville : *Histoire de Louis Philippe*, II. 28.
[2] *Ibid.*, p. 36.
[3] *Ibid.*, p. 35.
[4] *Ibid.*, p. 45.
[5] Thiers, Aix, September 1821. Bibliothèque Nationale, 20,601, No. 3.
[6] *Revue des Deux Mondes*, Loew-Veymars, 1835.
[7] *Le Correspondant*, 1922, Lacombe, p. 238.
[8] Simon, *Thiers*, p. 136. *Le Correspondant*, 1922, F. Benoit, p. 795. Mignet, Paris, December 13, 1821.
[9] *Le Correspondant*, 1922, F. Benoit, p. 794. Thiers, Liancourt, December 6, 1821.
[10] *Le Correspondant*, 1922, F. Benoit, p. 796. Thiers, Paris, December 23, 1821.
[11] *Bourgeois de Paris*, II. 307.
[12] Note in Mademoiselle Dosne's own hand on Thiers' bound copy of National-Bibliothèque. Thiers.
[13] Thureau-Dangin : *Parti Liberal*, p. 207.

[14] Thiers, Paris, to Madame Etienne, July 29, 1822. Bibliothèque Nationale, 20,601, No. 4.
[15] Thiers, Paris, to Rouchon, May 10, 1822. Musée Arbaud, Aix-en-Provence.
[16] L. Martin: *Thiers*, p. 21. Thureau-Dangin: *Parti Liberal*, p. 208.
[17] Simon: *Thiers*, pp. 137–38. Zervort: Thiers, p. 34. *Revue des Deux Mondes*, February 15, 1845, Sainte-Beuve.
[18] Thiers, Paris, to Rouchon, May 10, 1822, Musée Arbaud, Aix-en-Provence.
[19] *Ibid*. A propos of Thiers and his personal friendships among the painters, see *Revue de Paris*, July 1, 1924; an interesting article by M. Henri Malo entitled " M. Thiers et Les Artistes de son Temps."
[20] *Ibid*. Gérard: *Correspondance*, pp. 357–58, P. Thiers, Paris, August 26, 1827. Thiers, *Salon de 1822*, pp. 29, 30, 90, 91.
[21] Thiers, Paris, to Rouchon, May 10, 1822, Musée Arbaud, Aix-en-Provence.
[22] *Ibid*.
[23] Thiers: *Salon de 1822*, p. 14.
[24] *L'Album*, September 30, 1822. Thiers, p. 10.
[25] *Ibid*.
[26] *Memoires de l'Art Dramatique, Mistress Bellamy*. Thiers, xv–xvi.
[27] Thiers, Paris, to Rouchon, May 10, 1822. Musée Arbaud, Aix-en-Provence.
[28] Senior: *Conversations*, I. 62. *Le Correspondant*, 1922, Lacombe, p. 978.
[29] Senior: *Conversations*, I, 62–63.
[30] Ministre de l'Intérieur au Préfet des Hautes Pyrénées, December 29, 1822. Archives Nationales, F 7, 6934, 9994.
[31] Thiers, Tarbes, to Rouchon, December 19, 1822. Musée Arbaud, Aix-en-Provence. Thiers, Paris, October 2, 1822. Bibliothèque Nationale, 20,601, No. 4.
[32] Thiers: *Les Pyrénées*, pp. 1–3.
[33] Thiers, Tarbes, to Rouchon, December 19, 1822. Musée Arbaud, Aix-en-Provence.
[34] Préfet des Hautes-Pyrénées, Tarbes, December 19, 1822. Au Ministre de l'Intérieur, Préfet de l'Ariège, December 23, 1822; au Ministre de l'Intérieur. Bureau Militaire et de la Police, Préfecture des Bouches-du-Rhône; au Ministre de l'Intérieur, January 23, 1823. Archives Nationale, F 7, 6934, 9994.
[35] Bureau Militaire et da la Police, Préfecture des Bouches-du-Rhône, au Ministre de l'Intérieur, January 23, 1823, Archives Nationale, F 7, 6934, 9994.
[36] Thiers: *Les Pyrénées*, pp. 7, 8.
[37] *Ibid*., pp. 8, 9.
[38] *Ibid*., pp. 39, 40.
[39] Thiers, Tarbes, to Rouchon, December 19, 1822. Musée Arbaud, Aix-en-Provence.

AT PARIS

[40] Thiers: *Les Pyrénées*, pp. 50, 51.
[41] Quartier Leydeau, 2nd arrondissement, October 8, 1823. Archives Nationales, 6934, 9994.
[42] Lanzac: *Thiers*, p. 9. Frank: *Thiers*, p. 21.
[43] Thiers: Paris to Rouchon, May 10, 1822. Musée Arbaud, Aix-en-Provence.
[44] Quoted: *Le Correspondant*, 1922, Lacombe, p. 978. Senior: *Conversations*, I. 62-63.
[45] *Le Correspondant*, 1922, Lacombe, p. 39.
[46] Senior: *Conversations*, I. 64. Martin: *Thiers*, p. 24. Thureau-Dangin: *Parti Liberal*, p. 206. Contracts: Thiers and Cauchois-Lemaire, March 10, 1824. Thiers and Cotta, March 10, 1824. Thiers and Schubart, January 27, 1826. Thiers and Laffitte, January 27, 1826. Bibliothèque Thiers, fol. 546-47.
[47] Quoted: *Le Correspondant*, 1922, Lacombe, p. 40.
[48] *Ibid.*
[49] *Ibid.*, 1922, F. Benoit, pp. 799-800. Thiers, Paris, April 6, 1823.
[50] *Mémoires d'un Bourgeois de Paris*, II. 305.
[51] *Tablettes Universelles*, Bulletin Politique, October 31, Thiers.
[52] de Rémusat: *Thiers*, p. 28.

CHAPTER IV

THE RESTORATION AND THE "HISTORY OF THE FRENCH REVOLUTION"

> " *Toi qui deux fois leur dois le diadème,*
> *Toi qui deux fois languises dans les fers,*
> *Napoléon à cette heure suprême,*
> *Tu partageas leurs dangers, leur revers,*
> *S'ils sont tombés en héros de la France,*
> *Toi, tu mourus de lointaines climates,*
> *Par la poison d'une infame puissance,*
> *Mais les français vengeront ton trépasse.*"
> Verses printed in a pamphlet confiscated at Troyes, January 14, 1823.[1]

> " *Le discours du Monarque des Gaules*
> *A fait baisser les fonds et hausser les épaules.*"
> February 5, 1823.[2]

NAPOLEON had died in 1821, and his loyal adherents had mourned the passing of this vestige of the Revolution. Two years later the hopes of French Liberals for alliance with Monarchy seemed to have vanished also, and, like their Bonapartist fellows, they, too, mourned a lost cause. To many it seemed that the tradition of 1789 had gone never to return, and that, if the fight for liberty was to be continued, new parties must be formed and new political methods must be developed. " The time has come to prepare the ground and to sow the seed," wrote Mignet, the ever faithful friend of Thiers. " Politics and civilization are at a standstill, and so they will remain unless real men of action appear to lay the foundations of the nineteenth century." [3]

The old order of liberty *was* vanquished, but a new generation was just reaching maturity and soon its force would be felt. Metternich might congratulate himself

'HISTORY OF THE FRENCH REVOLUTION'

that Revolution was dead, but it would be revived in a new and more dangerous form. Jacobin, Girondist, and Cordelier were no more, but in their places came lawyer, *doctrinaire*, scholar, historian; in other words, it was Bourgeois staid and stodgy who now would take the lead. Ringing in his ears was the distant rumbling of the tumbrils as they passed to the guillotine, or the booming of the guns of *Vendémiaire*, and therefore he could not brook such a genuine Restoration as the Bourbons were envisaging. He would be moderate, he would not be radical, and he could never be reactionary. When the Old Régime began to raise its head, new régime in the guise of the Generation of the Nineties appeared to oppose it.

The years 1822–24 had witnessed an advance in the cause of Counter-Revolution in France; Louis XVIII and Villèle, his minister, had been following quietly the paths of Reaction. In Press, in University, and in Foreign Affairs, they had slowly turned back from anything bearing resemblance to Liberalism. The Press law of 1822 had hushed more effectively the voice of the Liberals; the cases of newspapers suspended because of indiscreet editorials were now to be tried before the royal courts, far from the influence of liberally inclined juries. The University had been muzzled by the appointment of a Churchman as Grand Master, and the École de Médicine, and the École Normale had been purged of their Radical leaders. Elections, too, in that year had been favourable to the Government, for Villèle, by clever manipulation of the electoral colleges, had obtained fifty-four Conservatives out of the eighty-six new deputies returned. But this was not all. A law providing for higher duties on imported goods had won the Ministry the support of the large industrials and landowners, and twenty-seven newly created peers swelled the chorus of those who approved of its policies. So re-enforced, Villèle now determined to make a Machiavellian stroke. The Chamber was dissolved and new elections proclaimed.

THIERS AND THE FRENCH MONARCHY

Again the wires that the minister pulled worked successfully; a new Chamber with only seventeen pronounced Liberals resulted, and when in April 1824 a law was passed providing that each deputy should hold his seat for seven years, the Government appeared to be approaching a plenitude of power and control. The only signs of protest to these measures were the echoes of small town riots in the provinces.[4]

In this fashion Counter-Revolution was steadily entrenching itself at home during the last days of Louis XVIII under the watchful eyes of his minister. Villèle's interests, however, were not confined to the internal affairs of France alone. He was concerned also with the re-establishing of the country in the eyes of Europe; he wished to remove the suspicion with which Austria, Prussia and Russia regarded the country, and to do this he must make France the obedient servant of these Holy Allies. The occasion for the accomplishment of this desire was already at hand.

In 1820 Revolution had broken out in Spain, and Metternich, as if to test the sincerity of the French Government's protests of sympathy with the old régime, imposed upon France the duty of doing battle with the Spanish Constitutionalists. All of the country had not supported this plan; it smacked too much of Austrian dictation, of Holy Alliance, and of Reaction to suit many Liberals. But when the French armies began to win victories, and when the Duc d'Angoulême was able to demonstrate that the Restoration, too, could wage war and uphold the military prestige of France, the Opposition began to weaken. The glories of Napoleon and the wonders of the Revolutionary armies began to fade before the actual accomplishments of the Restoration generals. There is no blinking the fact that the success of the campaign against the Spanish Liberals strengthened the Restoration Government in France in spite of the many protests that had been made over the original purpose of the expedition.

'HISTORY OF THE FRENCH REVOLUTION'

By the middle of the year 1824, therefore, Villèle, Church, University, and Chamber had set out upon an open policy of returning to the more reactionary principles of the Restoration. The stage was set for the entrance of the Ultras, who were no longer timid. Their first attempt had failed; it had been called the *White Terror*. Thanks to Villèle, another effort to raise the White Standard of old Bourbonism was now possible; Charles Count of Artois, leader of the reactionary Court party, might rule in France as soon as his brother Louis XVIII was no more. The King was fast ageing, and the deplorable event for which some of the Ultras were waiting was not far distant. As a matter of fact, it came sooner than even they expected, and on August 16, 1824, the King who had succeeded to the vacant throne of Louis XVI breathed his last. He was carried to the tomb with all the pomp that France could bring to grace his last journey. *Requiescat in pace*, chanted the priests. There were tears in many eyes, but in the eyes of the Ultras there shone the hope of another resurrection.

The Count of Artois assumed the name of Charles X. The selection of this title was not without significance for the future of France. A miserable predecessor of that name had learned nothing from the religious revolt that had occurred during his youth, and all the horror of the reign of Charles IX had been due to his failure or refusal to understand it. This latest Charles likewise had been taught nothing by the political upheavals of the French Revolution. He was himself the epitome of Conservatism. He was Ultra in politics, in religion, and in clothes. On the famous night of August 1789, when so many nobles had sacrificed their inherited rights, Charles had refused to renounce his privileges. In August 1824 his mind had not changed; he was determined to regain what had been taken from him thirty-five years ago.

Furthermore, in this determination Charles was not

entirely blinded by revenge. He had the means at his disposal to make at least a beginning. In contrast to the advisers of the Opposition, the counsellors of Charles were men of cunning and ability. Vitrolles, ardent Royalist, was a man of no mean political sagacity; Jules de Polignac was the head of a family famous for its loyalty to Louis XVI, and an experienced statesman. Neither one of them was animated by the spirit of ruthless revenge: to do them justice, these men and their followers were sincere. If they would not tolerate bargaining with the people, it was because they did not believe in the people. If they did not regard themselves and their new King as bound to the rules that had been established by the demands of the people, it was because they believed that Monarchy and its incumbents had a more divine sanction, that of God Himself. It is a mistake to regard the inner coterie of Charles's intimates as motivated by selfish interest alone. They believed in Monarchy by right divine as much as they believed in the Nicene Creed. More than all else, they were convinced that in 1824 the old régime could still be restored.

Possibly, in this last opinion, they were not entirely wrong. Had Charles been gifted with a real political sense, it is not unlikely that he might have established a more enduring reign, for the spirit of the pre-Revolutionary days was by no means extinct in France.

In the provinces many vestiges of the past survived; landholding continued to be the general principle and the peasants do not appear to have been much interested in political rights. The Revolution had not brought them prosperity; on the contrary, it had brought them the Terror with its representatives *en mission* and foreign wars. Monsieur le Comte and Madame la Comtesse were still the idols of many small rural communities in which even to-day the feudal spirit exists. In many localities the lord of the château remained the father of the little village of souls that clustered under the walls of his mansion. He continued to be their protector in

'HISTORY OF THE FRENCH REVOLUTION'

1824, even as he is still regarded as their friend to-day. These small village communities were still the centre of social life in the provinces. There were few towns of any great size, for the Industrial Revolution was yet in its infancy, and while the spirit of Liberalism could be found in these infant industrial communities, it was not yet very effective and not at all co-ordinated owing to the lack of communications.

Furthermore, the power of the Central Government extended its tentacles into the smallest villages, for Bonaparte had bequeathed to the Restoration an administrative system that might have been made to serve the cause of the Ultras themselves, and perhaps to secure for them a more lasting control than was actually the case. The Emperor had decreed that the prefects, magistrates, and police should be appointed by the Central Government. Even the prefects selected the mayors of the communes. This system had been taken over entirely by the Restoration, and it might have become a powerful instrument in the hands of the Ultras' King. The machinery for counter-revolution existed in 1824; but this was not the only advantage that Charles had.

Not the least important among other favouring circumstances was the psychology of the Liberal Opposition in 1824. The Liberal party was weakened, divided, and dispersed. La Fayette, the great living symbol of democracy, claimed alike by Extremist and Moderate of the Left, was out of the Chamber, and had gone to America to find consolation for his defeat in the honours that the young Republic desired to offer him. Manuel, a veteran of some twelve years' standing and patron of Thiers, had been expelled from the Chamber by reason of his opposition to French intervention in Spain. Only General Foy, who had so bravely covered the retreat of the French Army of the Pyrenees in 1814, and who had fought with equal courage from the floor of the House when, in 1819, the principles of the Revolution were endangered, remained in the Legislature. To his name should be added that of Casimir Périer, wealthy banker and man of iron. But these two could not control the Liberal Left. The General was feared because of his former association with Napoleon, and the capitalist, as a banker, was regarded as a man too intimately allied with the bourgeoisie. These men had not the confidence of the more Republican-minded followers of Manuel and La Fayette, and so the Opposition, lacking intelligent leadership, was incapable of effort. Probably many of them felt as did Guizot, the budding *Doctrinaire* who is said to have remarked to Manuel: " Far from believing that a change of dynasty is necessary, I should regard it as a danger. *Je tiens la Révolution de* 1789 *pour satisfaite aussi bien que pour faite.*"

Indeed Charles, the new King, must have been hopelessly misguided not to have been able to take advantage of such a situation and to mould it to his own designs!

This extraordinary failure of the King seems to have come from a complete misapprehension of the condition of public opinion in France. He under-estimated the fact of the Industrial Revolution. When he believed that it would die in its infancy, he forgot that it was healthy and that this new force would grow. He was not clear-sighted enough to realize that this new economic development would re-fertilize the effort of 1789. But more than all else, the King failed to understand his capital.

Charles judged Paris by the provinces, and in this he was grievously mistaken, for while Paris has led France, she has never been as the rest of France. The provincial hates Paris although he will eventually ape her modes and follow her lead. The city was then, and will be for all time, the centre of politics, intellectual effort, and art in France. In 1824 she boasted of seven hundred thousand inhabitants when few other French towns could claim as many as one hundred thousand residents. The administrative arm of the Monarchy might extend from Paris to the smallest commune and its mayor, but there was another arm that, with industrial growth in France, would begin to reach from the communes to Paris and thus exert their influence in the capital. This was a factor that appears to have escaped the notice of the reactionary king. Aix-en-Provence sent its sons to Paris. There were Doctors Arnaud and Messieurs de Lauris who, as time went on, sent other and lesser Mignets and Thiers from the provinces to the city that was at once the pride and hatred of France. And there, in the bourgeois salons of the *Chaussée d'Antin*, reigned the new men of the 'nineties, Villemain, Cousin, Rémusat, Duvergier de Hauranne, Carrel, and even in a lesser degree the intelligent little Thiers. Aided by their elders, Manuel, Laffitte, and Périer, who received them, these men began to make themselves felt and their opinions heard. Here was a growing force that all the pomp of a coronation at Rheims and the Laws of Sacrilege could not eradicate. The new Bourgeoisie and Industrialism had come to stay and must be taken into the reckoning sooner or later.

While the King was blinded to the social change that was coming over Paris, he was also mistaken in that he misconstrued the apparent silence of the Opposition. When the noise of the Clubs had temporarily subsided, and when only seventeen Liberals were seen and rarely heard in the Chamber, Charles felt that he was supreme. The subsidence of demonstration led him and his ministers to believe that propaganda against the Restoration was at an end. Confident in their security, King and Court were totally unaware of a novel form of opposition that was being slowly evolved under the very eyes of royalty by the new men of the 'nineties. In contrast to the practice of the past, it was an opposition of silence that consisted in a quiet, steady vote against the measures of the Government were they good or bad, in an effort to make it impossible for the Government to be a government at all. In fine, at the very moment when Charles and many others thought that Liberalism was vanishing, the means for its regeneration was coming to maturity. The Press was throttled, but Carrel could write seditious articles and some wealthy bourgeois patron of the Moderate Left would pay the fine. Guizot, Villemain, and Cousin might later be driven from the Universities, but they could still talk in the salons of Paris. Political editorials might be prohibited, but Thiers could write a history, and History has more than once served as an effective means of political propaganda. The fact that absolutism revived in France at the same time that the *History of the French Revolution* appeared is not without its significance.

There have been so many excellent studies, both contemporary and of a later date, treating of this first pretentious work of Thiers that a detailed criticism of the *History* would be merely a repetition of what has already been done. There is, however, an aspect of the *History* that has been too frequently neglected, and that is a consideration of the work as the product and result of the *milieu* in which its young author had lived and grown.

The *History of the French Revolution* began to appear at a very appropriate time. At the very moment when the reign of Louis XVIII was nearing its close, Thiers set to work. The elections so favourable to Villèle had just occurred. The full Restoration so desired by Charles of Artois and his coterie was on the point of accomplishment. Nobility was declaring its rights and proclaiming its virtues; in the *History*, Thiers recalled its vices. Monarchy was vaunting its recent victories in Spain for the cause of Holy Alliance and its principles, and Thiers recalled that liberated France had defeated Holy Alliance. Republican clubs thought on riot, and Thiers described the Terror and warned France of the danger of the multitude. It was revolutionary propaganda that this work contained, but it was propaganda for the best of the Revolution. It was sympathetic to an aspect, but in contrast to previous works on the subject it was not opposed to Revolution nor was it favourable

'HISTORY OF THE FRENCH REVOLUTION'

to its excesses. Thiers was preaching a sermon on Moderate Liberalism, the Credo of the new Bourgeoisie.

It was appropriate indeed that the two friends, Mignet and Thiers, decided to become historians about the same time.[5] The former's work appeared in 1824, and the first two volumes of Thiers' *History of the French Revolution* were issued in 1823. These earlier volumes do not bear the name of a single author on the covers. The publishers probably felt that Thiers was not yet well enough known, and it was at their request that Félix Bodin, formerly an editor of the *Constitutionnel*, was associated with the young author. It is very doubtful that Bodin had anything to do with the actual writing of the books; after the appearance of the first two volumes, Thiers alone figured as the author.

As soon as they had appeared, Thiers sent them to Étienne, and at the same time he wrote to his mentor:

"Très Cher Maître,

Here is my first fairly serious work, that is to say, my *History of the French Revolution*. I beg for the child the same welcome that you have already shown the father, and (then) they will both owe to you their small fortune. My two volumes have been confided to the *diligence* and they should reach you shortly. I hope that you will read at least one of them, for (then) your article could include that sort of criticism that you know (best) how to give, instead of a (mere) expression of friendship. A little criticism will do no harm, but haste especially will do wonders. If my two volumes sell, I shall have one or two thousand francs more. That is something for a young fellow who is without patrimony and without sobriety. Blow, therefore, in my sails; your testimony is one that will please me more than that of any other *littérateur*. I wish that you would allow me to place an 'É' at the end of the article. That is not necessary for the *connaisseurs* who can recognize you, but for the plain public it will be a mark of authenticity. I apologize for my egoism, but I am uneasy, as in a first *accouchement*." [6]

To his request for haste our *très cher maître* acceded, and his article appeared within a very short time; Étienne had followed to the letter the petitions of his protégé. From the sale of the first volumes Thiers did not make a fortune, for he had not yet acquired that remarkable art of negotiating with his publishers in such a way as to assure himself of a small fortune before the book was even written.[7] In his more mature years Thiers was an apt dealer in literary futures.

The subsequent volumes appeared in rapid succession and the young author was kept busy running all over Paris in search of his sources. Many of the latter were oracular, being conversations with survivors of the Revolution, a fact which accounts in great part for the peculiar charm of the *History*. It is, in fact, a mirror of the mind of that society in Paris of which the budding historian was becoming a part. It betrays their opinions, their hopes, and their ideals. It is an echo of the discussions that took place in the bourgeois salons of Paris where Bonapartist, Republican, and Constitutionalist foregathered. At times one can almost hear Talleyrand as he reads the lines, or Jourdan the general, or Baron Louis the statesman. With all these men and with many others the young historian talked. He plied them with questions Boswell-like, and from the living wreckage of the Revolution he gleaned his material. Sometimes he wearied his prey with his persistence. One day he encountered the brilliant Madame Gay. Ah! here was a chance to obtain atmosphere for the Directory!

Thiers : " What I regret not to have seen are the brilliant receptions during the Directory, the joy of meeting again, the need of social intercourse, the Greek *toilettes*. Tell me all about it."

'HISTORY OF THE FRENCH REVOLUTION'

And Madame Gay talked of the soirées, of Madame Tallien, and of Madame de Beauharnais. On and on he led her, farther and farther back, until the poor lady cried: " And are you not also going to ask me how they dressed and amused themselves at the marriage of Marie Antoinette? " This question appears to have silenced her relentless interviewer, for Thiers had made the mistake of asking her about things that had happened before she was born.[8]

These were golden days for the indefatigable worker, and he revelled in them. At last he seemed to be aware of his own potentialities. To Rouchon, faithful friend at Aix, he wrote :

" I am quite well, pushing away at my Revolution and preaching now for three years (the doctrine) that the Left lacks common-sense, that they are foolish as the *Émigrés*, and that it will take perhaps fifty years to re-establish an enlightened, indignant, and powerful public spirit. Philosophy, science, and industry alone will return to us our convictions and our powers, but it takes time for them to act. The petty instigators of riots are fools and idiots and are, for the most part, men who have been corrupted in one or two régimes and who wish the present one to terminate at once, because they are old and want to be prefects once again before they die. The youth (of France) alone hope for and look to the future because they still have years ahead of them." [9]

The above letter indicates quite clearly that the young Thiers did not purpose to write a purely narrative account of the great Revolution; in fact, he makes a full confession of his intentions in the first preface to Volume I.

" I propose to write a history of the memorable Revolution that stirred men profoundly and that divides them to-day. I have not blinded myself to the difficulties of the undertaking, for the passions that we thought had been quelled under a military despotism have begun to revive. Suddenly men who are weighted down with years and affairs have felt reborn within them the disagreements that they believed had disappeared, and they have communicated them to us, their sons and heirs. But if we have to sustain the same cause, we do not have to defend their conduct, and we can distinguish between the liberty of those who have served it well or ill, since we have the advantage of having heard those old men, who, still full of memories, still agitated in their impressions, reveal the spirit and character of their parties and teach us to understand them." [10]

In the earliest volumes at least, Thiers is loyal to this purpose, and throughout these books there is an unmistakable strain of political argument for a Government far different from that in existence in 1824. The young author is not inimical to the idea of Monarchy. His treatment of the unfortunate Louis XVI is kindly almost up to the last, but it gives him the opportunity to expound the virtues of his ideal government—*le roi règne et ne gouverne pas*—the famous limited kingship *à l'anglaise* that would soon become the rallying cry of those bourgeois (many of whom must have been readers of the *History*) who proposed to substitute Louis Philippe of Orléans for Charles X the Bourbon. In fact, Thiers is in haste to introduce the English system to his readers, and he does so at the earliest possible moment, when he introduces the Swiss banker, Jacques Necker, who had been persuaded by Louis XVI to try to disentangle French finances : " Necker was the only one who had not a place but a wish. He had always desired the English Constitution, *the best without a doubt that one could adopt as a means of accommodation between the throne, the aristocracy, and the people.*" [11]

'HISTORY OF THE FRENCH REVOLUTION'

A little farther on, while describing the efforts of the National Assembly at constitution-making, the beloved *gouvernement à l'anglaise* is discussed again :

> "The English Constitution was the model that appealed naturally to many minds, because it was the arrangement arrived at in England after a similar debate between the King, the Aristocracy, and the People. This Constitution consisted essentially in the establishment of two Chambers and in the royal sanction. But the minds of men in their first impulse go direct to the most simple ideas; a people that declares its will, a king who executes it, appeared to them as the only legitimate form of government. To give to the Aristocracy a part equal to that of the Nation by means of a high Chamber, to confer upon the King the right to annul the will of the Nation by means of his sanction, seemed to them an absurdity. *The Nation wills, the King fulfils.* Their minds did not go beyond these simple principles, and they believed that they wanted a Monarchy because they left a King as the executor of the National Will. Real Monarchy, as it exists even in the States that are called free, is the domination of one man who is restricted by the support of the Nation. The will of the prince here accomplishes all, and that of the Nation is limited to restricting the evil, either by disputing taxes or by appealing to the law. But from the very moment when the Nation can command what it wishes without the King's opposing a veto, the King is nothing more than a mere magistrate." [12]

In the second volume the discussion as to a desirable government is continued and concluded. The Constituent Assembly that drew up the first Constitution was succeeded in October 1791 by the Legislative Assembly. Before commencing his narrative of the Legislative's accomplishments, Thiers pauses and passes judgment on the work of its predecessor.

" The power conferred, it was necessary to reconstruct it in a just and suitable manner. But at the sight of this social scale at the top of which everything was lacking, even bread indispensable to human life, the Constituent Assembly experienced a violent reaction and desired to reduce everything to an equality. It decided, therefore, that the mass of citizens, once equalized, should express their will, and that the King should be charged only with carrying out that will.

" Its mistake was not at all to have reduced the Monarchy to a mere Magistracy, for there still remained to the King sufficient authority to maintain the laws, and even more authority than the Magistrates of Republics possessed. But its great error was to have believed that a King who possessed the memory of what he had been could resign himself to this new position, and that a people who had just come into enjoyment of a part of public power would not wish to assume all power. History demonstrates, in fact, that it is necessary to divide infinitely the Magistracies, or that, if one sets up a single power, it must be so arranged that it has no desire to usurp.

" When nations almost exclusively occupied with their private affairs feel the necessity of giving to a chief the cares of government, they do well to give themselves one. But then this chief, the equal of the English kings, with power to convoke and dissolve National Assemblies, only accepting their wishes or sanctioning them when they suit him, and only prevented from doing great harm, should really enjoy the greater part of the sovereignty. The dignity of man can still survive under such a government when each citizen realizes what he is worth, and knows that the great powers left to the prince were only abandoned to him as a concession to human weakness."

Aix had taught Thiers Revolution; his work for the *History* had converted him to the principles of Constitutional Monarchy, but in his opinion France of the seventeen-nineties was not ripe for such a government. The Revolution must follow its ordinary course before the ideal could be attained.[13] It was only in 1824 that the time had come, and in that year he undertook to proclaim the fact to his countrymen through the medium of this work of ten volumes.

In so far as there may be any real political significance to the *History*, it is to be found in the first two volumes. Considered as a purely historical work, however, they are in great part useless. They were done in haste; the sources, although they were general and varied, were not exact, for at the time the writer could draw only upon the impassioned testimony that was replete with explanations, apologies, and recriminations. When Talleyrand talked, he was explaining himself, and when others related their actions, they must have had in mind the criticisms that had been levelled at them. The treatment, too, is frequently uneven and there are obvious gaps. There is no mention of the origins of the revolutionary movement. The Philosophers are practically ignored.[14] Financial and economic considerations are reduced to a minimum, and there is only a vague mention of the irregularities of the feudal *impôts*.[15] These are only a few of the instances of omission and negligence that might be given.

But the bourgeois for whom his work was written were not scholars and received the results of his labours with acclamations. Simon relates that Thiers was not pleased with the applause of the Liberals.[16] Nor was he blinded to his shortcomings by Étienne's unstinted praise.[17] A change came over him; he became more serious in regard to his work and he desired to study his material more carefully; he wished to become a real *savant*.[18] Perhaps already the empty glory of academic laurels began to hover before him. He frequented Talleyrand more assiduously and he consulted Baron Louis, who helped him disentangle the financial intricacies of the period. He conferred with Jomenin and Jourdan on military matters. The same passion that he had formerly betrayed for the equestrian arts was diverted to the study of military strategy. He haunted the rendezvous of artillery officers and through them obtained admission to the manœuvres. Some of his friends were amused by what they regarded as his latest fad, but it was not amusing to Thiers; it was serious business, and it was a business that succeeded, for the beneficial results of his intensive venture into financial and military matters are apparent in the later volumes.

The later books of the *History* reveal Thiers as a writer of potent and dramatic ability. As a narrative they have not been surpassed, and the enthusiasm of the youthful author of twenty-eight knows no bounds. At times this latter characteristic carries him far. He becomes a hero-worshipper, and his heroes are indeed an oddly assorted lot. The young bourgeois from Marseilles is attracted by Bailly, the dutiful, the unselfish, " a plain citizen known only for his virtues and his talents, who presides over the great ones of the realm and of the Church." [19]

Thiers too was of the people. It is small wonder that he is captivated by Mirabeau, a *compatriot*, " né sous le soleil de Provence." [20] He is fired by the latter's power and eloquence, and fascinated by the sheer hideousness of the man. Another hero of a totally different character is La Fayette, whose loyalty to the King he upholds.[21] In the personalities of the later period Thiers does not find so much cause for admiration. To this there is one exception, Danton, and even in this instance Thiers has been credited with having expressed a good deal more

THIERS, WRITER AND HISTORIAN.

'HISTORY OF THE FRENCH REVOLUTION'

sympathy for the leader than seems actually to be the case.[22]

This hero-worship is for individuals, however, and never for *the people* themselves. He looks upon the Breton Club with a suspicious eye; he shows no special respect for the Jacobins. As for the mob, he gives his readers a very severe lesson on that subject when he is relating the events of November 1793.

> " It is with disgust, doubtless, that one beholds these scenes without restraint, devoid of sincerity, where a people changes its religion without understanding the old or the new. But when is a people sincere? When are they capable of understanding the dogmas that have been delivered (to them)? Ordinarily, what do they need? Large reunions that satisfy their craving to be called together; symbolic spectacles where they are reminded of the existence of a power superior to themselves; finally, feasts where homage is rendered to those who have nearest approached the good, the beautiful, and the great; in a word, ceremonies, temples, and saints!"[23]

It was not the mob that occasioned his enthusiastic outbursts; it was rather the steady and remarkable procession of able though unscrupulous men who carry the Revolution to its logical conclusion that inspires him. His admiration for these extraordinary " lords of a day " has been the basis for the charge that he was an apostle of success. It has been said by some of his bitterest critics that in his *History* he expressed his admiration for a man or a régime until failure set in and then he turned to an enthusiastic support of the successor. This comment is hardly just. The *History of the French Revolution* is an epic of patriotism written by an ardent young Frenchman in the full bloom of his love for his native land at the very moment when he perceived that it was losing its enthusiasm. Any deed or action accom-

THIERS AND THE FRENCH MONARCHY

plished by any of the régimes that redounds to the glory of the *patrie* is to him an evidence of the French genius in which he so sincerely confided. The successes of the Revolution are the occasions for an outburst of praise, but that is not to say that Thiers was fickle or that he believed in the abominable doctrine that the end justified the means. On the contrary, he has not allowed his enthusiasms to carry him too far, and in the course of his narrative he has not hesitated to pause and to express censure. An example of this may be found in his summary of the Terror, when the Convention was under the thumb of Robespierre. At the opening of the Terror the allied armies were threatening even the roads to Paris ; extreme measures were deemed necessary, and Robespierre established his practical dictatorship :

> " In order to continue as supreme dictators of this immense work, they destroyed alternately all parties, and in accordance with human nature they experienced the excesses of their qualities. These qualities were force and energy ; their excesses were deeds of cruelty. They spilled torrents of blood until, become unnecessary by the victory (of the armies), they succumbed. The Convention then assumed control and little by little they abated the extreme rigours of the administration. Reassured by victory, they listened to the voice of humanity and gave themselves over to a spirit of regeneration. All that was good and great they desired to attain to, but the (various) parties that had been weighed down under a pitiless authority revived under a kindly order. Two factions, in which men of infinite shades of opinion were confounded, both friends and enemies of the Revolution, attacked in turn the Convention. The first was vanquished at Germinal and Prairial, the other at Vendémiaire, and to the last day the Convention was heroic in the midst of danger. At the end they drew up a Republican

'HISTORY OF THE FRENCH REVOLUTION'

Constitution, and after three years of struggle with Europe, with factions, and with itself, they retired and gave France to the Directory.

"Their memory has remained terrible; but in their behalf there is one tremendous fact to declare, and all the accusations that have been raised against them fall; the Convention saved us from foreign invasion! The preceding Assemblies had bequeathed to them a France compromised, but the Convention gave to the Directory and to the Empire a France secure." [24]

The success of the work is familiar. From the date of its completion its author was recognized as a writer of merit. The undertaking and successful accomplishment of such a task led him to make a momentous decision; an historian he would be, and the *History of the French Revolution* would have a sequel. On April 2, 1826, he signed with Alexandre Schubart, publisher, a contract for the publication of a *History of the Consulate and the Empire*. This work was to begin where the previous history left off. It was to include at least four or five volumes. When it finally appeared it comprised twenty! Far different were the terms of this second contract; he was to receive three thousand five hundred francs per volume issued for the first edition of two thousand copies, and in the interval of its composition Monsieur Schubart agreed to advance sums of money that were to be arranged "à l'amiable." [25]

As a matter of fact, Thiers became distracted by more important matters, and when the sequel appeared he was almost twenty years older; Monsieur Schubart was not the publisher, and the fortunate Thiers received more than three thousand five hundred francs per volume issued. As well, his publishers advanced him over one hundred thousand francs during the period of its writing. Evidently the young Thiers had not studied finances under Baron Louis in vain!

NOTES TO CHAPTER IV

[1] Archives Nationales, F 7, 6934, No. 9881.
[2] *Ibid.*, F 7, 6934, No. 9885.
[3] *Le Correspondant*, 1922, pp. 802-3. Mignet, Paris, October 3, 1823, to S. Benoit.
[4] Archives Nationales, F 7, 6934, Nos. 9885-86.
[5] Thiers, Paris, August 12, 1822, to Rouchon. Musée Arbaud, Aix-en-Provence.
[6] Thiers, Paris, September 11, 1823, to Étienne. Bibliothèque Nationale, 20,601, No. 4³.
[7] Contract between L. A. Thiers and Lecomte et Durey, publishers, September 15, 1823. Bibliothèque Thiers, fol. 546-47.
[8] Malo : *Une Muse et sa Mère*, p. 150.
[9] *Le Correspondant*, 1922, pp. 805-6. Thiers, Paris, November 3, 1824, to S. Benoit.
[10] Thiers : *Revolution Française*, I. 1.
[11] *Ibid.*, I. 116.
[12] *Ibid.*, I. 136-37.
[13] *Ibid.*, II. 3, 4.
[14] *Ibid.*, II. 122-23.
[15] *Ibid.*, I. 94.
[16] Simon : *Thiers, Guizot, Rémusat*, p. 146.
[17] Thiers, Paris, October 9, 1823, to Étienne. Bibliothèque Nationale, 20,601, No. 4⁴.
[18] Thiers, Paris, August 12, 1822, to Rouchon. Musée Arbaud, Aix-en-Provence.
[19] Thiers, *Revolution Française*, I. 170.
[20] *Ibid.*, I. 117-20, 162, 179.
[21] *Ibid.*, I. 109-10, 177-97 ; II. 179-80.
[22] *Ibid.*, II. 199-200, 297-98, 303-4 ; V. 205-6.
[23] *Ibid.*, V. 201-3.
[24] *Ibid.*, VII. 385-88.
[25] Contract between L. A. Thiers and Alexandre Schubart, publisher, April 2, 1826. Bibliothèque Thiers, fol. 546, 547.

CHAPTER V

THE CRITICAL YEARS (1824-30)

THE years 1824-30 were critical years for Charles and for Thiers; during them both met their fate and set out upon those paths that determined their different destinies. The King experienced a baptism into the religion of Reaction, while the historian completed his education as a political journalist. Charles's initiation was in public, while that of Thiers was in secret and hidden from the eyes of most of his countrymen.

The spectacular coronation of the King had taken place at Rheims, where all the pomp and panoply of Church and royalty had been revived. Even the sword of Charlemagne was said to have been recovered to grace the sacring of this latest Defender of the Faith, and the holy oils that had been used to anoint the head of Clovis were believed to have been found to consecrate the new hero of Jesuit and Ultra. On the very eve of such an impressive occasion Chateaubriand had taken up his diary and written these words: " There are no hands virtuous enough to cure the King's evil; there are no holy oils powerful enough to make kings inviolable."[1] Which is to say that in 1824 two deadly parallels existed in France, Counter-Revolution and a revived Revolution. The coronation and the *History of the French Revolution* were the respective symbols of these two forces that within a short time would tear France asunder. So ill adapted to the nineteenth century were the tactics of those who upheld the principles of Rheims that the Revolution had only to wait until Ultra and King had heaped up a mountain of prejudice that one day would become top-heavy and fall upon the builders themselves. A strange sort of fatality seemed to pursue Charles X and his minister Villèle: every move that they made alienated some group in France, and this was true of those who would normally have supported them as well as of those who were their enemies by instinct or tradition. In the end the King pleased no one but himself and a very few of his coterie.

Charles himself had been an *émigré*, and one of his principal interests was to recompense those who he felt had been deprived of their property during the Revolution. From the very first day of the Restoration he and his Ultras had persistently demanded indemnification for their lands that had been confiscated. To return to them all or even part of the property was out of the question, and they had set a valuation on their losses. In this they had shown that, although adherents of the old régime, they were gifted with a good business sense. Their demand was not modest; one billion francs was the figure that they had named! It was utterly out of the question for the Government to pay outright such a sum, but some method of satisfying the King's party must be found, and to its discovery Charles devoted much of his thought. Such a problem, however, was not an easy one, for the louder the Ultras cried for indemnity, the greater was the fear of the Bourgeoisie for its own financial security. If the question was allowed to remain long without solution, the delay might affect the prosperity of the country and wreck the chances of the Monarchy. Charles was naturally impatient. At last, Villèle thought he had solved the problem, and he tried to better the situation by soft words in the coining of which he was so adept: " Security to the present holders, satisfaction for the *émigrés*." By this he meant that he would attack the purse and not the property of the Bourgeoisie through a reduction of the interest on Government bonds. These securities now paid five per cent.; hereafter they would yield only three per cent. This, said he, will make it possible to pay the

THE CRITICAL YEARS

interest on the billion that the King believes is due the *émigrés*. When announced in the Chambers the proposal created a furore. In the Deputies, General Foy and Benjamin Constant led the Opposition, while in the Peers, usually so docile, a vigorous protest was made by Chateaubriand and de Broglie. In spite of these efforts the measure was passed in 1825. Paris may have shrugged its shoulders at the coronation at Rheims, but many Parisians were not amused when their incomes were reduced by such a measure. The very class that Villèle had placated by his high tariffs in 1824 he had now antagonized.

The affair of indemnification must have occasioned not a little amusement to the young author, who was now filling the stalls of the Quai Voltaire with his *History of the French Revolution*. As a matter of fact, Thiers had narrowly escaped being concerned with the policy of the Restoration Government. In April 1824 he had carried on a rather odd correspondence with certain members of the Ministry who were at this time intent upon pacifying the Ultras in France. In fact, it is not at all unlikely that his affair with Villèle was due in part to the publication of the earlier volumes of the *History*. His researches had led him far into the field of economics. He had consulted frequently Baron Louis, a former finance minister of the Empire, and aided by the latter he had been enabled to present an intelligent analysis of the economic policy of France during the period of the Revolution.[2] At the same time he had had a hand in the publication of another work on finances. The Ministry had proposed a new system for the conversion of Government bonds. The proposal seems to have been sound, but it was an innovation and it was not acceptable to many of the Liberals. Paris was flooded with pamphlets on the subject, and newspapers discussed it in lengthy editorials. One pamphlet among others attracted especial attention because it bore the name of Jacques Laffitte, banker and

THIERS AND THE FRENCH MONARCHY

Liberal. It appears that Thiers, who had recently published an article entitled *John Law and His System*, participated in the writing of Laffitte's *brochure*. Contrary to the popular expectations, the banker and his young scribe supported Villèle's measure in no uncertain terms. These facts were brought to the attention of the Ministry, and negotiations were opened between the Government and Thiers. In April he received an anonymous letter asking him to write more articles in favour of the proposed measure. The wording was soft and ingratiating: "No one is more capable than you are," the unknown writer declared.[3] Though flattered, the astonished recipient of this unexpected communication did not lose his head. He suspected a trap and so he hesitated. Finally, he replied by requesting his anonymous correspondent to disclose his identity. The response that he received was even more flattering and offered the *Moniteur*, the organ of the Government, for the publication of the articles if Thiers would write them. The letter concluded: "As to the name of your correspondent, I hope that you will not make that a *sine qua non*. It should be sufficient for you to know that, next to the Minister of Finances, he is the man who would attach the greatest importance to your work. The young economist who has so truly said that in our modern society all is represented by gold, will not refuse to receive the price of a service rendered to his Country."[4] To this the "young economist" responded that he would be glad to comply because of the question involved and because of Monsieur Laffitte, to whom he owed what little he knew of finances, but first he must know the name of the writer and to what uses his articles would be put. This reply concluded the affair, and Thiers heard no more of it. As a matter of fact, Villèle himself was the author of the letters and he had even been seriously considering the possibility of offering Thiers a position in the Finance Department.[5] But for the facts of his extreme youth, his obstinate refusal to obey the suggestion of an unknown authority, and perhaps his political opinions, the young Thiers might have become a part of the Restoration Government. Would he then have launched the terrific attack that he inaugurated a few years after the episode had been concluded?

The indemnification of the *émigrés* quieted temporarily the Ultras, but there was another plank in their platform that had to be considered. Closely allied with Monarchy stood Church, and Church, too, had suffered by the Revolution in loss of property and prestige. Like the nobility, churchmen must be raised again to their former position of pre-eminence and respect. The King was blind to the fact that Catholicism when persecuted attains again and again its real perfection. Charles was a Catholic, but not of the liberal-minded, de Bonald type. He could never have understood La Mennais; it is doubtful whether he could have comprehended Lacordaire, Montalembert, or even the saintly Frédéric Ozanam. To him they would have probably seemed Abbé Gregoire all over again, or even Gobel, the remarkable Archbishop of Paris, who publicly abolished Christianity in the Archiepiscopal See of Paris. His well-intentioned efforts were ill-advised, to say the least of them. The first bit of religious legislation was almost a necessity; the Law of Sacrilege made it a capital offence to profane, steal, or mutilate Church property. But this law, wise in its purpose, extreme in the penalty that it inflicted, was merely a prelude to a policy of general religious toleration envisaged by the King. In the face of existing legislation the Jesuits were allowed to resume their activities in France. Great numbers of other religious orders returned, and the influence of the Church in the schools of France was facilitated. Hated by the Grand Master of the University, the courses of Guizot, Villemain, and Cousin were suspended, and the École Normale was closed a second time. These practices irritated not only the secular Liberal and the indifferent bourgeois, but they displeased as well not a few Catholics who were known as Liberal Catholics, who did not desire a return to Church privilege and the perilous alliance of Monarchy and Papacy. Possibly they were embarrassed by the untimely policies of Leo XII, who had come to the Papal throne in the previous year. These men, the advocates of a Gallicanism not unlike that of 1682, joined the opponents of the Government in their cries of protest. Popular replies to the reactionary measures of Charles and his friends took the form of demonstrations at the funerals of Foy and Manuel, the two Liberals, both of whom died in the course of the year 1825.

People's riots could be quelled by the police, but more drastic measures were needed to control the activities of the Press, where criticism of the Ultra régime was bitter and almost constant. The next concern of Villèle was, therefore, the Liberal newspapers. His weapon was a sweeping law popularly known as the " Vandal Bill of 1827." Its provisions would have required every newspaper to deposit with the Government the manuscript copy of every issue five days prior to its publication. The Act contained as well a declaration to the effect that previous regulations relative to " Liberal tendency " were to apply to all publications, magazines and books, as well as newspapers. Oddly enough, the greatest opposition came from the quarter where it was least expected. The Peers opposed vigorously the measure and finally brought about its defeat. When an earlier law re-establishing primogeniture was voted down, the defeat of the Government was celebrated with illuminations in Paris, and on the occasion of the loss of this latest proposal, the capital again indulged in rejoicings while the Government buildings remained dark and unadorned.

In brief, the two years of the partnership of Charles and Villèle had not resulted in popularity for either of them. The minister had begun with an unmistakable

THE CRITICAL YEARS

majority, but in 1827 he found himself confronted with a growing Opposition in both Chambers. Outside of the Legislative matters were not much better. The King had been insulted at a review of the National Guard, and the Government had replied by disbanding that organization. The Guardsmen had been compelled to doff their uniforms and pack them away for a more auspicious occasion that would come in July 1830, when the same Guardsmen had their revenge by forcing Charles to doff his crown.

The Guard abolished, the nobles and clergy reinstated, the Press throttled, the one remaining blot was the Opposition in the Chambers. In his handling of this matter Villèle made the greatest error of his career. In 1824 he had strengthened his hand by persuading the King to create new Peers and by calling for a new election. Evidently he believed that in 1827 history would repeat itself. Accordingly, seventy-six new peers were created and new elections were announced. But the latter failed to give the minister the support that he needed. He had alienated too much of France during those two critical years, and at the very moment of the crisis an event occurred that united for a brief time all of the different shades of the Opposition. It was the policy of Villèle in regard to Greek independence that caused his downfall.

Together with many other nations of Western Europe, the people of France had long sympathized with the heroic struggle that the Greeks had commenced in 1820 to obtain their independence from the Sultan. But Metternich, Holy Alliance, Charles, and Villèle had not allowed France to carry her sympathy too far. No official act of the Government had given the slightest indication of French concern. This had been left to individuals and to groups. French Liberals rejoiced in the war, for they saw in it the reflection of their own glorious Revolution. Catholics and Conservatives favoured it as a movement against the infidel. Poets, artists, and writers were thrilled at the possible revival of Classical Hellas. It is indeed odd that one particular writer, Thiers, has left no record of his sentiments at this time. From the first day of his administration, Villèle had encountered difficulty in restraining the enthusiasm of some of his countrymen. In 1825, when the massacres occasioned by Egyptian interference occurred, sentiment in France became almost too powerful to control. The cry was for intervention. But England, as usual, had preferred the method of diplomacy as a policy more advantageous to herself, and Villèle, faithful to Canning, managed to stand out against war. The French fleet might observe and police, but that was all. Then, in July 1827, came the great event at Navarino, when suddenly Russian, English, and French fleets struck a blow at the ships of the Pasha. At that instant Villèle's policy was discredited and his enemies arose. In despair he appealed to the country, and in its reply he read his own failure. He who in 1824 boasted of a mere Opposition of seventeen, in December 1827 found only one hundred and fifty supporters in the face of his two hundred and fifty opponents. On December 5, Villèle retired, and the Moderate Martignac succeeded him.

These affairs of religion and diplomacy did not affect especially the young economist with whom Villèle had corresponded in 1824. During the early days of Charles's rule, Thiers had remained faithful to his *History*, that is, as faithful as one of his variety of talents could be. Research of a sort and journalism claimed his attention. For the *Constitutionnel* there were articles to write; for himself, there were friends to be made and salons to be visited; art to be criticized and money to be raised by promises of wonders of histories to come. Political discussions were still mere incidents, and at first history and art were his chief concerns. The yearly salons he visited assiduously, and there in 1824 he resumed the education that he had begun in 1822. In literature and

THE CRITICAL YEARS

philosophy he had disdained the romantic and declared for the school of the natural; the same was true in regard to art.[6] There is ample evidence of this fact in the review of the Salon of 1824 published by him in midsummer of that year. He vaunted his admiration for Sigalon's " Narcissus," and praised that artist's avoidance of exaggerations in colour and in design. " You need not group the figures so that you cannot discover their condition or their situation; you need not deprive an old woman of her arm. It is not necessary to attach an arm to a horse's tail and display it upright without anything to support it. It is folly to say that Nature is disordered. Nature is abundant in accidents, but all (of them) are motivated by physical reasons. You need not place bodies in the air with nothing to hold them up. When Michael Angelo distributed his demons and his damned, he used a great number of accidents, but there is not a single one of them that contraverts physical laws."[7] To Thiers, the impressionists of 1824 were Jacobins in art, and he bore them the same grudge that he expressed for the Jacobins in politics in his *History of the French Revolution.*

The explanation of this passion for the natural is not difficult to discover. Even in these early years he prided himself on being a classicist, but was he aware of the fact that he was only a classicist *à la Renaissance?* It was the latter period that captivated him and that formed the basis for whatever taste he developed in art. " Although I consider that humanity in our days is as well organized as in the fifteenth century, I do not believe that there are two races like the Italian and two epochs like the fifteenth century."[8] So wrote the art critic who had not yet seen Italy and who had given only a cursory glance at the art of the Renaissance that was to be found in Paris! Small wonder, then, that this *connaisseur* found in Delacroix and Sigalon at least traces of that race and of that epoch that continued to be his passion for the remainder of his life!

If the naturalistic was his first basis for criticism, the historical was his second. In literature he had noted a marked tendency to reproduce the manners, customs, and characters of the past. In the Salon of 1824 he was delighted to discover the same thing. This fact he proclaimed aloud. His doctrine was that the real painter must be an historian; he must possess the historical sense; he must be correct in portraying the emotions of his subjects and the environment in which they find themselves. How he must have admired the awful historical realism of David, the Revolutionary painter! To Delaroche, and especially Scheffer, he gave the laurels for historical accuracy. In the latter he beheld the historical painter *par excellence*, and the portrait " Gaston de Foix " he regarded as a page from History itself.[9] What would he have said had he entered the Panthéon and beheld the portrait of good Sainte-Geneviève gazing over her beloved Paris, for all the world resembling a Syrian woman looking over a minareted city of the East?

It is impossible to take Thiers as an art critic entirely seriously, but that is not to say that he did not take himself seriously. On the contrary, from 1824 he began to interest himself in the careers and works of all the painters. His reviews of the Salons were enlivening and instructive, but they can hardly be regarded as serious or expert criticism. Nevertheless they are important, for in them there is a sign of a growth and a development. There is less bombast. His phrases are more concise, and he is beginning to develop that ability to make every word have a real significance and a real importance in the lines that he wrote. This change first appears in the Salon of 1824, and is more evident in his later articles for the *Constitutionnel* and for the *Encyclopédie Progressive*, a project of his friend Baron Cotta, to which Thiers and Mignet contributed. Of this later growth Thiers himself appeared to have been conscious. In fact he practically confesses to it in a letter to Rouchon at Aix, anent the latter's article for the *Encyclopédie:*

THE CRITICAL YEARS

"I have read your work and I feel exactly as Mignet does about it. Order, neatness, pictures—all is perfect. The descriptions of places, a detail so important in history and so very often neglected to-day, are wonderfully done in these chapters. I only hope for certain changes in style, not that I find yours lacking beauty, there is much of that, but I should wish for a little more freedom and a little more variety of language. There are some expressions that are peculiar to our section of the country and that should not pass beyond the Rhône or the Durance. There are others that are affected in their extreme simplicity and that recall too vividly the classical. That is an old habit that we acquired and of which increasing age should cure us. The ancients are sublime, my friend; for poetry and art I always turn to them, but we must not think of them when we write prose. They were not thinking of anyone and that is why they are so wonderful. A great writer must have a strong mind and one that is profoundly moved. That you have. Accustomed to write, compelled to say many things and at length, one does not consider overmuch the language to be employed; one uses it only as a medium, and then one becomes natural (in expression) and fluent. As Fénelon says, it is habit that teaches one to dress and not to decorate. But, I repeat, nothing is easier than that; everyone acquires it once he has learned it. Mignet, whose style was strained, has corrected it; I, too, had the same fault and I have it no longer. I am negligent, but that is not the fault of the method, it is rather the fault of my own careless self. Let yourself go and then re-read: I do not re-read enough." [10]

In December 1827, Thiers probably had occasion to repeat this advice to Rouchon in person, for in that month he set out for the Midi. The real motive for this journey is not entirely clear. His *magnum opus* completed, it would seem perfectly natural that he should leave Paris to rest among his own people, and to visit his mother who had remained at Aix.[11] There appears to be nothing surprising in his departure from Paris, but then we are not the watch-dogs of the Restoration. It is not necessary now to regard with suspicion everyone's move. There is no need to exercise a rigid surveillance over all the youth of Paris, and the authorities need not investigate the slightest sound, the opening of a door, or the stealthy tread of feet along a narrow *trottoir* in a dark street. Which is to say that in the latter part of the year 1827 Charles's Government was uneasy, and that Thiers, as one of the *Jeunesse Libérale* of Paris, was regarded as an *enfant terrible*, and was one of the causes of anxiety in official circles. Certain passages in the *History* and most of the articles in the *Constitutionnel* had made him an object of suspicion to the secret police. Then, too, Charles's minions did not like Thiers' friends. He went with bad company. His intimacy with Laffitte, with the lamented Manuel, with Étienne and with others of the Opposition was sufficient justification for watching his movements. The result was that his short journey, that lasted from December 1827 to January 1828, was closely observed by central and departmental authorities.[12] Monsieur the Minister of the Interior addressed to the Prefect of the Bouches-du-Rhône a request to watch Thiers and to ascertain the nature of his activities.[13] Evidently these orders were scrupulously observed, for on January 8, when he had begun his return journey to Paris, Monsieur le Préfet replied as follows:

> " Monseigneur, Sire Louis Adolphe Thiers, formerly a lawyer at the Bar of Aix, and one of the editors of the *Constitutionnel*, to whom Your Excellency called my attention in your letter of December 9, did not limit his stay to Aix. He went to

THE CRITICAL YEARS

Marseilles, where he remained for three days, during which time he was visited several times by Monsieur Borély, Vice-President of the Civil Tribunal, and by Monsieur Thomas, lawyer, one of the Constitutionalist candidates at the last elections, and by several other persons connected with the legal profession in that city.

"These relations are indeed ground for conjecture, and there is nothing to indicate that Sire Thiers came to Marseilles for private affairs—that the purpose of this visit was to communicate with these gentlemen, who are known for their extreme political opinions, and to inform himself from them of the spirit and opinion generally among the inhabitants of the city."

The Préfet also remarked that this apparently innocent object of their suspicions visited friends of the same shade of political belief at Aix.[14]

The above would seem to indicate that Thiers at least profited by his presence in Provence to obtain whatever information he could for his friends of the *Constitutionnel* at Paris. He had left Paris at the time of the Villèle crisis, and when he returned the Martignac Ministry was in power. He lost no time in reporting to his friends at Aix the condition of affairs in Paris and the difficulty that Martignac was encountering. In his letters Thiers tells them that the King had been so anxious to retain Villèle that he had given him *carte-blanche* to form a Ministry of any possible colour and that Villèle had even asked Laffitte if he would join with him.[15] As to the new Ministry, few believed that it would last long. It had no colour; it was grey; everyone was refusing positions offered by the new President of the Council, and some did not believe that it would even survive the opening of the Chambers.[16]

In fact, the Martignac Ministry found favour with no one. Charles X hated it, the Ultras despised it, and the

THIERS AND THE FRENCH MONARCHY

Liberals distrusted it. Thiers remarked of it: " Le nouveau ministère est tout de doublures." And yet it appears that Martignac made a genuine effort to better matters. He sought to placate the Liberal opposition by discreet concessions in regard to the University and the Press. Guizot, Villemain, and Cousin were reinstated in their professional chairs; a new and more liberal Press law was established. Censorship was abolished, as was the offence of " tendency." But the real measure of the new Ministry's Liberalism was found in the fact that trials of the Press were still restricted to the royal tribunals, where they were secure from sympathetic juries. One more gage of Liberal sympathies Martignac tried to give, and that was his re-enforcement of the Law of Public Education that forbade teaching by any religious orders other than those already authorized by the law. In reviving this regulation the minister was aiming at the Jesuits, whose activities had increased materially since the accession of Charles X to the throne. Such a system of contradictory concessions did not please all of France. The Right was offended, and the distrust with which the Left had always regarded Martignac was increased. In the columns of the *Constitutionnel* and the *Globe*, Thiers, Mignet, Duvergier de Hauranne, and de Rémusat continued to question the Government. Finally, they challenged the minister by calling upon him to give evidence of his good faith by declaring publicly his adherence to the principles of 1789. This cry was taken up by the Opposition. They waited, and to quiet them, a new electoral law was promised. Again there was a time of suspense. At last the promised measure appeared, only to occasion disappointment to those who hoped, rather sceptically perhaps, for good things from Martignac's " reform." The law accorded only a slight modification in the existing system by the establishment of provincial assemblies. The Royalists were angry; this was going too far. On the other hand, the Liberals were furious; this was not far enough ! On April 9 the

THE CRITICAL YEARS

Martignac Ministry fell, and its dissolution brought a time of evil forebodings. The men of the Opposition thought that they were prepared for the worst, but when the new ministerial combination was announced they discovered that their gloomiest anticipations had been more than realized. To the astonishment of the world, Polignac, but for the King himself the most Ultra of Ultras, was named President of the Council. The nomination of the latter was interpreted as a wilful throwing of the gauntlet by the King. It was a deliberate challenge from Reactionary to Liberal.

The years 1824–29 had been critical years for Charles and for his young contemporary, Thiers. During that time, the King had tried to re-establish by legal means the old régime in which he believed; but he had found that he could not accomplish a complete restoration by such methods and he was forced to resort to more questionable measures. In a different sphere, Thiers, too, had passed through a crisis. He had tried his hand at all trades, as historian, dramatic critic, and art critic. Particularly difficult had been the last year when, his *History* completed, he had felt the need of a compelling interest. Then it was that, finding it nowhere else than in Clio's arts, he had returned to her *culte* and set to formulating a plan for a monumental history. This work would go beyond the bounds of pure history; it would be something that was greater, more potent, something of which he had often dreamed, that would " be at one and the same time a poem and a philosophy." [17] Thiers, too, was not to escape at least the first fascination of that fatal desire that has ruined the prospects of more than one promising historian. But he was more practical than some of these unfortunates have been. If he would write of the world, he must first see the world, and lo! the door of opportunity was opened to him. Through the influence of Hyde de Neuville, Minister of Marine and son-in-law of Villèle, it was arranged that the young Thiers should travel on the ship *Favorite*, whose captain

THIERS AND THE FRENCH MONARCHY

was about to make a voyage of circumnavigation. Great was the enthusiasm of the prospective voyager! His plans were made, and all was in order when the hand of Charles the King at the Château designated Polignac as the successor to the unfortunate Martignac.

The minds and plans of many were disturbed by this unexpected action of the King, but probably no single individual was more affected than Thiers. He abandoned his *tour du monde* and decided to remain at his post among the journalists in Paris. The die was cast; into politics he would go, and the plan of a universal history was put aside, to be revived at a later period of inactivity. The years 1824-29 had whetted his appetite for the battlefield of political controversy, and his experience as a writer of history had taught him to admire the army. The virtues of these two courses he extolled at the very end of the year 1829. War and politics, he wrote, are the true portrayers of a man's character, for all his soul is in one or the other; "look at the works of the most famous poets, savants, and authors. Even their finest works will never reveal to you what was the real temper of their minds. There is only one thing equal to the art of war, and that is the art of governing." [18]

With these words Thiers took leave of his muse and abandoned his activities as historian and critic for seven years.

NOTES TO CHAPTER V

[1] Chateaubriand: *Mémoires d'outre Tombe*, IV. 179.

[2] *Vide* Chapter IV.

[3] Anonymous, Paris, April 4, 1824, to Thiers. Bibliothèque Nationale, 20,601, No. 8.

[4] Anonymous, Paris, April 10, 1824, to Thiers. Bibliothèque Nationale, 20,601, No. 9.

[5] Hyde de Neuville, 1866, to Mademoiselle Félicie Dosne. Bibliothèque Nationale, 20,601, No. 11.

[6] Thiers: *Salon de 1824*, p. 15.

[7] *Ibid.*, p. 18.

[8] *Ibid.*, pp. 10 and 12.

[9] *Ibid.*, pp. 20–23.

THE CRITICAL YEARS

[10] Thiers, Paris, May 30, 1826, to Rouchon. Musée Arbaud, Aix-en-Provence.

[11] Thiers, Paris, January 12, 1828, to Rouchon. Musée Arbaud, Aix-en-Provence.

[12] Prefect of Police, Paris, December 8, 1827, to Minister of Interior. Archives Nationales, F 7, 6934, 9994.

[13] Minister of Interior, Paris, December 9, 1827, to Préfet du Bouches-du-Rhône. Archives Nationales, F 7, 6934, 9994.

[14] Préfet du Bouches-du-Rhône, Marseilles, January 8, 1828, to Minister of Interior. Archives Nationales, F 7, 6934, 9994.

[15] Thiers, Paris, January 2, 1828, to Rouchon. Musée Arbaud, Aix-en-Provence. Chateaubriand (*Mémoires*, IV. 217) asserts that Villèle also approached Périer.

[16] Thiers, Paris, January 12, 1828, to Rouchon. Musée Arbaud, Aix-en-Provence.

[17] Thiers, Paris, August 12, 1822, to Rouchon. Musée Arbaud, Aix-en-Provence.

[18] *Revue Française*, November 1829: Thiers, p. 169.

CHAPTER VI

THE 'NATIONAL' (1830)

THE most immediate result of the appointment of Polignac was a change in the Opposition. Until August 1829 there was not any generally organized action against Charles X. Such action as had occurred had been sporadic and individual. Thiers as a member of the staff of the *Constitutionnel* might visit and consult with Borély and Thomas, the leaders of the Opposition in Marseilles, but when he did so, it was as one of a group in Paris and not as the emissary of a vast, organized, political machine. After the nomination of Polignac, however, groups of malcontents began to coalesce. But even this is not to say that real party machinery developed. What organization took place was entirely sectional, and was brought about under the guidance of regional leaders who appear to have acted quite independently of each other. In some places, even, the clubs revived, but these should not be confused with the earlier Carbonari sections in France; their purpose was not so radical nor were their methods so elemental. While opposed to the Government, these did not desire to overthrow it with bloodshed; instead they proposed to embarrass it by legal means. *The League of Breton Resistance*, for example, refused to pay taxes not sanctioned by the law. The Society known as " Help Thyself and Heaven will Help Thee " sought to obstruct legislation incompatible with the Charter. Perhaps the clubs under the direct tutelage of La Fayette and the Masons were somewhat more radical. All these groups, whether Moderate or partly Radical, did much to disseminate the spirit of opposition in France, but little to unify it, and practically nothing to educate it and to make it intelligent. Men confessed that they were discontented with the political actuality, but they could not bring forward a substitute that was entirely satisfactory. Many, except the workmen and *exaltés*, shuddered at the word Republic, for the years 1789–95 were still too vivid in their minds. While Charles and his Government were doomed, it is not unlikely that they would have survived longer had not a force arisen to educate the several public opinions, and to enlighten and lead an ignorant Opposition.

The first move in this direction had been made by the Republicans when they had inaugurated a new paper, *La Jeune France*, in June 1829.[1] But this paper was too radical to gain much support from the bourgeoisie; the banker and the industrial saw in its propaganda a menace to their own security. For the needs of these more cautious gentlemen, a moderate and less extreme system must be proposed and its safer theories disseminated. It was to this end that the *National* was founded during the latter part of the same year.

This latest addition to Paris journalism was an outgrowth of certain elements from the *Constitutionnel* and the *Globe*. The latter sheets had been advanced for the years 1820–27, but by November 1829 they had fallen far behind the aims and ideals of many of their subscribers and of certain young editors connected with their boards. But their stock-holders were conservative men who feared to jeopardize their business interests by countenancing all that the *Jeunesse Libérale* desired. It appears that Thiers actually tried to persuade the board of the *Constitutionnel* to approve the adoption of a more radical policy, but he failed in this attempt in spite of the support of Étienne and of Evariste Desmoulins.[2] When he was convinced that he could not transform the political programme of the *Constitutionnel*, he retired from its staff and joined with Mignet and Armand Carrel in the organization of a new sheet. The *National* became the organ of a new Opposition.

THIERS AND THE FRENCH MONARCHY

It stands to reason that Thiers would not have taken such a step without the advice of other men, older than he, more experienced, and better endowed with this world's goods. For the three to have founded a new paper alone would have been out of the question, for no one of them possessed a sufficient income, and as yet the position of none was assured in Paris. Of the three, Thiers was the best known and was regarded as a young man of promise. Mignet was already recognized as a competent and dispassionate historian, and Carrel had recently published a work on the Counter-Revolution in England that had brought him a certain notoriety. But no one of them was strong enough at that time to stand alone. There must, therefore, have been encouragement from powerful quarters that led the trio to attempt a new venture in Paris journalism, but it is difficult to discover exactly where the support that the *National* received originated.[3] Undoubtedly, Prince Talleyrand was concerned in it, for he acted as a pivot for that section of the Opposition with which Thiers had become identified. However, Talleyrand and even his garrulous niece, Madame la Duchesse de Dino, have been careful to leave no trace of this in the papers and letters that they have bequeathed to posterity. In spite of their silence, one may suppose, then, that Talleyrand advised and approved. During the short-lived Ministry of Martignac the Prince had carried on a brief flirtation with the Restoration Monarchy, but with the coming of Polignac, this remarkable navigator of the political seas sniffed the air and steered his ship straight into the harbour of Orleanism, where Sébastiani, Broglie, Villemain, and Molé had established themselves. Probably these men too were consulted. There remain Jacques Laffitte, that friend of Louis Philippe of Orléans and protector of Thiers, and the mysterious Baron Cotta of Cottendorff. Both of these men gave financial assistance to the plan.[4] But who was the first sponsor? Some would like to throw on old Talleyrand the onus of the entire affair. They present a possibility that is attractive. They take us to Rochecotte, the château of the Duchesse de Dino. There, in the country far from prying eyes, came Baron Louis, former associate of Talleyrand in Bonaparte's Government. With the Baron were two young men, Thiers and Mignet. And these three, in the presence of the old Prince and his niece, who, like her uncle, never missed a trick in the political game, arranged the plan for the *National* that was to prepare France to depose one king and enthrone another.[5] This story may be true in every detail; in its essence it most certainly contains the truth. Talleyrand aided them with his advice, and Baron Louis very likely gave them a more material blessing. But not a sou did the Prince contribute, for his personal fortune was indeed small. *A propos* of this, Chateaubriand remarks, " The Prince de Talleyrand did not contribute a sou; he only soiled the spirit of the paper by contributing to the common fund his share of treason and corruption." [6] Whether the scene at Rochecotte occurred or not, the fact remains that after the last of November, 1829, Thiers was an assiduous visitor wherever Talleyrand happened to be located, and that he held long and serious consultations with him.[7]

With support from these various sources, the three principal editors established the head-quarters of their paper in the Place des Italiens, rue neuve-Saint-Martin, No. 10. Within a very short time after its appearance, the *National* became the recognized authority to define and explain the policy of a large and growing section among the Left. In this way, an Opposition that was not united in any sense received an unconscious guidance and direction from the journal whose words they read with delight and whose suggestions they frequently followed, without, however, acknowledging in any way the leadership of the paper, its editors, or its stock-holders. The young editors inspired many readers who had become weary of the dull and old-fashioned platitudes of the

Globe, the *Constitutionnel*, and the *Courrier Français*. In fact it was not long before the example of the *National* reacted upon its more venerable and timid contemporaries; in time the *Tribune*, the *Temps*, and the *Globe* attempted to follow the pace set by the daring young journalists. Great must have been the amusement of Mignet and Thiers when, in April 1830, the latter paper was brought before the courts on a charge of radicalism.[8] This was the début of the *National*; what, now, was its real purpose?

Over this question there has been much discussion. In later years Armand Carrel became a radical Republican, and this has led some to infer that, from the very day of its inception the *National* was a Republican sheet. As a matter of fact, Carrel's case of Republicanism was very mild until the July Days. To discover the true colour of the paper, one must turn to the man who first presided as its editor-in-chief and to his friend, Mignet. Neither one of these two was Republican in 1830, and that is why Thiers broke with Carrel later in the year; furthermore, neither the editor-in-chief nor Mignet ever advocated violence against the existing Government until the July Days. Even his most hostile critics do not assert that Thiers wished a return to the early seventeen-nineties. In the first place, his bourgeois supporters would never have consented to such propaganda, and in the second place, it would have been contrary to his own political beliefs. He was still loyal to the opinions that he had expressed in the years 1823–27 when the *History* was being written. While he advocated Revolution, the methods that he and his friends advised were legal.[9] *Legitimacy* as represented by Charles and Polignac was their only enemy, and this must be reformed or else done away with entirely. But before either one of these solutions could be brought about, public opinion and public sentiment must be created, and the first step in such a task was to teach Frenchmen history and politics. Instruction, then, was one of the primary aims of the *National*, and in this respect the paper may be regarded as the continuation of the *History of the French Revolution*. To this programme Thiers, Mignet, and Carrel adhered faithfully.

To a certain extent the early policy of Polignac assisted the paper at the outset. It gave the young editors a breathing space and an opportunity to establish themselves in the mind of Paris. Contrary to popular expectation, the minister did not inaugurate immediately a drastic, reactionary policy. Due in part to his characteristic procrastination and in part to the timidity of certain of his colleagues, Polignac was at first inactive. He gave the *National* a chance to teach before it set about to attack the actual policies proposed by the hated Ministry. The first issue appeared on January 3, 1830, and contained a declaration of the paper's wishes for France. It goes without saying that Thiers was the author of this article. Evidently he had expended much effort and worry upon it. He writes to Chateaubriand: "If, in this first article, which is a source of great anxiety to me, I have managed to express opinions of which you approve, then I am reassured and certain of finding myself in the right way."[10] The noble recipient of this letter, however, regarded Thiers as an advocate of Republicanism even during these earliest days of 1830, but his eyes must indeed have been blinded by prejudice, for there is nothing Republican in the words with which the editor-in-chief of the *National* begins his first instruction as to the best government of France:

> "A king hereditary, inviolable, depositary of the Government, obliged to confide the exercise of the same to responsible ministers who declare for him peace and war, draw up the laws, and administer the public funds . . . a king thus placed in a region superior to petty ambitions, above public hate, where, when all is well, he enjoys the affection of his people, and is only punished by their silence when all is wrong. Beneath this king, a peerage which is

THIERS AND THE FRENCH MONARCHY

independent of the ministers by the fact of its hereditary character, and which its lights make dependent upon public opinion; a peerage richly endowed in a country of large estates, moderately endowed in a country of divided estates, filled with the most illustrious names, conservative both in its traditions and in its political maxims, and opposing a resistance to yield to the general impetuosity of human minds. Beside this peerage, an elective assembly composed of all the men distinguished in industry, arms, science, and art, sent up to represent the country and to proclaim the nation's mind, not to nominate ministers, but to have them nominated by the use of its votes; not administering of itself, but by means of those who have its confidence. Such an ensemble constitutes the most stable and free, the most balanced and vigorous (government). It is such (a government) that we should and do desire for France." [11]

This is Thiers' ideal of what he called "representative monarchy." It is the English system stated more concisely than in the pages of the *History*, featuring especially his beloved Peerage, for which he was to fight so valiantly in 1831. As to the kingly power, however, he has more to say, and it can hardly be questioned but that when he penned these words he was trying to make his readers compare his ideal king with their actual ruler:

"Such a king is not powerless as men like to say. For when he nominates his ministers, he has the power to show his sentiments, to realize his will, to stop and even to oppose the public will not for long or for ever, but long enough to give him an effect and an interest in the Government. Without a doubt he is influenced by someone. When are kings real masters? Instead of undergoing the influences of courtiers, of women, and of confessors (this king)

THE 'NATIONAL'

experiences the influence of public opinion operating on him gently and regularly. If that is real royalty, that is also real republic, but republic without dangers." [12]

How palatable this suggestion of the gentle and regular operation of public opinion upon the person of the monarch must have been to Charles X if he read these lines! Bold were the writer's words, and yet they were not bold enough to warrant police action. They were within the bounds of legality, for Thiers did not draw odious comparisons explicitly; all was by implication. But it was strong medicine that he was feeding his patients, and even this first article justified the comment that Lamartine is said to have made upon him at this time: " There is enough saltpetre in that little man to blow up ten governments!" [13]

These quotations from the leading articles in the first issue of the *National* display in clear and unmistakable characters the political and social creed of its editor-in-chief. He was not a Democrat nor yet a real Republican. In 1830, he was not even an advocate of bourgeois rule. In 1832, Thiers discussed his opinions with William Nassau Senior, and, referring to his doctrines of 1829-30, he said: " By birth I belong to the people; my family were humble merchants in Marseilles; they had a small trade in the Levant in cloth, which was ruined by the Revolution. By education I am a Bonapartist; I was born when Napoleon was at the summit of his glory. By tastes and habits and associations I am an aristocrat. I have no sympathy with the bourgeoisie or with any system under which they are to rule." [14]

In other words, when considering Thiers' representative monarchy, one should bear in mind that it included a peerage in which, he believed, reposed the safety of the nation.

These lessons in political science were continued in subsequent articles that appeared in the *National*. The aspect of his proposed system that became the greatest point of attack of his opponents was the kingship, and in most of the later articles he is concerned with explaining the nature of his ideal state. It is when studying this problem that the relation of the *History of the French Revolution* to the articles in the *National* stands out in a very definite and curious light. In fact, it is possible to see quite clearly the origin and development of that most famous *mot* of his : " The King reigns and does not govern."

The first intimation of the expression occurred in 1823, when the first volume of the *History* appeared. The author discussed the kind of monarchy that might have saved France in 1789, and in the course of a paragraph the following phrase appears : " The nation wills, and the King fulfils." [15] Seven years later, in the course of another instruction on government that appeared in the *National*, Thiers described his King in this way : " Again, in a word, he (the King) reigns, and the country rules itself." A subsequent discussion characterizes the monarch as follows : " The King does not administer, he does not govern, he reigns." Still later, he uses a different form of the same idea : " Thus the King reigns, the ministers govern, the Chambers judge " ; and finally, the concluding lesson ends with these words : " The King reigns and does not govern." [16]

To instruct the public in a new type of monarchy was the first purpose of the editors. Their second aim was to expose the character of the existing Government. This was done at first only by implication, but as the *National* began to prosper, its chief editor became more bold. As early as the third issue of the paper, Thiers had dared to make a direct reference to the Polignac régime. Even then, however, his words were chosen carefully, for there was the ever-present danger of the enforcement of the Press laws. Without Martignac's more liberal law, such a statement as Thiers made in the issue of January 5 would have brought censure upon him.

THE 'NATIONAL'

"The Ministry that suddenly came to surprise France on August 8 could not long hide from itself the fact that the majority in the Chamber would be opposed to it. In spite of some few uncertainties in regard to specific questions, this Chamber, formed in the midst of the generous outburst of 1827, could not betray its origin to the point of accepting a more lamentable Ministry, if that be possible, than the one which it had just destroyed. Any illusion that one may have had about it for an instant could not last, and since that time the new Ministry has found itself confronted with the choice of dissolving the Chamber or of itself retiring. All the statements that have been made since then have not changed the situation. To dissolve the Chamber, and in order not to see it returned stronger and more hostile, change by violence the electoral law, or else retire ingloriously, continues to be the existing and inevitable condition of the Polignac Ministry. The thought of dissolution by means of a *coup d'état* has been advised. One part of the Ministry, the most energetic, they relate, has consented to this plan." [17]

Here was the most sensational *exposé* of affairs yet published. It disclosed a deplorable condition in the Government, and it confirmed what appears to have been quite a general impression even as early as January—that the only resource of Charles to retain Polignac was by means of a *coup d'état*. This article was written on January 5; it was only a little more than six months later that the prophecy of Thiers was fulfilled.

The month of January had been a difficult time for the young adventurers in journalism. There had been financial worries, and to these had been added the positive knowledge that Polignac was watching them and waiting to take advantage of the first slip. It must have been hard for such daring spirits to rein in their enthusiasms and so avoid a summons to the courts. In January such an occurrence would have spelt disaster. Reviewing the developments of the weeks that had just passed, Thiers wrote: " I allowed myself to be hauled into this extraordinary enterprise by a series of bizarre circumstances that it would take too long to relate to you, but that were for me a sort of cruel violence. . . . So far, the plan has had complete success, but I am not sure that I shall not always regret the quiet of my studies which I hope to resume after a little while."[18]

If January had been a month of discretions, February was the period of indiscretions for the *National*. Once assured of a large number of subscriptions and conscious of a growing sympathy among the public, the three editors sent discretion and tact flying to the four winds. So far, the only form of action advised by the paper for the Opposition had been a legal resistance by means of obstruction of legislation, and by the refusal to pay taxes not authorized by the Charter of 1814. But in the second month of its life, Thiers changed his policy by facing in its columns questions that must have occurred to him and to his readers many times: If the present régime refuses our system, what then? How may we establish our own representative monarchy and avoid a repetition of the disastrous years, 1789-95? In answer to this last problem came the reply of Thiers, that there was such a thing as a bloodless revolution. One king might go; another might come, and long live the King! One king might go; another might come, and the beloved Charter remain the same except for electoral laws and other minor matters.[19] After all, what is heredity? A monarchy will allow of both heredity and election. One aids and purifies the other.

> " Heredity allows the bad to succeed the good; election arouses the country. Thanks to the combination of the two, one inconvenience corrects the other. One prince succeeds another, but he does

not govern; others give him those who will govern for him. So you have the unchangeable in order to avoid trouble, and the changeable to avoid merit.

"Such a combination is a form of systematic indifference as to persons. France, as a matter of fact, is indeed disillusioned in regard to persons; France loves genius, and she has seen what that cost her. *Simple virtues, modest and solid, that a good education can always assure in the inheritor of a throne, that a limited power cannot spoil, that is what France needs!* That is what France desires, and that, again, more for the dignity of the throne than for herself. For the country that has institutions that are well understood and organized has nothing to fear.

"The question is, therefore, one of *things*. Some day it may become a question of *persons*, but that will only come through the fault of the persons. The system is indifferent as to persons, but if they, in turn, are not indifferent to the system; if they hate, if they attack it, then the question will become one of things and of persons at the same time. But then it will be the persons themselves who will have raised the question." [20]

Enter Louis Philippe! *Simple virtues, modest and solid, that a good education can always assure in the inheritor of a throne, that a limited power cannot spoil, that is what France needs!* In the Palais Royal he lived, surrounded by his paintings and tapestries of the Revolution, and his children fresh from the public schools of France. Enter the school of 1688, the advocates of the deadly parallel between the House of Orange and the House of Orléans! *Egalité* and his disgraceful career were overshadowed by the pitiful actuality of a *Louis Seize à la manière de Charles X* (and how inglorious for the martyred Louis!).

The transition from Stuart to Orange suggested the change from Bourbon to Orléans. This was *Doctrinaire* at his deadliest, the modern scholastic hacking away at the foundations of a venerable civilization. Revolution was born again in France under the new " aristocracy " of capitalism. The culmination of all folly was reached when Thiers, in March, in referring to his beloved English system, was carried beyond the limits of all reason and pointed across the Channel to George IV with the words : " There is the model constitutional King ! " [21]

It was not to be expected that these more daring articles of the *National* would be allowed to pass unnoticed by the Government, nor is it reasonable to suppose that Thiers and his colleagues expected to escape official censure. Just previous to the appearance of the former's article on " Heredity," the *Globe* had had its experience at the courts because in one of its articles the possibility of a change in dynasty had been mentioned. Quite naturally, the editors of the *National* came to its aid, with the result that when the *National* was summoned, the *Globe* and other papers returned the compliment.[22] In fact, the summonses received by the various Paris papers tended to create a certain unity among the journalists of the capital. The reasons given for the calling of the *National* were the articles of February 19 (quoted above) and of January 18 that had contained the words, " The King reigns and does not govern." [23] While a trial in January might have checked their fortunes, in February the young editors had such support and sympathy that the event did not cause them the slightest concern. Public subscription paid the fine.[24] This was the first, but not the last, appearance of the *National* in the courts of the Restoration Government. They were summoned again in March and in May.[25]

The sudden activity of Polignac in regard to the *Globe* and the *National* corresponds with the emergence of the Polignac Ministry from its period of apparent lethargy. As a matter of fact, Polignac had not been inactive during the early days of his Ministry. He had been attempting to strengthen himself at home by a diplomatic *coup* in the

THE 'NATIONAL'

world of foreign affairs. He knew what a tremendous effect the inauguration of a successful foreign policy might have upon his fortunes. It would snatch from the very mouths of all the Opposition the charge of inefficiency and subservience to Holy Alliance. Accordingly he cast his line into the troubled waters of the East.

Ever since the time of the great Bonaparte, France had had her eyes on the Rhine and on Belgium. With this in mind, Polignac proposed to leave Turkey to the tender mercies of Nicholas I, if the Tsar would allow France to recoup along the north-eastern and eastern frontier. Had Polignac had time to reach such an agreement with the Russian autocrat, the life of the Restoration might have been prolonged. There is no question but that such a policy would have found favour with many Frenchmen; it would have satisfied at least the desires of Bonapartists and Republicans. But Prussia, scenting the danger, got in ahead of the minister of Charles. Berlin negotiated for Nicholas the Treaty of Adrianople and the Frenchman's scheme failed. In a desperate effort to cover his defeat, Polignac turned to a gigantic enterprise of conquest in Algiers and tried to force the Bey to make reparation for an insult delivered to a French consul as far back as 1827! At that time, the Restoration had let the incident pass. But this last desperate effort was hardly under way when disaster came to the Bourbon cause in France.

Unable to obtain any glory for his King outside the boundaries of France, Polignac turned reluctantly to internal affairs. The time had come when Charles and his minister must meet the Chamber, and neither of them was very anxious to do so. On March 2 the King opened the session. The Speech from the Throne was unfortunate, to say the least of it. It was haughty in its phraseology, and the attitude assumed by the King was almost overbearing. The whole affair was interpreted as a defiance. One sentence particularly was taken by the Opposition as a challenge : " If guilty inclinations raise against my Government obstacles that I cannot and shall not foresee, I will find the force by which to surmount them."[26]

The succeeding days in the Chamber were consumed by a long debate on the Reply to the Throne. Finally, the Address was completed and was accepted by a vote of 221 to 181. It had been written by Étienne, the friend of Thiers, and by Guizot. The Address was virtually a demand for the retirement of Polignac. Concord between Monarchy and people did not exist, it declared, and could only be obtained by the formation of a new Ministry.[27] On March 18, Royer-Collard, himself an adherent of Monarchy, presented the Address to the King. The reply of Charles was a curt refusal to heed the wishes of the 221, and after consultation with his ministers, the King dismissed the Chamber. A half-way measure towards conciliation was taken when the Ministry was reconstituted, but none of those who might have saved the Restoration was acceptable to Charles. Chateaubriand remarks of the Monarchy: " They seemed to have a horror of capable men."[28] Meanwhile, the *Globe, National, Tribune,* and *Courrier Français* redoubled their attacks.[29]

By this time, the greater part of the country had come to desire some sort of change. While the majority still adhered to a monarchical form of government, it wanted a Liberal King and a system according to a Bill of Rights. Many had come to favour the attitude of the school of 1688, whose principles had been advocated especially by the *National*. But all of the Liberal papers had succeeded in stirring up a general spirit of discontent, the first material effect of which was evidenced in the results of the new elections that were announced in the early part of July. Of the 221 who had voted for the Address, 202 were returned, while only 95 of the 181 opposed to it were re-elected as Deputies. The victory was unquestionably with the Liberals. The King and his Ministry could be certain only of 150 votes in the

THE 'NATIONAL'

Chamber. The crisis foretold by Thiers in his article of January 5 had come. What was the Government to do? should it retire or break the law? On July 20, the chief editor of the *National* published these words:

" Sinister rumours are abroad in Paris to-day. In spite of the general incredulity which people have shown until now, we are all struck with the thought that a *coup d'état* will be attempted before the end of the month." [30]

Within five days this second prophecy was fulfilled. The King had violated legality, and the time had come when, for Frenchmen, the question was one of *persons* as well as *things*.

" The system is indifferent as to persons, but if they, in turn, are not indifferent to the system, if they hate it, if they attack it, then the question will become one of *persons* and *things* at the same time. But then it will be the persons themselves who will have raised the question." [31]

NOTES TO CHAPTER VI

[1] Weill, G.: *Histoire du Parti Républicain*, p. 24.
[2] Laya: *Thiers*, p. 17.
[3] Thureau-Dangin: *Le Parti Libéral*, p. 461.
[4] Cotta, Stuttgart, December 31, 1829, to Thiers. Cotta, Stuttgart, January 31, 1830, to Thiers. Bibliothèque Thiers, fols. 546–47.
[5] de Gerainville: *Histoire de Louis Philippe*, pp. 225 sqq.
[6] Chateaubriand: *Mémoires d'Outre Tombe*, V. 186–87.
[7] Colmache: *Reminiscences of Prince de Talleyrand*, I. 56.
[8] Duvergier de Hauranne: *Gouvernement Parlementaire*, X. 386.
[9] Thureau-Dangin: *Le Parti-Libéral*, p. 476. Viel-Castel: *Histoire de la Restauration*, XX. 169.
[10] Chateaubriand: *Mémoires d'Outre Tombe*, V. 167.
[11] *National*, January 3, 1830: Thiers.
[12] *Ibid.*
[13] Quoted, Simon: *Thiers, Guizot*, etc., p. 164.
[14] Senior: *Conversations, Second Empire*, I. 39.
[15] Thiers: *Histoire de la Révolution Française*, I. 36, 37.

[16] *National*, January 20, February 4, and 19, 1830: Thiers. Senior: *Conversations, Second Empire*, I. 38.
[17] *National*, January 5, 1830: Thiers.
[18] *Le Correspondant*, 1922, pp. 812–13. Thiers, Paris, February 16, 1830, to F. Benoit.
[19] *National*, February 8 and 12, 1830: Thiers.
[20] *Ibid.*, February 19, 1830: Thiers.
[21] *Ibid.*, March 31, 1830: Thiers. March 4, 1830: Thiers.
[22] *Ibid.*, February 20, 1830: Thiers.
[23] *Ibid.*
[24] Simon: *Thiers, Guizot*, etc., p. 164.
[25] Viel-Castel: *Histoire de la Restauration*, XX. 322. *National*, May 9, 1830: Thiers.
[26] *Moniteur*, March 3, 1830.
[27] *Ibid.*, March 19, 1830.
[28] Chateaubriand: *Mémoires d'Outre Tombe*, V. 88.
[29] *National*, April 21, 1830: Thiers.
[30] *Ibid.*, July 21, 1830: Thiers.
[31] *Ibid.*, February 19, 1830: Thiers.

CHAPTER VII

EXIT CHARLES X (JULY 1830)

ON July 21 the *National* had signalled the *coup d'état*, and on the evening of July 25, that prophecy was fulfilled when Charles X signed, at St. Cloud, the four famous ordinances. As he laid down his pen, the King is said to have remarked : " There, Messieurs, are strong measures, and a great deal of courage will be required to enforce them. I count on you, and you may count on me. We have a common cause. Between us, it is a question of life or death."[1] The next morning the ordinances appeared in the official paper, and the plan of the Government for maintaining its control of France was exposed to the world. The first ordinance suspended the liberty of the Press ; the second dissolved the Chamber. The third changed the electoral system to the exclusion of the bourgeoisie and the advantage of the great landlords, while the fourth law called for an election according to the new system.[2]

These decrees caused surprise in Paris. The Liberal Press had long since warned the public of the possibility of such action on the part of the Government. As early as January 1830, Thiers had hinted as much in the columns of the *National*, but in spite of these prophecies, great was the excitement when the blow actually fell. Indignation ran high, and it should be remembered to the credit of some of the most loyal supporters of the Monarchy that they were not all unanimous in approving this latest move of Charles's Government. Marshal Marmont, to whom was given the command of the troops in Paris, is said to have remarked to Arago : " Well, the fools have gone beyond their limits. You have nothing to worry about, you who are a citizen and a Frenchman, but how much should I be pitied; I, who in my quality of a soldier may perhaps be forced to give up my life in the defence of acts that I abominate and of persons who for some time have seemed to be trying to fill me with disgust." [3] Probably Marmont was not alone in this sentiment. And yet, in spite of the disgust of Loyalist and Liberal, Charles and his partisans seemed to feel that there was a basis of legality for their actions and that this basis would bring many to their support. The ground for this contention lay in Article 14 of the Charter of 1814. According to this clause, the King was empowered to make " the necessary regulations and ordinances for the execution of the laws and for the safety of the State." [4] But it was certainly a very exaggerated interpretation of this provision that would permit a king to make regulations that would transform the character of the Monarchy. It was impossible to contend, as Charles virtually did, that Article 14 nullified all the other fundamental laws of the Charter.

Obviously, the ordinances affected principally three groups in Paris, the deputies, the disfranchised voters, and the Press. Of these, the Press was the first to take any action, while at the outset deputy and voter appeared to be struck dumb. The journalists were placed under very peculiar disabilities by the second law. For the publication of a periodical or newspaper a preliminary authorization was to be required, and this must be renewed every three months. Furthermore, the Government reserved the right to revoke its authorization at any time. This amounted to the temporary suspension of all publications from the evening of the twenty-fifth, and no paper could be issued until an application had been made and passed upon. Great was the need, therefore, of the Press, and it was quite natural that they should be the first to act. It is indeed with reason that the revolution that ensued has been called a " Newspaper Revolution"; at least two of the four July Days belong to the journalists and kindred trades.

Shortly after the appearance of the new laws in the *Moniteur* of July 26, a group of journalists representing the *Constitutionnel*, the *Temps*, and the *Débats* called at the law offices of Charles Dupin to consult about the legality of the disabilities that the Ministry had placed upon them.[5] A little later, Dupin was joined by several other lawyers, Merillon, Barthe, and Odilon Barrot. With these men Dupin went into consultation, and during their conference other members of the Press foregathered in the outer office. It was before quite an audience, therefore, that Dupin finally announced his decision: "The law alone is in force. The ordinances of July 25 are not able to abrogate it or to abolish it; these ordinances must not be enforced. If I were a journalist, I should resist by all means of fact and of law; and I add that, in my opinion, any paper that submits and requests the authorization imposed does not deserve to have a single subscriber in France."[6] These were bold words. Dupin was willing to urge them on, but he would not allow the journalists to take any action in his office, and so they adjourned to the bureau of the *National*, rue Neuve-Saint-Marc, No. 10, to deliberate.[7]

It was in the offices of Thiers' paper that the first organized protest of the Revolution was made. The Paris journals had latterly become leaders of public opinion, and now in the July Days, they reached the height of their power and might almost be said to have directed the first day of the Revolution. Out of courtesy to the paper whose guests they were, it was agreed that Thiers should preside at the meeting. But the fact that he acted as chairman does not seem to have prevented him from speaking frequently, and at length, from the floor! Various measures of retaliation were proposed, but none appears to have met with the support of the chairman until Monsieur Jean Pillet proposed that a collective protest be published. Again Thiers left the chair, this time not to combat but to approve. " Names are necessary; we must risk our heads," he declared.[8] The proposal was finally adopted. In the meantime, during the discussion, some of the more timid journalists left the room. After their departure, a committee was appointed to draft a formal Protest. Here was no excited group of enraged Jacobins, but cold, calm deliberation. If there was any excited man in the room, it must have been the little editor with the Provençal accent. Thiers, Chatelain, Cauchois-Lemaire, and de Rémusat were selected for the task of composing the Protest, and it was the first named who drafted the statement of the Paris journalists that was to appear in the morning.

The document as printed in the *National* was brief, concise, and to the point, written in its author's best and most lucid style. In a later age, he might have culled the archives for the dramatic draft of a decree of a Committee of Public Safety, but for this there was no time. As he wrote, however, the little man must have conjured up visions of Barnave, Couthon, or St. Just; or, possibly, ugly old Danton appeared to him and calmed his spirit. Whatever his inspiration, it was a happy one. Obedience to the Government, the Protest declared, is no longer a duty. For that body by its recent acts has violated the law and need no longer be obeyed. Article 8 of the Charter declares that the Press must conform to the law; it does not mention the ordinances. Article 35 states that the electoral colleges shall be determined according to the law; it does not specify that they shall be determined by the ordinances. Heretofore the Government has recognized these laws; now it has violated them. " To-day the Government has lost the legal character by which it commands obedience As far as our own rights are concerned, we will resist to the utmost. As for France, let her decide how far she ought to carry resistance against tyranny." [9] Appended to this statement were the signatures of representatives of

EXIT CHARLES X

the *National, Globe, Temps, Figaro, Constitutionnel,* and *Courrier Français*. With such words the Press of Paris would address its readers on the morrow, and the concluding phrase, " As for France, let her decide how far she ought to carry resistance against tyranny," would be the tocsin of a new revolution. But to-day Paris was quiet and silent. Charles X might return from a day's hunting and hear from Polignac that the city had not stirred. He might have one more night of freedom from anxiety.

Beginning with the morning of the 27th, however, ripples were visible upon the surface of comparatively serene Paris. The *National* and other papers appeared with Thiers' Protest printed in bold type. Extra editions were soon exhausted. From early morning, the boulevards and streets were thronged with groups of workmen with nothing to do, gazing into the barred shop-windows, reading extra copies of the *Temps* and the *National* that were distributed gratis, and prey to the whim of any passing moment. A drunken labourer or the sight of an elegant aristocrat might have led at any moment to a repetition of July 14, 1789. But, fortunately, July 1830 could offer no Camille Desmoulins, and aristocrats were all gathered at St. Cloud. For the present, these idle groups were enjoying an unaccustomed leisure, and the atmosphere was one of holiday, but soon that would become irksome and gradually the serious question of food for the family would present itself. For many of these labourers were destined to a longer holiday than they desired; they had been shut out of their shops. When they had gone to the scenes of their labour that morning, they had discovered placards posted on the doors, announcing the fact that the factories had been closed for an indefinite period. Apparently, during the preceding night, industrial as well as journalist had been at work. The first of the shops to adopt such a measure had been those closely allied to the journalists, the printers. At the suggestion of Monsieur Barthe, who had been one of the legal lights at Dupin's office on the 26th, a meeting of the printers had been called at the Café de la Rotonde. There it had been agreed to close the shops and to throw the printers on to the streets.[10] Other industries followed their example, and by midday of the 27th, labouring Paris was idle. But as yet its state of mind was not dangerous.

The first occurrence to arouse the mob to anything more than a passive interest in the novelty of the whole situation was the arrival of Government officers at the head-quarters of the *Temps*. Their purpose was to dismantle the presses. From the *Temps* bureau the mob followed the *agents* to the *National*, where the officers performed their duties, while Thiers watched serenely from behind his enormous glasses.[11] There can be no doubt but that he was enjoying the situation hugely. No sooner had the *agents* taken their departure than some machinist in the crowd set to work to assist the editor in reconstructing the presses. When the latter were again in order, Thiers prepared the issue for the 28th. This was to be printed on a single sheet. The issue of the 27th had sounded the tocsin, and the succeeding edition repeated the call in words more bold and, too, more impertinent: " We still can talk to France to-day. Yesterday, the Charter was torn into shreds, and those who found in it their guarantees lost them; yesterday, everyone was made free to act according to his power, and now no one should expect security save through using force." [12]

The morrow's issue prepared, Thiers and Mignet hurried from the scene of their labours and left Paris for parts unknown. In fact, there was good reason why the two young Liberals should flee the capital. They had been advised by Royer-Collard to leave at once, for warrants had been issued for their arrest as signatories to the Protest of July 26 which the Government regarded as seditious. In company with another of their colleagues, they took refuge near Montmorency

EXIT CHARLES X

at the house of Madame de Courchamp.[13] There they remained until the authority of the restored Bourbons had been driven from Paris. With the disappearance of the two writers the first Day of the Journalists ends.

In the meantime, the Paris mob had concentrated at two main points, around the Palais Royal, whose lord was absent, and in the vicinity of the home of Casimir Périer, where those Constitutionalist Deputies who had had the courage to remain were assembled. Marmont, appointed on the eve military Commander of the city by Polignac, sent two small detachments to disperse the mob. At the Palais Royal an officer, losing his temper, fired upon the crowd, and a riot ensued. Barricades appeared in the rue Saint Honoré, and Marmont sent to St. Cloud for reinforcements. The crowds did not interfere very much with the movements of the troops; they contented themselves with watching the soldiery, frequently even fraternizing with them. Towards evening, the uniform of the suppressed National Guard appeared on the streets. This was not without its significance. It boded ill for the morrow.

July 28 is properly called the " People's Day." The mob once turned out on the streets, the Deputies who remained seem to have made a feeble and not too sincere attempt at conciliation with the existing Government. Failing in this, they waited and allowed the people to drive the Ministry from power and the Royalist troops from Paris, before themselves taking up any constructive programme. As early as five o'clock in the morning, groups of armed men had appeared in the vicinity of the Porte Saint Martin and the Porte Saint Denis. Soon other parts of Paris presented the same aspect. During the night several arsenals had been raided, and arms and munitions secured. Actual fighting first set in, of course, in the crowded quarter of the Bastille and the Hôtel de Ville. By noon, the tricolour floated from the towers of

Notre Dame. Marmont, now thoroughly alarmed, concentrated his forces at the Louvre in preparation for an attack. At the same time he sent a message to Charles, apprising him of the situation and counselling an attempt at conciliation. From St. Cloud the King sent his reply; it was a curt refusal. By evening, the fighting extended to the Boulevards.

Meantime, what of the Deputies of France, those repositories and guarantors of law and order? Many had fled to their homes in the provinces, and the remnant that had remained in Paris was of the Constitutionalist party. On the evening of the 27th, some of them had met at the house of Casimir Périer, but the general confusion and the howling mob outside prevented their accomplishing anything. Again, on the morrow, these worthies convened at the house of Audrey de Puyraveau. To them came Laffitte and La Fayette. The presence of the banker and the general, both of whom were popular and whose Liberal opinions were recognized, gave a sense of assurance to the meeting. Some action must now be taken. Should an appeal be made to the King, or should a Provisional Government be established? Undoubtedly, the latter was the desire of the extremists. Probably La Fayette favoured this as much as he can be said to have favoured any definite policy at this time of his life. But the combined efforts of Périer, Sébastiani, and Laffitte won the day. A committee of five was appointed to visit Marmont and to present a protest through him to the King, against the Ministry that had issued and was seeking to enforce the ordinances. Gérard, de Lobau, Périer, Mauguin, and Laffitte set out for the Tuileries on their mission. Arriving there, they met with Arago, who joined his instances to theirs and besought Marmont to forward their Protest. To this Marmont consented, but, as he had foretold, the attempt failed. Both Charles and Polignac refused to communicate with this group of Deputies. Upon the return of the delegates to Puyraveau's house, the meeting

EXIT CHARLES X

decided to publish the Protest. The same thing occurred among the Peers, who had assembled at the hôtel of Pasquier. In the meantime, La Fayette had been dispatched to the Hôtel de Ville, where the Republicans were already in possession. During the night fighting continued in the streets, and when July 29 dawned, Paris was free from her detested King. The Royalist troops had evacuated their stronghold at the Louvre and were retreating in the direction of St. Cloud. The tricolour now floated above the Tuileries; Paris was in the hands of its citizens.

Monarchy had gone from the capital, but what was in its place? That was the serious question that everyone was asking himself on the morning of the 29th. As yet, nothing had been substituted, but unless the Deputies acted, a Republic was a possibility, even a likelihood. La Fayette held the Hôtel de Ville, and once there, he came under the influence of the Republican group. Bastide, Cavaignac, Thomas, and Joubert reigned at the Tuileries, and at the Café Lointier, the rendezvous of a very active group of Republicans, a proclamation calling for the election of a *Constituante* was in the process of composition. Consequently, when the Deputies reconvened at the house of Laffitte on that morning, one thing was uppermost in their minds—the necessity of establishing their control over the movement that they had allowed to break out and that they had done nothing to restrain. Obviously, if their predominance was to be established, they must set up a Provisional Government and make sure of the recognition of La Fayette and his party at the Hôtel de Ville before the latter had joined with the other Republican groups. Otherwise, the Constitutionalist Deputies would be outnumbered. Accordingly, de Rémusat was sent on an embassy to the Hôtel de Ville. He returned with a characteristically vague answer from the old General, but at any rate it was favourable enough to encourage the Deputies to act. Thereupon they set to work and

THIERS AND THE FRENCH MONARCHY

appointed a Provisional Government that was announced by the following Proclamation:

> " The Deputies present in Paris have met to remedy the great dangers that are menacing the security of persons and property.
> " A Commission was named to safeguard all interests in the absence of a regular organized Government. Messieurs Audrey de Puyraveau, Comte Gérard, Comte de Lobau, Mauguin, Odier, Casimir Périer, de Schönen compose this Commission.
> " The National Guard is in control of Paris at all points." [14]

It was well that these gentlemen spoke of the dangers menacing persons and property in the past tense. Wisdom dictated the statement that the National Guard was in control at all points; such was not the case, but it might be if La Fayette were made commander, for Republicans adored the old hero. The appointment of La Fayette might prevent the possibility of a union between the Hôtel de Ville Republicans and the desperadoes of the Tuileries.

When Dupin had drafted this Proclamation, it was spread over Paris. The Deputies were dealing desperately in futures, but only by dealing in futures could the possibility of any sort of Monarchy survive. In this way, a banker and an industrial became the temporary and uncertain masters of the July Revolution, and it is well to remember that the banker had managed the business affairs of the house of Orléans for twelve years.

A Provisional Government established and the means for restoring order in Paris set in operation, the next problem was the future of France. What should follow the temporary arrangement? One might expect that the answer would come from this same group of Deputies. As a matter of fact, this was the case, but it does not

EXIT CHARLES X

appear that the first to mention publicly the plan was one of its number. The journalists of Paris appear again on the scene.

With the success of the People's Day the two young gentlemen who had taken refuge near Montmorency returned.[15] Upon their arrival, they found much to interest them, and they set out to explore the new Paris that had come into being during their very brief absence. According to Thiers, this very simple promenade became a very momentous occasion. They walked along the streets, past the Tuileries, stopping often to speak to friends or even to exchange greetings with strangers, for the spirit of " Fraternité" was again in the air. They declare that they were impressed by the frequency with which they heard the word " Republic " pronounced. La Fayette was asserting it in loud tones, and one Monsieur de Laborde was forming a legion of Young Republicans. In the course of their walk the two young friends turned into the rue de Richelieu, where, in those days, there were many fashionable shops. Thiers remarked that the shopkeepers who had been furnishers to the King, or to the Duc or Duchesse de Berry, and who had proclaimed the fact in large gold letters, were now hastily removing the same from their shop-windows. As they went on, however, they noticed two shops whose windows were decorated with the coat of arms of the duc d'Orléans, and this was allowed to remain. Thiers was struck by this fact. " I said to Mignet, ' Do you think that they are considering the Duke of Orléans ? ' With that I went to Laffitte." [16]

It is indeed hard to believe that it had not occurred to these two that Louis Philippe might receive the crown of France. Otherwise, why the articles in the *National?* why the school of 1688 ? So much innocence could hardly go hand in hand with so much perspicacity as these two had shown. But, here again there is an element of truth in Thiers' statement that should not be forgotten. It is

THIERS AND THE FRENCH MONARCHY

evidence of the fact that there was no real, organized conspiracy for Orléans until July 1829. Time and time again, in later life, Thiers affirms this fact, and many others support him.[17] The Duke sought the throne, but he did not conspire in the earlier days,[18] and his candidacy does not appear to have been discussed openly even among his friends until the People's Day had driven the authority of the Bourbons from Paris. Then it was that the candidacy of Orléans, a matter that had undoubtedly been in the minds of many, became recognized as a desirable fact. The first men to mention it were, then, the originators of the July Monarchy, and these men were Laffitte, Talleyrand, Sébastiani, Thiers, and, to a lesser degree, Périer.

The name of Louis Philippe was first pronounced in public at the meeting at Laffitte's house on July 29. To this meeting came Thiers, newly returned to Paris. He tells us that as he entered the house, he was still impressed by the evidences of Republican spirit that he had beheld during his walk, but that once he found himself within the walls of Laffitte's mansion, where were gathered Deputies, bankers, and generals, he found a sentiment quite the opposite. All were opposed to any form of Republican rule. " You've got it," he cried, as he entered the room, " (the Republic) is spreading everywhere. You will not escape it. Only the Duke of Orléans can possibly get you out of this." In his opinion all concurred. But there was a difficulty, for none of them seemed to have the slightest idea what Louis Philippe would do or say to a proposal from them. They needed him to lead them, but would he come? Then it was that Thiers made a stroke for his beloved " representative monarchy." " What matter ? " he said, " *compromise him without consulting him.*" [19]

As was to be so frequently the case in later times, the daring of the little man swept the informal gathering. The older and more experienced of them accepted the proposition of one who was but a few years ago a complete stranger to them, and active conspiracy began. Most of the gathering retired to re-convene on the 30th, when they were to bring their friends with them. Only the arch-conspirators remained to draft the Proclamation with which Paris was to be placarded during the night. They had just completed their work when someone knocked at Laffitte's door. Old Régime in the persons of Marmont and a few Carlist peers had called to present the draft of a revocation of the ordinances to which Charles had at last consented! But the Deputies had gone home; the decision had been taken; and the presses of the *National* were being oiled to print for Parisians the momentous decree that had been declared by a small group of men not all of whom were Deputies. In the dim light Laffitte read to his latest visitors the draft of the Orléanist Proclamation, and the emissaries of the Bourbon Monarchy retired defeated. Thiers stayed by the presses until the Proclamations were through. Laffitte dreamed of statesmanship, and, off in his corner of Paris, Talleyrand saw again a stage on which he could play a part.

On the following morning, Parisians awoke to find themselves Orléanists. Every bill-board bore the poster relating the marvellous virtues of the great man who had lived so quietly and so modestly in their midst. Could the Duke have read it, it is doubtful whether even he would have recognized himself. The wording of the declaration was cleverly done, and even without his own assertion to that effect, one could be sure that it was the work of Thiers.[20] But it is difficult to find in the portrait the real Louis Philippe of the pear-shaped head —" la poire couronné " they called him—of the slow, heavy gait, the great wide-brimmed hat, and the inevitable green umbrella tucked under his left arm that his right hand might be free to greet bourgeois, labourer, and aristocrat as he sauntered down the rue de Rivoli. The glowing words of the youthful enthusiast who did not yet know him, and who had previously refused to meet him, created a new and altogether ideal Duke.[21] Perhaps it was just as well that Thiers did not know him, otherwise he would have been compelled to forget as much about the unprepossessing appearance of Louis Philippe as he, the historian, had had to forget about history when he had formed the thrilling words of the Proclamation:

> " Charles X can never return to Paris; he has shed the blood of the people.
> " The Republic would expose us to dangerous divisions; it would involve us in hostilities with Europe.
> " The Duke of Orléans is a Prince devoted to the cause of the Revolution.
> " The Duke of Orléans has never fought against us.
> " The Duke of Orléans was at Jemmapes.
> " The Duke of Orléans is a Citizen-King.
> " The Duke of Orléans has carried the tricolour under the enemies' fire; the Duke of Orléans alone can carry it again. We will have no other flag.
> " The Duke of Orléans does not commit himself. He awaits the expression of our wishes. Let us proclaim those wishes, and he will accept the Charter as we have always understood it, and as we have always desired it. It is from the French people that he will hold his crown." [22]

These sentences were well calculated to attract the public eye. The catchwords, Revolution, Jemmappes, Tricolour, and Citizen-King made fainter the already dim recollection of the disgraceful Égalité, Louis Philippe's father. Meanwhile, the subject of this panegyric was in hiding in the Parc de Riancey. Had he gone thither, like the prophets of old, to meditate on his mission, to protect his property, or because he feared the warrants of Charles X for his arrest?
Paris generally seemed to accept tacitly the sentiments

EXIT CHARLES X

placarded through the efforts of Laffitte and his lieutenant. But there were still difficulties and hindrances in the path of the new Orléanist party. La Fayette was an uncertain quantity, and no definite statement of attitude had emanated from the Duke or from any member of his household. The sooner the adherence of Louis Philippe could be obtained, the more likely it was that La Fayette would hand over the Hôtel de Ville to him. This, therefore, was the principal concern of the Deputies who foregathered at Laffitte's on the morning of the 30th. As he joined them, Béranger remarked: " The only subject of conversation this morning is your prince. His name is on every tongue." [23] But would the Duke come to Paris? Of this Laffitte felt quite sure, but Sébastiani and a number of others at the meeting expressed considerable doubt about it.[24] Time, however, was passing, and every minute lost by the Orléanists was a minute gained by Republicanism. Finally, Thiers and others urged that someone be sent to ascertain the sentiments of Louis Philippe. According to Thiers' statement, this was a difficult thing to manage, because there was no one at the meeting who was intimately cquainted with the Duke. Then it was that one of the group suggested that Thiers be selected to ascertain the sentiments of his Grace, and to discover if he would accept the Lieutenant-Generalcy of the Realm of France. To this proposal that young gentleman objected, protesting the fact that he was not even acquainted with their candidate. The reply to this settled the matter: " We will give you letters, and by means of these, you will present yourself in our name." [25] So it was that adventure again fell to the lot of the young journalist from Provence, and he became the delegate of bourgeois Paris in search of a king.

At first glance, the selection of Thiers may seem to have been an odd one. It is quite certain that he had never been presented to the Duke, and that once, on Étienne's advice, he had declined that honour. Laffitte, however, may have urged his nomination as the Commissioner of the Deputies on the ground that an invitation offered to Louis Philippe by one of the leading journalists of Paris might appear to be more of a direct request from the Parisians themselves. There is also another reason that may have occurred to Laffitte. His protégé was not only the friend of the Constitutionalist group; through his more radical colleagues on the *National*, he was also the friend of many Republicans, and the fact that Thiers, instead of a prominent member of the high bourgeoisie, had been selected might make Carrel and his associates more willing to accept the Monarchy.

With Monsieur Scheffer, who gave drawing lessons to the young princesses, Thiers set about the preparations for the journey to Neuilly, whither Louis Philippe's family had retired. Two horses from the stables of the Prince de Muskowa, son-in-law of Laffitte, were saddled for them. How grateful must Thiers have been for his recent lessons at Carreger's riding academy! The pair set out, accompanied by an officer of the National Guard. This officer carried passes from General Fagal to the military outposts, and the principal of the trio had in his possession a paper bearing Sébastiani's signature and a note from Laffitte that contained these words: " I beg Monsieur le Duc d'Orléans to receive Monsieur Thiers with all confidence, and to hear all that he is charged by me to say to you." [26]

Due to the fact that the passports had not been viséd, the two envoys and their escort experienced some difficulty, and were swept by the fire of the sentries several times, but they managed to reach Neuilly before the morning was spent.[27] Upon their arrival, however, Thiers had a great disappointment. He was informed that Louis Philippe had left in the direction of St. Cloud, where he possessed some property about which he was anxious. Finally, he succeeded in gaining admittance to the Duchesse Marie Amélie. This lady could not

EXIT CHARLES X

have been as ignorant and as unconcerned as she appeared to Thiers to be, for she had already interviewed at least one other delegation from Paris.[28] Dupin and Persil had seen her before the arrival of Laffitte's envoy, and it is not unlikely that Gérard and Talleyrand had communicated with the family early on the morning of the 30th. The Duchess began by protesting to her latest interviewer that the Duke was absent. Of this he did not appear to be convinced, and told her that the moment was decisive, and that no time could be lost. He broached the question of the Lieutenant-General. This time, the answer of Marie Amélie convinced him that Louis Philippe was really away. Having persuaded him of this, however, she made haste to assure him that she would gladly listen to whatever he had to say, and repeat it to the Duke upon his return. She then sent for Madame Adelaide, Louis Philippe's sister. This action on the part of the Duchess of Orléans indicates clearly her attitude to affairs in France. When, earlier in the day, Dupin had visited her and urged upon her rather violent reasons for pressing her husband to act, she had burst into tears and declared that she wished to remain a stranger to politics.[29] It is not unlikely that, in the case of this second interview, she wished to shift the burden. After her sister-in-law, Madame Adelaide, had entered, the future Queen of France sank completely into the background as far as Thiers' account of the interview is concerned. Madame Adelaide's was a far more masculine and active nature, and it was to her that Thiers addressed most of his remarks.[30] To her mind, the principal obstacle to her brother's acceptance of the position of Lieutenant-General was the fear that such an act would be regarded by the foreign Powers as a "révolution du palais." She feared the consequent anger of European courts. At this, Thiers called forth all of his young and audacious eloquence. It was Paris that called, it was not the Orléanists who sought. He conjured up his beloved " representative monarchy,"

THIERS AND THE FRENCH MONARCHY

and finally even hauled William of Orange into the drawing-room of the ducal house at Neuilly. Here was the supreme effort. If he could succeed in this mission, his own future was made. He extolled the virtues of public conscience and its glorious infallibility. Never would a family have had so divine and so certain a sanction to mount a throne. " All the world will know that you have not of yourselves sought the crown, for surely to-day it is so dangerous a possession that no one would seek it of his own accord." [31]

The eloquence of the Midi conquered, and finally Madame Adelaide, apparently overcome by the visions that the young magician had conjured up, turned to him, and said : " If you think that the adherence of our family will be of advantage to the Revolution—a woman is nothing in a family, one can compromise them—I myself am ready to go to Paris. There I will share the destiny of the Parisians. I make but one condition, namely, that Monsieur Laffitte or General Sébastiani come themselves to fetch me." [32] Thiers appears to have been satisfied with this declaration from one member of the ducal household. One can easily imagine the studied grace with which the little bourgeois delivered himself of these words : " To-day, Madame, you have placed the crown in your own house." Deserted son of the rue des Petits Pères, Marseilles, journalist, historian, and King-maker ! He then asked her to write to the Duke at once, and added thereto a little advice as to the arguments she should advance for his acceptance. One can see him so easily. He bows, begins to back out—ah ! just one word more ! And then, a word or two on government along the lines of " representative monarchy." Then, the final bow, the door closes behind him—and a shrewd smile comes over the face of the little man, for Madame Adelaide has betrayed to him a fact that he later puts into these words : " Louis Philippe n'a pas conspiré ; il a aspiré." [33]

No sooner had that strangely smiling, little bourgeois

EXIT CHARLES X

mounted his great horse, and galloped off to Paris than out from the palace at Neuilly sped the Comte de Montesquieu with the message for Louis Philippe, who was in hiding at Riancey.[34]

Meanwhile, Thiers, Scheffer, and the officer were hastening back to Paris to report to Laffitte and Sébastiani the result of the mission. They must have made good time, for, in spite of pickets, outposts, and sentries, they arrived at Laffitte's door a little before one o'clock. During the absence of the trio, the Deputies had established themselves at the Palais Bourbon, and thither Thiers hurried to make his report to his superiors. Like him, they interpreted Madame Adelaide's remarks as compromising the entire Orléans family. To give to the matter the appearance of certainty, they spread the rumour that one member of the Duke's family was expected momentarily, and that soon all of them would be in Paris. This done, they could refuse the last overtures of Charles in which the King had even consented to a Ministry that would include Marmont, Gérard, and Casimir Périer.[35]

At this point, the second adventure of Adolphe Thiers concludes with his retirement to the *bureau* of the *National*, where he dictated to Monsieur Martin, his secretary, the account of the greatest day that he had yet experienced.[36]

Parts of Paris were now eagerly awaiting the arrival of their hero, the Duke. What would these Parisians have thought if they had known that he who would declare in his first proclamation, " I have not hesitated to come and partake of your dangers," [37] had, once he was on the road to the city, actually turned back his carriage, and started off in the opposite direction ! [38] At last, however, the Duke arrived, and was received at the Palais Royal by Laffitte, Sébastiani, and those others most interested in his return.[39] He was welcomed cordially by these men, but one section of Paris held

THIERS AND THE FRENCH MONARCHY

aloof; La Fayette and his Republicans did not venture forth to greet him. And so it was decided by Louis Philippe himself that he would go to them. It was a perilous undertaking, and his supporters were uneasy.[40] The march to the Hôtel de Ville had its dangers, but for once in his life, a Duke of Orléans showed that he was capable of facing a trying situation. He rode through lines of silent and sullen men.[41] On he went to the hotel. There he dismounted, and climbed the steps to La Fayette's *bureau*. That march gave Louis Philippe the crown of France. Then occurred the famous scene—the old General and the future King, wrapped in the folds of the tricolour, on the balcony before the square hill of Republicans. Of this scene, that arch-cynic, Metternich, remarked: " A kiss is a slight effort to make to stifle a Republic; do you think that such a power can be expected of kisses in the future?"[42] To some Republicans it must have seemed to be the kiss of a Judas.

The return from the Hôtel de Ville was as triumphant as the previous march had been melancholy, and when Louis Philippe finally reached the Palais Royal, he felt far more secure than when he had set out. At once he set himself to his task. There were supporters to be gratified, friends to be made, and innumerable delegations to receive. During the first days there were very few trappings of royalty where royalty lived. No lackey in gorgeous liveries opened the doors. Common soldiers and volunteers in the uniform of the revived National Guard, or in no uniform at all, crowded the anterooms and lounged on the stairways, while the Lieutenant-General held council seated upon a tabouret. The Council room was open to all.[43]

It must have been in the midst of some such scenes that Thiers met for the first time the man in whose cause he had been so active. The occasion for one of their first encounters was an odd one. In fact, no one but Thiers could have thought of such a thing. He had found

EXIT CHARLES X

that not all of his friends, even some of his colleagues in the *National*, were behind the move of Laffitte. With Mignet and a few others who had joined him so heartily in his advocacy of the " representative monarchy," the little editor found sympathy for what had been done. Little did they realize at the time how undesirous Louis Philippe would be to have such sponsors. They were blinded, but not so Carrel, Cavaignac, Guinard, and Bauvilliers, who were ardent Republicans and who found themselves unable to reconcile their views to an acceptance of the Orléans régime. It was to these that Thiers now turned his attention. Having been presented to the Duke, he asked him to receive some of his discontented acquaintances, and to discuss their political difficulties with them. On the very same evening the interview took place. Perhaps the originator of this remarkable meeting may have been cherishing a hope that by such a presentation he might win this group of malcontents to the Orléanist cause, or at least effect an attitude of neutrality on their part.[44] If this was the case, he must have been grievously disappointed, for his Republican friends were not convinced by their talk with royalty. When the conference ended, several of them expressed to Thiers their disgust with Louis Philippe. He, amused at their discomfiture, held his sides, as he laughed and said, " J'ai fait là, ma foi, une belle ambassade." [45]

This may explain why Louis as King always seemed to distrust Thiers, his minister, and to classify him with the more radical element in the Chamber even when he was pleading the cause nearest to the heart of the monarch.

NOTES TO CHAPTER VII

[1] Viel-Castel: *Histoire de la Restauration*, XX. 540.
[2] *Moniteur*, July 26, 1830.
[3] Viel-Castel: *Histoire de la Restauration*, XX. 561.
[4] Anderson: *Constitutions and Documents*, Charter of 1814, Article 14.

[5] Dupin: *Mémoires*, II. 136.
[6] *Ibid.*, II. 137. de Rémusat: *Thiers*, p. 54.
[7] *Ibid.* Chateaubriand: *Mémoires d'Outre Tombe*, V. 205. *National*, July 29, 1830; September 8, 1830. Duvergier de Hauranne: *Histoire Parlementaire*, X. 535.
[8] *Ibid.*, X. 537. Simon: *Thiers*, p. 165.
[9] *National*, July 27, 1830: Thiers.
[10] *Revue d'Histoire Moderne*, III. 1901-02, Mantoux, p. 293. Festy: *Mouvement Ouvrier*, p. 27.
[11] de Hauranne: *Histoire Parlementaire*, X. 544.
[12] *National*, July 28, 1830: Thiers.
[13] Chambolle: *Retours*, p. 74. Dumas: *Louis Philippe*, I. 234. Chateaubriand: *Mémoires d'Outre Tombe*, V. 206.
[14] *Moniteur*, July 29, 1830; July 30, 1830. Dupin: *Mémoires*, IV. 140.
[15] Chambolle: *Retours*, p. 75.
[16] *Le Correspondant*, October 10, 1922. Lacombe, *Conversations*, pp. 22-24.
[17] *Ibid.* Thiers: *Monarchie de Juillet*, pp. 21-22. Beranger: *Ma Biographie*, p. 91. Falloux: *Mémoires*, II. 268.
[18] *Le Correspondant*, October 10, 1922. Lacombe, *Conversations*, p. 23. Louis Philippe's own words to Thiers.
[19] *Ibid.*, p. 24. For a different version see Chateaubriand: *Mémoires d'Outre Tombe*, V. 217.
[20] *Le Correspondant*, October 10, 1922. Lacombe, *Conversations*, p. 22.
[21] *Ibid.*, p. 24.
[22] The first placard printed the words "Le duc d'Orléans s'est prononcé." These words were changed to what follows in the text. Viel-Castel: *Histoire de la Restauration*, XX. 631-34.
[23] *Le Correspondant*, October 10, 1922. Lacombe, *Conversations*, p. 24.
[24] *Ibid.*, p. 24.
[25] *Ibid.*, p. 23.
[26] Thiers' Notes, July 30, 1830.
[27] *Ibid.*
[28] de Hauranne: *Histoire Parlementaire*, X. 594. Colmache: *Reminiscences*, I. 60. Dupin: *Mémoires*, II. 147.
[29] *Ibid.*, II. 149.
[30] Thiers' Notes, July 30, 1830. Bibliothèque Nationale, 20,601, Part II. 22.
[31] *Ibid.*
[32] *Ibid.*
[33] *Le Correspondant*, October 10, 1922. Lacombe, *Conversations*, p. 24.
[34] Chateaubriand: *Mémoires d'Outre Tombe*, V. 253.
[35] Dupin: *Mémoires*, II. 149.

EXIT CHARLES X

[36] Thiers' Notes, July 30, 1830. Bibliothèque Nationale, 20,601, Part II. 22.
[37] *Le Moniteur*, August 1, 1830.
[38] Chateaubriand : *Mémoires d'Outre Tombe*, V. 254.
[39] *Vide* Thureau-Dangin : *Histoire de la Monarchie de Juillet*, I. chap. i.
[40] L. Blanc : *Histoire de dix Ans.*, I. 166.
[41] Metternich : *Mémoires*, V. 22.
[42] *Ibid.*, V. 23.
[43] *National*, June 18, 1831. Thureau-Dangin : *Histoire de la Monarchie de Juillet*, I. 43.
[44] de Gerainville : *Histoire de Louis Philippe*, II. 379. Dumas : *Louis Philippe*, I. 268. Weill : *Parti Républicain*, p. 30.
[45] de Gerainville : *Histoire de Louis Philippe*, II. 380.

CHAPTER VIII

ENTER LOUIS PHILIPPE (1830–32)

THE visit of Louis Philippe to the Republicans at the Hôtel de Ville had determined the enthronement of the House of Orléans. It had been a courageous action that was fraught with danger.[1] La Fayette, ensconced in the seat of municipal authority, had been an uncertainty, but the coming of the Duke had won him, and with their appearance together on the balcony, the Provisional Government that had been formed under the old General faded out of existence. The menace of Republicanism then withdrew, and the Deputies, who had been gathered together by Casimir Périer during the crisis of the July Days, profited by a revolution in which they had not actively participated.

The power passed, then, from the Hôtel de Ville to the Palais Royal, and there, on the first day of August, the victorious Constitutionalist Deputies met to elect Pasquier their chairman and to inaugurate a new order. But modest indeed was the institution of the new régime to be; they were careful not to give too revolutionary a character to their proceedings. Had they done so, it would not have been in accord with Périer, the fastidious, for example. He was openly declaring that there had not been a revolution; what had occurred, he said, was only a change in the person at the head of the State.[2] But these words were a hollow mockery; let the coryphaei of the school of 1688 deny it ever so loud, the fact remained that there had been a revolution, and those who denied it would be the first to realize it in the August Days that would follow. In fact, the very first Cabinet that served the Lieutenant-General was proof positive

ENTER LOUIS PHILIPPE

of a greater change than his supporters would acknowledge. Strange indeed was the Ministry that they gave him. It was not a tricolour but a rainbow, for almost all of the various shades of political opinion had representation in it. Dupont de l'Eure was Minister of Justice, Gérard of War, Baron Louis of Finances, Guizot of the Interior, Bignon of Public Instruction, Jourdan of Foreign Affairs, and Sébastiani of Marine. Moderate Republicans, men of the Empire, representatives of the University and of the vested interests, all were combined into a glorious disunity. Dupont had been a member of La Fayette's Provisional Government; Baron Louis had served as Minister of Finances under Napoleon.[3] Gerard, Sébastiani, and Guizot, whose course at the University had been suspended by Villèle, were *Doctrinaires*. Over this ployglot Cabinet Périer presided as President of the Council, and Périer was a capitalist. It was under these auspices that the Bourgeois Monarchy set to work to establish its control.

On August 6, this Government and the Chamber assumed the task of government making. What an odd *Constituante*, and how different from that anticipated by the Café Lointier during the July Days! The throne was declared vacant, and the way was paved for the advent of a new dynasty. But before Louis Philippe could relinquish the title of Lieutenant-General for the more elegant name of King, the exact nature of the new monarchy must be determined; so the Deputies, who called themselves the elected of the people, turned to a revision of the Charter of 1814. In this business, however, the fathers of the new régime did not consult their constituents; they ignored blissfully the will of the people.

The first problem was that of the kingship. Thiers had written in the Orléanist Proclamation: "C'est du peuple français qu'il tiendra sa couronne," and this pious sentiment was inserted in place of monarchy by right divine. It was not sufficient, however, to deprive the

King of his sacred character; there was yet another attribute that the exiled Charles had claimed, and in virtue of which he had promulgated the fatal ordinances that had begun the July Revolution. This power reposed in Article 14, that allowed the monarch to promulgate special laws for the safety of the State. Such a privilege would be a constant menace to the Legislative Chamber, and the Deputies lost no time in abolishing it. Along with this clause went the suppression of the censorship of the Press and of the King's right to create extraordinary tribunals. Freedom of religion was declared, and the tricolour was substituted for the white flag of Bourbonism. Elections and representation were partially regulated. The electoral colleges and the Chambers might select their own Presidents. Twenty-five years was the age required to exercise the franchise, and a Deputy must be at least thirty years old. (The tax qualification for franchise was not lowered by one hundred francs until 1831.) As to the Chamber of Peers, those who had been nominated by Charles X withdrew; its hereditary character was not removed until December 1831, when the Peers became a Senate selected by the Crown from a limited class of distinguished men, the term of office being for life.

This was the work of the supposed *Constituante*. It was hasty, careless, and inadequate. The old machinery by which Charles X had sought to operate a return of the old régime was thrown out, but the " revised version " of the Charter of 1814 had many weaknesses. The Deputies accomplished little; their omissions promised much; and they left for their successors a long list of problems that became the battle-ground of later conflicts. It was well to remove the bases for such flagrant abuses as had been committed during the Restoration, but was it wise to leave unsolved a number of important questions concerning the Peers, franchise, electoral system, juries, the departmental and communal governments, and education? Would not the July Monarchy have been

ENTER LOUIS PHILIPPE

stronger if it had faced these matters at once ? May not that have been the reason for the apparently strange action of Thiers in practically forcing the Duke, on the very day of his triumph, to receive those whose opinions were regarded as *exaltées*, and to listen to their pleas ? Perhaps, however, Casimir and his deputies, older and wiser than Thiers, dared do no more without calling for a Constituent Assembly. This they feared to do because of the excited state of public opinion. The fathers of the Bourgeois Monarchy were confident that they must gain time in which Louis Philippe could win over the people and prove his worth; only when this had come to pass would it be safe to trust the people to legislate, through their newly elected representatives, a régime that was surely but moderately a monarchy. With such a makeshift Constitution the Duke of Orléans accepted the crown. There was a minimum of pomp as befitted the circumstances. His could be no *sacre* at Rheims, for there in 1824 the will of God had proclaimed Charles X the King, but Louis now ruled by the grace of Laffitte, Périer, and the latter's Deputies, and by the reluctant consent of La Fayette. " C'est du peuple français qu'il tiendra sa couronne " was a mere travesty.

It was, of course, to be expected that the *Jeunesse Libérale* should have a part in the new Government. Their labours during the July Days must be rewarded, and the August Days had hardly dawned when Villemain, Barrot, quiet Mignet, and effervescent Thiers received a recognition of their services. The latter did not return to his journalistic occupation after the July Revolution. At the *National* Carrel now reigned supreme, and his former colleague seemed to have been divorced from the Press and from history.[4] The Revolution had made him, and it appears quite certain that Thiers had made what he could out of the Revolution. During the July Days he had speculated and won. He had bought himself a magnificent establishment, the famous house on the Place Saint-Georges, but it is unlikely that his private fortune could have afforded such a residence. Part of the purchase was made by mortgage and part was made possible through the obliging character of his wealthier friends. But a palatial residence was not the only plum that he drew out of the revolutionary pie. Like Mignet and Barrot, he, too, entered the service of the July Monarchy, and in this service he remained almost continually for the following ten years.

His enemies assert that he did not enter upon a new career with any longings for the past; they do not believe that he entertained any regrets for the work that had once been so dear to him. Quite different, however, is the impression given by him a little more than a year after the formation of the July Monarchy. " If, in such times as ours, I may mention myself, I should say that I am not defending this monarchy for what it has profited me. For it, I abandoned my studies; I forsook my tranquillity, and I have had to endure recriminations. I have forsaken a quiet existence for an uncertain and troublesome career. But have we a right to consider our own welfare and our personal misfortune? Those who have been carried nearer to power by a revolution are not one whit happier than those who have been carried out of power by it. Eh bien: what matter? We cannot judge a régime by the good or evil that it brings to a country. In this way I am devoted to the new Monarchy, and I defend it as the source of future prosperity for my country." [5]

If duty was the impulse that called the writer of these words, certainly duty made him seek the welfare of his country in quarters that must have appeared strange to those of his acquaintances who had known him in his more youthful days. The protégé of Dr. Arnaud and of Monsieur d'Arlatan de Lauris deserted Carrel and the *exaltés* ; he even withdrew a little more from La Fayette and Laffitte. Along with Dupin and Guizot, he allied himself to Périer, who was the most Conservative in-

ENTER LOUIS PHILIPPE

fluence in the new Government. Hardly was the Bourgeois Monarchy under way than Thiers began to be identified with the advocates of *Résistance* to the more Liberal forces in the Ministry and in the Chamber. For this group, the Revolution of 1830 had gone far enough and should go no farther, and in this opinion Thiers concurred. A careful study of his writings shows very clearly that in his political beliefs he never passed beyond the bounds of " representative monarchy," and that he had always feared the influence of the lower classes. It was, therefore, quite natural that he should ally himself with Périer, and, if he ever had any doubts as to the wisdom of the *Résistance* School, the events of the August Days certainly removed them. Furthermore, as of old, he was a hero worshipper, and Périer became his great ideal. He had changed his gods just as he had changed his colours. " Of all the men of the July Days," he writes, " Périer is the most able and the most vigorous. Périer is an astute politician, while Laffitte only plays at politics. Périer is a tower of strength, while Laffitte is weak and timid." [6] It was through the former's influence that he secured a permanent occupation during the early days of August 1830.

The first official task of Thiers had been to act as a member of a commission whose duty it was to prepare a new law relative to the method of electing Deputies. For this task his studies of English methods had fitted him. It was Guizot, then Minister of the Interior, who named him on August 17.[7] But this was only a beginning. Soon Périer and Baron Louis, whom he also admired and whose acquaintance he had made while writing the *History*, nominated him as Under-Secretary of State in the Department of Finances.[8] By the month of November, Thiers was well established in Government circles, and he stood so high in the opinion of his chief that, upon the latter's retirement, he was recommended as the successor of the Baron.[9] Only his youth and inexperience prevented his appointment. It was in the

THIERS AND THE FRENCH MONARCHY

school of Périer, Guizot, and Baron Louis, then, that Thiers began his political education.

But the young Provençal was not the only one who embarked on a process of political schooling during the early days of the July Monarchy; the new King of the French was also receiving a cruel training in the art of governing.

Although the accession of Louis Philippe had been a comparatively simple matter, retention of the prize was not an easy task. In August 1830, the Deputies and some of the *Jeunesse Libérale* approved, but by many others he was regarded as " the King of the Barricades," an epithet that Louis did not relish but that was, nevertheless, at least half a truth. After all, his rule *was* the result of a revolution, and it was even more than that *révolution du palais* so dreaded by Madame Adelaide. There were those who asked, Did the crown fit? or, Was there a crown at all? All of France was not disposed to support what part of Paris had done. This was true of social classes as well as of parties.

In general, there was one class that was almost wholeheartedly in favour of the new dynasty; among the rising aristocracy, the product of the Industrial Revolution, the King found true friends. Even in this case, however, care should be taken to distinguish between the industrial banker and capitalist group and the more professional sections of the middle class. The first were privileged voters, but the latter were disenfranchised. In brief, it was from the monied interests that Louis Philippe received his greatest support.

There remained, however, the army and the Church. The Valois, Bourbons, and Bonapartes had military glory to attract the admiration of the former, but the Orléanists had only the speaker's dock for a *pavois*.[10] The army stood aloof, and so did most of the clergy. They were attached to Tradition, and to them Tradition meant *Ancien Régime*. These distrusted a king coronated

ENTER LOUIS PHILIPPE

without a sacring; they feared his law of general religious toleration. They resented the tacit denial of divine right, while the removal of the crucifix from the tribunals was interpreted as a dangerous approach to the infidelity of the first Revolution. Furthermore, the fact that a select group of the Church had gone over wholeheartedly to the Orléanist régime alarmed them. In La Mennais, Lacordaire, and their Liberal Catholic followers, most churchmen beheld a renaissance of that Gallicanism so dreaded by the Church and so dangerous to the integral faith of all Catholics.

It was in the political world, however, that the outlook was most serious as far as the welfare of Louis' family was concerned. Within a very few days, Republicans and Carlists, at first paralyzed by the rapidity with which the crisis had developed, regained their breath and became the implacable foes of the existing Monarchy. The Carlists, known from now on as Legitimists, shortly adopted a policy of obstruction. To impede the Government in all possible ways by participating in an almost continuous overthrow of Ministries, through alliance, if necessary, with men of the other extreme, became a favourite gesture of that party. To cast disparagement and doubt upon the truly sincere efforts by which Laffitte and Périer were attempting to restore public prosperity and confidence; to spread discouragement; in other words, to sacrifice the present for the past, was the permanent aim of these malcontents. And in their efforts they were not always unsuccessful, for they possessed an able leader of remarkable presence and forensic ability. Berryer, a bourgeois, and for that very fact all the more influential, was their leader. His only weakness was that in him passion predominated more often than reason. In themselves the Carlists were not dangerous, for their numbers were not great, but when allied with the Left, they presented a redoubtable phalanx. Of a totally different character and nature were their strange bedfellows, the advocates of a France more liberal than Louis Philippe, Périer and Laffitte had provided.

It would be a mistake to regard the Opposition of the Left as a solid unit in August 1830. In character and in organization it was still local, heterogeneous, and really lacking in unity. From it should be excluded great numbers in the provinces; it was in Paris that the centre of discord and Liberal Opposition existed.

Liberal Paris is generally taken to mean the Republicans or the Jacobins, but such a general term cannot be applied to the Liberals of the August Days. Most of the prominent Republicans had accepted reluctantly and sceptically the July Monarchy, and after the King had shown himself amenable to the project to abolish the hereditary Peerage, the majority of the Hôtel de Ville faction had resigned themselves to another attitude.[11] They asserted the opinion that France was not yet fit to be a Republic, and they devoted themselves to an effort to imprint upon the Monarchy as much of a Republican character as possible. Without doubt, many of them hoped, as did Béranger, that, in the end, Louis Philippe's rule would be ephemeral and would serve as a bridge to real Republicanism.[12] In this they were not disappointed eighteen years later. For the moment they had come to agree on two things; they would make a common demand, and they would employ a common method of bringing that demand to the attention of the Government and of the rest of France. They demanded a modification of the suffrage, and to keep the matter before the eyes of the people, they adopted a system of demonstration. This was the creed and plan of the Hôtel de Ville faction for the immediate present, and this platform was accepted at once by their leaders, La Fayette, Danou, and Auguste and Victorin Fabre.[13]

But it was not this section of Liberal Paris that first caused the new Monarchy so much anxiety. Beneath this group of old and experienced Republicans was a great disorganized mass of Liberals, and in their midst

ENTER LOUIS PHILIPPE

was to be found the source of most of the trouble. It was well for the July Monarchy that this lower stratum was disorganized, otherwise Louis Philippe might not have weathered the stormy month of August. It was among labourers and students that the basis for the Opposition was to be found.

The workers had played a preponderant part in the July Revolution. Bourgeois threw them out on the street and allowed them to do the work of driving Charles X from Paris. Theirs had been the sacrifice during the first days, and upon the conclusion of their work, they had retired to await developments. The remark of one of their class illustrates very clearly their general attitude at this time. Alphonse d'Herbelot relates that a friend bivouacked with a group of workers near Rambouillet, and that one of them said to him : " I know indeed, that out of what we have done, very little will come to us, and that we shall still die of hunger, or at the asylum. But we did it for the *patrie*, for you, I mean, who are a bourgeois and who will profit by it." [14]

It was only too true ; Louis Philippe's Government did not inaugurate immediately any remedial measure for labour; it had too much else to do; it only allowed Baron Louis a credit of sixty millions to meet the industrial crisis.[15]

The workers of Paris continued to suffer. Industrial and commercial depression increased. Failures were frequent, and even one wealthy member of the Chamber was forced to resign because of financial difficulties.[16] Louis Blanc relates, that before the July Revolution, the printing industry had employed about two hundred workers. These men earned from four to six francs a day. After the Revolution the shops remained closed for a fortnight, and when they were re-opened, only ten or twelve labourers were recalled. Six months later, they were receiving only twenty-five to thirty sous a day.[17] In an effort to remedy the situation, due to the fact that all industries appeared to have suffered in almost the same degree, the Government provided a mockery of public employment on the Champs de Mars.[18] Labour demonstrations before the Prefecture of Police were frequent.[19] But it was not the workmen who most embarrassed the Government. They were only the recruits; the organizers were drawn from what may be called the political wreckage of the Restoration.

Since the early days of the Restoration there had survived a group of dreamers, idlers some, and theorists. At Paris, in July 1830, the remnants of the Saint-Simonians, Fourierists, Socialists, and Communists had been aroused by the collapse of the régime of Charles X. With a stable Government, their renaissance might not have been a danger, but under the compromise rule of August, still in its most experimental stage, they became a source from which emanated " a venomous political poison." [20] For the most part, these Radicals included poverty-stricken youths, students, and members of the École Polytechnique, an institution always prominent in revolutionary upheavals in Paris. They were grouped around older men, former Republicans, Bonapartists, and Socialists, who became their political Nestors. Charles Teste, who kept a bookshop that bore the significant name of *La Petite Jacobinière*, Buonarroti, once a member of the Italian Carbonari and now a professor of music, and Voyer d'Argenson were their principal advisers. An odd assortment truly, but their spokesmen and leaders were even more strange. Among them were to be found Cavaignac, himself once a Carbonaro, Raspail, an apothecary from Carpentras, and Trélat, a surgeon.[21] Marrast was their representative in the Press, and Armand Carrel, once the associate of Thiers, allowed his paper to advocate their cause. Garnier-Pagès was their spokesman in the Chamber of Deputies. Enthusiasm and daring were not lacking to these men. Only one thing weakened their power, and that was the fact that they were not closely united and were very infrequently in accord with one another. But in spite of their divisions,

ENTER LOUIS PHILIPPE

they were agreed in one thing; they were all of one mind in their determination to attack the Magistracy, the Monarchy, and the Administration. Some of them were even bold enough to propose in the *Tribune* to overthrow the existing Chamber of Deputies.[22]

While they agreed in generalities, however, they differed in particulars. Each club had its own personal aims that must be gratified, and each organization had its own officers and methods. *The Society of Order and Progress* required that every man should have in his possession a rifle and cartridges. With these he was to direct the Government according to the lights of the Latin Quarter. "That," remarks a much-harassed Prefect of Police, "would not positively assure order." [23] Another club was called the *Condamnés Politiques*. It was composed of those who sought recompense for having troubled the social order during the Restoration. Fieschi, who attempted to assassinate Louis Philippe in 1834, was a member of this honourable company. Another club was known as the "Help Thyself and Heaven will help Thee Society." Of this group, Garnier-Pagès was the leader.

But the most important and influential of all these Paris organizations was the famous *Friends of the People*, who took their inspiration from what they had heard of the notorious Dr. Marat of 1789. Here were to be found the ablest of the young radicals, Cavaignac, Marrast, Raspail, Flocon, and Blanqui. Some of these men, so active in 1848, received their initial training during the August Days. Students, young men out of work, and social agitators made up the membership of this Society. In character it was distinctly Jacobin, and its members were vowed to strive for the establishment of a real Republic.

In contrast to the other clubs, the *Friends of the People* were practical in the methods that they employed to spread their doctrines. Their head-quarters were at the Peltier Riding School on the rue Montmartre, convenient to the sections where dwelt the labourers and small shopkeepers.[24] Here secret meetings and open forums were maintained. They established a bureau of propaganda that became, in a sense, a sort of Third Internationale. From this centre, they arranged for public demonstrations on convenient occasions and distributed incendiary literature. Affiliations were set up in Belgium and in Poland.[25] They possessed a paper, the *Tribune*. By means of such an extensive machinery the *Friends* were soon able to make themselves felt. It was this club that organized the greatest demonstrations of the August Days. On August 4, three thousand men marched at its instigation to the Chamber, and demanded that the Deputies resign their mandates and sanction new elections based on universal suffrage. For a moment, Conservative Paris was alarmed, and only the almost tearful pleadings of poor, old La Fayette and of Benjamin Constant persuaded them to disperse. On the following day, the *Friends* attempted a similar demonstration before the Press as a protest against the hereditary Peerage. On this occasion, the Government stepped in, and the President and Secretary of the Society were called before the police, but they refused to appear.[26]

Demonstration, however, was not their only activity. Located as they were so conveniently near to the quarter of the labourers, they began to pose as the protectors of this unrewarded class, whose condition was undoubtedly pitiable. They demanded for their new protégés political rights and an amelioration of their material condition. The Government may indeed have confined its attention exclusively to the necessities of the higher bourgeoisie, but it is equally true that the methods employed by its Radical opponents were not of the sort to gain the sympathy of the King's Council. Like the English agitators, they made protests against the introduction of machinery. The labourers were led to believe that this innovation was the root of all the evil. Demands were posted on the bill-boards of Paris, insisting on the

ENTER LOUIS PHILIPPE

substitution of manual for mechanical labour. The workers were told that the capitalists were flourishing; in reality, many of the latter were almost penniless because of the stagnation of industry that had set in immediately upon the conclusion of the Revolution.[27] This was a condition for which some held the clubs responsible. Under their guidance, demonstrations and labour troubles became an almost every-day occurrence. There were riots of the printers, bakers, locksmiths, and farriers. In some instances, factories were broken into and the machines were destroyed. At last, the *Friends* outdid themselves. Placards were printed demanding the overthrow of the Chambers. Then the Government had to act, but even then, its action was weak. The placards were seized, and the printers, together with the officers of the Society, were condemned to three months' imprisonment and three hundred francs fine.[28] The club was forcibly disbanded, but this was not a permanent measure; it revived before long.

The credit for this action against the *Friends of the People* must go to Guizot, who was ably supported by agile Dupin, so eager to win the favour of the King.[29] Even so little, however, was not accomplished without a rift in ministerial circles, for at the heart of the Government the forces for a conservative and orderly policy encountered opposition. Périer and Broglie supported Guizot, but Laffitte and Dupont de l'Eure were violently opposed to what he had done.[30] These last two, the representatives of the Left, could not forget that Liberal Paris had done much to make the " glorious week of July " successful. This was the reason why all that the Government could do was to fine the leaders and to bring about a temporary suspension of the clubs.

In the midst of this situation of discord stood Louis Philippe, supported by his capitalists and by those members of young France who, like Thiers, were of the *National* School. Prominent among these younger men was one who resembled Thiers in many ways, and who was destined to be associated with him on several momentous occasions. Odilon Barrot was a young enthusiast of undoubted ability. He was almost great; he was honest, but naïf and somewhat given to vanity. Consequently, he became the dupe of everyone, and especially the dupe of Thiers. In French history he is sometimes called a second Sylvain Bailly.[31] Barrot and Thiers were indefatigable supporters of the King during the critical days of August 1830, but they were young and had yet to make a name for themselves. Nearer to Louis Philippe stood the real thanes of his house, Duchatel, Laffitte, Périer, Broglie, and Molé, whose ideal was probably expressed most concisely in the words pronounced by Guizot at Lisieux: "Tout *pour* le peuple, sinon *par* le peuple." This was the ideal of the men who would aid the King to steer his ship between the passionate Berryer of the Right and the Ledru Rollin–Garnier-Pagès group of the Left that represented the clubs of Paris.

Unfortunately, it was not only in French waters that Louis Philippe must look out for dangerous shoals. The same was true of Europe, for the enthroning of the Orléanist family found even fewer sympathizers among the European States than it had found in France. The star of Metternich was still in the ascendant. That faithful watchdog of Counter-Revolution had opined that the Charter of 1814 was too Republican, and to his mind the revised version of 1830 was positively subversive. France had again had an attack of Revolution, and there was danger of contagion. In years past, the French disease had spread rapidly, and the experienced old physician to Europe's ills realized that the people of Holland and his precious Italians were likely to become infected, to say nothing of the Poles, who were straining at the leash of the Tsar, their King. As usual Metternich's prognostications were correct. Following the July Revolution at Paris, the Belgians revolted against the King of Holland; the Italians became aroused; and the Poles made another heroic endeavour to be free.

ENTER LOUIS PHILIPPE

From the very outset, Metternich seemed to anticipate the success of Belgium, and to prevent any further outbreaks, he sought to revive the Holy Alliance and to throw a sanitary cordon around France. In this plan the Tsar of Russia heartily concurred. Austria feared for her predominance in Italy, and Russia thought on Poland. Consequently, the Carlsbad Conference was called, and there Metternich pontificated while Nesselrode, the nuncio of Tsardom, responded with a fervent " Amen." But the requiem that these two Powers sought to sing over Revolution was not entirely successful, and this was probably because the celebrants were not entirely sincere.

Each had his own interests, secret interests, and each thought on different things. Metternich's anger at the insurgent Italians was not unmingled with a secret satisfaction; their action would give him a better excuse for an extension of Austrian penetration into Italy. On the other hand, storm as he might, may not the Tsar have felt that the extension of French influence into Flanders by means of the Belgian revolt would alarm Prussia to the point of declaring war ? Then what a glorious opportunity Russia would have in the East; a Western Europe conflagration would give the Tsar a freer hand. The principals at Carlsbad, then, were not entirely frank with each other; there were too many *arrière-pensées*, and it was the knowledge of this fact that saved Louis Philippe from Europe.

The King of the French was clever enough to perceive their insincerity and the reason therefor, and he was quick enough to take advantage of the situation. His own perspicacity and the astonishing rapidity of the Belgian revolt delivered him from the concerted attack that was being planned at Carlsbad. He appointed wise and experienced diplomats : to England, already favourably disposed to him, he sent old Talleyrand, who had befriended the English cause in Vienna in 1815. Through the latter, the French and British Governments came to a secret agreement not to tolerate interference in Belgium. In this way the French King gained two friends in Europe and was enabled to keep at bay the insincerely-minded, old gentlemen at Carlsbad. When, later, a French princess was married to Leopold of Saxe-Coburg, chosen ruler of the Belgians, the position of Louis Philippe in Europe was quite secure.

But while the Belgian revolt gave the King of France the opportunity for making friends abroad, it caused him a good deal of embarrassment at home.

Republican France failed to understand the wisdom of the Government's refusal to aid the Belgians by a declaration of war against Holland, and the extreme Liberals did not take this consideration into account. Instead, they declared that Louis Philippe was subservient to the dictates of the old régime, and they accused him of connivance with the Reactionaries in Europe and at home. As proof of their contention, they pointed to the fact that the ministers of Charles X were still unpunished. On October 17, Clubists marched again to the Palais Royal, this time to wreak their own bloody vengeance upon the ex-King's officials. Their demonstration was almost successful. La Fayette hesitated to turn his troops on them, and at first Barrot, Prefect of Police, refused to assist the Government in its efforts to prevent the massacre of the imprisoned ministers. This affair and the behaviour of the Government's agents led to a deadlock in the first Ministry.

Small wonder that Louis Philippe was uneasy. The firing of one gun by French soldiers in Belgium, or the shedding of a drop of the blood of the Carlist ministers might set the armies of Reaction on the road to Paris. And, as if to add to his anxiety, he heard from the terrace the terrifying chant of the Marseillaise, and the words of this uncomfortable song often drowned the cries of " Vive le Roi" that had so delighted his ears during the first week of his reign.[32] A compromise of some sort was necessary; to save himself from Radical, he must yield to

ENTER LOUIS PHILIPPE

Radical somewhat. He needed a mild Progressive, but not an energetic bourgeois like Périer. The present Cabinet could not last; Périer and Laffitte were too much in disagreement, and of the two, Laffitte was the more popular. On November 3, therefore, the King consented to a new Ministry under Laffitte; at the same time, he was confronted with a newly elected Chamber.

In character and tendency, Ministry and Chamber afforded quite a contrast. Laffitte was a man of compromises who inclined to the Left, through fear possibly rather than from sympathy. But it was not so with the House of Deputies. The elections were virtually a vote of confidence in the wise policy of the King. By them, the bourgeoisie had obtained a large majority, and the Chamber gave proof of its conservative temper by electing Périer, who was not of the new Cabinet, as its presiding officer. There was, therefore, a gap between Council and Chamber, and Laffitte, never a strong man, soon found himself embarrassed by the efforts of the Left to compromise him and to make him appear to associate with them.[33] In this attempt the men of the Left were aided to quite an extent by Dupont de l'Eure, who was a member of the Council and who was far more Radical than any of the others. The remaining members, Molé, Sébastiani, Soult, d'Argout, and Montalivet were known not to favour any more than Guizot and Périer a Progressive policy. It was not a Cabinet of agreement, but at least the Ministry had the virtue of public approval; Laffitte and Dupont were the two most popular men of the time, and the fact that the former, a successful man of affairs, was Minister of Finances, as well as President of the Council, restored confidence in the minds of many Parisians.[34]

The establishment of the new Ministry did not interfere seriously with the fortunes of Thiers, who had been occupied all the while in the Department of Finances. In fact, after a time it rather enhanced his opportunities, for

THIERS AND THE FRENCH MONARCHY

Laffitte was his friend, and so arduous did the latter soon find his task that he came to leave more and more of the direction of his especial department to his young acquaintance. His experiences with him anent the *National* and the *Constitutionnel* had only increased his confidence in Thiers, and the fact that the King had actually considered nominating him to fill the place of Baron Louis was an evidence that the retention of Thiers was approved by the Tuileries.[35] Within a short time Adolphe Thiers was named Secretary-General of Finances in spite of the protests of some of Laffitte's acquaintances, who objected to his youth and suspected his honesty.[36]

By November, the time of his appointment, the new Secretary was well known in official circles. During the month of August, he had stood for election from Aix and had won. Upon entering the Chamber, he had prepared himself to make his début from the Tribune. In September he was preparing his maiden speech. One can easily imagine the excitement with which he set about his work. He wished to be a great orator, but he realized only too clearly his weaknesses; he had not forgotten the amusement of his audience at Aix during his career as a young barrister. He had a high conception of the power of a real forensic ability. Once, when a student at Aix, he had expressed himself in this regard in the following words:

> " We have prostituted so often the most sacred things that now we are afraid of them. We dare not give ourselves over to them; we are always afraid of being duped by them. When an eloquent writer recalls them to our minds, we seem to be afraid to confess the real emotion (that he has evoked), for we are afraid of being accused of weakness. We have so often used words in all senses; there is no desecration that we have not given them. But should we, for that reason, regard as a dangerous seducer him who arouses in us feelings of which

DAUMIER'S CARTOON OF THIERS THE YOUNG STATESMAN.

ENTER LOUIS PHILIPPE

others have taken advantage to seduce us? No, fellow-orators, there is still a tongue that hypocrisy, lying, or charlatanism cannot mistake, an idiom that has never been found in the mouth of crime. Learn to find it; our souls tell us of it. You to whom nature has given the happiest mediums of expression, you who do not suffer from an inability to express the sentiments that move you, you whom nature has created orators, do not cease to hope. Believe in eloquence; man would be a beast if he ceased to be sensible to its effects." [37]

But on September 23, when he entered the Tribune to participate in the discussion of the budget of 1828, this budding young orator did not measure up to his ideal. Here was no impassioned Lally-Tollendal; instead, he fell far short of his model. He was still handicapped by the failings that deterred him at Aix, and his first speech is said to have delighted his enemies. The same accent, the quick, nervous gestures continued to distract his hearers. In addition, he had contracted or assumed bad forensic habits that may have been the result of his recent ramblings in the field of history. He was monotonous, pompous, copious, diffuse, and seemed to be incapable of repelling the insults of the Opposition.[38] His maiden speech did not convince his hearers that Thiers was an addition to the support that Laffitte's administration soon came to need so very sorely.

Previous to his appointment as President of the Council, Laffitte had been very well liked in Paris, but once in office, his popularity did not help him to control the situation. Essentially timid, he had pledged too much to the people and then discovered that he had gone farther than had been his intention. He had come into power because he had promised to bring about the trial of the ministers of Charles X, and on December 12, his pledge was fulfilled when the trial was begun in the Chamber of Peers. But evidently those Liberals who had been most zealous in their efforts to bring the Carlist officials to justice were not sure that Laffitte and the Peers would be harsh enough, and, to urge them on, the clubs resumed their demonstrations. It was only due to the quick action of Montalivet that the accused ministers escaped a worse penalty than the sentence of life-imprisonment that was passed upon them. The mob had nearly gained possession of them, and, in this crisis, again La Fayette and the National Guard had not behaved well. Their hesitating attitude had almost frustrated the efforts of the Government to maintain order and avert bloodshed.

This episode of the old General and the National Guard had been allowed to pass unnoticed by the easy-going Laffitte. He recognized the popularity of La Fayette with the clubs, which should have realized that, by 1830, La Fayette was more than ever a man of indecisions. He was still the hero of Liberal Paris. But if the President was afraid to reprove the General, the same was not true of the Chamber of Deputies, many of whom realized that the material interests of their constituents would remain in danger as long as the National Guard and its commander continued to be a force on whose sympathies the Radicals of Paris could rely. The affair of December 12 was immediately taken under consideration by the legislators, and a proposal was made to reorganize the Guard. Finally, the Deputies and King agreed to abolish the office of Commandant General, but, to spare La Fayette's feelings, it was agreed that the new law should not be effective until after the death of the old General.

Not all of the Ministry were in favour of the measure. The extreme Left supported them in their opposition to it, but the Cabinet had to yield. La Fayette retired immediately, but took the occasion to give public utterance to the platform of the Republicans when he demanded the abolition of the hereditary Peerage and the election of new Deputies on a basis of universal suffrage.

In this affair, Laffitte gained the favour of neither wing

ENTER LOUIS PHILIPPE

of the Chamber. To the Moderates, his concessions were too slight, while the Extreme Left complained of his weakness in not defending La Fayette. Similarly, his other policies failed to elicit approval. These concerned the system for municipal elections and direct taxation, and a lowering of the franchise qualification to two hundred francs in taxes. To one party, they seemed too timid; to the Moderates, they were too much. The Ministry encountered unfavourable comment from all directions, and prophets foretold another Cabinet crisis. Legitimist joined with Republican in discomfiting the perplexed President, with the result that the storm broke when news reached Paris of the revolts in Poland, Modena, and the Papal States.

The July Days in Paris had aroused the half-conscious desire for independence in north-eastern and southern Europe, and the insurrections that resulted gave more courage to the Liberals of Paris. Republicans dreamed of a general European revolution, and again the clubs were aroused to a fever of excitement. On every possible occasion they demonstrated their power. When the Counter-Revolutionists gathered at Saint Germain de l'Auxerrois to commemorate the death of the Duc de Berry, a mob sacked the church. Laffitte seemed to be paralyzed into inactivity, and again Louis Philippe and the Chamber took the helm. When the cries of Liberal Paris became louder for protection of the Belgian intervention, it was the King and not the President of the Council who mediated in France and Europe. In the early weeks of 1831, Louis Philippe was a really great King; his courage and wisdom saved France and Europe from a general European conflict. He established an agreement with Palmerston as to the neutralization of Belgium, and he silenced the Tsar by a clever and tactful explanation of the attitude of New France to the Polish insurgents. He forced his Ministry into adopting a strict neutrality in regard to Italy. Without the masterly intervention of Louis Philippe, the timid Liberalism of

Laffitte might have brought France to a second disaster as great as that of 1815.

But when the crisis had been safely passed, the situation between King and President was an impossible one. The tables had been reversed; it was Louis who had saved Jacques, and not Jacques who had saved Louis. Furthermore, not all of Louis' negotiations had been disclosed to the President. Frequently, the King had not taken Laffitte into his confidence. Once the latter realized this fact, a resignation was inevitable, and this was what the King had now come to desire. Montalivet, at Louis' instance, had even counselled Thiers to advise Laffitte to retire. Whether Thiers followed the suggestion of Montalivet is not known. At any rate, the day came, and on March 10 the Cabinet resigned. The banker had learned to his hurt that to handle the finances of the House of Orléans was one thing, and that to direct their policies was quite another. Louis Philippe and the Conservative section of the Chamber might now have a Ministry more to their liking. March 13 witnessed the return of Casimir Périer to the Presidency of the Council and the reversion of France to a definite and orderly system.

England hailed the arrival of a " stern and more forceful Ministry." Most of the Chamber was delighted to have the man who had acted as its presiding officer at the head of the Government, and Louis Philippe gave evidence of his personal satisfaction. But while moderate France was contented, there was an air of suspense in Paris, for it was known that the coming to power of such a man as Périer meant the inauguration of a war on all factions of disorder, the Extreme Left and the Extreme Right alike. Although Périer took a middle ground between Republicanism and absolute Monarchy, he was not the man to compromise with either.

It was a notable Cabinet, the *Résistance* Ministry. Périer assumed the direction of the Department of the Interior, and his colleagues included such experienced

ENTER LOUIS PHILIPPE

men as Sébastiani, Soult, Baron Louis, Admiral de Rigny, Barthe, Montalivet, and d'Argout. Under their guidance, the July Monarchy had a chance to catch its breath, and France was brought to the prosperity that Laffitte had promised but had not been able to accomplish. As a parliamentarian Périer was far superior to his predecessor and he exerted a very real control over the Chamber. His success was due in part to the fact that many of the Deputies were in favour of him, and in part to a very wise decision of the President to keep outside of the Ministry those who by reason of their situation or talents could be of use to him in the Chamber. He was above corruption and he served France only to be of benefit to her. He scorned the customary methods of defending his policies. He refused the usual practice of buying up the papers to support him and declared : " I have the *Moniteur* to register my actions ; the Tribune of the Chambers to explain them ; and the future to judge them." [39] It was under the ægis of such a man that the young Thiers began the serious part of his political schooling. It is significant that what Thiers learned under this wise man he never abandoned. From March 1831, the character of the Périer régime was indelibly impressed upon his political mind.

When Laffitte resigned, Thiers retired as Secretary-General of Finances and devoted himself exclusively to his duties as Deputy from the Bouches-du-Rhône, to which position he was re-elected in 1831. It appears that he was not unhappy when the preceding Cabinet fell. He had not been in sympathy with Laffitte's tolerant policy of *laissez aller*, and the sack of Saint Germain de l'Auxerrois that he had witnessed had filled him with a dread of the clubs. If in 1830 he was inclined to favour *Résistance*, by the opening of the year 1831 he had become a complete convert to it. The more unpopular his chief became, the more silent was Thiers, and as the Laffitte régime neared its close, the Secretary-

General became impatient to relinquish a position that did not give him a voice in the Cabinet, and to concentrate upon his duties as Deputy. But he was too mindful of what he owed his patron to abandon the President during the crisis, and it was not until the Cabinet had fallen that Thiers separated himself from Laffitte. On July 22, he wrote to Monsieur Thomas, the future Prefect of the Bouches-du-Rhône : " I want to do my duty, and I have begun it by breaking publicly with the Left and by declaring openly to Monsieur Laffitte that I am only a personal friend." [40]

Experience had taught Thiers much, but the greatest truth that the first six months had revealed to him was the danger of the Left. As always, whenever he had discovered a new lesson, he put it into words and passed it on to others. In 1831, Mesnier, a Paris publisher, issued a *brochure* that bore the title, *La Monarchie de Juillet, par A. Thiers, Deputé des Bouches-du-Rhône.*

This pamphlet was probably written shortly after his retirement from the Finances. Upon the fall of the Ministry, he had paid a visit to his mother at Aix, and then had established himself at 10, rue des Capucines, Paris. There he set to work upon the little booklet that was to be his political " Credo," a declaration of his adherence to the new Government and of his confidence in the Orléans Monarchy. It is, in great part, a reply to the two extreme wings of the Chamber, who were declaring that the Orléans family had not the sanction of popular sovereignty to rule France. His method was odd, and his thesis surprising. He acknowledged frankly that such a sanction had not been given to Louis Philippe, but, he countered, the consent of popular sovereignty would not have been wise or necessary in this instance. " Popular sovereignty calls into the Government the intervention of the masses, and these have never appeared except to upset the Government and to make it anarchical, violent, and bloodthirsty. On the other hand, the sovereignty of the majority calls in a factor true, natural, and legitimate,

ENTER LOUIS PHILIPPE

for then the nation, consulted not *en masse*, for that is impossible, but consulted consecutively in the persons of the electors, deputies, and peers, who represent the *élite* of the nation, replies and expresses a wish that is the real public desire. There is the true principle in virtue of which the country governs itself according to stable and regular laws." [41]

These are not the words of a friend of the clubs, of the *National* as it became after the July Days, or of any sectary of the Extreme Left. This statement, together with others that he put into the *brochure* relative to Périer's avowed declaration of peace as a necessary policy for France, showed that Thiers was a real henchman of the *Résistance* School.[42] And yet, although Périer admired him and appreciated his efforts, there does not appear to have been any great intimacy between them. The new President was not an easy leader to follow, especially for one who was as independently minded as was the Deputy from Aix. Delicate, proud, and accustomed to deference to his wishes, Périer must have found his young admirer in the Chamber very annoying at times, and he never admitted him completely into his confidence. Was this because he distrusted him or because he feared his youthful enthusiasm ? There were occasions, it is true, when the eagerness of the young Provençal went beyond the limits of discretion. Once, for example, Thiers, when speaking from the Tribune, referred to the Ministry and spoke of it as *nous*. At this, it is related, Périer was furious.[43]

The experience in Laffitte's administration had taught Thiers much, but of far greater importance was the practice that he received in the Chamber of Deputies during the personal rule of the great *Résistance* Ministry. It was then that the change came, and that he learned to discard the affectations of speech and the mannerisms that he had first assumed. It was a different Thiers who appeared in the Tribune on April 5, 1831, when he made a satisfactory defence of the financial policy of Laffitte and paid a felicitous tribute to the latter, as if to atone for the political break that had come between them.[44] The occasion was not an easy one, but he met it courageously and conducted himself well. It was not until August of the same year, however, that his talents as an orator really impressed the sophisticated audience of Deputies. Then it was that he rendered a really valuable service to the system to which he had attached himself.

The months of April, May, and June had been difficult. The activity of the Extreme Left within and without the Chamber had been relentless. In the Deputies there had been endless interpellations, and beyond the walls of that House, the clubs and radical newspapers had done their best to make trouble. Several demonstrations in favour of intervention on behalf of the Poles had upset Paris, and the instigators, Cavaignac, Blanqui, and Trélat, had been brought before the courts. The Press, too, had been made to feel the iron hand of Périer; the *Figaro*, *Tribune*, and *Ami du Peuple* had had their interviews with the magistrates. All of which goes to show that the President had made good his promise that law and order should prevail. Moderates were pleased with him, and so too was France, for the July elections had resulted overwhelmingly in his favour, and the agitators of the Left might have become discouraged had not the other political extreme become active. Legitimists had decided to block the success of Périer, and Madame la Duchesse de Berry, aided by the Duc de Cases, the Duc de Saint-Priest and Marshal Bourmont, had connived with their fellows in France to attempt a Bourbon restoration. Working from England and then from Italy they had met with considerable favour, and Counter-Revolution had actually appeared in the western corner of France. This development found Périer just as resourceful as he had been in the case of the Republicans; he dispatched an army into the Vendée to put down the conspiracy of the Extreme Right.

Policies as strong as these had, of course, aroused the

ENTER LOUIS PHILIPPE

discontented. One could laugh at Laffitte and eventually compromise him, but Périer was a man against whom one must carry on a serious and careful war. Accordingly, the Opposition abandoned a policy of ridicule and riots for a planned attack on the patriotism of the Government and on its infidelity to the principles that determined the Revolution of 1830.

To the minds of these men, there were two weak points in the policy of the Government. Why had France not given material assistance to Belgium or even, perhaps, annexed it? Why had France not aided the Poles to profit by her example and to become free? These were the questions with which Louis Philippe was confronted when he opened the session of the Deputies. His efforts to explain the wisdom of *non-intervention* were unavailing, and the effect of the royal discourse was weakened even more when news came that the King of Holland was about to invade Belgium. France is disgraced, cried the Deputies. France under Louis Philippe is still subject to Holy Alliance. These were the sentiments, couched, of course, in more courteous language, that the Extreme Left through Monsieur Thouvenel tried to insert into the customary Reply to the Throne. In the course of his arguments the Deputy of the Left had included the preceding Cabinet in his remarks. Then it was that Thiers, as a former member of the Laffitte administration, asked for the floor. On that day of August 9, 1831, he established himself as an orator of no small consequence and of great originality.

His method was novel for the orators of the 'thirties. He possessed none of the passion of a Berryer, none of his glowing phrases and persuasive eloquence. This new orator was not of the silver-tongued variety. He was clear, logical, and in his method of presentation almost didactic. He taught his audience its lesson. There was a hint of the schoolmaster in his art, and also an echo of the historian. Aix and Paris had made him at last, and each had left their imprint upon him. Frequently

THIERS AND THE FRENCH MONARCHY

he prefaced his arguments with a *résumé* of events that smacks of the *History of the French Revolution*. This is not to say that his discourse was dull and arid. It was relieved by witty little sallies directed at his opponents, who replied, as was then the custom, by caustic remarks addressed to the speaker in the Tribune. These extemporaneous quips of his delighted his hearers, and his apt and short retorts frequently put the laugh on the side of his interrupters. There was no sign of fear or of nervousness. One admirer and friend has described his appearance as he spoke from the Tribune in 1831 : " His half-hidden eyes would flash with profound shrewdness, while his set features and short hair made him resemble certain Roman busts to which energy and intelligence lend a kind of beauty." [45]

This may have been the impression that he made when he undertook to defend the Laffitte and Périer Ministries in August 1831. He declared that all that the Revolution of 1830 had guaranteed had been fulfilled, and he referred to the laws concerning the electoral system, municipal councils, and juries that these two Cabinets had put through. But the greatest part of the address was his defence of the foreign policy. He who had gloried in the victories of Revolutionary and Napoleonic armies became the advocate of a policy of peace, and supported the wisdom of Louis Philippe in not offering material and official aid to the Italian States, to Belgium, and to Poland. France had not committed herself to do so, nor could she have done so without involving herself in a general European war for which she was not prepared. There was nothing dishonourable in recognizing the fact that, for the moment, the only safety of the country lay in maintaining the peace of Europe. That was the great boon that France could offer to all oppressed humanity. His remarks anent Poland are especially significant :

> " As to Poland, one could not have the heart of a human being and not be touched by the sublime

ENTER LOUIS PHILIPPE

effort that this people is making, not hope that Poland will live again among the nations of Europe and protect the Occident. But has our own Government any reason to wipe out the reproaches that are being levelled against it in regard to Poland? It is possible to intervene in Poland by negotiation and not by war. *By war!* But one does not dream of such a measure! From the very moment that war is declared, from the very moment that the Poles resist Russia so heroically, what do we fear? That a new enemy may come in and destroy this unhappy nation; that Prussia and Austria, whose ill-will is well known, may each send 20,000 men to attack Warsaw from this side of the Vistula. What has prevented such a contingency that would have meant most certainly the ruin of Poland? It is peace; for before you could have brought her aid, Poland would have been erased from the list of nations. It is quite evident that you have only held the Prussians and Austrians in check by this policy of peace."

There speaks the logically minded Deputy from Aix, later the advocate of the principle of *sens commun* in politics. Continuing the same discourse, now speaks the historian, the pedant who was, with the possible exception of Guizot, the most didactically inclined member of the Chamber.

" In default of peace, would you declare war and go to Warsaw? Then you must cross the width of the Continent. Twice Napoleon went to Warsaw. The first time he had with him the army of Austerlitz that he considered the finest army in the world. He passed by Ulm, Austerlitz, Jena, along a path radiant with glory and—he almost failed. Again he went and failed. And you, before we even have an army, you want us to go to war in Poland!" [46]

THIERS AND THE FRENCH MONARCHY

The logic of the little historian prevailed, and at its conclusion, his speech was applauded with great enthusiasm.

At last he had arrived. Talleyrand was delighted with the success of his pupil, and Périer expressed his admiration in no uncertain terms. The public regarded him as one of the ablest and staunchest supporters of the wise policies of the President of the Council. From this time on, the *Résistance* Ministry looked to him for support whenever their programme was attacked by either political extreme. In fact, August 9 made him an important part in Périer's political machine that required more friends outside the Cabinet and in the Chambers. Guizot assured the Ministry of the adherence of the Constitutional Monarchists or *Doctrinaires* from the Right. Dupin, still loyal, rallied from the Left all those who could be gathered from the ranks of the old Opposition that had existed during the Restoration. Thiers, on the other hand, confirmed the timid and unstable, and controlled those who delighted to regard themselves as independents. It was at this period of his career that he inaugurated the remarkable but perilous practice of finding a support among the "floaters" in the Chamber whenever he needed it. This was a habit that led him in later years into dangers from which he so frequently escaped by a hair's breadth, and that won for him the epithet *l'oiseau sur la Branche*.

With Guizot, Dupin, and Thiers for his henchmen, Périer was safe for a time. The Opposition had little to offer in the way of leadership, and what guidance it received was not formidable. La Fayette was now too old to control them, and his behaviour earlier in the year had not increased his popularity with the Extreme Left. Odilon Barrot was only trying out his efforts at oratorical passion, and Garnier-Pagès, too, was not fully fledged. Mauguin was superficial and facile. But although the young Republicans were without able and experienced leadership, they were relentless in their

ENTER LOUIS PHILIPPE

attacks, and when, in the autumn of 1831, Talleyrand was able to announce the assurance of the neutralization of Belgium, they were somewhat discomfited, for the Brussels revolution had been saved, but not in the way that they desired. For the moment their continued complaints seemed groundless, but in the latter part of September, they found a cause. Sébastiani, Minister of Foreign Affairs, came to the Chamber and pronounced there those tragic words, *l'ordre règne à Varsovie*, which was a gentle way of announcing that the Russians had entered Warsaw. Upon receiving this intelligence, the Left burst into a flame of passion. Riots again, and even the Radicals in the provinces followed the example of Paris. Interpellations of the Ministry were renewed in the Chamber of Deputies, and once more Thiers entered the speaker's Tribune. Again he defended the policy of Périer, only this time with even greater intensity, for now that *système* had become his own, and he would continue it when he became a minister. The discourse of September 20 was a real success, and the results of his effort was the victory of the Ministry, when the Chamber passed an expression of confidence in Périer by a vote of two hundred and twenty-one to one hundred and thirty-six. From this date, the forensic activities of the President's lieutenant were almost continuous. On September 23, he defended the Government against the charges of laxity and indifference in regard to the legitimists' riots in the Midi of France, but his greatest effort came in October, when the matter of the Chamber of Peers was brought up for discussion.

So far, there had appeared to be complete accord between Périer and Thiers. Over the question of the Peers, however, there were surface differences. The President really favoured the idea that the Peers should continue to be an hereditary body, but Louis Philippe, on July 31, 1830, had virtually committed himself to the opposite principle, and Périer believed that the King must accomplish that promise. As long as it remained unfulfilled,

THIERS AND THE FRENCH MONARCHY

the Extreme Left possessed a grievance against the House of Orléans that was unanswerable. This was the opinion of Périer. On the other hand, the Deputy from the Bouches-du-Rhône believed sincerely in the virtues of an hereditary Upper House, and because he was not a member of the Ministry, he felt that he was free to assert his own opinions on a matter so near to his heart. Frequently, his critics are prone to assert that Thiers in 1831 was a time-server, but his actions in regard to the question of the Peers show him in an entirely different light. Although he was devoted to the *Résistance* School and had cast in his fortunes with them, he was still loyal to the principles that he had asserted at an earlier time. In his *History* and in the editorials of the *National*, he had frequently asserted his faith in the English system that allowed an elective Commons and an hereditary House of Lords. When, therefore, Périer's Government proposed to abolish such an institution in France, Thiers arose to protest. His arguments were practically the same as those that he had propounded when explaining his system of " representative monarchy " previous to the July Revolution. The Peers must be even as the House of Lords; an elective Chamber must be guided and advised by the more cautious minds of the nation. " You suggest the peril of a régime of privilege if the Peers continue to be an hereditary chamber, but what privileges have these gentlemen left to them now ? " [47] At the end of his discourse, the defender of the Peers gave an argument that was a threat, a threat, however, that must have brought a gleam of amusement into his own eyes as he uttered it : " If you deprive the Peers of their privilege of heredity, then the great families of France will have nothing more to do with that Chamber. Instead, they will throw themselves into the elective Chamber, just as, in former times, they piled into the palace of the Emperor." [48]

In spite of his efforts, however, the hereditary character of the Peers was abolished, and they became a house of

ENTER LOUIS PHILIPPE

men chosen by royal appointments from the *élite* of the nation. And so compromise crept into the Government even under the régime of Périer.

Other appearances of Thiers at this time were occasioned by the proposal to mobilize the National Guard, a measure to which he was opposed on the ground that it would alarm Europe, and by the discussion of the Budget of 1832, when he reported the opinions of the Budget Committee of which he was a member. It was during the latter address that he set forth his remarkable arguments in regard to the utter impossibility of cheap government. This speech was a masterpiece of clear reasoning and of common sense, and even his opponents paid tribute to the ability of the orator.[49]

During the interval occupied by Thiers' debates in the Chamber, Périer had had his difficulties outside the Legislature. The influence of the clubs had spread to the provinces, and the outlying sections of France became infected with the revolutionary fever. The translation of the ashes of General Ney to the Panthéon afforded an occasion for a tremendous demonstration conducted by the *Friends of the People*, and the trials anent this affair continued into April of the year 1832. At Lyons, the workers had rebelled against the capitalists over the question of tariffs. Government troops were even driven out of the garrison, and the merciless efforts of Bugeaud, the fire-eater, and the presence of the duc d'Orléans were required to reinstate the authority of the Government. In all of these repressive measures Périer was heartily supported by Guizot, Dupin, and Thiers, who was accused by Chateaubriand of having deserted his former Liberal colours.[50] Such Paris papers as the *Tribune*, *Quotidienne*, and *Gazette de France* decried the policies of the new triumvirate in the Chambers. Legitimists and Republicans joined the fracas, and Périer and his triumvirs were faced with the prospects of a formidable attack.

The year 1832 had opened inauspiciously with a riot

and a new European complication. In Paris, there was the plot of the Tours de Notre Dame;[51] in Europe, Italy made another attempt to shake off aristocratic rule. The Romagna revolted, and Gregory XVI appealed to Austria for aid. To this request Metternich acceded only too willingly, and Périer perceived at once what use that wily statesman might make of the situation to increase his hold on Italy. To counteract such a possibility, the President despatched a quota of French troops to the fortress of Ancona. This action was again supported by Guizot and Thiers in the Chamber. Boldly they faced the difficult question raised alike by Republican and Legitimist: was this in accord with the assertions of the July Monarchy that it would follow a policy of non-intervention, or was this a repudiation of this principle?

As a matter of fact, Périer had but short time in which to defend his action, and he bequeathed this problem to his political heirs. In April, 1832, the cholera broke out in France, and on May 16 the President of the Council fell victim to the disease. Great was the alarm of Thiers and Guizot; great was the delight of Legitimist and Republican, certain of whom actually proposed an illumination of Paris to celebrate the deliverance of France from an unscrupulous dictator![52]

One paper of the Left made the following comment on Périer's funeral: "The public profited by the first day of fine weather to take the air. There were countless *promeneurs* and many carriages on the boulevard. But there was no sign of mourning or of grief. Nevertheless, they had convoked the *ban* and *arrière-ban* of the *Juste Milieu*, without, however, being able to recruit more than fifteen hundred men."[53]

The King himself is said to have remarked: "Casimir Périer is dead; is this an advantage or a misfortune? Time will show."

For Thiers the passing of Périer was a stroke of fortune. He had been a silent observer, he now became an active

ENTER LOUIS PHILIPPE
participant in the problems raised by the first year of the July Monarchy.

NOTES TO CHAPTER VIII

[1] Metternich: *Mémoires*, I. 22 : account of General Belliard.
[2] Barrot: *Mémoires*, I. 215.
[3] Thiers: *Notes on the Cabinet*, September 1830. Bibliothèque Nationale, 20,601, Part II. 22.
[4] Note of Mademoiselle Dosne on Thiers' volume of the *National*. Bibliothèque Thiers, Paris.
[5] Thiers: *Monarchie de Juillet*, Avant propos, iv.
[6] Thiers: *Notes on the Cabinet*, September 1830. Bibliothèque Nationale, 20,601, Part II. 22. Zervort: *Thiers*, p. 81.
[7] *Ibid.*, p. 80.
[8] *Ibid.*
[9] Simon: *Thiers*, p. 167.
[10] de Cassagnac: *Histoire de Louis Philippe*, I. 8.
[11] Louis Blanc: *Histoire*, I. 353. Thureau-Dangin: *Histoire de la Monarchie de Juillet*, I. 20. Footnote. Weill: *Histoire du parti Républicain*, p. 69.
[12] Tschernoff: *Le Parti Républicain*, p. 224.
[13] Weill: *Histoire du Parti républicain*, p. 44.
[14] *La Jeunesse Libérale*, p. 211. d'Herbelot to Montalembert, Ivry, August 6, 1830.
[15] de Broglie: *Recollections*, II. 406.
[16] Thureau-Dangin: *Histoire de la Monarchie de Juillet*, I. 111.
[17] Louis Blanc: *Histoire*, I. 445.
[18] *Ibid.*, I. 454.
[19] *Ibid.*, II. 32.
[20] Guizot, *Mémoires*, II. 100-1.
[21] Weill: *Histoire du parti Républicain*, p. 49.
[22] *National*, September 11, 1830.
[23] La Hodde: *Sociétés Secrètes*, p. 32.
[24] de Broglie: *Recollections*, II. 409.
[25] La Hodde: *Sociétés Secrètes*, p. 35.
[26] *Ibid.*, pp. 38, 39. de Broglie: *Recollections*, II, 469 sqq.
[27] *National*, September 3, 1830.
[28] de Broglie: *Recollections*, II. 410.
[29] Guizot: *Mémoires*, II. 105-7.
[30] Thiers: *Notes on the Cabinet*, September 1830. Bibliothèque Nationale, 20,601, Part II. 22.
[31] de Cassagnac: *Histoire de Louis Philippe*, I. 126.
[32] *Ibid.*, I. 120.
[33] Dupin: *Mémoires*, II, 247.
[34] *Ibid.*, II. 248.

THIERS AND THE FRENCH MONARCHY

[35] Simon: *Thiers*, p. 167.
[36] Zervort: *Thiers*, p. 87.
[37] Thiers MSS., Sur l'Éloquence Judicial. Bibliothèque Thiers, fol. 543, 132-34.
[38] Simon: *Thiers*, pp. 174-75.
[39] Guisquet: *Mémoires*, I. 210.
[40] Thiers, Paris, to Monsieur Thomas, July 22. Bibliothèque Thiers, Paris, No. 43.
[41] Thiers: *Monarchie de Juillet*, p. 46.
[42] *Ibid.*, p. 91.
[43] Thureau-Dangin: *Histoire de la Monarchie de Juillet*, II. 41.
[44] Thiers: *Discours*, I. 25 sqq. April 5, 1831.
[45] de Rémusat: *Thiers*, p. 63.
[46] Thiers: *Discours*, I. 60-70; 70-71. August 9, 1831.
[47] *Ibid.*, I. 159. October 3, 1831.
[48] *Ibid.*, I. 183. October 3, 1831.
[49] Dupin: *Mémoires*, II. 353.
[50] Chateaubriand: *Mémoires d'Outre Tombe*, VI. 173-75.
[51] *Vide* Guisquet: *Mémoires d'un Préfet de Police*, I. 265 sqq.
[52] *Ibid.*, I. 457 sqq.
[53] *Tribune*, May 20, 1832.

CHAPTER IX

MINISTER OF THE INTERIOR (1832-35)

As the words attributed to the King indicated, the loss of Casimir Périer did not appear to Louis Philippe in the light of an unmitigated evil. Historians of the nineteenth century have not given full justice to that monarch's abilities. He was by no means content to be a figure-head, and once the *Résistance* régime had been instituted, the King had not been disposed to relish the domineering attitude of its chief. To the royal way of thinking, there had been too much Périer and too little Orléans. Consequently, during the days that followed Périer's death, it was Louis Philippe who took the helm.

At first the intention seems to have been to call a new Ministry. With this in mind, Talleyrand, ever faithful friend of the Government of the day, left his post at London and hastened to Paris to advise the King. On May 25, a conference was held at the residence of the Ambassador, and thither he convoked his faithful henchman and those indebted to him. At this consultation it was proposed to form a Cabinet of which Talleyrand, Sébastiani, and the triumvirate, Guizot-Thiers-Dupin, would be the shining lights.[1] It is unlikely that the King would have favoured such a combination; perhaps he feared to put Talleyrand in the saddle. At any rate, when Laffitte, Barrot, and Garnier-Pagès issued a strong protest against the formation of a Ministry that would establish a higher middle-class domination; and when the clubs showed their disapproval by a demonstration on the occasion of the funeral of General Lamarque, Louis Philippe decided to keep the control of affairs

THIERS AND THE FRENCH MONARCHY

in his own hands, and to continue himself the policy of Périer. During this period, the King's measures were as strong as if they had been the measures of the late President himself. When the rioting became acute in Paris, he declared the capital in a state of siege, and issued orders against Cabet, Laboissière, and Garnier-Pagès, who had instigated the Lamarque riot. Again, when Madame la Duchesse de Berry actually landed in the Vendée to encourage the Legitimist risings in the west, the party of the Extreme Right was given a taste of force by the arrest of Berryer at Angers. It was the King who stemmed the tide of Revolution during the June Days, and who kept his Cabinet in line with his policies by means of Montalivet and the fast ageing Sébastiani, who were his personal friends.

When the crisis of the late spring had been safely passed, Louis Philippe considered again the possibility of reconstructing his headless Cabinet. In this regard, Dupin, who was fast becoming discontented, declared that the principal concern of the monarch was to discover a chief who would not issue orders to royalty itself.[2] But this was not an easy task, for the men of July were either capable or hopelessly mediocre. Of the former, there were few and these were independently minded; of the latter, the numbers were legion, but they were as likely as not to become the creatures of the Deputies and to forget their duty to the King. The choice was narrowing down when, on June 28, Louis Philippe gave a dinner at Saint Cloud to which he summoned all those whom he regarded as acceptable candidates for royal favour. The list of guests interested political Paris; it included the actual ministers and Talleyrand, Bertin de Vaux, and Thiers, who, it was remarked, was now beginning to receive attention from the royal family.[3] Great disappointment was occasioned when the " Candidates' Dinner " failed to result in a new Cabinet, and the King continued his personal rule. In fact, it was not until October, 1832, that parliamentary

MINISTER OF THE INTERIOR

leaders and dissensions within the existing Ministry forced him to form another Cabinet.

The intervening months had not been successful for the Crown. Without Périer the Cabinet was incapable, and lacked the power to control the two extreme sections of the Chambers. The Republican papers gave themselves free rein and attacked relentlessly the Government. It was during this interval that the *Tribune* celebrated its sixty-second summons to the courts.[4] In the Chamber sedition was preached openly, and in the Cabinet the ministers were divided against each other.[5] This situation had encouraged the ambitious Dupin to strike for power. Resentful at what he chose to regard as the neglect of the King, he set about to force a way into the Ministry, or, failing in that, to form a new party of the Opposition that would drive the actual combination from power. Success crowned his first efforts, and certain members of the Cabinet were won over to his side. Finally, they proposed his appointment. To this suggestion Montalivet, Sébastiani, and d'Argout were strongly opposed, for they feared Dupin's personal motives, and they knew that the characteristic instability of his political opinions would make him unacceptable to the European courts. His appointment would change the Conservative colour of the Government policy. Within the Cabinet two parties developed, that of Dupin and that of Montalivet, and, due to these divisions, the members could not be brought to agree on any matter. A change was inevitable and necessary. Dupin had his followers, so had Montalivet, but there was a middle man who had the favour of both sections; the split in the Government cleared the stage for Thiers.

During the early days of this crisis, Thiers had been absent from Paris. Whether intentional or not, it had been wise. Twice the faithful Mignet summoned him from the country, where he had retired to study. Dupin desired him, so, too, did the King's party; here was opportunity beckoning him.[5] But Thiers, wary of Dupin's methods and mistrusting his policies, at first refused to make of him an enemy and declined to serve without him. There were interviews with Sébastiani, Montalivet, d'Argout, and even with the King himself. His conversations with the latter were not without their significance. Louis Philippe was afraid to take Dupin and preferred to settle the matter by taking Thiers. "Save me," said the King, "from this lawyer, Dupin. What will Europe say if they see me yielding to his demands? I shall dishonour myself, I shall endanger my negotiations, if I ask him to be President. Be my Pitt, and since Dupin wishes it, let him take the rôle of Fox." [7] The King was desperate, and he pleaded with Thiers to help him out of his political *impasse*. Dupin had made conditions that would have prevented the continuance of Périer's policies. Never a sincerely minded Conservative, he had become a Third Party man and was leaning more and more towards the Left. He had demanded the withdrawal of the King's most trusted ministers. Louis Philippe was in an agony of suspense. He recalled to Thiers, *avec une grâce et un esprit infinis*, the relations that he had had with him during the July Days, the Laffitte régime, and at the formation of the Périer Ministry. At these words, the former editor of the *National* must have trembled. Power was within his grasp, and yet he hesitated, and retired to the country to consider the matter.

Again a summons from Mignet, and this time the King said: "With what pleasure I see you again. You are my man, the one with whom I prefer to talk over affairs; with whom I shall very often have occasion to discuss them. We are destined to lose each other and to find each other often. Twenty times you will be my minister. I think that I have a long future ahead of me. Circumstances will force me to separate from you, but I shall come back to you again!" [8] These were the words of prophecy; they were far more true than either of them realized at the time. But they were almost promises, and Thiers began to weaken and almost to consent to go into the Cabinet with Montalivet and Sébastiani. At last, however, he informed the King that if he should ever enter a Ministry, certain of its members might have to be sacrificed in order to mollify the Opposition. He would decline to enter a Cabinet that was not representative of the mind of the Deputies. To this Louis Philippe replied that he would make such concessions as he advised if he would only find him his man, and he added: "At this very moment I should like to place you where you deserve to be and where the future will undoubtedly find you, but you are still too young and your importance is not yet fully recognized." [9]

These conversations were related by Thiers to his mother-in-law, Madame Dosne, and while they may not be verbatim reports, there are undoubtedly in them the essentials of truth, and they mark the sealing of an alliance between their reporter and the royal family. Out of them grew a friendship that was never entirely lost even during the trying days of the Guizot régime after 1840. For the present, however, they settled one thing: the Deputy from Aix could not yet be President of the Council. He had agreed, however, to find one for the King, and when this fact became known, he was the man most sought after in Paris. Even Guizot solicited from him the coveted post, but Thiers would not consider him, for, being a *Doctrinaire*, Guizot was too unpopular. Finally, however, the situations in the Netherlands and in the Vendée became acute. A Ministry undivided and capable of action must be found. At last a combination was agreed upon, and on October 11, 1832, Marshal Soult formed a new Council.

This latest Cabinet was not entirely a happy affair, but it was far better than its predecessor. The Marshal himself was docile, and the men who served with him were not of the sort to accept dictation from the King. Therein lay the power of Louis Philippe; he could control this new combination without their knowing it.

THIERS AND THE FRENCH MONARCHY

A President who was obedient and trustworthy, a Minister of Public Instruction (Guizot) who was a *Doctrinaire* and who disagreed with the Minister of Foreign Affairs (Broglie), who was of the King's school, and both of them in complete disaccord with the Minister of the Interior, who was none other than the parliamentary free-lance, Adolphe Thiers. Evidently, when the latter found a President for the King he discovered, as well, a soft bed for himself. He, at any rate, was secure, and so, too, was Louis Philippe, for Soult made a most unexpectedly successful début, due to the fact that the King of Holland respected his request that the Dutch troops be withdrawn from Belgium. This *coup* disarmed for a time even the Left, and gave the new Ministers an opportunity to become acquainted with their duties.

October 11 was a memorable date for the most recent appointee to the portfolio of the Interior. It marked a new phase in his political education. From that time until 1836, when he became President of the Council, Thiers was almost constantly in the Government. Minister of the Interior in 1832, he resigned to become Minister of Public Works in January 1833, only to resume his former office in 1834, when his services were required to meet a very difficult situation, a task for which he had proven himself eminently fitted.

When first he became a member of the Cabinet, he was not carried away with elation and delight at his good fortune. He was already a veteran in the Chamber and he bore the scars of battle and of hard, vigorous combat. His career as a parliamentary free-lance was not an easy one to continue. He was not a *Doctrinaire*, nor was he of the Dupin School. He was not a Legitimist, and he had already demonstrated his hatred of the clubs. At this period, he was essentially a patriot who had fought consistently for the security and dignity of the Monarchy in France and in Europe. But being a patriot without any party affiliations, he was open to attack and to suspicion. He was accused of being an opportunist, and

MINISTER OF THE INTERIOR

the latter charge was not without apparent justification when men recalled his political defection from Laffitte and from the *National*. Then, as now, the gladiators of the political arena did not understand that a man might change his tactics without altering one bit his essential beliefs. He was subject to certain family embarrassments in the person of a profligate father and a collection of natural brothers and sisters, and this made him the butt of *Charivari* and of the *Pilorii*. The calumnies that followed him throughout his life began to be thrown at him in 1832. It was indeed not without cause that, on the morrow of his appointment, he wrote to old war-horse Bugeaud, the Terror of the Lyonnais workmen, these words :

" Support me, I beg you. Give me courage, for I have need that people of heart support a young man calumniated and beaten by the winds of envy. Write me—I shall be so grateful for that. I am weighed down under the awful impression of the newspapers, and I write you with too much feeling, perhaps." [10]

But although it was with misgiving that he reached out his hand to grasp the portfolio tendered him by royalty, once he had it tucked under his arm he was fearless in the prosecution of his duty.

When he assumed the functions of Minister of the Interior, his activity was somewhat curtailed, for he had not charge of the administrative personnel, nor was he concerned with the departmental and communal governments. These were delegated to d'Argout, who was Minister of Commerce and of Public Works.[11] At first, the chief concern of Thiers was the matter of public security. In his speeches before the Chamber he had harped incessantly on this note, and now he found that the Government expected him to act as the chief policeman of the realm. Consequently, his duties brought him into immediate contact with the disruptive forces in Paris, and it was not long before they heard his threats and felt the bite of his sword. Educated in the school of Périer, he was recognized as an advocate of law and order, and he defended this principle as ably from the office chair in the Ministry of the Interior as he did from the floor of the House of Deputies. With the possible exception of Guizot, he was the most able protagonist of the Soult Ministry. Fearless to a degree, he spoke with a frankness that frequently took his opponents unawares. He was able to expose their grievances and their motives accurately and without fault. His speech of November 29 astonished his enemies as well as his friends. It was at one and the same time a remarkable diagnosis of the ills of the Left and a reply to their protests:

> "Unless I am much mistaken, here is what our opponents are saying every day: 'A revolution has taken place, but the Government is not heeding it, it is even denying it. It is tying itself up to the Restoration, to its system of civil administration, to its budget of a million, to its reactionary prejudices; it is continuing the latter's errors. What results? The Legitimists raise their heads; their hopes and audacities are reviving. On the other hand, the patriots are indignant and reasonably exasperated, and they are the ones who are persecuted.' So, they say, there is within the country a policy of consideration and leniency for the one, and for the other only anger and calumnies; without France, there is a policy of submission and subservience to the foreigner." [12]

Having enumerated the grievances of the Left, the orator then proceeded to one of those brilliant summaries of the benefits of the Monarchy. In glowing words he recalled the establishment of a constitutional system with a bicameral legislative, a lowered electorate, and a

MINISTER OF THE INTERIOR

foreign policy that was known as "non-intervention," but that was, in fact, the only programme that France could adopt if she were to live among the established European polity.[13]

In this speech, however, there was a personal note. Thiers was not only defending the Monarchy against the charge of disloyalty to the promises of July; he was also defending himself. He had been accused of unfairness in the administration of his Department. All the activities of the Interior, the Left declared, had been directed against his former associates and friends of the Left. To the intrigues of the Right he had given no heed. Such an accusation must have cut him to the quick, and it was, in part, to answer these that he had appeared in the Tribune of the Deputies during the latter part of the year 1832. He had had to defend his policies almost before he had inaugurated them. His first action as minister had aroused a storm of protest. As soon as he had assumed the direction of the Interior, he had sent out to the departmental police instructions in regard to the treatment of public meetings and demonstrations. The wording of these documents was exactly in line with that of Périer, whose praises he continued to sing.[14] Rioters of the Left he put into prison, but it is true he did not treat the *exaltés* of the Right in the same fashion. In making such a discrimination he was wise, for the performances of the clubs and of the Republicans were purely national, but the farce staged by the Legitimists had an international significance. Thiers might clap his Radical behind the bars, and the grizzly, old, crowned heads of Europe would wag a senile approval, but when the fair *prétendante* of Bourbonism tried to embarrass a Bourgeois King, these troublesome old monarchs would rub their hands with delight and utter their anathemas against the young upstart who would handle the royal lady too roughly. Austria, for example, was undoubtedly sympathetic to the cause of Maria Carolina, Duchesse de Berry and widow of the heir

THIERS AND THE FRENCH MONARCHY

of the exiled Charles X. Metternich was consistently favourable to all French pretenders who were not Bonapartes and might seriously alarm Louis Philippe. The old Chancellor at Vienna was enjoying his game of suddenly jumping out from doorways, waving a Bourbon white flag, and crying " Boo ! " at the French King whenever that monarch came to a sharp political turning. The Tsar hated the Orléans family and would have been delighted at its overthrow.

These facts were sufficient in themselves to warrant a moderate policy on the part of the French Government. It was by no means beyond the realm of possibility that drastic measures against the Duchess might have involved Louis Philippe in that war with the counter-revolutionary courts of Europe that he had so dreaded. But, on the other hand, there was the Left crying out that it was oppressed while the supporters of the Bourbons went scot free. Here was a situation that demanded a new kind of golden-mean procedure. Thiers must not offend the feelings of a critical Europe, and he must prove to the satisfaction of the Opposition that the July Monarchy did not hesitate to break with the Restoration. He must act, and yet not act too far. The Duchess was at last in the Vendée, and that section was making preparations to support her cause.

Fortunately for him, all of the Extreme Right did not approve of the behaviour of the Vendéans, but those that did approve were not negligible in quantity or in quality. Certain parts of the Church had espoused her cause, for that institution, ever attached to the old régime, was in great part still ultra-royalist. With the exception of the La Mennais and Montalembert group, few churchmen saw much hope for religion under the Orléanist rule. Prayers for the Duchess were even offered publicly in many churches of France.[15] Furthermore, other sections of France had become affected; the citizens of Aix and of Marseilles had been concerned in the conspiracy, for the presence of the fair leader

MINISTER OF THE INTERIOR

had even been signalled in the south of France.[16] One thing was certain, the movement could not be put down until Maria Carolina was safely and securely lodged in the care of the Government. To this task the Minister of the Interior devoted the greater part of his attention during his first term of office.

When he had assumed the portfolio, Thiers had found a clue. During the previous ministerial crisis, Montalivet, then in charge of the Interior, had had communications with one of the Duchess' entourage named Deutz. This agent had had a varied career. He began life as the son of a Jewish Rabbi. Later, he became a convert to Rome, a creature of the Jesuits, and through the latter, he was finally accredited to Maria Carolina, who accepted him as one of her spies.[17] Monsieur Deutz, however, was more concerned with personal gain than with the success of the cause of his fair patron, and he soon made overtures to Thiers. After the formation of the Soult Ministry, Deutz sent to Thiers an anonymous letter in which he proposed a meeting in the vicinity of the Champs-Elysées at a certain hour. There, for a consideration, he would divulge the hiding-place of the Duchess. The recipient showed the letter to one of his secret agents, and in spite of the latter's opposition to the plan, he decided to meet his mysterious correspondent at the stipulated time and place. Once he had gone in search of a Duke to make him a King; now he would go in pursuit of a Duchess to make her a prisoner. The affair was not without its dangers, and Thiers, ever cautious, took his precautions. He may have overdone the matter, for he tells us that he concealed two revolvers on his person and stationed his secret agents in the vicinity. Then he set out upon his second great adventure. A dark night, a drive along a silent street, the descent from the unlighted carriage, and the lonely walk to the designated meeting-place. The moment of suspense, and the relief upon finding that Deutz was alone and unarmed. There was no ambuscade after all! Deutz was most

THIERS AND THE FRENCH MONARCHY

compliant! The return to the hôtel of the Ministry, a hasty conference. The bundling of Deutz into the train for Nantes with the new Prefect, and lo! Madame la Duchesse betrayed and captured—and all for five hundred thousand francs drawn upon *fonds secrets*, the blessed, discretionary fund![18]

The capture at Nantes was made on November 6. Great was the dismay of the Legitimists, who tore down the placards announcing the event and offered prayers for the safety of their heroine.[19] France was flooded with pamphlets reviling her captor.[20] But prayers and pamphlets were of no avail; the royal captive was lodged securely at Blaye under the watchful eye of old Bugeaud. Whatever his methods in bringing her to bay, certainly the actions of Thiers after the arrest were worthy of only the highest commendation.[21] He was not bloodthirsty; he was tired of being a *Fouché* and was determined not to allow this case to become a second *duc d'Enghien* affair. His only desire was to keep his fair prisoner securely and comfortably at Blaye until such time when she could leave the country, or until her influence had decreased. Prospects of either seemed remote, when, as a matter of fact, they were nearer fulfilment than Thiers and Bugeaud believed. Suddenly it was discovered that the Duchess was with child, having contracted a second marriage secretly.

In this way the gods completed for Thiers the first task that he had encountered upon his coming into the Government, and the Legitimists, who had rallied to the cause of Maria Carolina, fell back into the usual divisions of Carlists, Dauphinists, and Henricinquists.

Although the Government was relieved from immediate danger from the Extreme Right by the indiscreet passion of the Duchesse de Berry, it found itself embarrassed by the general impression that the case had made. Republicans reviled Thiers for his leniency, while Legitimists denounced him as a cruel monster. He became the object of all the attacks of the Opposition. To quiet

MINISTER OF THE INTERIOR

this criticism and to save the Ministry it was finally decided that he should resign his post. On January 1, 1833, d'Argout went over to the Interior, and Thiers replaced him as Minister of Public Works. This change was not a defeat, for he entered upon his new functions at a very important time.

Until the formation of the Périer Ministry, the cry of both Oppositions had been that France was not prosperous and that no remedial measures had been undertaken with a view to bettering the economic condition of the country. Hindered by clubs and by a multiplicity of other problems, Laffitte had not been able to do much in this field of national interest. Under the able Périer, however, the industrial development of France had received attention. In Lille and in the districts of the Rhône and the Alps the factory system had been encouraged and more modern methods of communication had been undertaken. It was in relation to this growth in economic activity that the King had summoned in Paris a meeting of three Councils that represented respectively the agricultural, industrial, and commercial interests of France. As Minister of Commerce and of Public Works, Thiers presided at the formal opening of the Congress when, on February 15, he delivered an address of welcome on behalf of the Government. This was the second occasion on which he had expressed himself on the matter of general economic policy, and in this speech he laid down the principles that formed the bases for his later policies in this field of national enterprise. Tariffs, of course, were the principal questions; he declared that in regard to them he was a man of the golden mean. He was neither a high protectionist nor a free-trader. He believed in a middle policy between the two that should be determined according to the need of each separate enterprise.[22]

His greatest interest, however, was not in tariffs, factories, and railroads, but in something more akin to his character as a patriot. This man was not of the sort

THIERS AND THE FRENCH MONARCHY

who saw the glory of his country in dollars and cents, perhaps, even, he thought too little on that side of things; to Thiers, the glories of France meant dignity, beauty and military security. He must embellish France and, too, he must make her secure. Napoleon was his hero at this time, and it is not unlikely that his studies of Napoleonic literature influenced his own ideas. Napoleon had undertaken to give Paris magnificent buildings, stately vistas, and wide, open spaces; so, too, would Thiers. With this in mind, he upset the Chamber by demanding the modest sum of one hundred million francs. This request caused him no little difficulty in the Legislative, where he was attacked by the Left in the person of Arago. But his defence was so able, and the visions that he conjured up were so alluring that he won his point. Under his enthusiastic direction, the Arc de Triomphe, the Madeleine, the Quai d'Orsay, the Panthéon, and the basilica of Saint Denis were restored and completed. Possibly, in the Madeleine may be found just a suggestion of that predilection for the atrocious pseudo-classic architecture of the Renaissance school that he later developed. He added to the École des Beaux Arts, and, because of his friendship with the painters of the time, he became particularly interested in its development. He gave a ready ear to their suggestions. For a time, he was regarded as their patron, but when their little Mæcenas offered subsidies to such great men as Ingres, Delacroix, and Vernet, to induce them to go to Italy and make copies of great Italian masters for French art schools, they wearied of him! He enlarged the Collège de France and embellished the Place de la Concorde. But all of his interests were not purely æsthetic.

History had taught Thiers the value of an army, and at the same time that he was hobnobbing with painters, he was consorting with military engineers. Great maps and plans littered the long tables of his office. Over these he pored long hours, for he loved the game of war. France must be secure against her foreign foes, and Paris must be made safe from attack by both Reactionary and Clubist. The result of this venture into military interests was his wise proposal for the fortification of Paris, a project that was the occasion for more riots on the part of the Opposition, who did not view with equanimity the plan for a ring of forts around the capital. These forts implied, of course, the presence of more troops within the general vicinity of the city. Such a proposal did not meet with the favour of the more violently minded members of the two Extremes.

As Minister of Public Works he was successful, but he does not appear to have been satisfied. In fact, even as early as 1833, Thiers was not content with a reputation as an able administrator. Throughout his life, this little bourgeois asserted again and again that the affairs of the political world meant nothing to him; that what satisfied him were matters of intellect and taste. Whether these assertions were sincere is a question, but their frequent reiteration indicates that he was always desirous of being recognized as a man of letters and a patron of the arts. Even at his busiest moments his head was filled with grandiose designs for historical and literary productions. He would write a History of the World, a History of Florence, or, perhaps, a detailed study of Chinese art. He was ever the slave of an ambition to be recognized as a scholar and as an art collector. Amusing yet pathetic are some of his efforts. An unfinished History of Florence for which he collected copious notes, and employed the services of a secretary, Canestrini, in Italy, and the vulgar reproductions of Italian sculpture and painting with which he filled the spacious rooms of his house at the Place Saint Georges, are monuments to this phase of his interests. It was an ambition that was never entirely gratified, and that was always pushing him further into literary and pecuniary extravagances. Probably the nearest point to satisfaction of this desire was reached during the years 1833–34. In the latter year, the death of Andrieux caused a vacancy in the French Academy.

The procedure of election to the Academy is always a shock to anyone but a Frenchman. In accordance with the custom, Thiers proposed himself as a candidate for the Immortals. Some were amused at his audacity; he is still so young, they said. But others who knew that his chances were good were not surprised when it was announced that their candidate had received seventeen out of the twenty-five votes. On December 14, 1834, he was received into the Academy, and on this occasion, he delivered the customary eulogy of the man whose place he was to take.

It is not difficult to imagine the excitement of the young minister when he appeared before the brilliant assemblage of all the great in France. Facing him were old Talleyrand and Royer-Collard. Above him, in one of the boxes, Madame la Duchesse de Dino smiled down at him, and is it not likely that his mysterious affinity, Madame la Princesse de Lieven, *la belle russe*, was also there to witness the triumph of her latest conquest? Some related that his discourse was mediocre, and that again, he fell victim to that dangerous tendency to use too much rhetoric.[23] This, however, was not the opinion of the Duchess, who writes that Thiers enthralled his audience. Even she acknowledges, however, that the address partook more of the nature of a political argument than of a scholarly effort.[24]

Indeed, there was much that was personal in it, and the little candidate took this opportunity to assert before the wise men of France his loyalty to the Périer ideal of government. On that day he was far indeed from the intimate, little talks of revolution that he had had at Aix in the homes of de Lauris or of Arnaud. On this great occasion, Thiers was *patriote* and anti-revolutionary in politics, in philosophy, and in literature. And yet there is an echo of the historian of the French

MINISTER OF THE INTERIOR

Revolution and of the didactically minded editorial writer of the *National* in his words.

" Gentlemen, our eyes have really seen, our hands have really touched all these things and all these men. We have witnessed as bloody a forum as that of Rome. We have beheld the heads of orators displayed from the Tuileries where they had spoken. We have seen the old régime and the July Days." Enter now the ghost of Charles X ! " We have seen kings as unhappy as Charles I, more miserable than James II." Enter Louis Philippe ! " We behold every day the prudence of William." And then, suddenly, the hero of Thiers, Napoleon I himself, is hauled out of his mouldy tomb to grace the occasion. " We have seen Cæsar, Cæsar himself! Among you who hear me are men who have had the honour to approach him, to meet his flashing eye, to receive orders from his mouth, and to fly to execute them amid the smoke of battle ! " [25]

How Talleyrand's old heart must have leapt at those words. No wonder Madame la Duchesse records : " Monsieur de T. en était (enthousiasmé) à l'émotion." [26] Indeed, she adds, Thiers seemed to be talking to Talleyrand. Here was the moment of triumph of the young pupil, and he had not forgotten his debt to the man to whom he owed so much. But there was still a balance due the old prince. Would Thiers pay that ? or was this day of success to be the day of freedom for the new *académicien ?*

Throughout the discourse there was a distinctly personal note that was offensive to many. Thiers, they thought, was taking this occasion to pay off old debts and to make his own position clear to France. Certainly it was true that there were matters that needed explication. At least that was the opinion of the more liberally minded of his audience. Would the little statesman attempt to explain his own political evolution? That expectation of his enemies he did not fulfil in its entirety. There is, however, a curious passage in the address that refers to the *History of the French Revolution*, and that gives his own interpretation of that work as he saw it on that glorious December day of the year 1834.

> " When I was allowed to present myself as a candidate, I did so (at once). I devoted ten years of my life to writing the history of our great Revolution. I wrote it without hate, without passion, (and) with a great love for the grandeur of my country. When that Revolution had triumphed in its best, its most just and honourable aspects, I laid at your feet the portrayal of its long vicissitudes that I had tried to draw. I thank you for having received it, and for showing by that act that the friends of order and of humanity in France could acknowledge it. I thank you especially for having selected, from the midst of contention and of parties, a disciple of letters who has been temporarily separated from their service."

The latter phrase is said to have caused a smile of amusement among his detractors. And so, they said, it is farewell to his revolutionary heroes, to Danton and the Republicans, and long live the Golden Mean! To them, the speech of Reception was a second betrayal, an occasion to break definitively with his former associates, but those who knew Thiers intimately did not feel that it was any more than an effort to make his actual position clear at the very moment that it needed clarifying.

When he spoke these words, Thiers and the Government had just passed through another crisis during which he had been recalled to his former post at the Interior, where such a man as the one who had handled so successfully the Duchesse de Berry episode was sorely needed. The situation that confronted him had made him appreciate even more the virtues of a strong Conservative policy. Once the Legitimist intrigue had been averted, the problem of the Extreme Left became acute.

The year 1833 had witnessed a revival of the clubs. Aided by Trélat, Cavaignac, and Laboissière, the *Society of the Rights of Man* had renewed its propaganda. The *Tribune* assisted in spreading the doctrines of this organization, and the example set by the Paris chapter and its newspapers was followed by the provincial sections.[27] In spite of the assertions of Government papers to the contrary, matters were quite unsettled in France, a fact that did not escape the attention of at least one foreign observer.[28] Young Italy and Mazzini were at work in the country; a *Congrega Centrale* was established at Paris, and the Italian patriot was in active correspondence with Carrel of the *National* and with the *Tribune*.[29] From liberal centres in Italy and in Geneva, French Radicals were receiving encouragement. It was a time of new theories and new systems. Saint Simonism was rampant; Considérant was at Tours, and others of its agents were located in many of the industrial centres of France. Those who had not been affected by the over-idealistic principles of Saint-Simon had come under the influence of labour organizations known as *Mutualistes*, whose activities were signalled from Grenoble, Dijon, Strassburg, and Metz. The *Mutualistes* are said to have boasted of a following of five thousand. The year 1834, therefore, bade fair to be a troublesome year, and because of this, the lieutenant of Périer was returned to the Department of the Interior on March 25, just before the crisis was reached.

By the Radical leaders in the Chamber, Puyraveau, d'Argenson, and Garnier-Pagès, the reinstatement of Thiers was interpreted as a declaration of war on the part of the Ministry. His attitude to their former activities was well known; in his speeches he had not refrained from expressing a marked disapproval of their methods. Nor was he afraid to meet them. As he himself had said in 1832, even the victor of the Pyramids had faced revolts in his own country.[30] And, as Napoleon's future biographer, he may have found comfort in this thought; undoubtedly, it enabled him to bear the epithets of traitor and aristocrat with which the Left greeted him. His past experience had taught him much, and while he did not believe in a régime of privilege, he held to the doctrine of an equal opportunity for all men. But he went no farther; he was not so foolish as to think that all men were inherently equal in ability and in intelligence. He did not trust the masses, and so he repulsed their demands for universal suffrage; he was wiser than many in his own day and in ours, in that he believed that obligatory education constituted a danger. Thoroughly aware of what harm a little knowledge can bring, he refused to listen to their demands in this respect. As he himself put it, obligatory and general education was like building a fire under a great pot that was empty.[31] It was then, as a convinced and sincere Conservative and not as an Opportunist, that Thiers assumed the difficult task of stifling the Revolution that had again appeared in France. In April, 1834, his own strength and courage were severely tested.

In that year there occurred the famous revolt of Lyons. Its origin was not political, but the movement soon assumed a distinctly political character. It was the old story of the industrial transformation; the higher bourgeoisie had profited by the economic progress made since 1831, but the labouring classes, although steadily increasing in numbers, had gained nothing. The city of Lyons was the largest industrial centre in France, and it was natural that the labour situation should first become acute in that region. There had already been a serious riot anent the question of the tariffs, and for a time the workers had been masters of the town. This revolt had been quelled by reinforcements sent from Paris. Since the last trouble, however, the Republicans had been at work among the labourers and had turned the discontent of the Lyonnais into political channels, with the result that when, on April 9, 1834, the Government opened proceedings against several leaders who had been instigating a general strike, their fellows seized the opportunity to start a second revolt. Under their direction, the workmen gained possession of the garrison and forced the Government troops to evacuate the city. The example of Lyons was followed by the Radicals at Viènne, Perpignan, St. Étienne, Clermont, and Marseilles. By April 13, the situation was alarming, for the movement had spread to Paris and the Faubourgs Saint-Antoine and Saint Jacques became affected.

On April 11, the condition in the capital had led the Chambers to pass a Bill forbidding the formation of all associations except for commercial purposes without the authorization of the Government. But by April 13 law alone was not sufficient; force was necessary, and force was decided upon. At about eleven in the evening of that day, Thiers, after a conference with Guisquet, the Prefect of Police, hastened to the Hôtel de Ville, where Bugeaud had been placed in command. A visit to the latter always indicated trouble, and, as usual, Thiers was fired by the strong language of the old General. In this event Thiers was wise to follow his counsels. Together they set about to organize, with the aid of troops, a barricade that should shut off the disaffected Faubourgs from the rest of Paris. It was an undertaking fraught with peril. At the time, Thiers was wearing the costume of a minister, and this made him an easy target for the rioters who fired upon him. They missed their mark, but struck his secretary, who fell at the side of the excited young minister.[32] It was not until the following day that quiet was restored in Paris, and during the crisis, Thiers directed the operations himself, Bugeaud having been sent to Lyons, where his policy of the sword and no quarter was soon successful.[33]

His courage and quick action won Thiers the warm

support of Conservatives in both Chambers, and on April 15, at his request, they resolved themselves into a court of justice for the trial of the offenders. Once again the bourgeoisie had triumphed, and the Republicans, like the Legitimists in 1832, were crushed and silenced for some time to come. In part, the swift victory that the Government established over the rioters of April may be attributed to Thiers and Bugeaud, who understood each other so well; but there was another reason for the success of the Government, and it is to be found in the increased material prosperity of France at that time. Humann, Baron Louis, Périer, d'Argout, and Thiers had not laboured in vain, and when, on the first of May, just fifteen days after the labour crisis, the King inaugurated an Exhibition of Industry at Paris, the country seemed in the eyes of many to be on the high-road to peace and prosperity.

With the Republicans and the Legitimists silenced for a time, one might expect that the path of the July Monarchy would be a peaceful one. This, however, was not to be the case. Heretofore, Louis Philippe had enjoyed the support of a comfortable majority in the Chamber, and he and his *Résistance* ministers had been strengthened by a steadily favourable return at each election. But just at the moment when his Cabinet was about to vanquish completely its enemies of the two Extremes, serious divisions appeared in the Lower House.

Ever since 1832, there had been rumours of the formation of a new party. Vague mention had been made of a mysterious Third Party, but it was not until 1834 that its existence was recognized. The leader of this group, in so far as it had a leader, was Dupin, who was piqued by what he regarded as the Monarchy's failure to appreciate him and who early established an ascendancy over such Liberals as Sauzet, Passy, and converted Bonapartists. Of the latter, Étienne, the former benefactor of Thiers, was one, and his paper, the *Constitutionnel*, became the organ of the Third Party.

MINISTER OF THE INTERIOR

As to doctrine, this insurgent group can hardly be said to have had any; one writer had remarked that the Third Party was rather a state of mind.³⁴ Upon the death of Périer they had tried to gain power. Failing in this, they had broken from the *Résistance*, but they had not gone over to the *Mouvement*, of which Laffitte and Dupont de l'Eure were the leaders. On the contrary, they regretted the riots and intrigues of the Opposition; but they also condoned the programme of repression that had been inaugurated by Périer and was being continued by Thiers. They proposed a *via media*, not so much from conviction as from personal dissatisfaction. Like Dupin their leader, they were behaving like spoiled children.³⁵ But they sought to cloak their feelings by protestations of unselfishness and promptings that they declared came from their own consciences.³⁶ Virtue was the ideal that they claimed to follow, but their actions did not bear out this touching assertion of disinterestedness. They knew perfectly well that the King wanted to be the master, and that when he saw the existing Ministry getting out of hand, then their opportunity would come. At first they seemed to have relied somewhat upon the personal ambitions of Thiers and to have expected in the event of another ministerial crisis that he would turn to them in an effort to keep himself in power. They scoffed at his protests that he wished to retire to the quiet of scholarly pursuits, and they smiled at his reference to himself before the Academy as one *temporarily separated from the service of letters*. Probably Étienne knew his former pupil too well to take this remark very seriously. For the moment, their plan seems to have been to embarrass the Cabinet and to accomplish the conquest of Thiers and of the Ministerial power. It was easy to make a beginning, for the two ablest members of the Government were the most unpopular, Broglie, Minister of Foreign Affairs, and Thiers, who after 1834 stood in need of supporters.

Broglie bore the consequences of a policy for which

THIERS AND THE FRENCH MONARCHY

he was not entirely responsible. France could not intervene in European affairs, and because Broglie did not force her to do so, he was regarded as spineless. Left and Right attacked him for refusing to aid the Greeks when Mehemet-ali, Pasha of Egypt, turned against their oppressor, the Sultan. The fact that Mehemet had deserted the Ottoman ruler because of his own personal desires to carve out a kingdom for himself, and not from any sincere interest in the Greeks themselves, appears to have escaped the notice of the Opposition. Without considering the condition of France or the real purpose of the Pasha, the Opposition harped on the consequences of French abstention that had allowed Russia to entrench herself again on the Black Sea by coming to the side of the Sultan in his quarrel with Mehemet. Here was fodder for the guns of Dupin, and when Broglie allowed England to take the lead in the Iberian Peninsula and appeared to relinquish his support of the Spanish and Portuguese Liberal sovereigns, the attack on the foreign policy of the Cabinet was inaugurated. What had become of French prestige in European affairs? This was the slogan of the Third Party.

It was one thing to trap Broglie but quite another to corner the agile Thiers. At this time he literally lived, moved, and had his being in the recriminations that were being levelled at him. One might add that he also seemed to flourish as the green bay tree. Charges political and personal flew about Paris. Society disapproved of his entourage, especially since his marriage to a wealthy bourgeoisie whose father became *Receveur-Général* at Lille. The Vicomte de Launay ridiculed in the *Lettres Parisiennes* his intimates, and politicians questioned his handling of public funds.[37] To the former he was impervious, but the latter accusation worried him in spite of the assurances of his friends and his King.[38] To answer these charges he submitted to Louis Philippe a detailed report, to which that monarch replied by sending him a personal letter that asserted the royal confidence in

MINISTER OF THE INTERIOR

him and commended his loyalty.[39] But the accounting that Thiers rendered contained a list of expenditures from the *fonds secrets*. This prevented publication, with the result that he continued to be an object of suspicion to many in the political world for some time to come. However, he weathered the storm, and it was Broglie, not Thiers, who was the first victim of Dupin's new Party. When, in 1834, that Minister of Foreign Affairs negotiated a treaty with the United States providing for the payment of damages to that country for losses attendant upon the wars of Napoleon I, the Opposition joined with the Third Party to accomplish his retirement.[40] This first effect of the formation of a Third Party occurred just after the return of Thiers to the Interior when he was concerned with the labour troubles at Lyons.

Once again the King took the helm and prevented his new opponents from profiting by Broglie's absence to inaugurate action in favour of the Liberals in Spain. His answer to their protests that England had a monopoly in Spain would have been to urge an alliance with Austria, but he dared not utter such a wish, for Austria was too unpopular in France. Consequently, he avoided this pitfall by concealing the promptings of his heart. Before long, however, another matter forced him to call a new Ministry and give it a head. Louis Philippe seemed doomed never to be his own minister; at this time it was a matter of colonial policy that made him retire from the important position that he had assumed.

The July Monarchy had inherited the conquest of Algiers from Charles X, but, due to the difficulties that Louis Philippe had encountered in France during the year 1830, the beginning made in Algiers by the old Monarchy had not been followed up by the new. In fact, the development that had taken place in North Africa since the July Days had been due to individual initiative and enterprise. It was not until 1833 that

THIERS AND THE FRENCH MONARCHY

political France evinced very much interest in the matter, when the Peers adopted a statement setting forth the necessity of continuing the conquest. This, however, was not the sentiment among the Deputies, among whom the Third Party was advocating the use of French armies to aid the Liberal movement in Europe. In fact, few of the Deputies were inclined to favour any very pretentious policy in Algiers. Only those men who represented the vested interests were concerned, and even they were opposed to the recent methods that the Government had instituted. They called for the abolition of a military enterprise in that region and the substitution of a policy of real colonial development along more peaceable lines. Sympathetic with the latter view were two members of the Cabinet, Guizot and Thiers, both of whom soon found themselves at odds with the President of the Council, Soult, who was a soldier and who favoured the maintenance of a military régime in that colony. This division in the Cabinet, together with the machinations of the Third Party over the extravagant character of Soult's budget, led to a dissolution of the Ministry.[41]

In bringing about this latest crisis Thiers had played an important part. While he had not sold out to Dupin's cohorts, he had sought to save himself by publicly announcing that he was not in sympathy with Soult's plan for Algiers, and he merited the comment of the Duchesse de Dino: " Il n'y a jamais eu un dissolvant pareil à Thiers." [42]

When Soult retired, the King thought of Talleyrand, but Thiers told Louis that Madame de Dino did not wish it.[43] Determined not to lose his point about the maintenance of a military administration in the African colony, the King had to seek in many quarters before he found a man willing to observe his wishes. Finally, the choice fell on another man of war, Marshal Gerard.

Gerard was popular and should have been successful, but the very reason for his popularity became the cause

MINISTER OF THE INTERIOR

for an early break with the King. He was known as a Liberal, and when, in 1834, he announced that he favoured a Bill granting an amnesty to the Republicans, Thiers and Guizot, who saw in this a danger to the previous policy of *Résistance*, compelled the King to oppose him. In November, therefore, the Monarchy was faced with the necessity of constituting a new Council.

The return of Broglie was urged by Guizot, while Thiers, who had thus far sided with his future rival, now broke from him and selected Count Molé as his candidate for the Presidency. The tendency of Broglie to abstain from intervention in Spain and to allow himself to be tricked by Palmerston was too much for the little statesman. In reality, his own fingers were eager to grasp the power, but he dared not let it be known.[44] And it is unlikely that the King would have relished such a domineering Minister of Foreign Affairs.[45]

Between the two rivals and their candidates stood Louis Philippe. It was a difficult problem. He offered a portfolio to Thiers several times, but the latter persistently refused to enter a new Council without his former colleagues. Finally, in desperation, the King determined to try to do without Guizot and Thiers.[46] He made an abrupt move towards the Third Party, and for three days, his personal appointees exercised their functions, but, being unable to command a majority, they retired and the anxious King was forced to return to the *Résistance*. Again Thiers was summoned, and Louis Philippe asked him to join with Mortier, Guizot, de Rigny, Humann, and Duchâtel. After considerable hesitation he consented to do so, but he resumed his functions with a heart full of bitterness and with no great liking for his task, for he disapproved entirely of the royal policy in regard to Algiers and in regard to Spain. Subsequent events will show that this disapproval was sincere and was not simply an excuse for him to hack his way to power.

For a brief time the country was safe again in the hands

of the bourgeoisie, but the peace was not of long duration, for the Chamber, urged on by the Third Party, was resolved to discredit Mortier's combination, and the King soon discovered that, due to the attitude of Thiers, his Council was intractable. When Thiers behaved like a petulant prima donna, poor Louis Philippe tried to bring him to reason and to his will by flirting again with the Third Party. Between their King and their colleague, Mortier's companions had a wretched time of it, and when, in March, 1835, they were faced with the loss of their majority in the Chamber, they were happy to retire.

The experience of the past few months had taught the King one lesson; that it was unwise and dangerous to trust any others than the *Résistance* School. This recent venture among the more liberal had almost resulted in the acquittal of the Republican conspirators of 1835, and the King had no desire to give the Radicals any encouragement. Accordingly, on March 12, 1835, he returned to the pupils of Périer; Broglie succeeded Mortier with the distinct understanding that all of the policies of the *Résistance* should be resumed. But this did not satisfy Thiers, who mistrusted the Duke's foreign policy and became increasingly alarmed in regard to the isolation of France in Europe. Disgruntled and unhappy, he returned to his post at the Interior, but he came back at odds with Guizot and Broglie. It was only to serve the King and to assure himself of the final condemnation of the Republican rioters of 1834 that he resumed his task.

By these transactions during the crisis Thiers had not gained an enviable reputation. His break with Guizot and his hopping from one Ministry to another had detracted from the confidence with which many had regarded him. To many, his actions seemed inconsistent and selfish. His associates were of all sorts and kinds, of all colours and shades of political opinion. Even his old protector, Talleyrand, remarked after an evening spent at the Place Saint Georges: " Nous venons de

MINISTER OF THE INTERIOR

faire un dîner du Directoire." [47] Many of his friends were sycophants and were not his equals in intelligence and in ability. He was called " un petit roi des commerçants." But although at odds with many of his associates, he was still strong in the affections of the royal family. He had established a firm friendship with the young Princes, and if Louis Philippe did not trust him, he realized at least his value and his danger. For the sake of the family of the King, Thiers remained in the Cabinet of March 12. He still trusted the House of Orléans and regarded it as the symbol of his beloved " representative monarchy," but in Broglie, the newly appointed President, he had not the slightest confidence.

At the outset, however, the latter pursued a course satisfactory to Thiers and true to his promises. The Republicans were prosecuted with vigour, and on May 5 one hundred and twenty of their number were indicted before the Chamber of Peers. Great was the anger of the Radicals and the Third Party, but their protest availed nothing. The Ministry was serious in its relentless pursuit of disorder. As a matter of fact, there was indeed good reason for its determined attitude. In the spring of 1835 Radicalism was desperate. It appeared to be at the last gasp, but was none the less dangerous. As the year wore on the task of the Minister of the Interior became more absorbing, for he was determined to extinguish the flame of Revolution once and for all time. He would culminate the policy of Périer. The more absorbed he became, the more anxious and ill he appeared. He spent hours at his desk, and had more than the usual number of secret conferences.[48] Once, when in pursuit of a Duchess, he had delighted in his task, but now he was serious and harassed. Gradually it became known that the concern of the minister was not the prospect of another demonstration, but of an organized attempt to be made on the life of the King.

In commemoration of the July Revolution, a review of the National Guard had been planned for July 28.

THIERS AND THE FRENCH MONARCHY

When the morning of the event dawned, Thiers, very worn and agitated, interviewed the sons of the King. Joinville, the youngest, gives a very graphic account of their conversation. "'My dear Princes,' Thiers said, looking at us over his glasses, 'it is almost certain that an attempt will be made on the life of your father the King to-day. We have information from several quarters. It is (said to be) a question of an infernal machine near the *Ambigu*. It is all very vague, but it appears to have some basis. I have visited this morning all the houses in the neighbourhood. Nothing! Shall we tell the King? Shall we cancel the review?'" The Princes, Joinville relates, were convinced that their father would not consent to the latter plan. To this Thiers replied: "Watch over your father."[49] The brothers then mounted their horses to join their royal parent.

It all happened as Thiers had predicted. Fieschi's machine exploded, but all of the bombs did not explode; the King escaped unhurt.[50] Hardly a second later, Thiers appeared beside the Princes, his trousers covered with blood. He said: "Ce pauvre maréchal!" "Qui ça?" Joinville asked. "Mortier, il est tombé sur moi avec un cri 'Ah, mon Dieu!'"

The attempt on the life of the King filled France with horror, and the Conservative Ministry of Broglie found itself strengthened in the Chamber. Now it was Périer with a vengeance; all opposition must be crushed. It was even believed for a time that the Duchesse de Berry was implicated in the plot.[51] Sentiment ran high against the Republicans. Aided by the general confusion, Broglie, supported ardently by Thiers, who appeared to have lost his head, put through the September Laws.[52] This was the most reactionary legislation that France had known since the eve of the July Revolution. Special courts were allowed to try summarily all those who attacked the security of the State. The accused might be judged even when absent. A majority vote in a jury was sufficient for a condemnation. The liberty of the

MINISTER OF THE INTERIOR

Press was curbed by heavy fines for seditious articles. In putting through this legislation Thiers was merciless; he was at fever heat and ill.[53] He decried Royer-Collard; he openly condemned Republicans; he inveighed against Legitimists and all other sectaries of the Opposition. Finally, worn and exhausted, he demanded a leave.[54]

His political novitiate had had a tragic climax, but it was almost over. He had broken with Doctrine; he disliked Broglie. He was beginning to disagree with Guizot, whose principles were fundamentally the same as his, but who disagreed as to the time when they should be put into operation. In serving his King he had lost friends and made enemies; and, in 1835, he wanted his reward. As a matter of fact, it was not far off. In October, old Talleyrand wrote him from London: "This much I have obtained for you; many people think it too much. To me it seems all that you need. Profit by it quickly." [55]

Talleyrand had talked in England, and at last that uncertain ally of France would no longer oppose his policies and the gratification of his desires. Soon Thiers would replace Broglie as President of the Council.

NOTES TO CHAPTER IX

[1] Duchesse de Dino: *Mémoires*, I. 19, May 25, 1832.
[2] Dupin: *Mémoires*, II. 439.
[3] *Ibid.*, II. 441.
[4] London *Times*, September 4, 1832.
[5] *Ibid.*, September 15, 1832.
[6] Notes of Madame Dosne (dictated by Thiers), September–October, 1832. Bibliothèque Thiers, T. MSS. in 4°, 32.
[7] *Ibid.*
[8] *Ibid.*
[9] *Ibid.*
[10] d'Ideville: *Bugeaud*, I. 202-3. Thiers, Paris, October 12, 1832, to Bugeaud.
[11] Thiers: *Discours*, I. 468.

THIERS AND THE FRENCH MONARCHY

[12] Thiers: *Discours*, I. 476–77, November 29, 1832.
[13] *Ibid.*
[14] Thiers: Circular, Ministry of Interior, November 3, 1832. Archives Nationales, BB 18, 1210, 8074.
[15] Report, Secretary, Cours Royale, Paris, Department of Seine, October 9, 1832. Archives Nationales, BB 18, 1211, 8157.
[16] Thiers, Ministry of Interior to Keeper of Seals, November 14, 1832. Thiers, Ministry of Interior, to Minister of Public Works, November 19, 1832, Archives Nationales, BB 18, 1327, 7153. See also correspondance for May, 1832, same reference.
[17] Notes of Madame Dosne, October, 1832. Bibliothèque Thiers, T. MSS. in 4°, 32.
[18] Receipt from Deutz, November 17, 1832. Bibliothèque Nationale, 20,601, Part II., 18–27. Notes of Madame Dosne, November, 1832. Bibliothèque Thiers, T. MSS. in 4°, 32. *Le Correspondant*, September 25, 1922, p. 996. Thiers' account to Lacombe, May 22, 1861. Laya: *Thiers*, pp. 55–60.
[19] Report, Thiers, Ministry of Interior, to Minister of Justice, November 23, 1832. Archives Nationales, BB 18, 1211, 8161.
[20] Pamphlet (anonymous). Archives Nationales, BB 18, 1214, 8795. Pamphlet, *La Mode*, February 22, 1833. Archives Nationales, BB 18, 1334. d'Ideville: *Bugeaud*, I. 206–7. Thiers, Paris, to Commandant at Blaye, November 18, 1832. I. 210: Thiers, Paris, to Commissaire Special at Blaye, December 12, 1832. Dupin: *Mémoires*, IV. 16 sqq. Thiers: *Discours*, I. 509, January 5, 1833.
[21] Meniere: *Captivité de Madame la Duchesse*, I. 187. d'Ideville: *Bugeaud*, I. 204–5. Thiers, Paris, to Bugeaud, November 13, 1832. Thiers, Ministry of Interior, to Minister of Justice, December 26, 1832. Archives Nationales, BB 18, 1332, 8313.
[22] Thiers: *Discours*, I. 544–54, February 15, 1833.
[23] Zervort: *Thiers*, pp. 109–10.
[24] Duchesse de Dino: *Mémoires*, I. 302. Paris, December 14, 1834.
[25] Thiers: *Discours*, I. December 13, 1834.
[26] Duchesse de Dino: *Mémoires*, I. 302. Paris, December 14, 1834.
[27] Report, July, 1833. Archives Nationales, BB 18, 1339, 9747. Report, October, 1833. Archives Nationales, BB 18, 1339, 9699.
[28] London *Times*, August 11, 1833.
[29] d'Argout, Ministry of Interior, to Keeper of Seals, July 11, 1833. d'Argout, Ministry of Interior, Note, July 16, 1833. Archives Nationales, BB 18, 1337, 9101.
[30] Thiers: *Discours*, I. 492.
[31] Simon: *Thiers*, p. 180.
[32] Guisquel: *Mémoires*, III. 395.
[33] Report, Bureau du Lieutenant-Général du 2e Division Militaire, n.d. Bibliothèque Nationale, 20,602, 76.
[34] Thureau-Dangin: *Histoire de la Monarchie de Juillet*, II. 264.

MINISTER OF THE INTERIOR

[35] Madame Dosne's Notes, September–October 1832. Bibliothèque Thiers, T. MSS. in 4° 32.
[36] Dupin : *Mémoires*, II. 41.
[37] Viscomte de Launay : *Lettres Parisiennes*, I. 130.
[38] Duchesse de Dino : *Mémoires*, I. 235, Paris, August 29, 1834.
[39] Louis Philippe to Thiers, November 12, 1834. Bibliothèque Nationale, 20,601, Part IV., No. 4.
[40] Madame Dosne's Notes. Affaire d'Amerique, 1834–35. Bibliothèque Thiers, T. MSS. in 4° 32.
[41] *Ibid.* Crise ministerielle de Cabinet du 11 Octobre. Bibliothèque Thiers : same reference.
[42] Duchesse de Dino : *Mémoires*, I. 272. Valençay, November 4, 1834.
[43] *Ibid.*, I. 237. Paris, August 30, 1834.
[44] *Ibid.*, I. 237. Paris, August 30, 1834. Thiers, Paris, November 20, 1834, to Duchesse de Dino. Bibliothèque Nationale, 20,601, Part II., No. 77.
[45] Thiers, Paris, November 20, 1834 to Harrisse. Bibliothèque Nationale, 20,601, Part II., No. 78.
[46] Duchesse de Dino : *Mémoires*, I. 318–9. Rochecotte, March 12, 1835.
[47] *Ibid.*, I. 320. Rochecotte, March 12, 1835.
[48] *Ibid.*, I. 327. Berne, August 19, 1835.
[49] Joinville : *Vieux Souvenirs*, p. 71.
[50] Pégout : *Documents Épisodiques*, p. 21.
[51] Report, Ministry of the Interior, 1835. Archives Nationales, BB 18, 1240, 3911.
[52] Duchesse de Dino : *Mémoires*, I. 355. Paris, September 7, 1835.
[53] *Ibid.*, I. 356. Paris, September 7, 1835.
[54] *Ibid.*, I. 360. Paris, September 8, 1835. *Ibid.*, Paris, September 9, 1835.
[55] Talleyrand, London, October 22, 1835, to Thiers. Bibliothèque Nationale, 20,601, Part II., No. 80.

CHAPTER X

THIERS AND HIS RELATIONS

" I AM sprung from the bourgeoisie . . . I am a child of the Revolution." These words, Thiers when an old man, pronounced to his friendly and indefatigable interviewer, Nassau William Senior. No doubt when he uttered them he did so with a sense of pride, but at the same time he must have experienced a feeling of discomfort and of *malaise*. For he who became the intimate of Leopold of Belgium, of Talleyrand, and, later, even of that most incorrigible of aristocrats, Metternich, was very likely more of a child of the Revolution than he wished to be. Thiers and his relations are a perfect mirror of the topsy-turvy condition of French society in the second decade of the nineteenth century.

A bourgeois he was, and a bourgeois whose people had suffered and not profited by the Revolution. He was born into material poverty. But this was not all; Thiers as well was born into a moral poverty. He lacked the guidance of a father's hand. In fact, he may be said to have had all the disadvantages of sonship and none of its real advantages. Certainly, he knew none of its joys. Pierre Louis Marie Thiers, his father, evidently felt that he had satisfied all the requirements of paternity when he married the mother of his son exactly one month after the latter's birth. Life to Pierre Louis seems to have been a game, and his *wanderlust* appears to have increased when he found himself faced with the responsibilities that might devolve upon him now that Louis Adolphe had been added to a long list of natural and semi-recognized progeny. But this one son at least he had the grace to endow with legitimacy before he went his way to wander over Southern Europe in quest of adventure and further amorous diversions. It is not difficult to imagine what he did with himself. Very probably his life was much as it had been. Before the Revolution he had sought adventure in the Antilles. Upon its outbreak he fished in the troubled waters, seeking here and there a fortune, finding it and as quickly losing it again. He was in Spain, Italy, and Switzerland, in company with another like himself, a man from Toulouse who called himself the " Chevalier de Foinville." Pierre Louis and his " chevalier " dealt in food stuffs for the armies and spent the rest of their time in travel, associating with all the low castes of the Levant, and, once in a while, venturing north, where usually there was an affair with a dancer or a singer.[1] This was probably the sort of life led by Thiers' father after his son's birth. We hear little of him until Adolphe Thiers reaches a point in French public life where he might be of use to his extravagant parent.

It was in 1825 that the mysterious father seems to have crossed his son's path for the first time. The son, already prominent among the Liberal bourgeoisie and enjoying a certain fame as a journalist and writer, is made the object of a request for money. The episode is soon closed, but it is amusing. The young Thiers, already known as a gallant and a *bon vivant* himself, assumes towards his parent the tone of a grandfather and writes him a long letter reproving him for his excesses. How deplorable it is that a son of twenty-eight must expostulate with a father of sixty! How dares that father write of privations that he had endured when he deserted his unhappy wife! But the son will be merciful. Let us hear him speak himself: " When Monsieur Thiers (elder) has proven that he can do nothing for himself, that it is to maintain his life that he begs, and not to give himself over to further excesses, then his true sons will agree as to what they should do. Monsieur Adolphe Thiers will do so not from sentiment, for he recognizes only the love and duty that he bears to his mother." [2]

THIERS AND THE FRENCH MONARCHY

All this in the third person singular. Cold formality, and cold formality seems to have kept the profligate father silent for seven years. But after the July Revolution the opportunity was too tempting. Thiers junior had become a minister and a bright and promising future appeared to be in store for him. Like a pack of hounds Pierre Louis and other relatives pursued their prey. At Marseilles a paper entitled *Le Peuple Souverain* opened a subscription for the avowed purpose of rescuing the relatives of Monsieur Thiers from " famine and prostitution," while the father rushed to Paris to make new demands in person.[3] The visit to the capital was successful. Pierre Louis sold his silence and his consent to his son's marriage in return for 40,000 francs and the assurance of a pension of 600 francs for his natural daughter, Madame Brunet. For two years trouble between father and son continued, until finally, in desperation, the future President of the Council placed his father under the personal surveillance of Monsieur Floret, subprefect of Carpentras, with the distinct understanding that Pierre Louis must remain discreet and out of the public eye.[4] To this the father reluctantly agreed. He observed his promise until one morning when he read in the paper the announcement of his own death, inserted, it is unkindly rumoured, by someone at the instigation of his son. Only in 1843 was this burden removed, when Pierre Louis at last expired at the home of his daughter, Madame Brunet, whom Adolphe Thiers had presented with a tobacco shop.

Mention has been made of Pierre Louis Thiers' other natural children. Of these, only four seem to have concerned Adolphe Thiers. Madame Brunet seems to have been satisfied with her modest *boutique*, and Madame Rippert appears to have been quieted with a pension.[5] There remained two brothers, Louis and Germain. Both of these were the cause of considerable embarrassment to the statesman during the period of his political education. Of the two, Louis was the more

MADAME THIERS, THE MOTHER.

THIERS AND HIS RELATIONS

serious problem. Placed by Thiers in the supply service at Colmar, Louis was charged with theft. He was finally rescued and sent to Chandernoga by Thiers.[6] Germain, on the other hand, though not so bad a character, was still an encumbrance. Previous to 1832 he was concerned in a tobacco industry at Montargis. In 1832, when the Périer Ministry came in and Thiers became Minister of the Interior, Germain came to Paris and scandalized his brother by opening a shop in Paris that bore the sign : " Thiers, peintre en bâtiment, et frère de Monsieur le Ministre de l'Intérieur."[7] In 1835 Germain was sent to Calcutta. Nothing is known of the later relations of Thiers with his father's children.

When we turn to Madame Thiers, the mother, the problem is more difficult, for here, as in the other instances, there is an air of mystery. With Madame Thiers, however, there is also a hint of tragedy. Marie Madeleine Amic was of respectable bourgeois stock, but poor. Disappointed in her hopes for a happy married existence, deserted by the man whom she loved, she and her parents devoted themselves to the education of Louis Adolphe, her son. In spite of their poverty they procured for him the best schooling available, and in his early days, Thiers seems to have been devoted to his mother and to his maternal grandmother.[8] " Mes deux mères," he calls them in a letter to Rouchon, his friend at Aix.[9] Madame Thiers lived at Aix with her son while he was studying at the law school. Then came the separation, a separation that he seems to have regretted very genuinely.[10] After the death of his grandmother in 1824, Madame Thiers visited him in Paris, but the visit seems to have been spoiled by her son's apparent reluctance to have her with him and by the police inspections and questionings to which the Government of the restored Bourbons subjected her.[11] For the Bourbons had already begun to suspect Thiers. In 1833, the relations between mother and son appear to have become strained. At this time Thiers wrote a curious letter to Rouchon *à propos* of his

THIERS AND THE FRENCH MONARCHY

coming marriage. He besought Rouchon to ask his mother for the formal consent demanded by the law. He seemed to foresee difficulties.[12] Evidently Madame Thiers consented, for the marriage was celebrated, but we find the surprising statement that when, in 1836, Madame Thiers, the mother, came to Paris to live, she received a small pension from her son, and stayed in a house near the magnificent hotel of the Place St. Georges, the doors of which were always closed to her.[13] Finally, she moved to the Batignolles, and her son, so engrossed in affairs and so completely taken up by his new relations, saw her but little. In fact, one must suspect that Thiers substituted another interest for that which he should have had in his own family. After 1833 Thiers' real family became his wife's parents, Monsieur and Madame Dosne.

Among the group of wealthy bourgeois prominent in Paris in the early 'twenties was Alexis Dosne. Monsieur Dosne was a banker and industrial of Lille, who married in 1811 a Parisian named Euridice Matheron. Mademoiselle Matheron was the daughter of a cloth merchant.[14] She had spent her childhood in the Faubourg Montmartre, but she dreamed of the Faubourg St. Germain, and there her marriage to Alexis Dosne, a very prosaic man of affairs, finally placed her. Madame Dosne soon set up a salon. Her *habitués* were mostly those who belonged to the " Juste Milieu " or to Orleanism. She was brilliant, ambitious, and domineering, and it was not long before her hotel at the Place St. Georges became a rendezvous for the rising generation of journalists, writers, and men of affairs. About the year 1822, young Thiers, who, since his arrival at Paris had renounced his revolutionary enthusiasms and had donned the colours of Talleyrand's school, was presented at the house.[15] It was Madame Dosne who took possession of Thiers, and when she saw in him certain possibilities, she was not mistaken. She was an able manager. Balzac calls her " une espèce de Père Joseph en jupons." [16] Thiers and the able hostess of the

MADAME ADOLPHE THIERS.

Place St. Georges were of the sort to be congenial. He with his past of the rue des Petits Pères, Marseilles, and she with her memories of the Faubourg Montmartre and a clothing shop; both with the Faubourg St. Germain before their eyes! It was not long before the two became firm friends. In fact, a great intimacy developed between them, an intimacy to which certain scandalous sheets made uncomplimentary allusions. Between the years 1822 and 1833 the friendship grew apace, and in 1833, Madame Dosne prepared to add to her rôle of a confidante that of a mother-in-law. The young Thiers was betrothed to Élise Dosne.

Thiers as a lover is disappointing. There is not much romance; there is too much reason. He writes to his friend, Rouchon, asking him to break the news to his mother, who was then residing at Aix:

"I write you at a very important time of my life. I am to marry a young person, lovely, amiable, *raised for me with infinite care.* She is not even too young for a man of thirty-five years who has a healthy body but a mind worn and fatigued by the immense cares of government. I shall not be able to give her all that a young girl expects, but she is devoted to me; she has been brought up by her mother who has taught her that it is her duty to live for me alone. She is attached to me; she has placed all her pride in me. I think that I can make her happy. What is not less precious to me is her family, in whom I find repose, confidence, consolation, and all that I need more than anyone and more than ever. Her fortune will be very great some day, especially for me, who have nothing, and I am proud (of that), for I have made nothing (out of my position)." [17]

The writer then gives instructions as to how to obtain his mother's consent. There must be haste, haste! For what? For a happy married life or for ease?

THIERS AND THE FRENCH MONARCHY

Certain writers have unkindly remarked at this point that Thiers was in debt. Certainly, he had many demands on his purse;[18] there was his mother's maintenance, and the keep of his father and sisters. At any rate, the marriage was celebrated on November 5, 1833, with great pomp. The marriage contract was signed by five pages of distinguished witnesses, including such men as the President of the Council, the Duc de Dalmatie, Guizot, Broglie, d'Argout, Gérard, Sébastiani and the faithful Mignet.[19] Not content with this showing, a mandamus was issued allowing the record to be transported to the Tuileries for the signatures of Louis Philippe and of Marie Amélie, the Queen. The Faubourg Montmartre had arrived at the portals of the Faubourg St. Germain. A brilliant future was assured Madame Dosne. And the repose of Thiers, too, was secure, for the Deputy of Aix brought his wife in furniture and effects 10,000 francs, and a house valued at 60,000 francs but mortgaged for one hundred thousand, plus a house at Aix, while Élise Dosne brought a trousseau and furniture at 10,000 francs and 300,000 francs dowry.[20] In this way, Thiers found a new interior in which he was happy in spite of the scorn of his more aristocratic friends. Talleyrand's niece, the Duchesse de Dino, complained : " Since his marriage, Thiers lives in a sort of solidarity with the smallest people in the world, ill-famed, pretentious, parvenu par le coup et non pas arrivés ! " [21]

In his wife Thiers found all the satisfaction that he sought. She was lovely, and her beauty was frequently commented upon. In later days, she graced his salon well and performed ably and gently her social duties. But she seems to have been overwhelmed by her indefatigable and restless husband. Unlike her mother, she never sought to interfere in politics.[22] In fact, politics do not seem to have interested her. This may be accounted for either by her extreme youth, for at her marriage she was only sixteen, or by a rather indifferent

MADAME DOSNE.

health that frequently caused Thiers and Madame Dosne much alarm.

In marrying Mademoiselle Dosne, however, Thiers allied himself to an important influence in his life that should not be overlooked, though care should be taken not to exaggerate it. To a certain extent, Madame Dosne was worthy of the title that Balzac gave her. She watched over Thiers, she protected him, she advised him.[23] Her letters are replete with warnings and suggestions. She read the French and English newspapers assiduously, and she seems to have been possessed of a remarkable political sagacity.[24] She gloried in the fame of her son-in-law and daughter. " I read yesterday an article describing your reception in Berlin. The article gave me great pleasure, first because it gave me news of you, and then because I saw that people appreciate you both. My *amour-propre* was flattered to read that ' Monsieur Thiers and his lovely wife arrived at twelve o'clock in Berlin.' " [25]

The Salon Thiers–Dosne became a great political centre and served its purpose in shaping the fortunes of the young statesman who stood, in 1835, on the threshold of his first political experiment. During the years following immediately upon his marriage the hotel of the Place St. Georges, " a coquette démeure," as the gossipy Viscomte de Launay calls it,[26] was the particular centre of the " Juste Milieu," and for another type of nobility so characteristic of Parisian society of the year 1834, that Heine calls the " chevaliers de l'industrie." [27] Here the cohorts of true Orléanism met. Madame de Flahaut and Madame de Lieven were the only serious rivals to the Place St. Georges, but there was a distinct difference between their salons and that of the Thiers–Dosne *ménage*. Madame de Flahaut was merely a rallying-point ; the charming Princess de Lieven ruled, yet did not govern, but Thiers and, at times, Madame Dosne through him exercised a very real power.[28] In fact, contrary to the usual custom, the hotel at the Place St. Georges appears to have been the scene of almost continuous receptions. Thiers and his family received nearly every evening, and never went out except when they had a *loge* at the Théâtre des Italiens. At these receptions Madame Dosne usually presided. Even so hostile a critic as the Duchesse de Dino comments upon her striking appearance and her masterly air.[29] With her received Madame Thiers and Mademoiselle Félicie Dosne. In these days, we are told, Madame Thiers appeared to carry the weight of the whole company on her shoulders, but this was probably due to the fact that she was still so young.[30] Her father, the prosaic Monsieur Dosne, made his appearance very infrequently. During the early part of the evening even the young statesman himself was not visible, at least not visible to the uninquiring eye. But if one sought him, he might be found asleep in a fauteuil in an obscure part of the salon. For Thiers had formed in his youth a habit that he continued to observe in his later years, the practice of a siesta after dinner. There in a retired corner the distinguished young hero rested while his guests passed softly by his peaceful form and respected his slumber. In a little while, suddenly awakening, he would jump up, stretch himself, and approach the different groups, salute the ladies and, as if the rest had rejuvenated his thoughts, become the most brilliant conversationalist in the world.[31] He was always courteous and obsequious, and always accompanied the ladies to their carriages when they made their departures. He was known as a charming and agreeable host, and he never distinguished between the really worthy and the ignominious and plutocratic bourgeois who thronged his salon.

Thiers in his salon was always a success, but Thiers in the rôle of a young man of society, outside the Place St. Georges, was not always so successful. He had continued to acquaint himself with the usual accomplishments and diversions of the young Parisian of his day. He did not relinquish his avowed or assumed fondness for horses after his first entry into public life. It pleased

THIERS' RESIDENCE ON THE PLACE SAINT GEORGES.

him to demonstrate his equestrian ability at the promenades to which the King invited him. These usually took place at Compiègne, at St. Cloud, or at Fontainebleau. He disliked to ride in the open landaus with the older and more important guests. He preferred to ride on his horse beside them in the company of the young Princes. Mounted on a horse called " Vendôme " that he, with his meridional accent, persisted in calling " Vanndomme," he loved to ride ahead of the cortège at triple galop, vie with the Prince de Joinville, his particular favourite, and display his prowess. If, by chance, he passed a peasant girl who smiled up at the little minister as he galloped by, he would rein in abruptly, drop a handful of money into her hand, and off he would go at a terrific pace, jumping fallen trees and ditches and playing the gallant with all his heart and soul.[32]

Sometimes, however, he was not so successful in his performance. The younger son of King Louis, Joinville, who seems to have had a real affection for the King's Minister, recalls an incident that occurred on the occasion of the restoration of Napoleon's statue to the column on the Place Vendôme. To this ceremony Thiers had looked forward with eagerness. It was the time of his great interest in Napoleon, and the incident is not unrelated to the final recognition of Napoleon when his ashes were returned to France in 1842. Thiers was at this time an unconscious advance agent of Bonapartism.

" The troops, the National Guard were under arms ; the military band with drums and a magnificent drum-major at their head were massed at the foot of the column. We approached, *en grand cortège*, via the rue de Castiglione. In front of us was the column surmounted by the statue that was covered with a veil destined to fall at a given signal. Upon our arrival at the scene, Monsieur Thiers, *en grand uniforme*, wearing a hat with waving plumes and mounted on

THIERS AND THE FRENCH MONARCHY

'Vanndomme,' spurred his horse, left the cortège *au grand galop* and passed before my father, crying shrilly in his high falsetto, ' I bear the King's orders.' He accompanied these words with a wave of the hat that unkind tongues declared he had copied from the pose of General Rapp in Gérard's painting, ' The Battle of Austerlitz,' at the Louvre. At this gesture of his, the drums began to beat, the band struck up, and the veil fell from the statue. But Monsieur Thiers was no longer master of ' Vanndomme,' who, wild with enthusiasm, charged head down, upset the drums and the magnificent drum-major, and (tore off) with the little minister hanging on to him like a monkey at the Hippodrome." [33]

Sometimes, Thiers' love for the theatrical nearly occasioned his downfall. This was true in society, but never in the Tribune, whose principal occupant he so soon became.

NOTES TO CHAPTER X

[1] F. Benoit: *Correspondant*, 1922, p. 789 sqq. Zervort: *Thiers*, p. 9. Halevy: *Courrier de M. Thiers*, p. 11. Senior: *Conversation*, Second Empire, I. 137-38.

[2] Thiers, Paris, 1825, n.d., to P. L. M. Thiers: *Correspondant*, 1922, p. 809.

[3] F. Benoit: *Correspondant*, 1922, p. 790.

[4] Thiers, Paris, to his father, July 14, 1832. *Correspondant*, 1922, pp. 815-16.

[5] F. Benoit: Thiers, *Correspondant*, 1922, pp. 815-16.

[6] F. Benoit: *Correspondant*, 1922, p. 790.

[7] *Ibid.*, p. 789.

[8] Thiers, Paris, to M. Amic, June 4, 1824. Bibliothèque Nationale, 20,601, No. 5.

[9] Thiers, Paris, to Rouchon, April 22, 1824. *Correspondant*, 1922, pp. 803-4.

[10] Thiers, Aix, to F. Benoit, September 17, 1821. *Correspondant*, 1922, p. 792.

[11] F. Benoit: Thiers, *Correspondant*, 1922, p. 791. Ministry of the Interior, F. 6934, 9994, Archives Nationales: Ministry of Justice, Affairs Criminelles, BB 18, 1138, Archives Nationales. Correspondence

THIERS AND HIS RELATIONS

between Minister of Interior, Prefect of Bouches-du-Rhône, and Ministry of Justice.

[12] Thiers, Paris, to Rouchon, October 18, 1833, *Correspondant*, 1922, p. 817.
[13] F. Benoit: Thiers, *Correspondant*, 1922, p. 791.
[14] Documents *re* Dosne Family, Nos. 3, 6, 7, 8, 15, Bibliothèque Thiers.
[15] F. Benoit: Thiers, *Correspondant*, 1922, p. 787.
[16] Balzac: *Revue Parisienne*, July 25, and August 25, 1840.
[17] Thiers, Paris, to Rouchon, October 18, 1833. *Correspondant*, 1922, p. 818.
[18] A. Martin, Paris, to S. Benoit, March 16, 1833. *Correspondant*, 1922, pp. 816–17.
[19] Marriage contract—Thiers' documents. Bibliothèque Thiers.
[20] *Ibid.*
[21] Duchesse de Dino, *Mémoires*, I. 120.
[22] F. Dosne: *Correspondances*, pp. 8–22. Madame Dosne to Thiers, Lille, August 12, 1841. Thiers to Madame Dosne, Berlin, August 17, 1841.
[23] *Ibid.*: Madame Dosne, Lille, to Thiers, August 15, 1841.
[24] *Ibid.*, p. 56: Madame Dosne to Thiers, September 4, 1841.
[25] *Ibid.*, p, 30: Madame Dosne to Thiers, Coblentz, August 21, 1841.
[26] *Viscomte de Launay*, I. 42: December 15, 1836.
[27] H. Heine: *Lutèce*, p. 130.
[28] *Viscomte de Launay*, I. 42: December 15, 1836.
[29] Duchesse de Dino: *Mémoires*, I. 34. December 11, 1833.
[30] *Ibid.*
[31] Beaumont–Vassy: *Société sous Louis Philippe*, p. 307.
[32] Prince de Joinville: *Vieux Souvenirs*, p. 68.
[33] *Ibid.*, pp. 69–70.

CHAPTER XI

PRESIDENT OF THE COUNCIL (FEBRUARY–AUGUST, 1836)

UNPLEASANT as the experience must have been for Louis Philippe, the attempt of Fieschi was not an unmitigated evil for that monarch. Human nature is surprising in its actions and positively astonishing in its reactions. Attempt to assassinate your sovereign, and the assassins themselves are likely to weep with delight when he emerges from the mêlée covered with dust and blood but safe and sound. The most hardened *incroyant* will raise his hat and shed tears as the funeral cortège of a cardinal passes by him. In 1836 human nature had not changed, and that is why the King of France was more popular after the attempt on his life than before it. France was shocked, and Louis Philippe and his ministers were clever enough to administer strong potions while their patient was still in a state of collapse. Alarmed by the thought of what might have happened, the Chamber was docile for once and, at the instance of the Council, reactionary legislation was proposed and passed in record time and almost with unanimity. The Fieschi affair and the September laws that followed it seemed to establish definitely the régime of the parliamentary bourgeoisie. They had beheld their cherished system endangered and they forsook their liberal pose to rally to the Monarchy. But that is not to say that there was complete understanding between Louis Philippe and his bourgeoisie; they might approve of his laws but they did not approve of his diplomacy.

In the very beginning of the Orléans rule, French diplomacy had not been brilliant and forceful, but it

PRESIDENT OF THE COUNCIL

had been wise and timely. Discretion had been necessary in 1830. But that, said the bourgeois, was five years and four months ago. Now, in December, 1835, matters were different. France was pacified, prosperity had come, and many Frenchmen were no longer satisfied with a policy of discretion that does not always contribute to national dignity. In short, with the revival of the country came a great wave of sentiment for the re-establishment of French predominance in European affairs. The nation was restless. From time to time, a King must don his armour and ride his horse, and if the King does not do so, he may find another astride his charger. Already in 1835, some people were harking back to the " glorious days " of the Empire, the Napoleonic legend was becoming popular; to counteract it, the Crowned Pear (as the King was called) must become a Little Corporal.

Louis Philippe was not ignorant of this sentiment, and he realized the necessity for satisfying the desires that it represented. So, too, did his counsellors and friends. But King and counsellors differed in their opinions as to what methods should be adopted, and the counsellors, alas ! were not even in agreement among themselves on this matter. The King himself wished to avoid all possibility of foreign complications. He feared old Metternich, and betrayed a ridiculously pathetic desire to win the good graces of that Prince by serving Austrian interests in the Near East, and by refusing to be pushed too far in the reluctant support that he had given to Palmerston's familiar policy of encouraging Revolutions wherever they appeared. In this latter practice he was not unwise. Wherever an uprising occurred, there was England, patroness of Liberty, and there, too, British influence and commercial interests were established. Louis Philippe had not come to the throne of France to aid in the building of the British Empire ! Consequently, he sought to avoid a more intimate alliance with England, and to palliate the ambitious demands of his people by

THIERS AND THE FRENCH MONARCHY

constructing museums of war and celebrating magnificently the fêtes of victories won during the Revolution and the Empire. He offered them Mars on a leash and not Mars triumphant. This, however, was not the procedure desired by the public, by the Third Party, by de Broglie, and by Thiers. These men were realists and they looked to a more material satisfaction.

Since 1832 there had been no more loyal Conservative than Thiers. He had proved his adherence to the Périer system by his relentless pursuit of Legitimists and clubs; he had been responsible in great part for the severe September laws. So far, he had pleased the King, but there was another side to the story. While he agreed with Louis Philippe in that he was not a warm partisan of an exclusive English alliance, he favoured the adoption of a more forceful foreign policy. Now that France was strong and prosperous, he relinquished his support of discretion so dear to the heart of the King, and advised a more active participation in European affairs. In this he was at one with de Broglie, who was still at the head of the Government, but the Duke desired to participate at the side of England and to strengthen the English alliance by concerting with Palmerston in regard to the Near Eastern question. To Thiers, such a plan was sheer blindness. France must not follow too closely the lead of England; she must begin to look out for herself. Opportunity for France was not in the Eastern Mediterranean. The door to a glorious future was nearer at hand; it might be found on the Pyrenees. It was there that France had a legitimate reason for action.

As early as 1834, France and England had guaranteed the constitutional régime of the young Queens of Spain and Portugal. They had promised to come to their aid if their position became precarious. In 1836 the time to fulfil that promise seemed to have come when the young Queen's security was endangered by the attempts of two reactionary pretendants, Don Carlos and Don Miguel, to overthrow them. As usual, England was exploiting the

PRESIDENT OF THE COUNCIL

situation in the Iberian peninsula to her own advantage, while Thiers desired that France should take this opportunity to act independently if need be, and to give real support to the Liberal Governments.

But neither the policy of his President of the Council nor the plan of his Minister of the Interior was entirely satisfactory to the King. Of the two men, the personality of Thiers made more appeal to the monarch. At least, the former would not oppose his cherished desire for a reconciliation with Austria. Of de Broglie's sincerity Louis was uncertain and found him *difficile* and *maladroit*.[1] Displeased with the chief of his Cabinet, he watched him carefully and he could not have been very unhappy when a slight incident made it possible for him to release the Duke. A rash Minister of Finance, without consulting his chief, proposed to reduce the interest on Government bonds. This measure was met with a howl of rage from the Chamber and a violent opposition on the part of a number of his fellow-colleagues, among whom was Thiers. The latter had sniffed the winds, he had foreseen a storm, and he was not going to founder with Broglie's ship. Ever resourceful, he seized a life-boat and boarded a ship of his own. The debate that ensued gave him an excellent opportunity to break with the Cabinet and so become free to participate in any new Council that might be formed. His attack was tremendous and he made a dramatic departure from the policies of the unwise Monsieur Humann. Madame de Dino witnessed the spectacle from a box in the Chamber of Deputies, and after its conclusion she wrote to Thiers, who, in spite of his success, had appeared ill during the proceedings. His reply was as follows: " I am worn out. . . . In those few minutes I expended several years of my life. I have never encountered such stubbornness; it requires an iron will to surmount such an *entraînement* as that which you witnessed (in the Chamber) to-day. I am sorry that you heard me. Those figures must have bored you and they must have given you a sorry idea of

THIERS AND THE FRENCH MONARCHY

the Tribune. You should hear us and judge us only when we are at our best and not when we are settling our accounts. I am uncertain of the result, and, save for the King, I rather hope for the retirement of the Ministry."[2] His wishes were granted when, on February 4, the Chamber forced Broglie to retire.

After Broglie's retirement the ministers who had served under him tried to form from themselves another Cabinet. This effort was made at the request of the King, who wanted to prevent the possibility of the Third Party entering into power.[3] But their efforts came to naught, for differences of opinion that had not been very apparent during their term of office now became evident, and when the attempt was abandoned, each man was free to act according to his own ideas. Few of them, however, had any immediate prospects of returning to the portfolio that they had relinquished. In fact, only two of them appeared to have any support in the Chamber; of these, Thiers was one, while the other was Duchâtel.[4] Guizot, oddly enough, did not count, and from the date of the fall of the Broglie Cabinet, the rivalry of Thiers and Guizot began. While the former, without any real party affiliations, had to find his support from the Left, the latter became again the leader of the Conservatives, but in February 1836 he was not powerful enough to oppose his rival's nomination as President of the new Council.[5] This is not to say, however, that Thiers was the first selection of the King. There were two long weeks of suspense before he grasped the prize that he had so long desired.

The first efforts of the King were with Humann and Molé. Failing with these, he turned in despair to the Third Party, but Dupin, its leader, could not find men who were willing to serve with him. The choice was narrowing down, but Louis Philippe did not wish to take Thiers unless he could separate him from his former colleague of the *Doctrine*.[6] Périer and Broglie had been too independent to suit the taste of that monarch and

THIERS, PRESIDENT OF THE COUNCIL.

PRESIDENT OF THE COUNCIL

he was too clever a statesman himself to think that Thiers would be an obedient servant.

Meanwhile, that object of the royal meditations was not worried. He had broken with his former colleagues, and his plan was now to remain aloof and to let events take their course. On February 7, there was a great dinner at the Place Saint Georges, and the *convives* remarked upon the contrast between Thiers, the retiring Minister of the Interior, and de Broglie, the defeated President of the Council. " Thiers never once touched the ground. He flapped his wings, like one who is sure to enter his cage whenever he wishes. He talked of travels; he wished to go to Vienna, Berlin, Rome, and Naples. He proposed to leave in April. . . . Monsieur de Broglie had a gloomy and defeated air." At any rate, if there was not a Ministry to enter, there was a History to return to! The project for the *History of the Consulate and the Empire* had not yet been undertaken. But Thiers himself, and others wiser than he, knew that it would probably not be History. On February 13, Royer-Collard remarked to him: " You are not possible to-day; but in a week you will be necessary, indispensable, absolute."[7] The prophecy was true. On February 21, Thiers entered upon his duties as President of the Council.

To all of his men in his first Cabinet the President was superior. Many of them were older, but few had had as much experience, and none was so able before the Chamber. With him were associated Montalivet as Minister of the Interior, Sauzet as Keeper of the Seals, Passy as Minister of Commerce and Public Works, Pelet de la Lozère Minister of War, Admiral Duperré Minister of the Navy, and d'Argout Minister of Finances. At the outset this combination offended few and satisfied less. The *Doctrinaires* were represented by Maison, Duperré, and d'Argout, who had served in the preceding Cabinet, while Pelet de la Lozère, Passy, and Sauzet had been taken from the Third Party. The new President himself acknowledged frankly that his Council was a golden mean between the *Doctrine* and the cohorts of Dupin.[8] This fact itself was the *raison d'être* for the Ministry and accounted for the nomination of Thiers as its head. It was not the effort of Talleyrand that had brought his protégé to power;[9] it was the logical sequence of events. The King was weary of the *Doctrinaires* and could not take the Third Party, whose leader was headstrong and rash and whose views alarmed him. Thiers, on the other hand, was a man of no permanent party affiliations, who possessed friends in both and who had the largest following in the Chamber. And so he was called at last to the post to which his own actions and the King's promises had long since predestined him, but he was not acclaimed as a hero who would save the country.

The Ministry was not received with any great show of cordiality by the Chamber, but at this, some of his friends rejoiced, for they feared that an early success might cause the young President to lose his head.[10] The *Constitutionnel* was lukewarm and spoke the mind of the *Doctrine* when it declared : " If the personnel of the new Cabinet were not satisfactory, the country would accept it because of that which is not to be found in it."[11] The Royal Family, and especially Madame Adelaide, were confident of its success. France accepted it with tolerance and settled back to watch developments.[12] At least, the Ministry would not be dull, and its head would provide food for gossip and for entertainment. But this was not the attitude of Europe; there the sentiments in regard to the new Government were more definite. Prussia alone was completely satisfied.[13] England hesitated, suspecting that Thiers might not be so docile and easy a Minister of Foreign Affairs as de Broglie had been. There had been too much patriotism and too little interest in the welfare of England in the remarks of the Deputy. His most hostile critic, however, was Metternich, about whom all the Courts of Central and Southern Europe rotated. To Metternich, Thiers was a *révolutionnaire pratiqué*.[14] In brief, whether favourably disposed or not, no one in Europe was indifferent to his policy, and all awaited with interest the first official declaration.

The new President did not keep his audience long in suspense. On the day after the formation of his Council, he appeared before the Chamber and made clear his attitude to France and to the Monarchy : " As for myself, I must tell you at once, so that all of you may hear, for I do not wish anyone to be in doubt about it : I remain what I have been, the faithful and devoted friend of the July Revolution. *But I am convinced of this great truth, that to save a Revolution, you must prevent it from going too far.*" [15]

In other words, the new Government would not abandon the Périer principles in which its chief had been schooled. The preceding Cabinet had not fallen over any question of Legitimists, or Clubs, or Republicanism, and this President purposed to continue the same policy. He would repress all elements of disunion and " oppose an invincible barrier against disorder." [16]

There was nothing in this to alarm Royalty, *Doctrine*, or Metternich. To them his remarks were perfectly orthodox, but they may have caused some perturbation among certain sections of the Left, the adherence of which had enabled Thiers to reach the pinnacle of government.

It was evident, at any rate, that his internal policy would not be revolutionary, but in the matter of foreign affairs, the appointment of Thiers implied a change of conduct on the part of France. Commenting upon this aspect of the Cabinet of February 21, 1836, Metternich said :—

> " Monsieur Thiers is in every way a very dangerous man. He has certain faults that are common to all Frenchmen and he lacks experience in the handling of political affairs. The cart that he drives is always veering from Right to Left, and he will have many severe lessons before he learns how to keep it

steady. Thiers should have remained Minister of the Interior. He understands how to manipulate parties in France. But it is different in the case of Europe. Strange combination of revolutionary doctrines, journalistic audacities, and governmental despotism, this Minister represents his country to his country; but he is not fit to represent it before Europe." [17]

As a matter of fact, nothing could be more unjust. Throughout his administration, Thiers was experimenting, but he had an aim that was quite evident as well as a policy that was logical and consistent. Inspired with the ideal of grandeur for his country, he could not tolerate the equivocations that French diplomacy had pursued since the death of Périer. In fact, whenever he had been free to express himself on this matter, he had spoken his mind. His belief that France was being degraded in the eyes of Europe had been one of the principal reasons for his hesitation to enter the preceding ministerial combination; and in time, it became the explanation for his desiring the downfall of de Broglie's Council. In his disapproval of the line of diplomacy adopted by de Broglie both the King and the country participated, but the reasons of Louis Philippe were somewhat different from those of Thiers. Both of them feared that an intimate alliance with England might drag France into war on the side of the British against Russia over the question of control in the Near East. King and President were convinced that France should not be bound to take part in a war from which the country would gain slight advantage, and which might precipitate a general European conflagration.[18] For Louis Philippe, there was the reason of peace; for Thiers there was the reason of French independence. To the latter, the exclusive alliance of France with the democratic nations had brought the country nothing but a quasi-servitude. To a certain degree, the French Monarchy was becoming the handmaiden of England. This condition could not continue, he said. While he respected and desired the maintenance of English friendship, he did not wish that union to prevent alliances with other nations.[19] What he proposed to do was to remain on good terms with the British Government, and to establish an *entente* with Austria that would counterbalance the disadvantages of the too exclusive understandings that had been established with the leading democratic nation of the North. The latter bound France, but two alliances would allow her a greater latitude of action. This was his policy; what now was the purpose?

These new conditions would enable his country to take a more active part in the affairs of those nations bordering on her frontiers, the conditions of which were naturally of great importance to her and to her dynasty. The maintenance of Belgian independence was a prop to the July Monarchy. Again, Louis Philippe was weakened if the Reactionaries in Spain succeeded in driving out the Constitutionalist Queens, while Swiss democracy was an aid and a menace that must be watched and controlled. Heretofore, Thiers reasoned, France could only have acted in concert with England and not without her. But the diplomatic revolution that he envisaged would enable the country to act freely and unhindered, according to her own traditions and needs. In brief, the President of the Council sought to substitute action for discretion, independence for dependence. He purposed to continue the Périer system as far as internal policy was concerned, but he hoped to do this under cover of a more brilliant action abroad that would quiet the Ultra Liberals and satisfy their growing desire for French predominance. One is tempted to draw a parallel between this system of the Cabinet of February, 1836, and that of Napoleon. It is not impossible that here, again, is found the influence of Thiers' historical studies upon his policies as President of the Council.

These were the aims of the new Government, and at

first, the Chamber that he had been called to tame and to rule was in no condition to offer an effective resistance to his policies. There was not the slightest evidence of unanimity among the Deputies. Politically the condition was pitiable. " Paris is going to become more and more difficult to live in, for, aside from the great dynastic divisions that separate society, we shall now have all the factions to which disappointed personal ambitions have given rise; faction Molé, faction Broglie, faction Guizot, faction Dupin, and finally, faction Thiers. And everyone of them as hostile and bitter as are the Legitimists and Orléanists. . . . They hate each other and tear each other apart." [20]

Such a situation was not of the sort to appal the new President of the Council; in fact, it is not unreasonable to suspect that he enjoyed it. He beheld the Chamber entrapped in a sort of impassable *status quo*. " The Chamber cannot recede and does not wish to advance any farther. It is obliged to stop right on my ground." [21] But, confident as he was, he was also perfectly aware of the fact that this was only a temporary condition, and that, sooner or later, faction Guizot and faction Broglie, even possibly faction Molé, would join together against him and form again a *Doctrinaire* Opposition from the moderate elements of the Right. With the Left, too, there was the danger that, in time, Barrot would gain followers from the more timid Liberals and from the Third Party. Guizot of the Right Centre and Barrot of the Left Centre were the two irreconcilables; between them was the logical place for a line of cleavage to develop in the Chamber. The agile Thiers must avoid falling into this political no man's land. He was the prize, swinging on the tree; beneath stood Guizot and Barrot trying to capture him as he swung above them. That became the game that was played in the Deputies from February, 1836, until their adjournment on July 12. But Thiers, smiling and serene, clung to his branch and did not let go. Never for a day did he really commit himself to one party

PRESIDENT OF THE COUNCIL

or the other, and the blows that they struck to dislodge him were ineffective.

It was a game, and one in which the little minister seemed to take great delight. Whenever he needed it, he found a majority, and oddly enough, these rather dangerous tactics were facilitated after March, 1836, when a few of his bolder adversaries among the *Doctrine* launched an attack in which they attempted to cast doubt upon his honesty. During that month, the Cabinet presented a Bill calling for funds to complete the work of restoring the monuments and buildings of Paris. This undertaking had been inaugurated by Thiers when he was Minister of the Interior in 1833. At that time he had been granted a credit of ten millions. But the work required four millions more, and this sum his Finance Minister now requested. After an unsuccessful attempt to frighten the President by a threat delivered through an investigating committee, Jaubert laid the charge before the Chamber. The affair caused the object of the attack some annoyance, but he cleared himself by an admirable defence before the Deputies and emerged from the contest stronger than ever, for some of the *Doctrine* broke from the party to show their disapproval of this method of trying to intimidate the Cabinet into submission to their wishes.[22] From this time on, he had a greater number of floating votes from which to draw a majority when he needed it.[23]

Meanwhile, the Left had not been inactive. It attacked his plan to defer again the reduction of the interest on Government bonds.[24] But his greatest trial of strength occurred when Guizot tried to force him to admit that his initial speech as President of the Council was a declaration of policy in line with that of the *Doctrine*.[25] Desperate in their inability to compromise him, both Oppositions redoubled their attacks. Blinded by personal prejudices and jealousies, they opposed his plans for tariff revisions and for railroad extensions.[26] In all these minor engagements Thiers found a majority and won his point. Import duties were changed according

THIERS AND THE FRENCH MONARCHY

to the principles that he had outlined in his address when, as Minister of Commerce, he had welcomed the National Council of Industrials and Tradesmen. Tariffs were regulated according to the needs of each industry or trade. Suburban lines were built to tie the outlying communities with trade centres. Throughout this early period of his administration he held his own, but in June, two debates gave him the opportunity of establishing a more positive control over the Chamber.

The first occasion was brought about by the Extreme Right, a small group that possessed only twenty-five representatives among the Deputies. In June, d'Argout, Minister of Finances, presented his budget for the ensuing year. Berryer, the Legitimist leader, used this discussion to attack the Monarchy as well as the Ministry. It was a fortunate incident for Thiers. Berryer attempted to demonstrate that the Orléans Monarchy that had talked so much of economy was, in reality, a more expensive affair than the Restoration. In spite of the suppression of the Royal Guard and the Swiss Guards and the abolition of salaries to the Peers, the total budget of the July Monarchy from 1830 to 1835 far surpassed that of the preceding dynasty. This attack brought Liberals of all colours to the side of Thiers; even Laffitte came to his aid. On June 15, the President himself closed the defence by a brilliant speech in which he silenced the Extreme Right by demonstrating that a fair part of the expenses of the existing Monarchy had been incurred by paying off the debts of the one that had preceded it.[27] Poor Berryer had his accusation thrown back at him, and the Right was quite discomfited. During the debate Thiers again took occasion to pay a glowing tribute to Laffitte, whose protection during the early years of his career had meant so much to him. This *politesse* was a tactful stroke and, of course, delighted the Left. At the conclusion of the discourse the President was accorded an ovation. So great was his success that even Guizot was forced to admit that his rival had gained considerable

PRESIDENT OF THE COUNCIL

ground.[28] The discussion of the budget had given him one victory, but soon it would bring him another occasion to gain more supporters.

Attached to d'Argout's financial measure was an estimate of the sums needed to continue the expansion of French power in Algiers. France was still inexperienced in the science of colonization; there had been a great difference of opinion in the country concerning what should be done with the North African province. In the eighteen-thirties, men were not yet the adept colonial builders that they became later, and there were few at that time who regarded the matter as a man of modern France would view it to-day. Of these few the President of the Council was one, and the recommendations that he proposed show that he was far in advance of his countrymen. He did not agree with the Industrials and Conservatives, who desired the conquest of only the coast. Instead, he advocated an extensive conquest of Algiers and of the surrounding country. He pointed out that the future power of France lay in establishing her sphere of influence in North Africa. Russia and England were already in possession of the Eastern Mediterranean. Because of their presence, France could never expand beyond Alexandria, if indeed that far. The Western Mediterranean was still an open field for colonizing; to make such a policy permanent in character, French influence must penetrate beyond the Algerian coast into the hinterland. He went even farther in his declarations, and reminded his hearers that a more active participation in Spanish affairs was a necessary preliminary to the permanent hold on Algiers.[29] His logic and his common-sense won him the day, and it is due in no small part to Thiers that France was enabled to begin a plan of colonization that was of untold advantage to her later in the century. But the immediate advantage was the fact that he had again discovered a majority.[30]

These successes of the month of June increased the general impression that Thiers had come to stay, a belief in which he himself appears to have had some confidence. He had passed through all his measures and had avoided political alliances of too entangling a character. To a certain degree, he had broken up the Opposition of the *Doctrine*; it had not remained a unit during the discussions of the spring of 1836. But he had also been supported by considerable numbers of the Left, and while he did not regard himself as bound in any degree to the latter, some of his opponents declared that they suspected him of having pronounced sympathies with the more Liberal sections of the Chamber. These older men of the *Doctrine* still thirsted for an opportunity to embarrass him, and the fact that Guizot had ably supported him in the debate about Algiers had not turned them from their purpose. The time had come when he must pay for that hazardous practice of finding his support on occasion and for not being one of them. A man without a party is always disliked, but a man who boasts that he has no party is positively suspected. The blow came when Thiers least expected it.

On June 25, only a few days after the victories in the Chambers, Louis Alibaud made his almost successful attempt to take the life of Louis Philippe. At first, Thiers did not realize how much this affair might effect him and the parliamentary control that he had just established. On June 27, he wrote to Montebello, the French envoy at Bern: " If I were thinking only of my personal condition, I should be perfectly satisfied with the political situation." [31] But within a few days, he had begun with Montebello a correspondence the nature of which must have caused him much alarm. The investigation that he, as President, instituted soon revealed distressing facts that placed some of his friends of the Left in a very bad light. It was not very long before it was established that the Alibaud attempt was the act of an individual, but that, at the same time, the moral complicity of the Press of the Left was undeniable. Although they were not party to a conspiracy, the

PRESIDENT OF THE COUNCIL

actions and words of certain Deputies of the Left had encouraged such *exaltés* as Alibaud. At the same time it was discovered that many desperate organizations had been re-formed in France during the spring of 1836. Some were asking: " What of Thiers and his avowed adherence to the Périer régime; what of his earlier expressions against the elements of disorder ? " The words, " I will oppose an invincible barrier to anarchy," were thrown back at him, and when Montebello himself disclosed to the unhappy President the existence of correspondence between the refugees in Switzerland and a central revolutionary Committee at Paris, his anxiety became acute.[32] " This perseverance of crime, even after Fieschi, has filled the entire world with an extraordinary anxiety. It alarms especially those of us who are responsible agents and who hardly know what precautions to take, what measures to ask of the Chambers." [33]

To the President, the situation created by the Alibaud affair had a personal significance of no mean import. It embarrassed him because of the relations that he had had with the Left; for from that quarter he had gained much of his support. But his own embarrassment was the delight of the *Doctrine*, for it gave them the opportunity not only to attack the man himself, but as well to discredit a foreign policy that he had pursued and that they believed was undignified and fraught with danger. To Thiers it was a Great Design on which hung the future welfare of France, and so he was willing to make concessions to save it. With a desperate effort he started the ministerial pendulum on a swing back to a definite Conservatism.

All Europe was perfectly aware of the fact that Thiers desired to inaugurate a foreign policy of reconciliation. And yet the very fact that this was common knowledge made difficult his debut in foreign affairs, for while the President wanted a *rapprochement* with the more Conservative Courts of Europe, he was not seeking an exclusive alliance with Austria. Nor did he wish to

THIERS AND THE FRENCH MONARCHY

break completely the bonds already established between England and France.[34] In the Chamber he had to steer between Guizot and Barrot, while in Europe he must sail his ship between the Liberalism of Palmerston and the Ultra-Conservatism of Metternich. Even if he had not wished to adopt such tactics, the European situation would have forced him to do it, for upon his assuming the power, he was confronted with a number of important problems touching foreign policy that had been bequeathed to him by the preceding Ministry. Of these, the most important were the cases of Cracow and of Switzerland.

In 1815, Cracow had been granted independence under the protection of Russia, Prussia, and Austria. But this privilege had been accorded to the city on two specific conditions; it was understood that no army should be introduced into the city, and that its citizens should not harbour political offenders who had escaped the police of the three bordering States. It appeared that the terms of the agreement had not been observed. Inevitably Cracow became a centre of the movement of Polish independence and an asylum for political refugees. Europe soon took cognizance of this state of affairs, and three days after the dissolution of the Broglie Cabinet, the three " protecting Powers " established a governing council that undertook the rule of the city and the expulsion of all the agitators who had gathered within its walls. At this action Cracow protested, and five days before Thiers assumed office, the three Powers had begun an advance towards the city.

This was the problem that confronted the new President of the Ministerial Council on February 22, 1836. France expected that Thiers would sympathize with the offending city; this would have been in accord with the desires of Barrot and his group of the Left. But Monsieur de Sainte-Aulaire, French Ambassador at Vienna and himself a Conservative, warned the President of the temper of Metternich and counselled moderation.[35]

PRESIDENT OF THE COUNCIL

In principle this advice was followed, and the Government restricted itself to a middle policy that appeared fair to the Liberals and that did not offend Conservatives in France and in Europe. Thiers satisfied his natural desire for action by demanding that the town be evacuated by the three Powers as soon as possible, and that the prosecutions of the agitators be reduced to the minimum. At the same time, he arranged for the reception in France of those refugees whose presence could be tolerated no longer in Cracow.[36] This action partially reassured the Left as to the future attitude of the Cabinet to Liberal movements in Europe, and it interfered in no way with the interests of the three Powers most concerned. With Cracow he encountered little difficulty, but Switzerland was a more difficult problem to solve.

Like the former, Switzerland, too, had become a haven of refuge for political offenders. Once within the confines of that Republic, the exiles renewed their activities, and soon that peaceably inclined country became a hotbed of foreign political conspiracy. There grew *Young Europe*, *Young Italy*, *Young Germany*, and even *Young France*. Previously, Périer and, after him, Broglie had adopted towards Switzerland the same attitude that they had assumed towards Piedmont. They had tried to observe the principle of *non-intervention*. This inaction on the part of France had irritated Austria, and after 1832, that irritation had increased until internal affairs in France brought a change. In 1834, Fieschi had made his attempt on the life of the French King, and Louis Philippe came to desire an alteration in the policy of his Government. He had been playing with fire that had nearly burned his fingers; it was unwise to deal gently with it in France, and foolhardy to tolerate its continuance in a neighbouring country where many other Fieschis were thriving. Consequently, the attitude of Paris to Geneva ceased to be friendly, and the King of France was eager to find a minister who would rid him of the anxieties that his neighbour was causing

THIERS AND THE FRENCH MONARCHY

him. When Thiers became President of the Council and Minister of Foreign Affairs, he pleased his master by expressing himself in no uncertain terms to Monsieur de Montebello, the French envoy at Bern : " Switzerland has become a centre of revolutionary agitation, a place whither flock the offenders of all nations. Everywhere else, the Revolution has been laid low by law and order and cannot raise its head." [37]

With this sentiment Montebello agreed,[38] and when he was instructed to extract a promise from the Swiss Government that it would arrest the most dangerous fugitives, he lost no time in seeing that his demand was enforced.[39] But in June, 1836, the instructions that he received were even more severe. Louis Alibaud had attempted to assassinate the King, and the connivance of the Radicals at Geneva was suspected. This time, Montebello was asked to make a formal demand that the *exaltés* should be expelled. France would arrange to transport them across the country to the coast, where they could embark for England.[40] It was even rumoured that Thiers had introduced into Switzerland a spy to pry into the relations of the Swiss Government with the Radicals, but when the President was confronted with this statement by his political enemies, he denied it indignantly, declaring that he had never known " le misérable." [41] These early successes had reassured him, and the little minister now began to talk in a louder and bolder tone. He was definite in his statements in regard to the Near East; France would enforce peace on Greek, on Pasha, and on Sultan : " Inform the Sultan and the Pasha that the first to break the peace will have us to deal with. There, in a word, is our policy as expressed to Constantinople and to Cairo." [42] But in his mind all these questions were subordinate to another of far greater significance.

The greatest interest of the President was not centred in Cracow, Geneva, Athens, Constantinople, or Cairo, but in Vienna, St. Petersburg, and Berlin. His other policies were simply the reflection of his desire to bring about a change in the attitude of these three Courts to France, to accomplish a reconciliation with the aristocrats, and to establish a rehabilitation of French diplomacy. The Teutonic stodginess of the Court of St. James did not appeal to him; he longed for the brilliance of Vienna and the glittering jewels of the Court of Russia. *There* was dignity, and there he wished to see his France again. To this end all other lines of his foreign policy converged at first. He must create a good impression, he must show that he was not too revolutionary, and then he could aspire to an intimate alliance with the aristocratic Conservatives of Europe.

The medium by which this new alliance was to be effected was daring, to say the least of it. Thiers desired to see the grandson of regicide Philippe Égalité married to a Hapsburg! He would seek the hand of an Austrian Archduchess for the heir to the French throne. He would break for ever the " matrimonial blockade " that Europe had set up against France.[43] Such a change would give the monarchy more *éclat* at home and consolidate its position in Europe.[44]

The stage had already been set for this bit of comedy; the object of the Duc d'Orléans' affections had already been selected by his royal mother. Marie Amélie had chosen the Archduchess Maria Theresa, a daughter of the Archduke Charles of Austria. Before the coming of Thiers, the Queen had intimated as much to de Broglie, but that minister had been too much impressed by the difficulties to make headway. The present Emperor, who had just come to the throne, was *difficile* and at times almost imbecile. Consequently, it was Metternich with whom Broglie must negotiate, and Broglie was not eager to enter into conversations with the latter on such a delicate subject. He was aware of Metternich's dislike of the House of Orléans and he knew that Metternich had an ally, the Tsar, who would be even more opposed to such a match. But in February, 1836, all this was changed; Broglie resigned, and the magnitude of the problem did not disturb in the least the buoyant optimism of Thiers. A Paris journalist was not afraid to enter where the polished Broglie had feared to tread! The very fact that he was a parvenu gave him an advantage; inhibitions were unknown to him. He had been careful to show how very conservative he could be, and he imagined that the mildness of his debut had impressed Metternich. As for the Tsar, he would see about that matter when the time came. Nevertheless, he must have scrutinized carefully the reports of Sainte-Aulaire at Vienna and of Bresson at Berlin. For once in his life, Thiers was the most cautious man in Europe.

When inaugurating such a change of policy, the President was careful to proceed gradually and not to shock too suddenly the sensibilities of Metternich and of the Tsar. During the latter part of February it was announced that the Duke and his brother had expressed a desire to make a *grand tour* of Europe. The French emissaries accordingly were advised to ascertain the attitude of the various European Courts to such a plan, for it would never have done to force the Princes upon the hospitalities of Berlin and Vienna. Reports from the former capital were most favourable; Bresson recounted the friendliness of the Prussian King and of Ancillon, his minister.[45] The same was not true of Vienna, for Metternich hesitated to commit himself, and Sainte-Aulaire, the French Ambassador, advised Thiers against a too precipitate action.[46] This news from Austria did not surprise or discomfort the President; for the moment, his greatest concern was the attitude of the Tsar.

Nicholas II had always disliked the House of Orléans, and just at the moment when Thiers was about to attempt a *rapprochement* with Austria, an event occurred that irritated the Autocrat of All the Russias. The Spanish Reactionaries under Don Carlos interfered, and,

PRESIDENT OF THE COUNCIL

in an attempt to discredit the French Cabinet in the eyes of Conservative Europe, published abroad the real purpose of the journey contemplated by the young sons of Louis Philippe. The reason for their action was the fact that they knew Thiers to be in sympathy with the Constitutionalist Queen whose overthrow they were trying to accomplish. This created an embarrassing situation for France. To meet it, the President sent to his agents a letter instructing them what to say. France, writes Thiers, is not begging for a marriage alliance, but the French Government is thinking of marrying off its Princes. He adds: " It is at Vienna that there are Princesses galore; I can enumerate at least three. *My Young Princes* will be seen and will see; there is the truth. You know as much about it as I do. If the trip should have no other results than to show that our Princes are well received at the palaces of Legitimate Princes, and to bring together the reigning families and their subjects, the advantages would be considerable." [47] To the hopes that were expressed in these lines, de Barante, from St. Petersburg, could give only scant encouragement. " The Tsar has not changed in his attitude of reserve and malevolence," he wrote, but at the same time, he acknowledged that in this attitude the Tsar was almost alone. The Court favoured a more friendly feeling towards the July Monarchy.[48]

In spite of unfavourable reports from Russia, Louis Philippe and his minister had already decided that the time had come to put their experiment into operation. In May, the Duc d'Orléans and his brother set out upon their journey.

Their task was not an easy one; where Orléans did not seek a wife he sought to establish friendship for France. But for this double task he was eminently fitted; he had great personal charm and was intelligent, attractive, and gracious. Their first stop was at Berlin, where the princely pair met with an immediate success; they were cordially received and the Court was delighted with them.[49] If there had been any feeling of distrust in Berlin towards the bourgeois King of France, it appears to have been dispelled. " Your King has been pleased to show in a fashion that can be understood by the whole world the union that exists between himself and the Continental Powers," the Prussian King remarked to Bresson. " I responded immediately. This is only the beginning; the future will show us the result. I have performed my part, and it has been as easy as it was agreeable, thanks to your Princes, who, I repeat, have won the hearts of all of us." [50] Even Ancillon, the Prussian Minister, wrote to Thiers a glowing account of the good impression that the brothers had made.[51] At Paris, the King of France, Égalité's son, beamed with delight, and praised his President for the success of his plan.[52]

In Berlin the favour of the Court had been gained, but in Vienna the Princess was yet to be won. The section of Paris that supported the Ministry awaited eagerly the news from Austria, but Thiers' former friends of the Extreme Left were angered at a policy that they interpreted as indicative of a reactionary tendency on the part of the Cabinet. " Monsieur Thiers is now the very humble servant of the *grands seigneurs* of Hungary, Prussia, and Russia, who are graciously pleased to forgive him for being, after all, only a humble plebeian like ourselves." [53] But if the success of Thiers' efforts at Berlin annoyed his more Radical opponents, the almost immediate conquest of the Viennese Court aroused them to a condition of positive rage.

In Austria the Princes comported themselves in such a manner as to delight their royal parent and his minister. Almost from the day of their arrival their popularity was assured. Only in Metternich did they encounter any coldness, and whenever the object of their visit was mentioned even in the vaguest terms, that old statesman would talk of the Imperial Family and its wishes.[54] But Thiers was not deceived by such ruses;

PRESIDENT OF THE COUNCIL

he knew that, with such an Emperor, the wishes of the Imperial Family, to which such frequent references were made, were nothing less than the desires of Prince Metternich and those of his friend, the Tsar. As well, a weakness in the Metternichian armour began to appear; the Archduchess Theresa and her father had given evidence of their approval of the young heir to the French throne. This fact gave the French Government courage, so that it was not long before Sainte-Aulaire was instructed to make an attempt to force Metternich to commit himself on the question of a marriage. Rather unwillingly the Ambassador set out to perform his task. To his surprise the Austrian Chancellor agreed to discuss the matter with the " Imperial Family," and he finally consented to comply with the request of the French Government to write out before Sainte-Aulaire the draft of the reply that he would make " if the Emperor and the Imperial Family were well disposed."

On June 10, Sainte-Aulaire received the letter. " I have submitted to the Emperor the note that your Excellency did me the honour of sending me. His Imperial Majesty desires to leave the Archduke Charles free to consult his own wishes and those of his august daughter. If their decision is favourable, I am to discuss with Your Excellency the political difficulties that the question will present." [55]

With such words Old Régime addressed Revolution; Metternich wrote to Sainte-Aulaire for Thiers. Negotiations were opened immediately, but they were closed almost as abruptly. On July 25, the hopes of Louis Philippe and his President were dashed to the ground when Louis Alibaud made his attempt on the life of the French King. This incident raised again the ghost of Revolution before the eyes of Metternich, and it was a far more serious check to the fortunes of the Thiers Ministry than any attack of the Liberal Press or Deputies' opposition. Thiers must retreat before the revived scorn of Metternich, and Thiers' retreat was never a dignified process—threats and then a desperate attempt to save himself by pursuing with relentless vigour a totally new policy and interest, often even at variance with the earlier plan. Frantic letters by special courier to Sainte-Aulaire; warn Austria of the dangers that she will run if she refuses to stand by the King to whom she has just proffered the hand of friendship![56] But threats availed nothing. To Metternich's mind, an alliance with France had always been undesirable, and Alibaud's attack made it an impossibility, for it betrayed the inherent instability of the Bourgeois Monarchy. He wrote to Apponyi: "The events of the year 1830 separated our two Governments completely, and this separation was not one of theory but of absolute fact."[57] When Thiers heard of this comment of the old Chancellor, he remarked: "There those Austrians are, just as I have always known them! It is with exactly such a spirit as theirs that, for half a century, people who walk backwards spoil everything."[58]

It had been through no fault of the President of the French Council that the marriage policy had failed, and that Metternich had slammed the door again in the face of France, but it might have caused his own overthrow had he not had another policy to which he could now turn the attention of France. If a foothold in European polity could not be gained through marriage alliances with Austria, France could force an entrance by asserting her interests in Spain. Thiers has been credited with saying: "Monsieur Metternich need not worry about me. If I am too much Holy Alliance in regard to Switzerland, I shall make up for the fault as far as Spain is concerned."[59]

This is not to imply, however, that Thiers took up the matter of French intervention in Spain simply to avenge himself. Spain and its desperate situation had long been in his mind, and at the very beginning of his administration, he was more concerned about the

PRESIDENT OF THE COUNCIL

fate of the Spanish Queen than about the Austrian marriages. Nevertheless, it must be admitted that his Spanish policy became more drastic after the failure of the marriage proposal. Or did this change come about because of an alteration in Spanish affairs and a change in the attitude of the King? With the latter he had never been in agreement as far as the affairs of the Iberian Peninsula were concerned. As early as 1835, he had counselled a more active participation in Spanish affairs, and the difference between himself and the King had become evident to many. Again, when Don Carlos actually began an armed attack on the power of the young Queen Christina, Thiers had demanded that General Harrispe, Commander of the Army of the Pyrenees, be instructed to make an effort to capture the Pretender and bring him back into France. This action would have been completely in agreement with the Treaty that England and France had made with Spain and Portugal in 1834. But both Soult and Gérard believed, as did all of the old school army officers of the Empire, that only disaster could come to French armies in Spain. The country that had begun the undoing of Napoleon might easily do the same to Louis Philippe, they thought.[60] To Thiers this was mere superstition, and he chafed under the restraints, but could do nothing, for in 1835, he was only a much disgusted Minister of the Interior. He nursed his Spanish interest in silence, and his friends suspected that once in power, he would revive the question.

Hardly had the Ministry of February, 1836, been formed, when the Comte de Rayneval, French Ambassador at Madrid and an ardent adherent of the Constitutionalist Queen, broached the subject of French intervention to the new Minister of Foreign Affairs.[61] In fact, it is not at all unlikely that Monsieur de Rayneval was indiscreet and had given the Queen's party more hope than Thiers' actions or remarks had justified, for both the Ambassador and the Spanish Government

THIERS AND THE FRENCH MONARCHY

betrayed evident disappointment at the first official attitude of Thiers. The early days of his Ministry were days of extraordinary caution ; he must not alarm the King, of whose pacific intentions he was well aware, and he must not offend Vienna by championing too vigorously the defence of a Liberal cause. Evidently, he had made promises to the King to this effect, for his reply to Rayneval's first communication was to counsel moderation :

> " Madrid is right in considering me a very sincere partisan of the Queen's cause. But to-day, I consider the active intervention that I advised so strongly last year as very dangerous and almost impossible. Times seem to me to have changed, and I have told you in my previous despatches why I thought we should refuse to send a French army across the Pyrenees. *It is, of course, distinctly understood that I do not make that promise of yes or no irrevocable for the future.* But to-day and for some time to come, I do not think the thing proposable. I understand your reasons ; I admit the truth of all that you say ; I am inclined to believe that Spain will work out her own salvation alone ; and I am not of those who disapprove of the judgment that you have made in regard to affairs in the Peninsula. But there is something more powerful than all argument, and that is impossibility. It is an impossible thing to make the Chambers countenance intervention, and without the Chambers to bring the King around to it. Consider that as certain and absolute." [62]

This letter may account for the fact that many critics of Thiers have held that at first, he yielded to the King and then broke his promise, and that then, had he been honest, he should have retired. On this score, his own memorandum in regard to the earlier period of the negotiations, covering the time between February and June, is enlightening :

> " I did everything that I could do for the cause of the Spanish Government; I held it to be a thoroughly French matter. I believed, in fact, that a counter-revolution in Madrid would be a greater catastrophe (for us) than a counter-revolution in Brussels, and for my own part I should have used all possible means to prevent it. I even desired to quit the Cabinet over the question of intervention; if I have not done so, it is because they have allowed me some small assistance for the Government of the Queen, because I may be able to obtain better still, and because the condition of France and the embarrassments of our Cabinet have commanded me to endure the yoke rather than to give rise to another ministerial crisis (by resigning)."[63]

Convinced that the maintenance of a Liberal Government in Spain was a *sine qua non* to the permanence of the Constitutional Monarchy in France, he did not relinquish the purpose of eventual intervention in the Peninsula, but he realized that first he must win the Chambers to his view, and that then the Chambers would win over the King from a policy of inaction to the support of the Liberals.

As time wore on, however, Thiers' policy of waiting until France was converted became very embarrassing. Rayneval's letters became more insistent, and in April, 1836, he even informed the President that the Spanish Government was on the point of forcing from France a formal refusal to participate, by sending a demand for immediate intervention.[64] Upon receipt of this alarming intelligence, Thiers tried to arouse the Chambers, and to avert the contemplated action of the Queen's Cabinet by delivering before the Chamber a speech on the Spanish situation. His discourse was received quite cordially by his audience, and Rayneval reported that the impression made by his utterances before the Chamber had been favourable in the Court of the Constitutionalist Queen.[65] The little President was playing hard for time. The Chamber was learning its lesson very slowly, all too slowly, and Louis Philippe was stubborn. But during the month of May he still hoped; a month later, however, he became desperate.

In June a succession of insurrections in the Peninsula rendered the Spanish problem even more serious. Frantically the minister besought the King to allow an increase in the numbers of the Foreign Legion now gathered on the Pyrenees. In this request he was strongly supported by the King's son and heir, the Duc d'Orléans. The request was finally granted, but not at the instance of Thiers. Failing in his own efforts to persuade the obdurate Louis, he had finally had recourse to the astute Leopold, King of Belgium and son-in-law of the French King. It was the Belgian monarch who undoubtedly saw in Spain a dangerous example of what might have arisen in his own realm, and who obtained the royal sanction for the demand of Thiers.[66]

To obtain even a slight increase in troops that *might* be used in Spain had been a long process, and in the meantime, the condition of the Peninsula had become even more aggravated. The Constitutionalist party supporting Christina had split over the question of what sort of Constitution was necessary, and the country was threatened with a double civil war.[67] Here was a dangerous advantage for Don Carlos and the Ultras. The possibility of a disastrous repercussion on the Orléans monarchy alarmed Thiers. The hopes of the French Legitimists arose with the fortunes of the Spanish reactionaries. Again Thiers pleaded with the King, and again the Duc d'Orléans added his instances to those of the President. A little more concession was wrung from the monarch, and a special emissary, Monsieur Bois le Comte, was sent by Thiers to Queen Christina. This gentleman was to inform the anxious Queen that the Foreign Legion would be increased and would become an active army, and that either Bugeaud or Clausel would be named as commander.[68]

Royal assent to these arrangements had been obtained only with great difficulty; Louis Philippe feared to increase the Legion and he disliked Bugeaud and mistrusted his impetuosity.[69] Nevertheless, Orléans and the President had won and Thiers was able to inaugurate a policy that he called "indirect intervention." But the interpretation placed upon this phrase by the President was entirely different from that held by the King. "A French general, ten thousand French soldiers, two or three thousand Portuguese, and five thousand English," hardly deserved such a modest epithet, and yet Thiers was not satisfied with the arrangement. Because this "was the only feasible plan," he wept, though he acknowledged in the same breath that he was consoled by the remarkable success of the recruiting at Paris.[70] This last remark made it appear that Frenchmen were learning the lesson that he had tried to teach them.

So far, the policy of the President had succeeded, but the King was becoming weary of the President's protestations of Liberalism and of his insistences. There were good reasons for the King's annoyance. We are now in August, 1836, and the events of the weeks preceding that month had only served to convince the King of his insecurity in France and in Europe. June 25 had nearly cost him his life and he was tired of being Liberal even in theory if not in fact. Metternich had slammed the door in his face. In fine, Thiers had brought him neither security at home nor respect in Europe. As well, he had lost the confidence of his slow-moving, corpulent master. From the end of July, Louis Philippe had been watching the movements of Thiers by means of the faithful Montalivet, who was a member of the Cabinet. The information that the

THIERS AND THE FRENCH MONARCHY

latter conveyed to him had led the King to suspect that Thiers had not been entirely honest with him. In fact, it is not unlikely that the President had felt it best to keep Louis in the dark in regard to some of his actions. He appears to have been playing to force the King's hand. There was the matter of Bugeaud, for instance. Thiers admired him, while Louis' feeling was quite the opposite, but the President was determined to have his man. In the letter to Rayneval relative to the reinforcements to which the King had at last consented, Thiers remarked : " Finally, none of your letters to me must ever give the number of 10,000 Frenchmen, unless you wish to bring about a catastrophe. Mention the number only in general terms. Do not yet pronounce the name of Bugeaud." This letter was written on August 12. Evidently the King had not yet approved Bugeaud's nomination, else Thiers would not have advised the Ambassador to forego the use of his name, and yet Bugeaud had already received his appointment from Thiers, by a letter bearing the date of August 3 ! [71]

Such practices must have been a sore trial to the royal patience. Threats of resignation were now a matter of daily occurrence, and between the King and the President the feeling of mutual distrust became acute. Louis Philippe accused Thiers and his friends of publishing orders to which he was not party, which pushed France nearer hostilities than he had ever intended to go, and which he must, therefore, openly deny. Thiers replied by letters full of explanations that were not convincing.[72] A break was inevitable, and when on August 24, General Lebeau, Commander of the Foreign Legion, announced in agreement with Thiers that a French army would cross the Pyrenees and enter Spain, the astonished monarch, without consulting his minister, published an official denial of the fact in the *Moniteur*. He followed this up with a demand that the recruits whom Thiers, without consulting the King, was assembling at the foot of the Pyrenees be disbanded.[73] On

PRESIDENT OF THE COUNCIL

August 29, Louis Philippe was glad to accept the resignation of the President and of six of his colleagues.

To his friends, the retirement of Thiers came as a disagreeable surprise. He had had no quarrel with the Chamber of Deputies, for it was not in session. By them his action was interpreted as a personal quarrel with the King, to whose elevation he had contributed six years previously. His greatest supporters, the Talleyrands, were much perplexed, and their attitude may have represented the sentiment of many of his acquaintances : " You break with the King—is it because of that hideous Spain ? How despicable she is, and how we have cause to detest her ! If only you had repulsed her from the first day. We are sad, anxious, and concerned about you. . . . To resign from power is not always regrettable, but to see you leave the King and the Ministry for a cause that will not excite the slightest sympathy in France ! " [74]

But to the retiring President there was a reason more subtle than that of Spain. " I wrote in the *National,* ' the King reigns and does not govern.' I acted on it. I never allowed Louis Philippe to interfere with me when I was his minister, and therefore my time of office was short and interrupted." [75]

NOTES TO CHAPTER XI

[1] Madame Dosne's Notes. Affaire d'Amerique, p. 67. Bibliothèque Thiers ; T. MSS. Fol. in 4°., 32.

[2] Quoted, Duchesse de Dino : *Mémoires,* II. 8. Paris, February 6, 1836.

[3] Quoted : *Ibid.,* II. 9. Paris, February 6, 1836.

[4] *Ibid.,* II. 11. Paris, February 8, 1836.

[5] Thureau-Dangin : *Histoire de la Monarchie de Juillet,* II. 439.

[6] *Ibid.,* II. 435.

[7] Duchesse de Dino : *Mémoires,* II. 11. Paris, February 8, 1836. *Ibid.,* II. 17. Paris, February 13, 1836.

[8] Thiers, Paris, February 29, 1836, to Sainte-Aulaire. Bibliothèque Nationale : 20,607, 15.

[9] Duchesse de Dino : *Mémoires,* II. 22. Paris, February 22, 1836.

[10] *Ibid.,* II. 23. Paris, February 23, 1836.

THIERS AND THE FRENCH MONARCHY

[11] *Le Constitutionnel*, February 23, 1836.
[12] Dupin: *Mémoires*, III. 201.
[13] Bresson, Berlin, March 11, 1836, to Thiers. Bibliothèque Nationale, 20,608, 58.
[14] Metternich: *Nachgelassene Papieren*, VI. 138. Metternich to Apponyi, May 17, 1836.
[15] Thiers: *Discours*, III. 242. February 22, 1836.
[16] Metternich: *Nachgelassene Papieren*, III. 243. Same date.
[17] *Ibid.*, VI. 147. Metternich to Apponyi, August 22, 1836.
[18] Thiers, Paris, February 29, 1836, to de Barante. Thiers: Paris, February 28, 1836, to Sébastiani. Bibliothèque Nationale: 20,608, 13; 20,607, 7.
[19] Thiers: Paris, February 29, 1836, to Sainte-Aulaire. Bibliothèque Nationale, 20,607, 16.
[20] (*a*) Duchesse de Dino: *Mémoires*, II. 23. Paris, February 24, 1836. (*b*) Thureau-Dangin (*Histoire de la Monarchie de Juillet*, III. pp. 8–9, footnote) estimates the division in the Chamber as follows: 150 devoted to the former Cabinet, 50 devoted to *Réunion Gaméron*, 70 to Third Party, 70 to Odilon Barrot, 70 to the Extreme Left, and 20 to the Legitimists.
[21] Thiers, Paris, February 29, 1836, to Sainte-Aulaire. Bibliothèque Nationale, 20,607, 15.
[22] *Moniteur*, March 16, 1836. Thiers: *Discours*, III. 367 sqq.: May 14, 1836.
[23] Guizot: *Lettres à sa famille*, 160. June 18, 1836.
[24] Thiers: *Discours*, III. 252 sqq.: March 21, 1836.
[25] *Moniteur*, March 24, 1836. Duchesse de Dino: *Mémoires*, II. 30–31: Paris, March 24, 1836. II. 32, Paris: March 27, 1836.
[26] Thiers: *Discours*, III. 317 sqq.: April 20, 1836. III. 331 sqq.: April 21, 1836.
[27] *Ibid.*, III. 551 sqq.: June 15, 1836.
[28] Guizot: *Lettres à sa famille*, 159.
[29] Thiers: *Discours*, III. 501: June 9, 1836. III, 537: June 10, 1836.
[30] *Ibid.*, III. 619: July 5, 1836.
[31] Thiers, Paris, June 27, 1836, to Montebello. Bibliothèque Nationale, 20,607, 163.
[32] Montebello, Berne, July 3, 1836, to Thiers. Bibliothèque Nationale, 20,606, 20.
[33] Thiers, Paris, June 30, 1836, to de Barante. Bibliothèque Nationale, 20,607, 88.
[34] Thiers, Paris, February 29, 1836, to Sainte-Aulaire. Thiers, Paris, February 28, 1836, to Sébastiani. Bibliothèque Nationale, 20,607, 16; 20,607, 7.
[35] Sainte-Aulaire, Vienna, February 28, 1836, to Thiers. Same to same, March 9, 1836. Bibliothèque Nationale, 20,606, 96 and 100.
[36] Thiers: *Discours*, IV. 473: June 2, 1836.
[37] Quoted, *Moniteur*, February 3, 1847.

PRESIDENT OF THE COUNCIL

[38] Montebello, Berne, June 12, 1836, to Thiers. Bibliothèque Nationale, 20,606, 5.
[39] Quoted, *Moniteur*, February 3, 1848.
[40] Thiers, Paris, June 27, 1836, to Montebello. Bibliothèque Nationale, 20,607, 163.
[41] Thiers, Paris, September 8, 1836, to Montebello. Bibliothèque Nationale, 20,607, 130.
[42] Thiers, Paris, May 13, 1836, to de Barante. Bibliothèque Nationale, 20,607, 130.
[43] Thureau-Dangin : *Histoire de la Monarchie de Juillet*, III. 74.
[44] Thiers, Paris, April 24, 1836, to Sainte-Aulaire. Bibliothèque Nationale, 20,607, 85.
[45] Bresson, Berlin, March 11, 1836, to Thiers. Bibliothèque Nationale, 20,606, 106.
[46] Sainte-Aulaire, Vienna, April 13, 1836, to Thiers. Same to same, Vienna, April 30, 1836. Bibliothèque Nationale, 20,606, 108.
[47] Thiers, Paris, May 2, 1836, to Bresson. Bibliothèque Nationale, 20,607, 123.
[48] de Barante, St. Petersburg, June 11, 1836, to Thiers. Bibliothèque Nationale, 20,606, 14.
[49] Bresson, Berlin, May 23, 1836, to Thiers. Bibliothèque Nationale, 20,603, 43.
[50] Bresson, Berlin, May 15, 1836, to Thiers. Bibliothèque Nationale, 20,603, 42.
[51] Ancillon, Berlin, June 3, 1836, to Thiers. Bibliothèque Nationale, 20,601, 20.
[52] Louis Philippe, Versailles, May 23, 1836, to Thiers. Same to same, May 30, 1836. Bibliothèque Nationale, 20,604–5, 161 and 168.
[53] *National*, May 3, 1836.
[54] Louis Philippe, Neuilly, June 19, 1836. Bibliothèque Nationale, 20,604–5, 187. Sainte-Aulaire, Vienna, May 27, 1836, to Thiers. Bibliothèque Nationale, 20,606, 119.
[55] Note attached Sainte-Aulaire, Vienna, June 12, 1836, to Thiers. Bibliothèque Nationale, 20,606, 143.
[56] Thiers, Paris, July 6, 1836, to Sainte-Aulaire. Bibliothèque Nationale, 20,607, 207.
[57] Letter of Metternich attached to Louis Philippe, July 30, 1836, to Thiers. Bibliothèque Nationale, 20,604–5, 223.
[58] Thiers, Paris, August 8, 1836, to Sainte-Aulaire. Bibliothèque Nationale, 20,607, 361.
[59] Quoted, Thureau-Dangin : *Histoire de la Monarchie de Juillet*, III. 99.
[60] Madame Dosne's Notes. Bibliothèque Thiers : T. MSS. Fol. in 4°., 32.
[61] de Rayneval, Madrid, March 5, 1836, to Thiers, Ministère des Affaires Étrangères, 771, 70. See also Miguel a Alava, Paris, March 3, 1836, to Thiers, Ministère des Affaires Étrangères, 771, 73.

[62] Thiers, Paris, March 31, 1836, to de Rayneval, Ministère des Affaires Étrangères, 771, 150.
[63] Thiers' notes on Spain, June 9, 1836. Bibliothèque Nationale, 20,602, 74. See also Granville, Paris, May 6, 1836, to Palmerston, P.R.O.F.O. 27, 521, 169.
[64] de Rayneval, Madrid, April 17, 1836, to Thiers, Ministère des Affaires Étrangères, 771, 201.
[65] de Rayneval, Madrid, June 12, 1836, to Thiers, Ministère des Affaires Étrangères, 771, 380. See also Thiers: *Discours*, IV. 492 sqq.: June 2, 1836.
[66] Madame Dosne's Notes, 84 sqq. Bibliothèque Thiers: T. MSS. Fol. in 4°., 32. Thiers, Paris, August 15, 1830, to Leopold. Bibliothèque Nationale, 20,607, 273.
[67] Isturis, Madrid, August 5, 1836, to Thiers. de Rayneval, Madrid, August 9, 1836, to Thiers, Ministère des Affaires Étrangères, 772, 48 and 50.
[68] Bois le Comte, Madrid, August 9, 1836, to Thiers, Ministère des Affaires Étrangères, 772, 58.
[69] Thiers, Paris, August 15, 1836, to Leopold. Bibliothèque Nationale, 20,607, 273.
[70] *Ibid.* Also: Thiers, Paris, August 12, 1836, to de Rayneval, Ministère des Affaires Étrangères, 772, 67–70.
[71] *Ibid.* Thiers, Paris, August 3, 1836, to Bugeaud. Bibliothèque Nationale, 20,607, 241–271.
[72] Louis Philippe, Neuilly, August 15, 1836, to Thiers. Bibliothèque Nationale, 20,60405, 228. Thiers, Paris, August 16, 1836, to Louis Philippe. Bibliothèque Nationale, 20,607, 275.
[73] Thiers, Paris, September 8, 1836, to Monsieur Étienne. Bibliothèque Nationale, 20,607, 301. Thiers, Paris, August 29, 1836, to Bois le Comte. Bibliothèque Nationale, 20,607, 291. *Cambridge Modern History*, X. 496.
[74] Duchesse de Dino, Valençay, August 29, 1836, to Thiers. Bibliothèque Nationale, 20,604–5, 85.
[75] Senior: *Conversations Second Empire*, I. 38.

CHAPTER XII

CLASSICIST AND COALITIONIST (1836-40)

SHORTLY after the retirement of Thiers, the King remarked to Werther, the Prussian Ambassador, " Ask your King when judging me to consider the difficulties of my position. . . . I had to take Monsieur Thiers for six months in order to show France exactly what he is worth. It requires infinite patience and persistence to steer my ship." [1]

Undoubtedly, Louis Philippe was glad to be rid of a second Périer who had almost involved him in a war. But the feeling was mutual. Périer Number Two was glad to be rid of his King, and for a time, there was a coldness between the Tuileries and the Place Saint-Georges. However, it was not a sentiment that changed in any way Thiers' belief in Monarchy or even in Orleanism. While he may have wished to operate on the system, he did not desire its death. He was still loyal, but he had had a surfeit of all things political. He desired a change of scene and needed a change of interests. He wanted to rest, but it is unlikely that he planned to abstain from politics in the future. He would retire temporarily from the field of battle, and this he could do with honour, for his had not been a parliamentary defeat. It is even possible that his recent experience had taught him what some of his contemporaries had already perceived. " Monsieur Thiers is never so powerful as when he is on the ground ; the ministerial pedestal does not become him. On the contrary, fighting (from the floor) gives him force ; his brilliant mind, his happy phrase, give him at once the prestige that he lost as minister. Monsieur Thiers is tremendously powerful when he is not a minister." [2]

THIERS AND THE FRENCH MONARCHY

Whether he was ever sincerely of this opinion himself, one will never know, but the fact remains that in later years, he was always reluctant to form a Ministry and appeared to prefer a Deputy's bench to the *fauteuil* of the President of the Council. At any rate, after the fatal month of August, 1836, Thiers' entire attention was not given to politics. Between 1836 and 1839, he was frequently *en voyage* and only returned to Paris to participate in a crisis in the Chamber. After his retirement from Government councils he was determined to play, and his playground was far from the political turmoil of Paris. It was Italy that now claimed his interest.

It has been customary to regard Thiers' passion for Italy as a sudden pose and the direct result of his quarrel with the King, a turning from France to Italy in a spirit of pique. As a matter of fact, the interest that he betrayed for Italy was rather the result of a gradual development, and it had appeared before the date of his controversy with Louis Philippe. As early as 1832, he had made a short visit to Italy, but was recalled by the death of Casimir Périer.[3] Then after his dismissal by the King, he set out to resume his acquaintance with that country. On the 12th of September he boarded ship at Toulon, and three days later he was at Rome, where he was initiated into the wonders of the Eternal City by Ingres, then Director of the Academy of France. Later, he went on to Florence, and returned to Paris in November.[4] This second and more lengthy sojourn whetted his appetite, and he began to make plans for a stay of several months. The following year these matured, and, accompanied by his wife, he went direct to Florence. There he and Madame Thiers established themselves at the Villa Castelli and he threw himself into a new existence with all his characteristic enthusiasm.

" I have become a man of letters and a philosopher. As Bossuet, the classic, puts it, I am enjoying the

CLASSICIST AND COALITIONIST

sight of human things through monuments and books, that is, through the men of the past. I even pretend to divine what I am told only a half of. And as that is the manner of history, I think that I understand the past quite well. Thanks to this variety that harms no one, neither Guizot, nor the King, nor Prince Metternich, I should be very content, busy, and quite happy if family cares did not worry me. I will make every effort, therefore, to remain what I am now. I wish to enlarge my spirit, to elevate my intelligence. That is more easily done in retreat than elsewhere, for in retreat one reflects, one studies and is interested. If, when I become more worthy, a good rôle should be offered me, *à la bonne heure!* But it is not worth the trouble to pass one's life between a King who demands and a Chamber that refuses, to be attacked incessantly by the Tuileries and the Palais Bourbon, by people who know nothing of you and who impute to you their own particular wrongs. . . . I write this from the bottom of my heart, and as I have had the happiness of discovering that my family shares these sentiments with me, I shall continue as I am; so you will see me entirely free this winter." [5]

Emancipated from the service of his King, Thiers in 1837, as so often in later life, was called by another power, Clio, his muse; to her he was preparing to give his entire service. At first, however, he did not write: he breathed in what he chose to call "antiquity." He revelled in the memories of Florence, of the Renaissance, and of the great classical age. His letters were filled with his enthusiasms; sometimes, even, the latter seem to have gone beyond the limits of the reasonable. His rhapsodies were as extravagant as his speeches had been during the earlier years. On the present he looked with disgust. France, he writes to Étienne, reminds him of a garish cabaret that bears the sign "Salons pour cent converts." [6]

THIERS AND THE FRENCH MONARCHY

Into the mind of this ever-active young man came a thousand plans; too many for all of them to be accomplished. He would continue the Revolution and write of Napoleon; he would write a history of this glorious Florence, where he was living with his charming wife and his books. Opportunities for both projects were not lacking, and Thiers was not the man to allow opportunity to go by. He had espoused a wealthy wife, and had plighted his troth to Clio; one would aid the other. Then, as now, riches would open many doors that appeared to be irrevocably closed. There was another advantage; a Bonaparte was in Italy, and to Italy Thiers had come. Considering the nature of the two men and their respective needs, it was quite inevitable that there should be a meeting.

Jerome, the youngest brother of Napoleon I, was residing in Italy. Jerome desired to return to France; Thiers desired to see some documents that were in the possession of the Prince. So, to Quarto Thiers went. He saw his precious manuscripts, and left as payment, the advice that the Prince appeal personally to the King to remove the edict of banishment.[7] Evidently, Jerome was impressed with his visitor, for, after his visit he sent him an ornament that had belonged to the Emperor. This gift the historian acknowledged with feeling, and in the course of his letter, he made a rather surprising statement: " I am, you know, one of the Frenchmen of to-day who is most attached to the glorious memory of Napoleon I, and I will be happy indeed when I see the return of his relatives reconciled with the peace of our own country, and the maintenance of its government."[8] Other letters of an even more definite nature followed: " Furthermore, if I am recalled to the post that I formerly occupied, I will use my influence with the King to bring near to their fatherland the French who are barred from it, and who are worthy to see it again. The friendship that you have allowed me to conceive for you and for your family is recent, but it will be real and lasting."[9]

CLASSICIST AND COALITIONIST

Shortly after his interview with Jerome Bonaparte, the health of Madame Thiers permitted him to travel, and they returned north via Cauterets. At Valençay, they stopped for a visit to the Duchesse de Dino. Almost the entire Thiers family descended upon the Duchess. With Thiers were Madame Thiers, Madame Dosne and Mademoiselle Félicie Dosne. As usual, Monsieur Dosne was absent. Madame Thiers was unwell; her critical hostess called it nerves, but found her otherwise quite gracious and pleasing. It was the mother-in-law that Madame de Dino disliked. " Un son de voix vulgaire; et des expressions triviales aux quelles je ne puis m'accoutumer. La soirée a été lourde and pésante, malgré les enthousiasmes de M. Thiers sur l'Italie. Il m'a paru très frappé de Valençay, et je les crois tous fort aisés d'y être. Heureusement le temps est beau; je n'ai jamais tant invoqué le soleil ! "[10] With Thiers Madame la Duchesse was visibly impressed. " He speaks much of his forty years and of the coldness of age. But I pay no heed to this; if provoked, he could easily cross swords."[11] To the hostess, as to so many others, it was an odd family, and she was not sorry when they were gone.

1837 had given Thiers new ideas, and 1838 saw them put into operation. Again the *ménage* Thiers–Dosne set out for Florence, and again Thiers revelled in the past. This time, however, he had returned with a very definite purpose that was already under way. Italy had enthralled him, but not in the way that one might expect. It is strange, indeed, when one considers his early revolutionary background, that his sympathies were not aroused by the spirit of the Risorgimento, echoes of which must have reached him at Florence. In fact, even in later years, with one brief exception, Thiers was never an enthusiastic friend of Young Italy. Perhaps his previous experiences with French Liberals and their Italian conspirators, account for this fact.

THIERS AND THE FRENCH MONARCHY

Nor was he attracted at first by the strictly classical age. While sojourning in Florence, it was the age of the Medicis that first captivated him, and it was their history that inspired him. His letters to France announced the fact that he had begun work on a History of Florence. This was not a sudden resolve, for there is evidence that this project may have been in his mind before 1838. In two of his earlier addresses, there are obvious references to Florentine history.[12] Apparently the Consulate and the Empire was not sufficient to occupy the remarkably active mind of this young man of the world! With the aid of a secretary, he might carry on researches in another field. One Giuseppe Canestrini, who had been highly recommended to him, was employed to go to Florence, and collect the material that Thiers indicated. The faithful secretary was first charged with the purchase of books that he forwarded to Thiers, wherever he happened to be.[13] Of these there must have been a quantity, for there is a large collection in his personal library, and one bill made out to *Sua Excellenza Il Signore Baron Thiers* lists six hundred and fifty volumes, valued at one thousand seven hundred and thirty-six francs, and weighing in total two hundred and twenty pounds![14] The busy little historian consulted and annotated extensively Malespini, Villani, Machiavelli, Machionne di Coppe Stefani, Muratori and countless other authorities.[15] But there were problems that these secondary works could not answer. Herein lay the usefulness of Canestrini, who consulted Florentine scholars, and delved into the libraries and archives. This was history-making *de luxe*, and the fortune of the Dosnes must have been called in to pay part of the expenses attendant upon his labour. To judge by the mass of notes accumulated by Thiers, the Florentine History must have been well under way, when politics intervened, and the project was finally abandoned.[16]

While this historical undertaking was never completed, the researches were not lost, for they brought the historian

CLASSICIST AND COALITIONIST

again under the charm of Renaissance art. His previous experience in the criticism of paintings in the Salons of 1822 and 1824, served as a preparation for what was to come, and it was during this interim of freedom from ministerial duties, that he began the practice of collecting painting and sculpture. But copies they were, and poor copies at that.

> "If I had wanted to buy pictures, I should have been bankrupt; my small fortune would have been swallowed up. I bought two or three originals, but they were of little value, and I stopped. Even if I had had the wealth of our greatest financiers at my disposal, I would not have done much more. Look, now, at the celebrated collections of our time. Those that cost enormous sums, do they give you even a suggestion of that delight that you experienced at Florence, Rome, Madrid, Vienna, or Dresden? Certainly not! *Eh bien!* it was the memory of so many lovely things that pursued me, distressed me ceaselessly, and that gave me the idea of this *petit musée*, so complete, that surrounds me." [17]

And so the much-frequented hotel of the Place Saint-Georges became a *petit musée* for those gigantic reproductions in oil, plaster, and bronze, that delighted the heart of the little bourgeois.

As time went on, however, he became more catholic in his tastes, and then it was that he made the amazing discovery that there were other periods as great as the Renaissance, and other civilizations than the Italian. Once he delivered himself of the following pronouncement:

> "The true barbarians are those who call the rest barbarians, those who think that they possess the exclusive monopoly of art and of taste. When you read Sanscrit and Chinese you discover admirable

poetry; do you think for a minute that a country can have poets and not have painters? While we must respect the Greeks as being first in all these things, yet we must open the doors to all the world, and allow each people to display its attainments. . . . God has not disinherited any part of the universe. One country possesses the sense of form, another that of colour; one has inherited philosophy, and another some other wonderful accomplishment." [18]

So far his work in preparation for the History of Florence had carried him; it brought him back to his interest in art. But it gave him as well a new ambition for a new undertaking. In later years he acknowledged that his studies in Florence had led him to plan a complete history of the art of the world! [19] That is why, at the Place Saint-Georges, examples of Chinese workmanship, for which he had developed an especial fondness, were mingled with Italian, Greek, Roman, Persian, Japanese, Russian, and Indian. To acquire this variegated collection, he expended large sums of money and considerable mental effort, for he was an intelligent collector; no matter over how wide a range of interests his collecting extended, he was at pains to cover it with reading and careful study. In a niche beside his bed, where stood, incidentally, a camp-bed belonging to Napoleon, was a library as extensive and as varied as his *objets d'art*. There might be found the Bible, the Koran, Horace, Plautus, the Sayings of Buddha, Bossuet, Calculus, Astronomy, Machiavelli, and La Mennais. In brief, the *petit musée* of his home became a monument to that extraordinary multiplicity of interests that filled the life and thoughts of this little statesman *en retraite* and *connaisseur à l'occasion*. And it was during the interval between his first and second Ministries that he allowed his whims and fancies to have full sway. To his friends, his enthusiasms at this time were delightful, but they made him an easy target for his enemies, and the latter delighted to call attention to these newest vagaries of Thiers. Chateaubriand, for example, remarked : " Du reste, M. Thiers mêle à des mœurs inférieures un instinct élevé; tandisque les survivants féodaux, devenus cancres, se sont fait régisseurs de leurs terres, lui, M. Thiers, grand seigneur de la Renaissance, voyage en Athéus, achate sur les chemins des objets d'art et ressuscite la prodigalité de l'antique aristocratie ! " [20]

The pursuit of studies in art and in Florentine history, however, was not without interruption. There was an obligation to his publishers that was still unfulfilled ; the *History of the Consulate and the Empire* had not yet been written. How much he actually accomplished with the latter during these years of comparative abstention from politics, is uncertain. In 1837 he had visited Jerome Bonaparte, and had obtained what he could from that Prince. After that, there is silence as far as the French history is concerned, until 1838, when the stay in Florence was nearing its end. Then it was that Thiers received an interesting piece of news, that decided him to make a bold stroke. He had consulted Revolution in the person of a Bonaparte, and lo ! here was an opportunity to consult Reaction in the form of its leader, Metternich himself.

When the young Thiers heard that Metternich was resting at Como, he packed off his family, the delicate wife, and the indelicate Madame Dosne, and to Como they went. A pretext for this journey was not lacking. The Thiers had been invited to attend the celebrations in connection with the coronation of the Emperor Ferdinand as Lombardo-Venetian King, and it was with this as an excuse that the Thiers–Dosne *ménage* approached the temporary retreat of Metternich, the great statesman. There, at Como, on August 25, the bourgeois who ten years previously had never met with Royalty, encountered the Prince who had been his greatest enemy in Europe, and the most faithful watch-dog of the old aristocracy.[21]

The conversation must have been interesting. One

THIERS AND THE FRENCH MONARCHY

can easily imagine the curiosity of those who witnessed the meeting of the two. Monsieur Thiers, nothing daunted, plunged at once into the breach, and assured Metternich that the real purpose of his visit had been to meet the Prince. In fact, as soon as he had retired from the Government, he had vowed to avail himself of the earliest opportunity. He wished to reassure the Prince as to one particular matter; he had renounced for ever a political career and was resolved to spend the remainder of his days in literary pursuits! It is related by an onlooker, that the old statesman to whom these remarks were addressed, did not appear to receive this last declaration too seriously. After these preliminaries on Thiers' part, Metternich took the lead in the conversation. He tried to keep it off the domain of politics. He discoursed on a great variety of subjects. His talk, however, did not appear to interest his interviewer, for Metternich relates, " Perceiving that my discourses on the arts and remarkable vegetation of the country only interested him moderately, I embarked on the subject of the philosophy of society. This topic exhausted, *mon interlocuteur* jumped pat into politics." [22] Monsieur Thiers wished to make an explanation of his foreign policy during his late administration. In spite of apparent differences, there were certain points of agreement between himself and Monsieur Metternich! Monsieur Thiers desires to assure His Excellency that *now* he is entirely without *parti pris*. This assertion gave the veteran an opportunity to deliver to his young interviewer a long sermon on the evils of the liberal Opposition in Europe.

At this point the conversation ended, but it was not without result. Metternich now recognized the genius of the man whom formerly he had despised, and the agile Thiers had made a wedge into the wall of reserve that the older man had tried to throw around himself. At a later date, the Prince was to open to his young acquaintance all the resources of his mind, and those of the Archives at Vienna as well. At least, a trail had been blazed on the way to information for the *History of the Consulate and the Empire*. Following this interview, the Thiers returned to Paris, and soon the calls of his various Muses were drowned by the clamours of the Opposition in the Chamber.

During the greater part of the years 1836-38, Thiers had been absent from France, and had repeatedly declared that he did not want to hear of politics. Nevertheless, in spite of these protestations, his friends had continued to keep him well informed as to the condition of affairs in France. Mignet had kept him *en rapport* with everything; Madame Dosne had been receiving her usual batch of political correspondence and newspaper clippings, which she had studied so assiduously, and Thiers himself, again a Deputy, had made it a point to be present at the openings of Parliament, and at the most important debates. Until the latter part of 1838, however, he had not felt that his continued presence in Paris was necessary. It was only upon the return from Como, that he began again to devote himself almost exclusively to studying and participating in, a very peculiar situation that was developing between the Crown and the Chamber of Deputies. It was a situation that made its first appearance after the resignation of Thiers in September 1836.

This overthrow, it will be recalled, had not been accomplished by the Chamber. In fact, when his Council retired, the Deputies were not even in session, having been adjourned on July 12. Louis Philippe and his President had parted company because they could not agree on the question of policy in regard to Spain and Portugal. In other words, it was an affair of royal prerogative, in which the King had won. Consequently, that monarch was determined to retain the power that he had gained, and this decision made the selection of a new President a very difficult problem. It was with his own power in mind, that the choice of the King

finally fell on Count Molé, who was a man of the Empire and not of the *Doctrine*.
The composition of the new Council was of the sort to satisfy the King. The presence of Duchâtel, de Rémusat, Guizot, and the ever-faithful Montalivet assured Louis of the sympathy of the Government, and he expected them to do his will, and relieve him from the embarrassments in which Thiers had left him. To accomplish this task, Molé set about to undo the work of his rash predecessor in regard to Spain. France must be disarmed, and so the army on the Pyrenees was disbanded. As a gage of the intention of the King to remain strictly conservative, the President then negotiated successfully the marriage of the Duc d'Orléans to Hélène of Mecklenburg. These two acts restored the confidence of the more reactionary Powers of Europe, while even in France the *Doctrinaires* applauded. The support of the latter augured well, for Molé needed a majority. But the adherence of the *Doctrine* was destined to be of short duration. While Guizot remained in the Ministry they were loyal, but when the portfolio of the Interior fell vacant, and the King refused to transfer Guizot from the Ministry of Public Instruction, the former's allies became cold to Molé, and upon Guizot's resignation, they joined with him in the demand that the King recall Broglie and Thiers. To this request Louis refused to give an ear, and the breach between the Government and the *Doctrine* became a fact. Molé must find new supporters and sympathizers.
Both the King and his President felt that this would be a comparatively easy thing to do, for at the beginning of his administration, Molé had announced a general policy of conciliation, which implied the abandonment of the repressive measures that had been instituted by the men of the Périer school. On June 10, 1837, the Government celebrated the wedding of the Duc d'Orléans by issuing a general amnesty to the Republicans. From Geneva and from England, the banished Liberals poured

into Paris. At the same time, Molé tried to conciliate the bourgeoisie by encouraging the development of industry and commerce. To him is due the credit for the development of Modern France. It was under his direction that wise measures were undertaken to construct bridges, canals, highways, and railroads. The material prosperity of the country was considerably advanced; within her boundaries, France appeared to be content and the Opposition was silent. The success of the Ministry had not been limited to internal policies, however. The joint efforts of France and England had saved Belgium and Greece, and had even aided the cause of oppressed Italy. In the latter case, Molé had withdrawn the troops sent by Périer to Ancona, on the condition that Austria should draw in her lines. On the surface, the years 1836-38 had been happy years; Molé was a wise and able administrator. He was a good peacemaker, but he did not know how to fight a parliamentary war, and under the surface a storm was brewing, born in great part of petty jealousies, that veiled what should have been a patriotic approval of some of Molé's wise plans. The storm centre was the King and his President, and the source was the Chamber of Deputies.

Molé did not represent any large faction in the Chamber, and he had not been called by them. He had been selected by the King, while Guizot, a real leader, had been ignored. According to the saying of the time, Molé was the King's valet. To many, his Council appeared to have no legal right for existence, for Thiers' Cabinet had not been overthrown by a vote of the Chamber, but by the desire of the King. These two objections gave a semblance of reason to the remarks of those who declared that the fundamental principle of a parliamentary system, on which the July Monarchy had been founded, was violated. This last criticism was made by the cohorts of Guizot and Thiers.

At first, however, neither one of the leaders participated

very much in the growing opposition. In December 1836, it is true, Thiers, in his capacity as Deputy from the Bouches-du-Rhône, was present for the opening of the Chamber, but this was quite natural, for he knew that the discussion would revolve around the policies of his Cabinet. When the matter of a Reply to the Address from the Throne was broached, he did not hesitate to defend his former policies, and to attack those that Molé had substituted for them. He characterized the Count's attitude to Spain as disloyal to the Treaty of 1834, and contrary to the principles of his own Government. He branded his methods as feeble and cowardly.[23] Before his merciless diatribe, Molé was helpless. Doubtless the new President felt much as did Alexis de Tocqueville, who remarked of Thiers, " Je vous réponds que cet-homme-là a le diable dans le corps assurément." As to Molé, when faced with Thiers, the same commentator writes, " What was the Ministry doing? It was disappearing from its bench; you would have needed a microscope to find it, it had been reduced to such infinitesimal proportions." [24]

The discussion of January 14, 1837, told; it displayed the weakness of Molé, and re-established the influence of Thiers. He was on the ground again, and he felt his power. From the spring of that year, he began to command more and more of a following, and, as his strength increased, he was able to dispel the doubts of those who had come to suspect him during the preceding year. At the same time, a situation was developing in the Chamber of Deputies, that would eventually consolidate his power. All that he had to do was to remain quiet, and allow the *affaire* to grow. Perhaps, after all, political discretion as well as æsthetic interests, advised the sojourns of Thiers in Italy.

There were, in the main, four principal factions in the Chamber: the Left, the Right, the Left Centre and the Right Centre. Four orators superior by far to all their contemporaries, were the leaders of these sections. They

CLASSICIST AND COALITIONIST

were, respectively, Barrot, Berryer, Thiers, and Guizot. Of these four, no one was in the Ministry, and all were discontented. Jealousy of those in power was one reason for their opposition. When the Viscomte de Launay lamented : " How is it that a century that gives us such enormous flowers, can only produce great men who are so small," her plaint was not without some justification.[25] But disappointed personal ambition was not the only cause of their antagonism to the Government. Barrot, Left, opposed the Molé régime because it appeared to him to be nothing but a feeble repetition of Charles X and Polignac, so great was the ascendancy of Louis Philippe over the President of the Council. Berryer, of the other extreme, opposed the Government on Legitimist grounds. Thiers, Left Centre, saw in the existing system a menace to his " representative monarchy," while the Right Centre under Guizot did not favour the Ministry for the same reason. In these four men was the nucleus for an enormous Opposition, and what had Molé to meet it ? Practically, there was nothing left but the support of Thiers' personal enemies. Of the latter, there were not a few who were under the leadership of Émile de Girardin, journalist and politician. Girardin did not trust Thiers' views, and he had suffered much at his hands. When the latter had discovered that Girardin was opposing his measures, he had taken advantage of an erroneous registration to have him disfranchised, and from that time, the indignant editor had opposed Thiers in the Press. His attacks had been aided by his wife, the able Delphine de Girardin, who, under the pseudonym of the Viscomte de Launay, wrote clever and scandalous accounts of the little statesman and his family.

It was a time of the reign of personal animosities, and Thiers, with all his qualities of political *finesse*, knew how to exploit the situation and to profit by it. While appearing to avoid as much open controversy as possible, he and his friends, among them Vivien and Cousin, were quietly at work, and as early as 1838, when he returned from Italy, he evidently felt that he would soon be master of the discordant spirits in the Chamber. In February of that year, he remarked to Royer-Collard: "You must believe me when I say that I am the only man who is capable, powerful, and in condition to dominate this situation. Furthermore, I will not enter into power until they open both doors to me."[26] Even Delphine, herself, must acknowledge that at a certain *soirée*, Thiers gave every evidence that he was confident in the future: "Monsieur Thiers was calm and dignified. He had relinquished the practice of going here and there to shake hands with everyone. He behaved no longer like an affluent elector. He had the attitude that best suited him, that of a statesman who had a future ahead of him."[27]

The first notable step in the revival of his power, came in January 1838, when Thiers again attacked the Government, and when Barrot with his followers from the Left, relinquished temporarily their more radical demands, and rallied to his support. During a discussion over the Reply to the Address from the Throne, Thiers resumed his criticisms of Molé's policy in regard to Spain; on this occasion, he actually accused the Court of permitting Counter-Revolution to re-establish itself in the Iberian Peninsula.[28] Such a charge was, of course, one that would bring the Barrot Republicans to his side. When this alliance with the Left was under way, the advocates of a Coalition movement, who were none other than Rémusat, de Hauranne, and others of Thiers' friends, brought about a reconciliation of Thiers and Guizot. By March 1838, the Coalition of the Left, Left Centre and Right Centre was a *fait accompli*, but it was not a union that would appeal to men of a really sincere frame of mind. Royer-Collard characterized the reconciliation of Thiers and Guizot as *une union impie*.[29] The Viscomte de Launay called Thiers a *Mirabeau-Mouche*, and Guizot she apostrophized as a glass of sugared water.[30]

In reality, the Coalition was a union of insincerities.

CLASSICIST AND COALITIONIST

Nevertheless, there were certain reasonable bases for the alliance of two such outstanding rivals as the agile little leader of the Left Centre and his pedantic colleague of the Right Centre. While their differences were great, there were certain points of agreement between them, and no one was more adept at discovering these happy *vias medias* than Thiers. If he had been able to persuade himself that he had much in common with Metternich, how much easier it was to make himself and Guizot believe that they were working for the same noble purpose! And yet, the grounds of their reconciliation had a certain foundation.

In 1838 and 1839, while Thiers, as leader of the Left Centre, was acting in defence of all progress compatible with the principles of the July Monarchy, Guizot became the leader of the more conservative. Both were Liberals, and both agreed as to "representative monarchy," but, while Thiers believed that the time had come to change it from theory to fact, Guizot was not quite convinced of the advisability of such a programme. The one was endeavouring to conciliate those whom the Revolution of July had offended, and the other was undertaking to satisfy all those who were more exactingly conservative in their interpretation of the word "democracy." Of the two, Thiers, of course, was the bolder. In brief, he would have had a Conservative policy carried out by Liberals, while his rival desired to see a Liberal policy carried out by Conservatives.[31] But in 1839, these fine similarities in spite of differences, were not so apparent; it was only after the year 1840 that they became so marked.

The plan of the Coalition was not a complicated plot. They sought to drive out Molé by the accusations that they brought to bear against his administration. Briefly, these charges were put forth in six speeches that Thiers delivered during the month of January 1839. On January 7, the Reply to the Throne came up for discussion. *A propos* to this debate, Guizot arose to justify the Coalition on the ground that it had been formed by patriots,

THIERS AND THE FRENCH MONARCHY

who believed that the policy of the existing Ministry was detrimental to the country and to the throne. To this, Molé replied by calling to mind the undoubted material benefits that his policy had brought to France. After the President's defence, Thiers mounted the Tribune, and opposed to Molé's thesis, the supineness of the Government in regard to Spanish affairs, and the resultant coldness of England, because France had not co-operated with her and observed the engagements of the Quadruple Alliance of 1834. This policy, he declared, was losing to France an ally, and allowing England a predominance in Spain, that was a blot on French honour. The speaker, however, did not confine himself to foreign affairs. He went further and denounced the *laissez-aller* policy of the President in regard to the Radicals, citing the general amnesty in particular, which, he declared, had resulted in the revived propaganda of the Radicals throughout France. Within and without, the dignity and influence of the throne had been jeopardized.[32] By a second speech on January 9, anent the same matter of the Reply, Thiers reduced Molé to a state of inarticulate helplessness by a rapid succession of ridicule, that made the Chamber rock with laughter.[33] The subsequent speeches concerned the question of Belgium, and the fact that France had been left out of the final settlement, and the evacuation of Ancona by the French troops.[34] The next of his January tirades was a brilliant résumé of the reasons for the coldness of the English to France, the blame of which he laid entirely at Molé's door, while his last speech raised the question as to whether the Ministry had been acting according to the principles of parliamentary government.[35] In brief, there was not a single phase of the Molé régime that Thiers did not touch upon.

Refreshed and inspired by his sojourns in Italy, the little statesman had returned to Paris with more than his normal accumulation of energy. He was tireless in his effort. Eighteen more times he inveighed against the Government, and twelve times Guizot brought his more

CLASSICIST AND COALITIONIST

serious and pedantic oratory into play. Between them, they weakened the power of the President. Urged on by the growing animosity of the public, the Coalition redoubled its efforts. The tide was fast turning against the Ministry, and in a desperate effort to save this Cabinet, the King consented to call for new elections. These resulted overwhelmingly against the Government, and on March 8, 1839, Molé resigned.

The collapse of the Molé Cabinet brought Louis Philippe face to face with a difficult problem. He must yield to the Opposition, but he was determined at first not to select any one of their leaders to head a Council. Consult with them he must, and as Thiers was really astride the Coalition, he turned reluctantly to him. How far away the time must have seemed when the King had said : " You are the man with whom I prefer to discuss affairs ! " It was a disgruntled King who now summoned the little bourgeois Deputy of Aix. Louis was the vanquished, and Thiers the victor.

Many and long were the communications that passed between them.[36] After several unsuccessful attempts the King was brought to ask Thiers to sit in a new Cabinet, but the latter was unwilling to accept. He refused to be subordinate to another who was not of his own party of the Coalition. He urged the appointment of Barrot, but to this suggestion the King turned a deaf ear. Thiers was adamant to his almost pitiful entreaties. He was inpatient with the King, and he had too much else to do.

During the crisis of March, his activities were tremendous. To the palace he must go to interview an anxious King, to the Chamber to safeguard and exhort his uncertain flock, and then he would return to the Place Saint-Georges, where *Madame-Mère*, his precocious mother-in-law, had been entertaining important callers during his absence, promising them favours, secretaryships, and embassies. Even when her famous son-in-law appeared, this lady would not withdraw, but would remain for the interesting conversation that followed ;

THIERS AND THE FRENCH MONARCHY

and, if she disagreed with her illustrious *gendre*, she would not hesitate to remonstrate with him.[37] Then, too, there were interesting little seances *dans l'intimité*, when from his study he directed his cohorts, and set into operation measures to control the opinion of his constituents. Through friendship, or through business relations, he was dictator to the *Journal des Débats, Constitutionnel, Siècle, Messager, Courier Français*, and other papers. Balzac describes a *matinée chez Thiers* during the year 1839, in the following fashion :

"Every morning, Messieurs Cardonne, Grimaldi, Boilay, Veron, Walewski, Léon Faucher, Chambolle came to the rue Saint-Georges, to the hotel of Monsieur Thiers, to receive their orders, and to be informed what kind of articles to write. Monsieur Thiers was aided by two of his assistants, Messieurs Martin and Sainty; the task of the latter was very difficult, being to translate into good French whatever Monsieurs Thiers wrote. There, with Madame Dosne presiding, the cakes that were to be swallowed by the public, were buttered." [38]

Balzac, who was a friend of the Girardins, was for that reason, very hostile to Thiers, but there was a hint of the truth in what he wrote. Thiers as a Deputy, behaved much like a general and exercised a very real sway. In 1839, so great was his power that, although only a Deputy, he was able to prevent the presentation at the Cómedie Française, of *L'École des Journalistes*, a travesty of himself and of Madame Dosne.

Among the conferences held by the Deputy of the Bouches-du-Rhône, was a dinner given by him to the leaders of the Opposition on March 19, just when the crisis was at its height. There, the great men of the Chamber met for the purpose of drawing up an ideal programme for the future Ministry, the composition of which was still in doubt. Some of the clauses in this document are significant. " The new Ministry, representing the opinions of the Left Centre, will not proclaim itself the continuator of the Ministry just resigned." " The laws of September will be maintained." " No proposition for electoral reform will be made for the present; that question will be left for the future." This latter agreement removed the principal difference between Thiers and Guizot. " No armed intervention during the present condition of affairs in Spain, but in the event of serious incidents, the Cabinet reserves a complete liberty of action." [39]

Naturally, such a programme was not the sort to appeal to the King, and in spite of their elaborate preparations, the Coalitionists were not called upon to form a new Cabinet. In place of one of their number, Louis Philippe selected Marshal Soult, who undertook to find colleagues acceptable to the Chamber. This effort required two months of searching. At first, acting upon the King's instructions, he sought out Thiers, but the latter replied that, since the King had declined to accept the programme of the Coalition, he could not be expected to make any further sacrifice of his opinions than he had already made.[40] The sacrifice to which he referred, was the fact that he had consented to a postponement of electoral reform in order to maintain his alliance with Guizot.

At the same time that the parliamentary crisis was at its height, another matter of serious import developed. In his speech of January 7, Thiers had signalled the revival of Radical agitations, and had ascribed it to the unwise amnesty policy of Molé. Just at the critical moment, his remarks were justified. The Republican-Socialists, freed from the ban of the Government, became active again. It was a return to the Radical club movement of the earlier 'thirties; the followers of Buonarroti's principles had organized a new society known as the " Seasons." The leaders of this organization were Blanqui, Barbès, and Trélat, all of whose names had been made

THIERS AND THE FRENCH MONARCHY

familiar to the police in August 1830. Previous to Molé's retirement, they had resumed their familiar practice of demonstration, and on May 12 they quite outdid themselves. A small riot in the rue Saint-Martin became a revolt that resulted in an attempt to gain control of the Hôtel de Ville, the seat of municipal authority in Paris. Although this movement was checked in time, it was serious enough to alarm the more conservative of the Deputies, who beheld in this affair, a dangerous result of the general ill feeling against the Government, that had been aroused by the influence of the Coalition. Many deserted Molé and his opponents, and left them to fight out their quarrel alone. They went over to the support of Soult, in an effort to put down the unhappy divisions that had been due in great part to the personal interests of Thiers, Guizot, Barrot and Dupin. But neither the new Ministry nor the Conservative group that rallied to it, was able to silence the passions that the speeches of these four men had aroused in the provinces. Taught by the latter, many Frenchmen had come to regard the policy of the Government during the last three years, as one degrading to France. They demanded the regeneration of the country through the formation of a Coalition Cabinet. As a result, Soult's power was weak and uncertain. But this was not the only effect of the antipathies to the Monarchy, that were aroused by the unwise leaders of the Coalition.

The general discontent made possible the revival of the hopes of other parties that, until 1839, had been negligible. Among them were the Bonapartists. The *culte* of Napoleon I began to grow. The pathetic death of the Duc de Reichstadt in 1832, had brought the matter again before the eyes of the public, and the spectacular performances of Louis Napoleon, first in Switzerland and then, in Strassburg, kept the Bonapartist cause alive in the minds of Frenchmen. At the same time, the theatres began to produce plays relative to the Empire, and in verse, as well as in prose, the Napoleonic legend was

CLASSICIST AND COALITIONIST

becoming a fad. It cannot be denied that an unconscious contributor to this movement, was the foremost leader of the Coalition, who, when he was not in the Tribune, was at his desk in the house on the Place Saint-Georges, working away at his *History of the Consulate and the Empire*. And, when, a little later, his romantic enthusiasms carried him to the point of proposing to bring back to Paris the body of the Emperor Napoleon I, he was only feeding the dangerous tendencies that were already prevalent in France. For once in his life Thiers, the apostle of what he called " common sense," must have been deaf to its appeal, when he disregarded the eloquent words that Lamartine delivered before the Deputies, anent the proposal to bring Napoleon's ashes to France :

"But whether you select Saint-Denis or the Panthéon or the Invalides, remember to inscribe on this monument, where he must be at one and the same time, soldier, Consul, legislator, Emperor; remember, I say, to write the only inscription that is possible for this unique man, and for the difficult times in which you live : *à Napoléon seul* ! '

" These three words, while recognising that this military genius was unsurpassed, will make it evident to France, to Europe, and to the world that, while this generous nation honours her great men, still, she knows how to distinguish their faults from their services . . . she knows even how to distinguish them from their party, and from those who become a menace in their name ; and that, when she raises this monument, and as a nation receives within it this great memory, she does not desire to see arising from these ashes, war, tyranny, *prétendants*, and imitators ! " [41]

How true were these words of the " solitary orator of the Chamber " ! The future fortunes of Louis Napoleon were founded and grounded in the divisions aroused throughout France, by the disgruntled leaders of the Coalition.

As is so often the case, at the time only one man sees ahead, and the rest are blinded by the brilliancy of their particular enthusiasms and petty ambitions. Consequently, while many of their followers rallied to the King in the hope of establishing peace and concord in the country, the ruthless parliamentary leaders continued the policy of hacking their way to power, by spreading dissatisfaction among their constituents. " France is disgraced and isolated in Europe," they cried. And the provinces took up the echo. It was the development of a situation in the Near East, that gave an appearance of truth to their slogan, and that presented to their leader, Thiers, the opportunity to re-enter into power through wide-open doors.

For some time England, the ally of France, had been watching anxiously the increase of Russian power in the Balkans and at Constantinople. The Treaty of Unkiar Skelessi, 1833, bound the Tsar and the Sultan in a defensive alliance of the most intimate character. By it, Russia enjoyed an almost exclusive influence at Constantinople. But England, too, had made gains in an easterly direction. Her influence in the Ionian Islands was supreme, and in Greece British power was extensive. These advantages had whetted the appetites of commercial England, and now, British merchants, under the ægis of Palmerston, were casting their eyes on Trebizond, and even, on the great Porte itself. Then it was that a quarrel between the Sultan and his ambitious vassal, Mehemet-Ali, Pasha of Egypt, gave England an opportunity to offset the rival power of Russia.

Mehemet desired to extend his rule into Syria, and his efforts in that direction had met with such success, that the Porte had finally decided to make peace by offering to invest him with the hereditary power in that district. This arrangement would have raised the Pasha to a

CLASSICIST AND COALITIONIST

position practically independent of the Sultan. Here was the opportunity of the astute Palmerston; a proposal to help the Sultan and to mediate for him, might cause the balance of Turkish favour to swing from Russia to England. The first move was to sound out France; if that country agreed to the proposal, England would be free to act. In the meantime, the Tsar, scenting a danger to his own influence, attempted a speedy accommodation between the Porte and Egypt, but this effort of Russia was checked when Soult declared that the Egyptian matter was not an exclusively Russian affair, and that France and all the other nations of Europe had a right to participate in the negotiations. So far, England and France had acted in agreement, but at this point, discord developed between the two countries. Palmerston planned to win the Sultan by snubbing the Pasha, and to this plan France refused her consent. The Pasha had given the latter country many commercial privileges, and was very popular among Frenchmen. His popularity, incidentally, had been increased and spread by the influence of Thiers, who regarded him as a second Napoleon, and who saw in the Egyptian question an opportunity for France to regain her lost prestige in Western Europe polity.

When, therefore, Soult showed signs of yielding to Palmerston's scheme of snubbing the Pasha, the Opposition demanded that he assume the contrary attitude. The fight was on. To all appearances it was the fight of Thiers for himself, for many of the important Coalition supporters deserted him. Again, in the parliamentary debate that ensued, he made the charge that the Ministerial Council was timid and subservient to England. His accusation had at least the appearance of truth, and he was quite certain of a majority. In fact, he had felt confident of his position ever since June 1839, and in this belief his friends, and especially the faithful and cautious Mignet, concurred.[42] To many he had become the embodiment of French patriotism, and he was praised as the man who sought to revive the honour of France. The municipal council of Aix voted to erect a monument to its Deputy : " le premier parmi les hommes d'État." [43] With the certainty of victory, in January 1840, Thiers mounted the Tribune to attack again the policy of the Government. It was a still more experienced and adroit orator who now commenced his final drive to power.

> " At the last séance of the Chamber of Deputies, where he (Thiers) staged his discourse-act, you would have beheld him ascend the Tribune with a constrained and discontented mien. Why ? Because it was late and the Chamber was already deserted, and Monsieur Thiers does not like to raise the curtain and perform before empty benches. He must have about him voices that respond to his voice, faces that animate him, and hands that applaud. *Then* he is in the Tribune. Beside him, not the usual parliamentary glass of water, but a glass of water and wine, to make his voice stronger and more penetrating. He begins by speaking so low that you can scarcely hear him. His voice will return when the time comes ; Quintus Sextus will throw away his crutches. The quality that is the peculiar characteristic of Monsieur Thiers as an orator, can hardly be called his eloquence, for that word has too majestic a meaning ; it is rather something vivid, easy, flowing, and familiar that he alone employs. He does not pose, and so he is free in his movements, and he appears to be the least embarrassed person in the world. When he finds that the attention of his hearers is distracted, he retraces his steps ; he is so sure of himself that he asserts and repeats the same things almost in the same words, without fearing to annoy his hearers. Monsieur Thiers never employs figures or metaphors. He uses the words for what they are worth and does not change them from their ordinary meaning. This

CLASSICIST AND COALITIONIST

familiarity of language is, perhaps, one of the most important reasons for his success." [44]

It was probably such an impression as the above that he made when, on January 13, he directed a last blow at the ministerial combination that had replaced Molé.[45] Soult's policy in regard to Palmerston and Egypt appeared weak and dangerous to the Opposition. They were determined to overthrow him on the slightest provocation. Accordingly, when the Ministry proposed a Bill that provided for the dowry of the King's son, the Duc de Nemours, Thiers and his cohorts arose to take this occasion to force Soult to retire by refusing a measure so dear to the heart of Louis Philippe. The *dot* was the occasion; the real cause was the relation of Palmerston and the minister. France must act by herself, the Coalition had said. They did not wish to go so far as war, they only desired to overthrow what they regarded as a spineless and subservient Ministry.

NOTES TO CHAPTER XII

[1] Quoted, Hillebrand : *Geschichte Frankreichs*, I. 636.
[2] Vicomtesse de Launay : *Lettres Parisiennes*, I. 269.
[3] Maugin : *Chroniques*, p. 3.
[4] *Ibid.*
[5] Duchesse de Dino : *Mémoires*, II. 169–70. Valençay, July 26, 1837.
[6] Thiers, Florence, July 2, 1837, to Étienne. Bibliothèque Nationale, 20,607, 40.
[7] Prince Napoleon : *Monsieur Thiers et les Napoléon*, p. 5.
[8] *Ibid.*, p. 7. Thiers, Florence, July 21, 1837, to Jerome Bonaparte.
[9] *Ibid.*, p. 8. Thiers, Cauterets, August 29, 1837, to Jerome Bonaparte.
[10] Duchess de Dino : *Mémoires*, II. 189–90. Valençay, October 10, 1837.
[11] *Ibid.*, II. 191. Valençay, October 13, 1837.
[12] Thiers, *Discours*, I. 179. December 13, 1834 ; October 3, 1831.
[13] Thiers' Notes. Bibliothèque Thiers, Fol. 549,220. *The History of Florence*.
[14] *Ibid.*
[15] *Ibid.*
[16] Canestrini himself published a History of Florence at a later date.

[17] Quoted, Blanc: *Cabinet de Monsieur Thiers*, pp. 9–10.
[18] *Ibid.*, pp. 47–8.
[19] *Ibid.*, pp. 73–4.
[20] Chateaubriand: *Mémoires d'Outre Tombe*, VI. 175.
[21] Metternich: *Nachgelassene Papieren*, VI. 261. Metternich to Apponyi, April 21, 1838.
[22] *Ibid.*, VI. 269. Metternich to Apponyi, September 6, 1838. See also Diary of Princess Mélanie, No. 1309, August 25, 1838.
[23] Thiers: *Discours*, IV. 76, 77, January 14, 1837.
[24] Alexis de Tocqueville, Paris, May 14, 1837, to Gustave de Beaumont. Château Tocqueville.
[25] Viscomte de Launay: *Lettres Parisiennes*, II. 195.
[26] Alexis de Tocqueville, Paris, February 16, 1838, to unknown. Château Tocqueville.
[27] *La Presse*, February 17, 1838, Madame de Girardin.
[28] Thiers: *Discours*, IV. 207: January 10, 1838.
[29] Duchesse de Dino, *Mémoires*, II. 222. Paris, March 22, 1838.
[30] Viscomte de Launay: *Lettres Parisiennes*, II. 115: March 6, 1839. *Chroniques*, I. 263–4, January 12, 1839.
[31] de Rémusat: *Thiers*, pp. 83–4.
[32] Thiers: *Discours*, IV. 279–81: January 7, 1839.
[33] *Ibid.*, IV. 287 sqq.: January 9, 1839.
[34] *Ibid.*, IV. 303 sqq.: January 11, 1839; 334 sqq.: January 14, 1839.
[35] *Ibid.*, IV. 356 sqq.: January 16, 1839; 369 sqq.: January 19, 1839.
[36] Louis Philippe, Paris, to Thiers, March 10, 12, 26, 29, 1839. Bibliothèque Nationale, 20,608, 112, 114, 116, 118.
[37] *Revue Parisienne*, pp. 114–15: July 25, 1840. *Ibid.*, p. 124: July 25, 1840.
[38] *Ibid.*, pp. 119–20: July 25, 1840.
[39] Dupin: *Mémoires*, IV. 7–8.
[40] Thiers, Paris, March 20, 1839, to Duc de Dalmatie. Bibliothèque Nationale, 20, 608, 147.
[41] *Moniteur*, May 27, 1840.
[42] Mignet, Paris, June 23, 1839, to Thiers. Bibliothèque Nationale, 20,608, 12. Mignet, Archambault, Bourbon, July 19, 1839, to Thiers. Bibliothèque Nationale, 20,608, 129.
[43] Monsieur Aude, Maire, Aix-en-Provence, August 10, 1839, to Thiers. Bibliothèque Nationale, 20,608, 91.
[44] Pinard: *Histoire à l'Audience*, pp. 138–9.
[45] Thiers: *Discours*, IV.: January 13, 1839.

CHAPTER XIII

THE SECOND MINISTRY (1840)

THE refusal of a dowry to the Duc de Nemours was not meant as an act of hostility to the royal family of France. At least, that was not the intention of the majority who opposed the measure of Soult. To their minds, the unfavourable vote was only an expression of final disapproval of the latter's policies in general. Both Louis Philippe and his President of the Council had tried to respond to the desire of the nation for a truly active foreign policy, but their efforts had not taken the direction that the people had been led to desire. When French civilians in Mexico and in the Argentine had been ill-treated, the Government had blockaded the ports of the offending Powers. When a revolt led by Abd-el-Kader had broken out in Algiers, the Government had undertaken to put it down. Even when Russia had sent Monsieur de Brünow to London to negotiate an entente with England, Soult had appointed Guizot to counteract Russian influence at the Court of St. James and to prevent a settlement of the Mehemet-Ali matter without consideration of France. But to the minds of many in the Chamber and in the provinces, these were feeble attempts to make French opinion respected in Europe, and the country was not satisfied, with the result that the Coalition triumphed by a vote of two hundred and twenty-six to two hundred and twenty. There had been so little discussion, that the Ministry itself was astonished at the defeat. It was a bewildered President who carried his resignation to a still more perplexed King.

In all times of crisis, the Place Saint-Georges had been a rendezvous for the friends and enemies of Thiers. The year 1840 was no exception to the rule. Those who were not his sympathizers, called at the house in the hope of discovering what was going on and for the purpose of consulting and observing that remarkable political barometer, Madame Dosne, *la reine de Paris*.[1] February again beheld her shining in the political firmament of Paris, and her salon became the scene of many important discussions. Her son-in-law, she asserts, abstained from intrigue, but wherever he and his wife were to be found, there were groups of aspirants praising the wit of the Deputy from the Bouches-du-Rhône and flattering his charming lady.[2] At this time, it was in the salons of others that Madame Thiers shone; at the Place Saint-Georges, it was her mother who was the centre of attraction. There *Madame-Mère* talked with men of all party colours, and learned what her precious *gendre* was expected to do.

By the twenty-second of February, there were signs that the latter might again be called to head a Council. On that very day, Thiers informed Madame Dosne that his name was on the list of every possible ministerial combination. Out of the confusion, he would be sure to draw some sort of a plum.[3] He consulted with Molé and with Broglie, but found that he could not agree with the one, and that the other had given up politics. The King had even intimated that he was desirous of talking with the Deputy, but Thiers had resolved not to go to the Tuileries unless he was commanded. At last, on February 25, the expected summons came.[4] One can easily imagine the touching family scene at the Place Saint-Georges; the joyful tears of Madame Dosne, the anxious looks of the lovely and delicate Madame Thiers, and the confident, placid air with which the leader of the Coalition set out to obey the summons of his King. The result of this interview and others that followed upon it, was the Second Ministry of Adolphe Thiers.

There can be no question but that he was glad to grasp again the power, and there can be no doubt that he manœuvred to obtain it. Nevertheless, there is another

DAUMIER'S CARTOON OF THIERS THE STATESMAN.

reason for his second elevation. It was expressed by the Viscomte de Launay in terms that are not entirely flattering :

> " To be fair to Monsieur Thiers, he is not the only one who loves to be minister, and if he manages to become one so often, it is because he has as accomplice all the active part of the nation, of which he is the natural leader and the true representative. We are an envious people who love to make fun of our masters, we allow ourselves to be led only by those whom we really disdain. We resemble those husbands who, blindly jealous of their independence, resist the counsels of their wives, and follow the caprices of their mistresses. They defy the former because they recognize their common-sense and fear their authority. They obey the latter without realizing it, for they find them unworthy to command. The superiority of the wives is their weakness and the mediocrity of the mistresses determines their power. . . . We are frank Republicans who hate all crowns —crowns of kings, of counts, crowns of laurel, crowns of ivy, even haloes of purity. We are jealous democrats who hate all nobilities ; nobilities of birth, conduct, and of *tenue*. We suspect every man who has a distinguished air. A great superiority is unbearable, unless we can ridicule it and belittle it. In France, we love Monsieur Thiers precisely because he is poorly born, poorly made, and poorly brought up, and because of that, we forgive him for being intelligent and for having talents and generous sentiments. It is his faults that make his virtues endurable ! " [5]

In spite of the hostility that inspired this comment, there is a grain of truth in what Delphine De Girardin wrote. The fact that Thiers had so obscure an origin, was one reason for his continued success and popularity.

THIERS AND THE FRENCH MONARCHY

But that is not to say that the Ministry of February 1840 was received with any great show of enthusiasm. There were many who were sceptical, and foremost among these was the King himself.

A vote of the Chamber had forced Louis Philippe to call into his Government some of the very men who had tried to put an obstacle in the way of the marriage of his second son. Consequently, he did not greet his new ministers with any great show of cordiality. " Well, Messieurs, I am forced to endure you and to submit to my own dishonour. . . . You force yourselves upon me. . . . You place my children on straw. . . . At last, I am a constitutional king, *il faut bien passer par là*." [6] If the King did not actually utter the words, they were at least, on the tip of his tongue. And their truth became painfully real to him when Thiers, as President, declared, in his speech of March 4, that, under this Ministry, France would have a truly constitutional government.[7] This pronouncement must have filled the royal cup of unhappiness to the brim. But Louis and his circle were not alone in their misery. A constitutional minister and a disgruntled King were faced with a dissatisfied Chamber of Deputies.

It had been Molé and Passy who had carried the vote of the 226, but neither one of them was included in the combination that Thiers and his monarch finally evolved. The Left Centre was represented by Pelet de La Lozère and Vivien, while the *Doctrine* or Right Centre could only point to Charles de Rémusat. " Where was Guizot ? " these latter asked. The answer did not please them. Monsieur le Président du Conseil had left him at London, where he might be valuable, and where he was out of Monsieur's way ! Left Centre and Right Centre, then, were uncertain quantities, as far as a ministerial majority was concerned. And while the Centre parties frowned, the real Democrats of the Left recalled the repressive September laws and glowered at the little statesman who *would* be President. Fortunately for him, each faction

THE SECOND MINISTRY

hated the other, and he lost no time in trying to establish his control over a divided Legislative.

His first move was to silence the opposition of the more recent social classes by establishing reforms that would remove the causes for their complaints. With this in mind, he extended the economic measures of the Molé régime, by laws relating to factory reforms and to the reduction of the National Debt. To the industrials, he threw out the sop of legislation for the increase of seaports, for railroad expansion, and for the more rapid development of Algiers. When these laws were under way, Thiers then ventured to test his strength by forcing a vote of confidence on the part of the Deputies. It was a hazardous experiment, but, like so many other bold strokes of his, it succeeded.

In his initial speech of March 4, the President had promised to give, at a later date, a more detailed explanation of his policy. The time came to make a specific pronouncement when Charles de Rémusat, Minister of the Interior, proposed a measure appropriating one million francs as a complement to the *fonds secrets* for 1840. Of this question, Thiers decided to make a vote of necessity and of confidence. As was the custom, the measure was first discussed in committee. The discussion of the measure had necessitated the appearance of the President before the Committee, and once he was before them, these gentlemen began to interrogate him as to the specific intentions and sympathies of his Council. To their question, Thiers replied that his Cabinet was neither Right nor Left, Right Centre nor Left Centre. It was, he asserted, a Ministry of *transaction*, that represented all parties.

This statement alarmed the minority who represented the Right Centre, and who saw in Thiers' words an intimation that he would not follow their dictation. Consequently they expressed certain reservations in their approval of the Council, and intimated their fear, that a Cabinet whose members had not been selected from the old majority, might make more concession than was advisable to the Left, on whose goodwill and support it had been dependent when it was created. The hesitation of this group, however, did not interfere with the measure, and it passed through the Committee without difficulty. But, although the majority had signified their approval of Rémusat's Bill, Thiers was not satisfied, for he beheld in the hesitation of the Right Centre, an attempt to discredit his Ministry in the eyes of all of the Right. He reasoned, and correctly, that this party was manœuvring to form a Coalition against him. When, therefore, the Bill was presented to the House, the President took the opportunity to make a public definition of his policy, and at the same time to persuade the various parties in the Chamber to unite behind him. He was hunting a majority with a vengeance, and the gun that he used was the word *transaction* that he had let slip when the matter of Rémusat's request for additional *fonds secrets* was being discussed in committee. The meaning of this word he now set about to define.

It appears that in his own mind Thiers himself was *transaction*, a symbol of the reconciliation of all party differences, and of their consecration to the welfare of France.

" I do not believe that there exists (in this Chamber) one party that is devoted exclusively to order, and another that is pledged to disorder. I think that all of you who are here desire order, only you understand it differently. There is no absolute difference between you, then, and, if you try to raise this difference, what will be the result? You will be committing the very mistake that brought about the downfall of the Restoration. The Restoration believed that if it ever approached the Opposition, if it even discovered one matter of agreement with the Opposition, it would be lost. Under this delusion, it fought a miserable fight and perished.

THE SECOND MINISTRY

And who was in this Opposition that the Government repulsed? None other than the illustrious Casimir Périer, who saved the social order in his country. We must have no exclusion. Allow me to say that if, in 1830, I threw myself into the arms of friends of order, into the midst of those who are called the friends of order, I did so, because I believed that order was endangered. Later, my convictions separated me from them and threw me into the Opposition. Messieurs, I have seen all of you working for the same purpose; I have seen that there is no one (of you) who is marked out for order or for disorder, that you are all only the friends of the country; and if you now seek to introduce this word *exclusion*, it will bring misfortune to him who pronounces it. . . . I believe that, in this Chamber, there are none but good citizens, and that what they need, is to be enlightened as to each other. Some hold that there are dangers, but these are non-existent. Others believe in possibilities that are not yet born. All that you have to do is to bring about a *transaction* between these (divergent opinions). A Ministry that desires to show you the real condition of your minds shall, if it is heeded, render a great service." [8]

The discourse of March 24, appealed to many, who, as patriots primarily, were above all selfish demands of party. Many of the phrases, however, were not pleasing to the Extreme Left, for to the thinking of these gentlemen, there was too much angling in more conservative waters. Else, why should Casimir Périer be lauded? And what could "possibilities that are not yet born" mean, but another delay for electoral reform? Some of the leaders of the Left were not won by the eloquence of the President. They were coldly *réaliste*. It was Lamartine who arose from among them, to break the spell of the word *transaction*.

The speech of the poet-politician was not tempered

with mercy, and he treated the proposal of reconciliation as foolhardy and dangerous. He turned upon Thiers and cried dramatically : " Whence come you ? From the heart of our political enemies. Where is your support ? Among our adversaries. And without, what forces back you ? Those that calumniate you with the greatest obstinacy." [9] Lamartine's invectives also struck at Barrot, and he charged the latter with having betrayed the cause of the Left, by his recent approval of the formation of the Thiers Ministry when he could have prevented it.

The effect was exactly what Thiers desired ; Barrot's partisans drew nearer the Ministry. Only a little persuasion was needed, a few promises and a few engagements for the more distant future. A slight alteration in the September laws that would allow a greater latitude of freedom to the newspapers, and the announcement that electoral reform would be considered at a later and more convenient time, was the price that the President paid for the support of Barrot's section of the Left. It was a cheap purchase. Thiers gained his majority, and his Cabinet received the vote of confidence that he needed.

The policy of *transaction* was introduced principally, because the Ministry must turn its attention to a matter of foreign affairs that might have grave consequences, if France should be suffering from any great divergence of opinion.

Ever since the final settlement of Belgian independence, the problem of the Near East had been absorbing more and more the attention of the Western European statesmen, and when the ambitious Pasha of Egypt set into operation his plan to extend his dominions to Syria, all Western Europe became alarmed. As a natural consequence of her engagements with the Sultan, Russia had come to the side of the Porte at once. Logical as this step was, England had become alarmed, and had asserted her right to participate in the settlement of the quarrel. There-

THE SECOND MINISTRY

upon, Russia had opened negotiations with England for the purpose of agreeing upon a plan of joint action, and the logical result had been that France, fearful of losing her already small voice in Mediterranean affairs, began to assert her right to participation in the Sultan–Pasha controversy. The names of Palmerston, Brünow, Pasha, and Sultan had been frequently uttered in discussions in the Chamber of Deputies. Even as early as 1835, Thiers, as Deputy, had advocated a firm stand against an Anglo-Russian entente, and had advised, in the event of such an alliance, that France give material assistance to the Pasha. But in February 1840, he was not inclined to believe that such drastic measures would be necessary. The King and his President had come to a complete understanding, in which they remained until Palmerston's antics of July 1840 upset their calculations.

Before Louis Philippe gave Thiers his commission, he had gone over the entire ground carefully, and both of them believed that they had foreseen all the possible complications that might arise.[10] They were one in desiring the maintenance of the Turkish Empire, but at the same time, they acknowledged a benevolent interest in the cause of Mehemet-Ali, for from the Pasha, France had gained considerable trade advantages in Syria, and many had come to believe with Thiers, that France would never have the preponderance at Constantinople that she might have in Egypt. Thiers, in fact, even maintained that Alexandria was the logical place for the establishment of a French sphere of influence in the Mediterranean.[11]

Having been convinced of this opinion, Louis Philippe and the Cabinet were determined to prevent the crushing of the Pasha, by the united efforts of England and Russia. In the spring of 1840, however, neither the King nor the President believed that it would be necessary to use other than diplomatic pressure. They did not think that the two Powers would ever resort to arms against Mehemet-Ali, and for a time, the policy of the French Government consisted in keeping a careful watch on what passed between the young Queen of England and the Tsar. All that official France sought to do, was to gain time.[12] But, if this was to be accomplished, unofficial France must be diverted. This the Government attempted to do, by entertaining the public with glowing reports of the activities of the army in Algiers where the Abd-el-Kader revolt was being suppressed, and by the amusing negotiation of Louis Philippe and Thiers, anent the proposed return of the body of Napoleon I to Paris. It was *à propos* of the latter affair, that Madame Delphine de Girardin launched her remarkable description of Thiers as " the poetical statesman."

" Your patron, Monsieur Thiers, what is he in politics ? A great poet, and that is all. What is he seeking in his dreams of government ? Poetical effects always. He sends our warships across the seas to St. Helena, to *demand* the ashes of the great Emperor, in order that the hero of battles, brought back in triumph from the land of exile, may sleep under the sky of the fatherland, surrounded by his old soldiers. Is that a really serious political idea ? No, but it is a poetical conception, full of grandeur.

" He has constructed a large funeral carriage, that in its lugubrious immensity, passed through the streets of Paris, and carried to a glorious tomb the venerable relics of the victims of July. The names of the heroes were inscribed on an elegant column from the top of which Liberty takes her flight. Is that a really serious political programme ? No, but it is a poetical idea, mythological even, and it is very beautiful.

" He sends to the Pasha, as a mysterious ambassador, Monsieur le Comte Walewski. Is that a really serious political idea ? No, but Monsieur de Walewski in Egypt . . . there is a poetical touch that attracts him.

" Monsieur Thiers solicits for his young wife the

THE SECOND MINISTRY

grand *cordon* of Marie Louise; by dint of persistence he obtains it. Is that a political stroke? No, but it is a graceful, poetical idea to decorate a pretty, little woman with a ribbon white and amaranthine. At least, it is a revolutionary idea.

"Ah! we cannot hear Monsieur Thiers bragging about his revolutionary sympathies, without our blood boiling! That, to us, is absolutely fatuous. He revolutionary? In reality there is not a more conservative and retrogressive administrator in the world. Monsieur Thiers governs entirely *à l'ancienne mode*, by means of a state of siege, a *cabinet noire*, all the old traditions of police, all the old practices of the bureaux, all the antiquated decorum of the ministries; great magnificence, fine dinners, obsequious bows before ambassadors; diamond orders, red sashes, all the old frippery of the Empire, minus the glory, and of the Restoration, minus the dignity. As well, not one reform, not one new idea; of the development of democracy, not a word; of electoral reform, not a word; of the agricultural interests, not an idea; of the welfare of the people, not a thought. What would you! These things are not bright enough for Monsieur Thiers. They have not enough theatricality about them, and their production would not bring him much honour; a statesman who aspires to poetry, must necessarily despise them, they seem to him of the earth, earthy, and cold. Perhaps, they can only have an attraction to a *poet* who aspires to statesmanship (Lamartine)." [13]

While Thiers and his master were bragging about their successes in Algiers and were making remarkable preparations for Napoleon's belated funeral, they were secretly studying the affairs of the Pasha and the Sultan. In fact, much of their personal attention was being given to this perplexing problem. The result of their cogitations was the opening of secret negotiations with the Egyptian

THIERS AND THE FRENCH MONARCHY

Government. For this, the moment was propitious; France was diverted, and Victoria's Government was resting while the young Queen was on her honeymoon with Albert. Palmerston had decreed that the Pasha might only have Egypt, and that he would not be allowed to exercise authority over Syria. Then it was, that Thiers tried to save Mehemet-Ali from the threats of the English and the Russians, by attempting a direct arrangement between Constantinople and Cairo.[14] To cover his tracks, the French Minister issued definite instructions to his envoys at Constantinople and at Alexandria, to be careful not to appear to mediate. "You must not even suggest to the Viceroy too formally a direct arrangement with the Porte, for such counsel would arouse, in England, an antagonism that it would be well for us to avoid. It is enough if we bring Mehemet-Ali to understand how much it will be of advantage to him, if he facilitates the efforts of those who are working to make the attitude of the Porte more favourable to him." [15]

The result of this procedure was seen in June, when the Grand Vizier, Kosrew Pasha, enemy to Mehemet-Ali, was removed from his post, and the Pasha of Egypt responded by sending to the Sultan his most able ambassador, Sami Bey.

This scheme for a direct arrangement was almost a *fait accompli*, when Palmerston heard of the improvement in the situation. The latter believed, or pretended to believe, that this had been done by France with the intention of reaping all the benefits that would accrue to her as peacemaker. To him, the efforts of the French Government appeared to be directed towards the exclusion of Austria, Russia, and England. Proof positive of this, seemed to be the fact that Thiers had almost concluded a separate entente with Prussia in regard to the affairs of the Near East. Had this alliance come to pass, the success of the French plan might have been assured. Both King and President were confident of a favourable outcome.[16] But both of them had failed to take into

THE SECOND MINISTRY

account the temper and character of Palmerston, and while Thiers was eagerly concentrating on a direct arrangement between the Sultan and the Pasha, Palmerston was making efforts to thwart him.

The English Premier, enraged at what he called the selfish policy of France, instructed Ponsonby, his agent at Constantinople, to send emissaries to Syria, to stir up a revolt against Mehemet-Ali. At the same time, unbeknown to Thiers and Guizot, French Ambassador at London, he called a secret conference of Russia, Prussia and Austria. On July 15, he delivered his blow at France, when the four Powers signed the Pact of London that called on the Pasha to evacuate Syria within ten days. If this order was obeyed, the Powers declared that Mehemet-Ali might retain Acre, but if he ignored their demand, he should be deposed. To give force to the proclamation, an English fleet was despatched to the Syrian coast.

The announcement of this ultimatum dumbfounded Thiers, and angered him. He saw in it an utter disregard of France, and an attempt to re-establish her isolation in European affairs. But there was a more personal element in the matter; Thiers interpreted Palmerston's move as an effort to bring about an estrangement between Louis Philippe and his Council.[17] The world was perfectly aware that the French King would support his President, only as long as there was no likelihood of hostilities, but the former's fear of war was equally recognized, and, it was believed, once the phantom of Mars appeared upon the scene, that the King would take to cover. Palmerston's shrewd calculations were not mistaken.

From the date of the publication of the London Pact, the position of the French Ministry became an extremely difficult one. It was, now, no longer possible to divert the attention of the French public from the unfortunate affair of Mehemet-Ali, and Palmerston's action only increased the desire for national grandeur

THIERS AND THE FRENCH MONARCHY

and prestige that had been fostered in France during the period of the Coalition. But although it rallied many rash patriots to the side of Thiers, it lost him again the sympathy of his King. The President, however, had learned a lesson in 1836, and, even in July 1840, he did not want war as a means for re-establishing the influence of his country. Had this been his desire, he would have attempted to call the Chambers in August. He still adhered to his promise that he had given the King, when he resumed the functions of President of the Council; he would not be as rash as he had been in the Spanish affair.

With this in mind, he set about to obtain a modification of the London Pact. He even went so far as to instruct Bresson at Berlin, to ask the interposition of Prussia.[18] When this failed the President advised the Pasha to consider the sacrifice of Syria, in the hope that Palmerston would then relent.[19] But both London and Cairo were obdurate. Thiers had reached an *impasse*. Pacific methods had failed him, and his only resort was to threaten. In despair, he visited the King and asked him to call the classes of 1836, and 1839, to arms, and to demand war credits. The fleet should be increased, and preparations undertaken for the fortification of Paris. He assured him that these measures were only threats to Palmerston, and that they did not mean actual hostilities. To these requests, Louis Philippe, so peace-loving, gave a reluctant consent. But the King was becoming uneasy. During the last days of July, Guizot wrote to Thiers : " Que fera la France ? " The President sent the question to the King. Louis Philippe replied : " Laissons faire." By the end of August, the royal mind was much disturbed. He wrote to Thiers : " Please moderate the tone of the papers." [20] But Monsieur le Président was no longer in the mood to moderate. He saw his dream for France endangered and he feared the ridicule of his opponents. Someone had asked Madame de Lieven, that lovely Russian spy of whose wiles he had been warned, what

THE SECOND MINISTRY

Russia was doing about the scrape of the President of the French Council, and she had replied : " Nous rions." [21] These remarks, and others of a similar nature, irritated him and goaded him on. He wrote to Bresson, that he could not control the Press of Paris.[22] He seemed to be losing his hold. His weaknesses made him the butt of his enemies and supplied fodder for the guns that they trained on him. Beholding him in such a predicament, the Girardin–Lamartine combination could not restrain themselves, and the Viscomte de Launay sharpened her quills to write : " Monsieur Thiers believes in the *grand seigneurs*. When a lord condescends to write him in order to mystify him, he is flattered. When a great lady deigns to call at his house in order to make fun of him, he is flattered. When he is girded with a *grand cordon* of any colour, he is flattered. But you know how they treat those who allow themselves to be flattered. *Tout flatteur vit au dépens de celui qui l'écoute*, and it is for that that we are going to have war, after twenty-five years of peace. God protect France." [23]

Thiers was desperate, but the good-natured King was resolved not to be pushed too far. His attitude to his President was slowly changing from vague uncertainty to actual suspicion. At times, even, Louis Philippe was guilty of duplicity. He allowed Thiers to continue his warlike preparations, but, in private, he remarked to Saint-Aulaire, who came to him after a long conference with the President : " There you are, well instructed, my dear Ambassador ! Your official theme is excellent, but for your own private instruction, let me tell you that I will not allow myself to be carried too far by my little minister. At least, he wants war, and I do not want it ; and when he will not allow me any other resource, then I shall break with him rather than break with Europe." [24]

It required no small amount of courage for the King to take such a stand. He must face not only the anger and the ruses of Thiers, but also the opposition of his own sons and of Leopold of Belgium, his son-in-law, all of whom were at the time heartily in favour of Thiers' policy. He refused to increase the army to six hundred and thirty-nine thousand men, and to mobilize three hundred of the National Guard. He became convinced that Thiers desired war, and he did not agree with Metternich's more accurate diagnosis of the matter : " I never would believe that Monsieur Thiers wants war. He is not a fool. He wants to make a noise, that is all." [25]

Let Thiers cry *war* as loud as he might, let him declare that the Pact of London had revived the Holy Alliance, he did not really desire hostilities. It was a policy of bluff, and in this practice, Guizot and others supported him.[26]

But if the President of the French Council was bluffing, Palmerston was serious. On September 11 Beyrouth was bombarded by the English fleet, and with the aid of Austria, English and Turkish soldiers were landed in Syria. The Sultan proclaimed the deposition of the Pasha. These acts cast Thiers' words back into his teeth. It was time for France to decide what to do.

Conservatives began to wonder if the little President had not gone too far. Some questioned, if he had not been the dupe of Palmerston. Guizot, Duchâtel, Broglie, and others began to withdraw their support from the Council, and when this defection began, Louis Philippe took heart. Thiers found his King more *difficile* and less *aimable*. He spent hours arguing with him. Madame Dosne is almost lachrymose in her description of the scenes that were enacted daily at Auteuil, during the first days of October. " It was like a son speaking to his father, trying to convince him of the dangers that he and his dynasty would run by breaking with the really National party of the country . . . making a complete sacrifice of all personal considerations in order to facilitate a change of Ministry, if the King so desired. The King, eloquent, affectionate, and moved by the sight of such devotion, said to Monsieur Thiers : " There ! if you wanted to be my peace minister, you and I could arrange everything." [27]

THE SECOND MINISTRY

But Louis Philippe would not hear of war, and the President, more than ever convinced that the matter was not a ministerial question, but one of more serious import, continued his entreaties. At last, on October 6, the King consented to send Thiers' Memorandum protesting against the acts of the English Government. At the same time, however, the monarch uttered these words: " I still declare that if I can find a way of getting out of this peaceably, I shall take it." The Note was forwarded on October 8, and, at the same time, the Chambers were convoked for October 28, when the situation was to be exposed to them. The success of the President's policy now hinged on the King's Speech to the Legislative. Thiers desired him to mention the increase of the army, and to declare his firm resolution to negotiate, if necessary, " à tête de cette force." But Louis Philippe refused, and it was for good reason that he declined to join in his minister's plan. He had received encouraging news from England, viâ Belgium, where Leopold, his son-in-law and Victoria's " dear uncle," had been intervening in his behalf. As well, he had conferred at Eu with his Ambassador to London, and he had found Guizot more to his taste in this affair than Thiers. This last was a great blow to the President, for he had been led to believe that Guizot was in complete accord with him.[28] Leopold's news and Guizot's words confirmed the King, who now announced that he would not include in his Speech from the Throne, the phrases that Thiers desired. The result was immediate; the Cabinet of March 1 resigned and Guizot hastened from London to Paris, to assist in the formation of a new Ministry.

The actual events of the Second Ministry of Adolphe Thiers are not nearly so important, as their significance. On the face of it, the Cabinet of March 1, 1840, appears to have been a failure. A ministry, avowedly constitutional, failed and yielded to royal prerogative. Again, as in 1836, Thiers was not thrown out of office by the

THIERS AND THE FRENCH MONARCHY

Chamber, and this fact is not without its importance, as far as the political evolution of the little statesman is concerned.

1822–29 had taught Thiers Orleanism, but he was only an Orleanist, because he believed in " representative monarchy." 1830–40 gave him the opportunity to teach France this lesson in the science of government, but that part of France that could vote, would not listen, and the most unsatisfactory pupil of all had been Louis Philippe. He had begun by trying to enforce this sort of rule through the *Resistance* Party, and he had failed. Again in 1840 he had attempted to establish it through the Left Centre, and had failed. In each instance, the cause for his lack of success had not been the party with which he had been associated, but the King. Consequently, the next logical development was for Thiers to join the Dynastic Opposition. And with this group, he was associated, after October 1840. In fact, from that date, the ex-President became an opponent of the King, although he was none the less a believer in Monarchism, in which faith he remained until the last day of his life. But, unlike his associates, Thiers was not a *coup d'état* monarchist, for his ideal was " representative monarchy," and for it, the consent of the intelligent majority of the country was necessary. That is why he betrayed no enthusiasm for the plots of Prince Louis Napoleon, who, after February 1848, became the rallying point for an Imperial restoration in France. The years that followed 1840, are, therefore, another stage in the political development of Adolphe Thiers, but, they are the age of a more mature accomplishment, and not a period of experiment in governing, as a more detailed study of his efforts will show. In 1840, he beheld his ideal monarchy endangered both by the King and by statesmen, and from that time, he devoted himself to saving it and to driving its enemies from power.

To the minds of many of his contemporaries, Thiers appeared to have failed in 1840. Balzac, for one, attri-

THE SECOND MINISTRY

butes this failure to the fact that he tried to do things without the advice of *Madame-Mère*.[29] This verdict is a great injustice. While Madame Dosne was a great factor in his earlier successes, and while he often sought her counsel, and as often did not have to ask it, for it was offered freely, he never was dominated by her. And, too, the word "Failure" cannot be applied in this case, for, while his Egyptian policy was disowned by his successors, there were many other accomplishments of his administration that remained.

Thiers had done much between March and October 1840. Underneath all the tumult and excitement of the diplomatic warfare that he carried on, there was a steady progress. The little minister was busy laying foundations for a greater France. To win the Centre parties, he urged the increase of railroads, the building of the great port of Saint Nazaire, and the development of the French marine to North and South America. During the critical months of July, August, and September he obtained extraordinary credits for the army and navy. He increased the fortifications of Paris. He raised the salaries of the officers, and improved the *matériel* of the war forces of France.[30] Aided by the co-operation of the Duc d'Orléans, the armies that later won their victories in the Crimea and in Italy, received their first training and development. Assisted by Bugeaud, with whom he did not always agree, he made the colonization of Algiers a permanent policy.

These are things that are often lost in the smoke of political hatreds and passions in which France has had no rival until recent times. These are facts that should be remembered along with the wild plunges and temerity of the little man who was so daring and so dangerous, that, even to-day, he is left by France to slumber in an obscure grave, in *Père Lachaise*.

THIERS AND THE FRENCH MONARCHY

NOTES TO CHAPTER XIII

[1] *Revue Parisienne*, July 25, 1840, p. 108 ; Balzac.
[2] Madame Dosne's Notes, p. 173. Bibliothèque Thiers : T MSS. Foli in 4°., 32.
[3] *Ibid.*, p. 176.
[4] Louis Philippe, February 25 and 26, 1840, to Thiers. Bibliothèque Nationale, 20, 611, 273 and 274.
[5] Viscomte de Launay : *Lettres Parisiennes*, III. 73-4 : July 31, 1840.
[6] Regnault : *Histoire de Huit Ans*, I, 16.
[7] Thiers : *Discours*, IV. 464 : March 4, 1840.
[8] *Ibid.*, IV, 489 : March 24, 1840.
[9] Quoted. Regnault : *Histoire de Huit Ans*, I. 29.
[10] Thiers, Paris, April 20, 1840, to Guizot. Bibliothèque Nationale, 20,613, 592. Thiers : *Discours*, November 25, 1840.
[11] Minautz, Consul, Alexandria, May 2, 1836, to Thiers. Ministèr des Affaires Étrangères, 5, 222.
[12] Thiers, Paris, March 7, 1840, to Guizot. Bibliothèque Nationale, 20,613, 572.
[13] Viscomte de Launay : *Chroniques Parisiennes*, II. 99-100 : December 5, 1840.
[14] Thiers, Paris, March 12, 1840, to Guizot. Bibliothèque Nationale, 20,613, 574. Guizot, London, March 12, 1840, to Thiers. Bibliothèque Nationale, 20,610, 27.
[15] Thiers, Paris, March 17, 1840, to Cochelet. Bibliothèque Nationale, 20,613, 576. See also Thiers, Paris, April 17, 1840, to Cochelet, 20,613, 589. Thiers, Paris, April 17, 1840, to Sainte-Aulaire, 20,613, 590. Guizot, London, April 18, 1840, to Thiers, 20,610, 61. Thiers, Paris, April 28, 1840, to de Partois, 20,613, 596. Thiers, Paris, April 28, 1840, to Guizot, 20,613, 597. Cochelet, Alexandria, May 26, 1840, to Thiers, 20,609, 6. Same to same, June 15, 1840, 29,609, 12. Bibliothèque Nationale.
[16] Thiers, Paris, July 3, 1840, to Cochelet. Bibliothèque Nationale, 20,613, 614. Thiers, Paris, July 30, 1840, to Guizot. Bibliothèque Nationale, 20,613, 610. Thiers, Paris, July 4, 1840, to Bresson. Bibliothèque Nationale, 28,613, 616.
[17] Thiers, Paris, July 4, 1840, to Guizot. Bibliothèque Nationale, 20,613, 622. Duchesse de Dino : *Mémoires*, II. 332. Carlsbad, July 17, 1840.
[18] Bresson, Berlin, July 25, 1840, to Thiers. Bibliothèque Nationale, 20,608, 302-4.
[19] Thiers, Paris, July 29, 1840, to Cochelet. Bibliothèque Nationale, 20,613, 601.
[20] Louis Philippe. Saint Cloud, July 26, 1840, to Thiers. Bibliothèque Nationale, 20,611, 353. Louis Philippe, Eu, August 22, 1840, to Thiers. Bibliothèque Nationale, 20,611, 354.

THE SECOND MINISTRY

[21] Czartoryski, Paris, August 6, 1840. to Thiers. Bibliothèque Nationale, 20, 608, 75.
[22] Thiers, Paris, August 6, 1840, to Bresson. Bibliothèque Nationale, 20,613, 638.
[23] Viscomte de Launay : *Lettres Parisiennes*, III. 76, July 31, 1840.
[24] Quoted, Thureau–Dangin : *Histoire de la Monarchie de Juillet*, IV. 345.
[25] Sainte-Aulaire, Marien Baden, August 10, 1840, to Thiers. Bibliothèque Nationale, 20,612, 542.
[26] Guizot, London, August 1, 1840, to Thiers. Bibliothèque Nationale, 20,610, 210. Bresson, Berlin, September 17, 1840, to Thiers. Bibliothequè Nationale, 20,608, 316.
[27] Madame Dosne's Notes, 1840, pp. 194–5. Bibliothèque Thiers : T MSS. Fol. in 4°., 32.
[28] Guizot : *Mémoires*, V. 264–72. See also Madamoiselle Dosne's copy of Thureau-Dangin, MSS. notes on v. IV. p. 346. Bibliothèque Thiers, 8°., R 18. Louis Philippe, Paris, October 19, 1840, to Thiers. Bibliothèque Nationale, 20,611, 287.
[29] *Revue Parisienne*, August 25, 1840.
[30] In all, between July 29 and September 21, 1840, Thiers demanded 120,194,250 francs for military and naval development. Calmon : *Histoire Parlementaire des Finances de France*, IV. 172–3.

CHAPTER XIV

LEADER OF THE DYNASTIC OPPOSITION (1840-46)

THE return of Guizot from England, and his subsequent appointment as a member of the Council, marked the reconciliation of Louis Philippe and the *Doctrinaires*. To effect such a reunion, each of the contracting parties had had to make sacrifices; the King must consent to *Doctrinaire* theories of government, while Guizot and his circle must relinquish all pretensions to a strong nationalistic foreign policy, and accept the more pacific system desired by the King.

The establishment of an Orléans–Guizot *entente* had but one inevitable and logical effect upon the retiring President: from the time of its formation, Thiers became a member of the Dynastic Opposition. In fact, there was no other place in the Chamber where he could go. But, although he was forced by circumstances into the Opposition, the behaviour of himself and that of his friends, was never fractious. Their criticisms, rarely bitter, were thoroughly in the line of constitutional opposition, and at first they made no attempt to embarrass the new Government. It was inevitable, however, that a conflict should come, for Guizot's Government was committed to the undoing of Thiers' strenuous foreign policy, and once this policy was put into operation, the retired minister, or his friend de Rémusat, must take the floor in defence of their measures.

The first task of Guizot was to settle the complications that had arisen out of the Near Eastern crisis. He must calm England and save the honour of France at the same time. It was on November 25, 1840 that he exposed his plan to the Deputies. At once, Thiers and Berryer

LEADER OF DYNASTIC OPPOSITION

of the Right, arraigned the new Cabinet.[1] The defence of the ministerial party was not of the most high-minded sort, and they even accused Thiers of having used the crisis that he had created in July, 1840, to make money on the Exchange.[2] Finally, Guizot won his point in the Chamber, when the Deputies gave him the vote of confidence that he desired, and on July 13, 1841, the quarrel of the Sultan and the Pasha was settled, when Mehemet-Ali was allowed to retain Egypt and France was admitted into the European concert. This initial foreign policy of the Guizot régime did not win him any great popularity, for it was clear to the world that France had been humiliated. In the meantime, his early efforts at internal administration were not any more successful.

Guizot had announced that he would repress all signs of anarchy and would abide by the September laws. He instigated a very rigid enforcement of the Press laws, and even applied their principles to all sorts of publications. In brief, he tried to outdo Périer, but Guizot, the schoolmaster, had neither Périer's personality, nor his political acumen. He was cold and harsh, unfeeling and inconsiderate. He failed to realize that a necessary corner-stone to a policy of repression in France, was popularity. The latter qualification, he possessed to a very small degree. His methods were not relished by the Chambers, not even by his friends, and he had the unfortunate ability of driving his opponents into the arms of the extremists. Barrot, often amenable, became an *enfant terrible* in the Legislative, and Thiers was driven by the minister into making his first pronouncements, that favoured a slight modification in the September laws, whose chief guardian he had been, and into advocating a minimum enlargement of the electorate.[3]

The personality of the new Minister alienated many of the most able statesmen in France, and within a short time, he could command but few worthy men in the political world. But it was not only the question of a lack of personal magnetism; Guizot lacked, as well, vision and tact. His blindness caused him to ignore social changes, the consideration of which might have been of assistance to him. Instead, they became in time the agents of his own embarrassment. This minister detested anything new, and, something new of which he was not cognizant, was growing up under his very eyes.

A new social evolution was in the process of development among the bourgeoisie. In that stratum of society, two new groups were developing, the Catholic bourgeoisie and the Aristocracy of Business. In the one reposed a new and revived Faith; in the other a new wealth and a new economic view-point.

The fathers of the former had been born of the eighteenth century and had been steeped in Voltaire, Rousseau, and religious scepticism. But, as is so often the case, the second generation became absolutely different. Where the fathers had been atheists, the sons became Catholics. The latter upheld the Church, its Faith and its freedom, and in upholding its freedom, they demanded that the right of the Church to teach, be recognized. They opposed the *monopole universitaire*, the exclusive predominance of the State in matters of public instruction. In other words, these men were of the generation that frequented Saint Sulpice, the centre of the Catholic revival, listened to Lacordaire, attended the courses of Montalembert, and of the saint-like Frédéric Ozanam, and that applauded the articles of Louis Veuillot, when they appeared in the new Catholic paper *L'Univers*. Here was a group of growing, intelligent, patriotic, Catholic youth, loyal to the throne and to its avowed principles of democracy, who saw in the Orléans Monarchy but one great contradiction—religious freedom did not exist. And to their minds, the régime of Louis Philippe would be a lie, until it allowed the Church the right to instruct its children. Monsieur Guizot, on the other hand, chose to ignore them as long as he could. He did not go to Mass, he attended

LEADER OF DYNASTIC OPPOSITION

the *Temple*, and when he thought that he saw in the Catholic Revival the nucleus of a revived Bourbon Opposition, he was only giving another proof of his blindness.

In contrast to the Catholic bourgeoisie stood the new class, so often called the *Chevaliers d'Industrie*. They were born of the Industrial Revolution that had been encouraged and aided by the Périer, Molé, and Thiers régimes. These men were not concerned with religion, but with gold. They had entered upon a race for wealth. They were conservative by instinct, but indifferent to the form of the Government. They would favour the adoption of any policies that were novel and productive of comfort and pleasure. Their spokesman before the public was Émile de Girardin, business man, Deputy, editor of *La Presse*, and husband of the brilliant Viscomte de Launay. They, too, had their preachers and professors. They were carried away by the zeal of Thiers, the reasoning of Jaubert, and the eloquence of Lamartine, while the cold, pedantic phrases of Guizot disgusted them.

Here were elements for a new Opposition, and gradually these men drew nearer to the Moderate Republicans of the Left Centre. Dissentient bourgeois, persecuted young Catholics, and disappointed party leaders slowly came closer to those who had for some time previously been demanding electoral reform, less stringent laws, and labour legislation. This was, in part, the origin of the Dynastic Opposition.

Oddly enough, Guizot did not make any attempt to win either group; perhaps, he was too proud. At any rate, the only notice that he took of them was to warn his *Doctrinaires* against them, and to redouble his efforts to maintain his control of those two hundred thousand electors who paid two hundred francs in taxes. Probably, he could have established an honourable agreement with one group or the other, but he preferred to retain his hold on the older classes by the distribution of

THIERS AND THE FRENCH MONARCHY

Government favours, and by trying to maintain the law that Government functionaries might sit in the Chamber of Deputies. Apparently, the dream of this cold calculating minister was a Chamber of Deputies composed of the judges of the courts, *huissiers*, Government clerks, and secretaries! As a matter of fact, it never became so bad as that, but that was one of the methods that he used to ensure his control, and it became one of the principal charges that the new Opposition brought against him. Guizot's system, however, was not put to a test, until the reopening of the Chambers in December 1841.[4]

In the meantime, the elements of the Opposition were beginning to coalesce, under the leadership of Thiers. While he was not yet definitely allied with Barrot, the former had established close relations with the leaders of the Left, through his friendship with Duvergier de Hauranne, descendant of the famous man of that name, who had been the friend of Jansenius and of Arnaud. Like his forbear, de Hauranne was a man of letters and a *publiciste*, and he boasted of political and religious principles as advanced as those of the Left Centre. Through him, therefore, Thiers was able to come into contact with the Barrot group, and with him, Thiers consulted as to what he should do during the approaching session of the Chambers. De Hauranne counselled more activity:

> "I believe that by talking more, you will increase your influence rather than diminish it. In England, the parliamentary chiefs of the Ministry or of the Opposition, are always ready to give their attitude on everything, on finances as well as on policy, on legislation, as on commercial matters. You are the only man in France who can do that, and Monsieur Guizot, who in politics, is your only worthy rival, cannot combat with you for a minute on other subjects. When we were with Guizot, and against

LEADER OF DYNASTIC OPPOSITION

you, it was a principle that we recognized and that made us very angry. 'Guizot,' we said, 'is good for a storm and when discussion has reached a certain point, but when affairs in general are to be discussed he is no good, while Thiers holds his own on this new ground.' I hope, then, that as chief of the Opposition, you will not abandon this powerful means of action no more than you did when you were chief of the Ministry. Excuse me, I beg you, if I send you sermons. You know that is my *specialty*, and that, in the party, I am both preacher and whipper-in." [5]

When the Chamber opened, Thiers followed his friend's advice; he attacked Guizot concerning the final arrangements made with Mehemet-Ali.[6] His speech was able, but he did not let himself out; he was waiting for a better occasion that came in February, 1842. At that time, Guizot had to stand his first test of strength.

On December 20, 1841, he had agreed to a treaty with England in regard to the Right of Search. This treaty, and others that had preceded it, had been drawn up against those who were still carrying on an illicit traffic in slaves. The New Convention allowed more extensive efforts on the part of the signatory Powers. France was undoubtedly in favour of the abolition of such a nefarious practice, but, in 1842, the Opposition feared that England, who possessed the largest fleet, might, by such an arrangement as the treaty provided, obtain a superior right to police the seas. When the results of the negotiation were presented before the Chamber, therefore, Billaut attacked it, and Thiers seconded his efforts. The latter exposed to his colleagues the dangerous precedent that might be established if English ships were allowed to search French boats.[7] The attack of the two men, who were reinforced by Berryer and Barrot, caused the Ministry to withdraw the treaty. Guizot's power was endangered for a moment, and English sentiment against France ran high. In a few days, the Minister was almost in the position that Thiers had experienced with Mehemet-Ali. But the Cabinet was saved, when the King intervened, by dissolving the Chamber and by calling for new elections.

It was an opportune time to ask for the opinion of the country. The last proposal of the Government had been to establish a network of railroads in France, and this proposal, it was believed, would bring the embarrassed Council the votes of the industrials. In such a hope, however, the King and his ministers were not entirely justified. Sectional interests blocked the plan. Thiers, as Deputy from Aix, favoured the proposal, if it would mean the establishment of a direct communication between Provence and the Île de France, and, like him, each Deputy was concerned with the needs of his own region.[8] Thus it was, that the local interests of the Deputies prevented a real gain in popular favour for the Monarchy. On July 9, the elections were announced. The result was significant, but Guizot failed to note its real importance. While the Ministry gained a majority of seventy-five, its support from Paris was considerably decreased. The capital returned only two ministerial candidates, and the remaining ten candidates from that district, were from the Left. It was the provinces that had reacted to Guizot's system, and had given him their support.

Nevertheless, the election was not the victory of Guizot but of the King. Greater than Guizot at this time was Louis Philippe, who could count on the loyalty of Thiers and his followers, if not their sympathy. But the pedant Minister did not perceive this fact, and an event that occurred in July 1842 should have made it evident to him and to his King. Had both of them realized it, Guizot could have retired, and the rule of Louis Philippe in France might have been saved.

On July 13, the Duc d'Orléans, son of the King, was killed in a carriage accident. The tragic death of the

LEADER OF DYNASTIC OPPOSITION

heir to the throne, caused great sorrow throughout France. All regretted the gracious, pleasing, and able prince, but not very many realized at the time, that the accident was a blow to the July Monarchy itself. His popularity, common-sense, and liberal sympathies might have stemmed the tide and checked the pernicious practices of Guizot. But, by his death, an awful gap was created in the royal succession; a King, already sixty-nine years old who had as his heir, an infant of four years.[9] All of France was anxious, and especially all of those who were sincere adherents of the July Monarchy. Louis Philippe could not live for ever, even now he was showing signs of age; and the Regency that seemed destined to come, might result in the control of affairs slipping into the hands of the Legitimists, or, even, of Republicans.

All eyes were turned to Neuilly where the bereaved King was closeted with his distressed family; but many eyes too turned to the Deputy from Aix, who had so frequently asserted his loyalty to the Crown, in spite of the fact that he was the leader of the Dynastic Opposition. Would he stand by his colleagues, or by the King? It must have hurt the proud Guizot, if he realized it at all, that next the King, Thiers was the most-discussed man in France during July and August 1842. The very peculiar position that the Deputy occupied and the sentiment of many Frenchmen in regard to him, is clearly indicated in a letter written to him immediately after the death of the Duke.

> " We wish that you were at Paris; you are one of the greatest props of this dynasty, and the terrible blow that it has received has weakened it. Unless I am very much mistaken, the death of the Duc d'Orléans changes all situations, and modifies seriously public feeling. For several years, your strong point has been the reaction of national sentiment against the foreigner. We knew that you were strongly

THIERS AND THE FRENCH MONARCHY

opposed to the King from the moment that he had to pronounce for or against intervention. Many intelligent people thought that the King, founder of the dynasty, was forgetting that a little war made *à propos* and under favourable circumstances, renders thrones popular and solid. France was not brave for the moment, but she was beginning to feel that she had made enough sacrifices for peace, and the blind hatred of England that was evident everywhere, showed itself in a disposition, not intelligent but undeniable, to turn our regards and actions to internal matters. You could control and direct this movement, and if the occasion should not come under the present King, you were regarded as necessary for the (coming) reign of the Duc d'Orléans, who was more forceful than his father.

" Until that time should come, the various shades of the Opposition gave you their voices in the Chamber and tried to make use of you. But their efforts were without danger to the dynasty, and even from the beginning, they could be turned to the profit of your own ideas. The Legitimists thought to check the King by supporting your opposition to a systematic peace, and by demanding your support to increase the number of their Deputies. The Republicans, who have no leader, liked to say that your only fault was a lack of ambition. The Dynastic Left obtained your support for certain internal reforms and hoped, mistakenly, to make you go one day beyond the limit that your common-sense had set. . . . But now, there is no second reign. According to the views of an old man, we will have, perhaps, the unpopularity of a regent. We will certainly have the weakness of a child. Will France, who had not enough energy to risk the chances of a war, when the succession was assured, have the courage, now that her dynasty will be endangered from within by Republicans and

LEADER OF DYNASTIC OPPOSITION

by *prétendants*? Will not the first danger be from the Legitimists? What great rôle may the Opposition play in such a situation? The Extreme wings become menacing, suspect, and they compromise their allies. National feeling, already so feeble, is snuffed out by the uncertainties of the country. The death of the King hangs over our heads; will it be the signal for a general panic? . . . You are the support of the dynasty against the Legitimists. You are the only minister who can control the interior. You have in this respect, I think, the confidence of the King and the country; there is no doubt of it. I do not speak for anyone. I have no commission to write you. But I believe that the hour is a solemn one. You know that I am devoted to you. I repeat what I hear many say: they declare that your mission from the very day of July 13, is to retrieve for the Crown its popularity and its security." [10]

That Thiers heeded the plea of the editor of the *Constitutionnel*, who wrote the above letter, subsequent events will show.
He first learned of the news from Mignet, and, when the latter wrote him, he issued a summons even more imperative than that of Merriam :

" I suppose that you will leave Vichy and come here, as soon as you receive this sad news; all those who have been in your position, or in positions less important, are sure to return. Man of the July Revolution and of the Dynasty, you must be here at a time that is so critical for both of them. You must see the King; you must be present at the funeral of the Duc, and you must be a party to the question of the Regency that will be raised. Think much on the conduct that you shall observe. It is one of the most important moments of your life.

THIERS AND THE FRENCH MONARCHY

Do not hesitate to come; (your presence) is the desire of all your friends. . . . Prepare to render greater services than ever to your country."[11]

It was a serious Thiers who set out at once for Paris. There can be no doubt of his admiration for the Duke, with whom his relations had always been pleasant.[12] His feeling, too, for the King was sincere and profound; he was visibly touched by the sight of Louis Philippe at Neuilly.[13] But, sad as the situation was, there remained a more serious question in the mind of the Deputy; the future of the kingdom of France and the part that he should play in determining it. As Merriam had written, a weak Regency might end in a Republic or a Bourbon Restoration; the triumph of the Extreme Left, or of the Extreme Right, with both of whom Thiers had flirted. 1842 would be the test, and out of it, Thiers emerged more of a patriot than a politician.

Never for a moment, does there appear to have been the slightest doubt in his mind as to the course that he should pursue. He was inclined to fight for a strong Regency in spite of the certain opposition of both extremes. If necessary, he would take the part of the widowed Duchesse d'Orléans, over whom Republican and Legitimist were hoping to gain an ascendancy. His interview with the King decided him. Louis Philippe was opposed to the plan that, upon his own death, his daughter-in-law should be Regent. The wise monarch feared the rule of a woman, and he desired that the Duc de Nemours, who was less popular than his lamented brother, but serious and capable, should be named as Regent. To this plan Thiers agreed, and he pledged the King his entire support. It was understood, however, that their conversation should be kept a secret. Otherwise, some of Thiers' associates might suspect that he had come to Neuilly to arrange a comfortable berth for himself.[14]

Having given his promise to support Nemours, and to

LEADER OF DYNASTIC OPPOSITION

desist, for a time, from his policy of Opposition, Thiers went his way. His task was not an easy one, for it was certain that his pledges would lose him many of his followers. He declared, however, that he was resigned to a retirement from politics, after he had fulfilled his engagements to the King, and to the accomplishment of these he now set out to work with all his customary energy.[15]

The Place Saint-Georges became a sort of general head-quarters for all of those who were loyal to the House of Orléans. There they received their orders. Poor Madame Dosne was furious that a torpid liver kept her at Vichy. " Oh that the cursed *saison d'eaux* was ended, and that I could bring you your wife and watch over *tous mes petits à la fois*. I hope to be in Paris by the last of the month, and even sooner, if anything of importance occurs."[16] Until then, she and Madame Thiers will only have the consolation of displaying their new Court mourning at Vichy! Perhaps Madame Dosne hoped that the tragedy might again bring her son-in-law into the Government. Others suspected that this might be the case.[17] But there does not appear to have been even an official hint of such an appointment at this time. Meanwhile, Thiers was continuing his labours for the King. He gathered at this house the editors-in-chief of the *Courrier*, *Siècle*, and *Constitutionnel*, and made them promise not to embarrass the plan that the Government proposed to recommend in regard to the question of the Regency.[18]

In August, the King's desire was laid before the Chamber. It provided, in the event of the King's death before the young Duc d'Orléans had attained his eighteenth year, that Nemours should assume the Regency. Up rose the coryphæi of the Opposition; Lamartine and Ledru-Rollin howled it down. Tocqueville attacked it calmly and dispassionately. Finally, on August 20, the climax of the debate was reached, when Thiers arose to deliver one of his finest speeches. 1842 and 1870 are the high-water marks of his career. The patriot, eloquent, and inconsiderate of party, or of self, appears. It required courage to deny so flatly his suspected Republicanism, to define his avowed Liberalism, and to explain his belief in the King, although he was leader of the phalanx that opposed the royal policies.[19] It was by a call to loyalty, a truly spiritual, political argument, that he won his audience.

His efforts triumphed, and the cause that he supported was victorious. He had merited well of his King. But although he won his case, he lost many political allies, and he retired from the scene to turn again to his studies. His retreat, however, was a glorious one, for the plaudits of many Frenchmen followed him. " You are a patriot above all ; " " You love your country much ; " " You are loyal to your King." [20] Six years later, he was to make another retreat, but how different it would be ! With one or two unimportant exceptions, he refrained from parliamentary debates from August 1842 to January 16, 1844. He had observed his promises to the King, and now, he would refrain as long as possible from embarrassing a dynasty that must have time to recover from the great crisis that it had just traversed.

When Thiers retired into the bosom of his family, it was not to rest; there was a task of another sort before him. When the Regency crisis was at its height, he had written to Madame Dosne : " I believe that I am the only one who can save the country, but I need retirement and quiet. I need to give others a rest from me, and myself a rest from them. . . . The example of the Duc de Broglie attracts me. I am tempted to devote myself to the pursuit of my own satisfactions." [21] These satisfactions were none other than the studies for the *History of the Consulate and the Empire*, for which he had been making preparations ever since 1838.

In 1841, he and Madame Thiers had made quite an extensive tour of Germany. Incidentally, it was the first journey that had not been graced with the presence of

THE STUDY OF THIERS AT THE PLACE SAINT GEORGES.

LEADER OF DYNASTIC OPPOSITION

Madame-Mère. In search of data for Napoleon, they visited Cologne, Berlin, Dresden, Austerlitz, Vienna, and Prague. Their efforts were facilitated by the courtesy of the German officials who received them as semi-public personages, and afforded them all the privileges accorded to retired officials of a foreign Government. It was the visits to the battle-fields that gave Thiers his greatest delight. To his secretary, Monsieur Martin, he wrote of one excursion :

" I spent an entire day, the 8th, at the battle-field of Austerlitz. I know it well now, and the study was one of the most interesting that I have ever made. You cannot understand great events without visiting the places themselves ; you cannot estimate the tact and *sûreté de l'esprit* of Napoleon, unless you examine the physical conditions that determined his conduct. This is especially true of Austerlitz. A quarter of a mile ahead or behind, and all would have been lost instead of marvellously won." [22]

The travels in Germany had increased his desire to begin writing, and, after August, 1842, this became his principal occupation. Perhaps also the words of advice that Mignet sent him made him increase his pace : " I hope before your return to public affairs, that you shall have finished your History. But hurry ; politics may yet seize upon you, your vows and own wishes to the contrary." [23] And so, Thiers became again a man of letters. Where before, in his study, he had entered long discussions on political matters and played a whole orchestra of newspapers, he now devoted himself to researches, pored for hours over great maps that littered the room, and kept his secretary copying notes or receiving dictation, at a furious rate. His conversation was entirely about armies, navies, imperial administration, commissaries, and military tactics. What he had studied in the morning, he discussed in his salon in the evening. In the summer he entered his study at five. His library, which served as a work-room, was long and well lighted. On the walls, hung enormous reproductions of Italian masterpieces. Atop the book-cases were busts of great men. Down the middle of the room, ran a long oak table on which he could spread maps of great size. He developed a passion for maps. In this room, he worked until the late afternoon, when he rested and, then, prepared himself to go to the theatre, to attend a *soirée*, or to receive at home his friends and admirers.[24]

But Thiers was still a man of fantasies and of varied caprices, and history was not his only interest. He varied his work with other hobbies. He gathered a collection of tropical plants and rare birds. He had two gazelles that were his particular pets. At one time, he was engrossed in the construction of a model of a palace which, he said, he and his wife would build at Rome, whither they would retire to spend their declining years. These were his extravagances, and they were harmless, for they were *extravagances de l'esprit*; he never indulged in the more fashionable distractions of gambling, and of frequenting the races.

While Thiers was discussing art, history, tropical plants, and architecture with those who called to see him, Madame Dosne, who could not understand these things, but retained her interest in politics, was keeping a weather-eye open for an opportunity for her son-in-law. She was impatient with his resolve to abstain from debates. She read the papers assiduously, and kept him advised on *affaires*. Her salon became known as " L'asile où l'arsenal, peut-être, de nos hommes politiques mécontents et desenchantés." [25] If Thiers did not always participate in her political discussions, it was probably because *Madame-Mère* was becoming more Radical than her son-in-law, and was rapidly developing sentiments that were almost Republican.

During the period of Thiers' retirement, matters were

LEADER OF DYNASTIC OPPOSITION

not going well with the Government. Guizot's party was holding its own, but that was all. How different the story of the succeeding years might have been, if the King had only joined with those who came to his side during the crisis of 1842! But Louis Philippe could not take them, for he was not bold enough to pursue the course of diplomacy that they desired; he could not bring himself to abandon the policy of concessions on which he had embarked. And so, these continued. Between 1842 and 1844, France yielded to England on several occasions, and the efforts that the Government made to obscure these affairs by continuing the conflict of Algiers, and by planting French influence in Guinea, Madagascar, and Tahiti were not successful. Frenchmen of the Opposition were well aware of the situation, but for the moment, they remained silent. Two matters, however, aroused them to the point of making a vigorous protest, for both of them appeared in the light of dangerous indications of a tendency on the part of the Government to accept dictation from London.

When the British Government objected to the establishment of a Franco-Belgian Customs Union, Guizot and his companions abandoned a project that might have been of great commercial advantage to France. Again, when Queen Victoria announced that she could not approve of the match, Louis Philippe meekly stopped the negotiations for a marriage between his son, the Duc d'Aumale, and a young Princess of Spain. These incidents made silence too painful, and as the opening of a new session of the Deputies drew near, preparations were begun by the Opposition to resume their attacks on Guizot.

Again, Thiers began to emerge more frequently from his seclusion, and his friend Duvergier de Hauranne redoubled his efforts to encourage this practice.

" I begin to hope," wrote the latter, " that, at the next session, I shall be free. I desire it very much for many reasons. It is not only because, like you, I am disgusted with political affairs and very uncertain in regard to the future. But, without pretending to break the Cabinet immediately, there is an attitude to be taken, and a party to be re-formed. That is worth the trouble of two or three months, and I learn, with pleasure, that you think as I do. . . . You are struck with the ruin of our military conditions; and I am especially impressed by the daily increasing dullness and stupidity of our diplomacy, and by the lowness in spirits, corruption of character, and general deadness of our internal situation. If that continues, the *reign* (to use Lamartine's word) will have the honour of having reduced France to the rank of a secondary Power, and of having destroyed, in their essentials, the institutions for which we have fought for fifteen years." [26]

The *reign* referred to Guizot's régime, and the attack that must be made on it, began as soon as the Chamber convened.

The first matter to be discussed by the Deputies, was the Reply to the Throne. Louis Philippe had been unwise enough to declare in the Address with which he opened the Parliament, that order had been maintained everywhere, and that France was extending her influence beyond her borders with every confidence. Guizot, who had inserted this phrase in the King's Speech, was thinking of Algiers, Madagascar, and Tahiti. Had he forgotten the fate of the Customs Union with Belgium and the Spanish marriage? If the memory of the Minister was poor, that of the Opposition was good, and they undertook to refresh his mind. An occasion for so doing was afforded when Guizot's minions proposed that the following phrase should be incorporated in the Deputies' Reply: " There, Sire, is France as she has been under your reign, and as she has become through the systematic and logical development of her institutions. We con-

LEADER OF DYNASTIC OPPOSITION

template, with profound thankfulness to Providence, the prosperity of our country."

This was too much for Gustave de Beaumont, the friend of Alexis de Tocqueville, and he proposed for this sentence a substitute that he claimed was more sincere. " We trust that, fortified and wisely developed, these institutions will assure to France the benefits of a parliamentary government, a government, the care of which is given to us and which we should maintain in all its integrity and purity." [27] Beaumont then proceeded to discuss the decline of clean political methods in France, and the decadence of a genuine parliamentary system.

Following Beaumont, Thiers arose, and proceeded to break his self-imposed silence. He compared the government of France under Guizot to that under Molé, when the principle of " representative monarchy " was entirely lacking. Concessions must be made to public opinion.

" Since order was re-established in France, that is, since 1836, I have always thought that the real system of government consisted in the art of making concessions that were *à propos*. . . .

" Now, you will say to me : but what concessions ? In order to create this broad basis of government, in order to attract what are called intermediate opinions, in a word, to gain votes, are you going to give over the institutions of the country to another rearrangement, as one gives children something to destroy, in order to keep them occupied ? No, without a doubt. If, in our institutions, there is nothing to reconsider, we must not destroy anything, even to gain votes. As to myself, I am not fond of innovations. One of my most honourable friends, who is no longer a Deputy, but who serves his country well in Greece, said, ' I hate progress.' Messieurs, I will not use those words ; I regard them as extravagant, but I will say that, in a time so commonly regarded as a period of progress, I have a certain fear of progress. Therefore, I need not be suspected of a taste for reform; but when I see what is happening around us, I speak frankly, I am not among those who hold that there are no reforms to be made; on the contrary, I am convinced that there are reforms, useful, important, safe, and urgent." [28]

These remarks were received warmly by the Left. Once Achilles-Thiers left his tent he wended his way towards the tent of Barrot. But this was not the final step towards an actual union, for Thiers had not yet discussed definitely the matter of electoral reform. Although silent on this question, he referred, however, to another sort of reform, the mention of which must have struck home, for it was a direct thrust at Guizot's methods:

"There is a dependence of Ministry to Deputy, of Deputy to elector; this is an honourable and excellent dependence. It is that of public opinion based on the appreciation of the country's interests. That sort of dependence I do not repel. But there is another sort that is becoming more general in France, and that alarms me. It does not exist in England. On the day of an election in England, there are hideous scenes, scenes of debauch which the gold of the aristocracy makes possible. Yes, there are hideous scenes, but on the morrow, the members of the Parliament are free, completely free. With us, on the other hand, election day is a day of sobriety . . . but on the morrow, the dependence begins; it continues and increases from election to election; for services rendered, the obligation to recompense them increases. I do not wish to exaggerate here these references to corruption, of which a man of the government should only avail himself with great care. I do not cite facts that have struck everyone. Beware of one

LEADER OF DYNASTIC OPPOSITION

thing; *often* a government of favours is called an absolute Government. With truth, it has been said, and we have seen many examples of it in history, that in an absolute government, which is the government of the Court, one must please in order to succeed. Take care that the ' representative government ' in whose train we are following, does not become the government of favours reversed, and that, in order to please above, it fails to please below." [29]

This was enough for one day, but at the end, the indefatigable orator announced that at a later date he would attack the foreign policy of the Guizot Ministry. At least, he had the good grace to allow his rival the time to prepare his defence!

Thiers had collaborated with Beaumont when he denounced the internal policy of Guizot: his allies in his assault on French diplomacy, were Billaunt, Duvergier, de Hauranne and other leaders of the Left. The fact that Thiers and these men found themselves so often in agreement, was not without a significance for the future; for Thiers, it meant the formation of a new political party, and for Guizot, it meant the development of a *bloc* of the Centre parties that would eventually wreck his every move. Oddly enough, it was the Minister himself, who hastened the completion of this new Opposition. More concessions to England were the cause.

France had established a protectorate at Tahiti. This act had displeased the British Government and its subjects, for in Tahiti there were many British colonists. The latter resented the action of the French Government and, led by one Pritchard, attempted to arouse among the natives, a spirit of opposition to their " protectors." The effort succeeded, and the British agent finally excited the native rulers to such an extent that an insult was given to the French officials. Admiral Du Petit Thouars avenged the insult, and later one of his officers arrested Pritchard. At this, England demanded satisfaction, and, to the astonishment of the Left and the Right alike, Guizot agreed to pay an indemnity. About the same time, France yielded to the demand of the British Government that she settle her quarrel with Morocco, a disagreement that had developed incidental to the pacification of Algiers. Great was the anger in the Chamber when these facts became known, and in January 1845, the full force of the union against Guizot, that had been gradually developing among the Deputies, was felt for the first time. Molé, Montalivet, Lamartine, Ledru-Rollin, and Thiers stormed the Government.[30] During this debate, when Thiers delivered his diatribes in which he accused the Government of gross negligence and weakness in regard to Morocco, Tahiti, and English dictatorship, the session had to be suspended because of the applause afforded him.[31]

Thiers and Guizot were now avowed enemies, and yet, there was a sort of chivalry of frankness between them, that is quite typical of the two men. Some time after the fray of January 21, 1845, Guizot met his opponent, by chance, at the house of Madame la Princesse de Lieven. As the Member of the Council shook hands with the leader of the Opposition, he remarked: " You want to overthrow me. But I warn you, we are not willing and you will be forced to throw us out by the door." To this Thiers replied: " If that is absolutely necessary, I am prepared to take that course. It is an extremity that I contemplate without the slightest horror." [32]

Guizot's foreign policy lost him the support of even the Moderates of the Chamber, and the numbers in the Opposition were increased by the addition of another group that he had alienated by his policy in regard to education.

Ever since 1840, the party of Young Catholics, of which Montalembert was the leader, had been crying out against the Government's practice of enforcing State

LEADER OF DYNASTIC OPPOSITION

control over all the educational systems in France. As early as 1841, Guizot had tried to pacify them by a Bill on Public Education, that was presented by Villemain, Minister of Public Instruction. This measure would have abolished the *monopole universitaire* that required all children of the middle class to attend State colleges and to hold a certificate of the State University for a bachelor's degree. While this concession would have been a gain, there was a clause that subjected all members of faculties in free colleges (those not controlled by the State) to examinations to determine their moral and intellectual fitness. This section of Villemain's measure so displeased the Catholics, that the Government withdrew the Bill. Encouraged by Guizot's retreat, Montalembert's group began a campaign for the Liberty of Public Education. Louis Veuillot pleaded their cause in the columns of the *L'Univers*, and various associations were formed to assist in arousing interest in a question that must have appealed to many liberally minded men.

But, when the clerical forces became active, anti-clericalism revived. The activities of the Church in spreading propaganda for its cause, led men of the Left to take alarm, and, when some of them discovered a counter-cry, the fight was on. The revival of the Church question led to the discovery that, contrary to the law, the Jesuits were back in France, and that schools of the order were quite numerous in certain sections of the country. Then it was that the Radicals began to howl, and Guizot found himself between Montalembert's Young Catholics on the one hand and a growing anti-Jesuit party on the other. To extricate himself from this uncomfortable position was the Minister's principal necessity, and to accomplish this, he must quiet the one by means of the other. He practically promised the Catholics that he would abolish the *monopole universitaire*, with all its objectionable features, if they would consent to the exclusion of the Jesuits. As a move in this direction, Villemain proposed, in 1844, a compromise, to the effect that any Frenchman might open a school upon submission of evidence as to his intellectual and moral capacities, and even this evidence would not be required of those who belonged to free seminaries, as long as those seminaries remained no larger than they were in 1828. There was, however, one more clause that provided that no person was entitled to enjoy any of these privileges who could not show that he did not belong to "any religious congregation not legally recognized in France." This proposal created a furore among the Deputies. The Left declared that Guizot had betrayed the University, while the Catholics cried out that they had been tricked by the Minister. In June, the matter was debated in the Chamber. Thiers opposed the Government's plan, and Montalembert and Berryer attacked it, though from a different angle.[33] Again, the Ministry withdrew its measure, and announced that another law would be forthcoming.

In preparation for another effort to extricate itself, the Government removed Villemain from the Ministry of Public Instruction, and Salvandy, a more moderate man, replaced him. The effect of Salvandy's appointment appeared shortly afterwards, when the distinctly Radical lectures at the University were suppressed. The courses of Quinet and Michelet, against whom Montalembert's followers had protested, were closed. This action was followed up by a ministerial order of December 7, 1844, which increased the Royal Council on Public Instruction by seventy members. These tactics alarmed the Left. Would Guizot yield to the Church after all? Many believed that this was the case, and the deposed Villemain, together with Cousin, Hébert, and Dupin, began crying out against Church influence.

This situation was too good a one for Thiers to allow to pass, and, on May 2, 1845, he joined the Left and staged a scene by which he may have hoped to drive out the Guizot régime. On that day, he began his famous interpellation of the Ministry in regard to the Jesuit

LEADER OF DYNASTIC OPPOSITION

order. He traced the vicissitudes of that society in France since 1790. In fact he delivered a complete history of their order. It is said that he rarely composed his speeches beforehand, but this could hardly have been the case with the oratorical performance of May 2, when he demanded the enforcement of the existing laws against this order.[34] The result of the interpellation, was the vote of the Chamber to form a Committee to frame a new law against the Society of Jesus.

Thiers and his colleagues had thoroughly aroused public opinion, and supporters flocked from all sides; even Émile de Girardin upheld him in the *Presse*.[35] He was fast entrenching himself, too firmly, perhaps, on the side of the Left. But he had salved his conscience by declaring that he was not attacking the Ministry from any party point of view; he declared that he was only protecting the laws of France, and trying to prevent the Cabinet from making a mistake that would cause it to lose the power that it had hitherto enjoyed! He protested his sincere respect for religion, but admitted that he felt " un amour jaloux pour les droits de l'état."

Naturally, Guizot did not place much confidence in Thiers' avowal that he was trying to protect the Ministry! The Minister perceived that, if he yielded one inch to the Jesuits, or even himself supported them, Thiers, supported by a pack from the Left or the Right, as the case might be, would have the Ministry cornered.[36] Guizot was seeking a loophole for escape, and his search was successful. Through Rossi, he attempted to persuade the Pope to advise the Jesuits to retire from France. On July 6, the Pope consented, and the Government issued a notice to this effect. Some houses were closed, and their numbers went to other establishments of the order. The Catholics, astonished, yielded to Rome, or rather to Guizot through Rome, and Thiers and the Left ceased their cry " Aux Jésuites." The Ministry had again won its point; both Catholics and Opposition had been tricked.

THIERS AND THE FRENCH MONARCHY

One effect of the affair " Aux Jésuites " was to bring the various elements of the Opposition closer together. Having failed in his attempt to oust Guizot by this question, Thiers resorted to a more definite alliance with Barrot, in the hope of breaking the Conservative majority that supported the President.

Their plan was to demand a moderate electoral reform that should be obtained by doubling the number proposed, and to set the franchise at one hundred francs. When this programme became known, the number of Guizot's supporters began to dwindle, with the result that, when Thiers attacked him for agreeing to stand by England in her opposition to the annexation of Texas by the United States, a bare majority upheld the Government.[37] On this occasion Guizot actually talked of resigning, but the prayers of the King dissuaded him from carrying out his threat. Louis Philippe had now reached his seventy-second year, and it was becoming increasingly difficult for him to tolerate changes of ministers and of policy. He clung to Guizot, and, in an effort to make his continuance possible, he dissolved the Chamber on July 6, 1846.

Once again, the elections were well managed by Duchâtel. Superior functionaries of the Government were the ministerial candidates for Deputies' chairs; Guizot's system of obtaining a majority was now manifest to the world. Against this practice, Catholic and Liberal alike protested. The organs of the Opposition blared forth their protests. Through *L'Univers*, Montalembert and Veuillot demanded Liberty of Instruction and " clean government." Electoral Reform and Labour Legislation became the cry of the *Réforme* and the *Presse*. Although they understood these things differently, the entire Opposition, united in denouncing the " reign " of Guizot. Amid the bedlam, might be heard the sharp phrases and shrill tones of Thiers, who played a whole orchestra of newspapers. Through his friendship with Léon Faucher, he controlled the *Courier Français*. Sometime previous, he is said to have remarked of the latter : " I am sure of his devotion. Madame Thiers and my mother-in-law receive Madame Faucher." [38] He could influence the *Constitutionnel* through Veron, who used to come early in the morning to the Place Saint-Georges to discuss politics, while Thiers shaved himself. His acquaintance with Marrast, kept him in close touch with the *National*, now that Carrel was no longer there to oppose him. These were the principal supports of the Opposition, but there were others, less evident, perhaps, but really effective.

The talk of electoral reform and of Labour legislation had enlivened the interest of the nation, and the events of the year 1845, had quickened its sympathies for the Opposition. In response to the encouraging statements of Thiers, Barrot, and the newspapers, there had been many Labour demonstrations that should have embarrassed these leaders who were playing so desperate a game. The small *commerçants* of Paris, Beziers, Toulouse, Bordeaux, and Rouen had leagued against the united competition of the larger houses.[39] The carpenters at Tours had struck.[40] In Lyons, labourers had established their own paper, *L'Écho de l'Industrie*, in which they were airing their grievances.[41] At Nantes, carpenters, ironworkers, butchers, and riveters had joined in strikes to demand more wages, and at Clermont-Ferrand there had been a serious demonstration of stonemasons and builders.[42] All of these troubles had occurred between August 26 and October 30 of the year 1845, and there were as many upheavals during the latter part of the same year.

This condition of unrest affected not only politicians and industrials, but it was spreading among the general reading public. It was reflected in the literature of the Forties. Hugo, Béranger, Georges Sand, and Eugène Sue wrote of the common people, and described their lot. The works of the historians, Michelet, Lamartine, Thierry, and Thiers, treated of the rise of the lower classes. As able a political scientist as Alexis de Tocqueville

THIERS AND THE FRENCH MONARCHY

described, in a work of superior merit, the experiment of democracy across the Atlantic. Unconsciously, perhaps, but, nevertheless, certainly, these writers and their fellows aided the cause of Reform. But, in spite of the growing army of the Opposition, Guizot won the elections in August, 1846. It was, however, the last victory, and it did not discourage or disrupt the Opposition. Certainly, the spirit of its leader was serene and confident, even though he himself suffered a temporary reversal of fortune. A change had come over France, but Guizot refused to recognize either the fact or its durable character. This much, Thiers recognized, and it gave him courage. On August 22, he wrote a very interesting letter to Mignet :

> " My dear friend, I have wanted to write you for several days, but my work, the Chamber and a crowd of things that always come up during retreats (and I am making one at present) have prevented me from realizing my desire. To-day, before working, for I am at present writing a book of my *History*, I will give you a few bits of news of the day.
> " I passed three weeks at Havre. I have rarely worked so hard as I did there, for, beside from seven to eight hours for my *History*, I gave as many to the lumberyards, ports, propellers and engines ! All that delighted me as instruction and as national service. I found the workers admirable. Havre is the only French port that has all the grand airs of England. During one tide I saw arrive and depart fifty large vessels. I can assert from the bottom of my heart that I do not regret my loss of power, but at Havre I was sorry not to be Minister of the Navy ; one could do many and valuable things. But the administrative incapacity of our Government passes all imagination. If I had the time I would tell you things that would astonish you ; my informants were agents of the Government, the Chamber of Commerce

LEADER OF DYNASTIC OPPOSITION

composed of Conservatives. Havre has charged me to defend all its interests, and along with that it has named a Deputy who is of the ministerial party, but who, they say, is foolish, incapable, and ignorant of the first things about the country. But they elected him in pursuance to a sort of docility of which they are not conscious. That is the spirit of this day. The time of mutiny is passed; the age of docility has come. It, too, will pass in its turn; but in the meantime the power does what it wishes, does not do what it does not wish to do, and is the master, as Napoleon was in his time; not because it has glory, merit, or any particular utility, but because this is the hour of domination. Whoever is provided for to-day will be the master for the time being.

" I am that one of all statesman of to-day whom the electors have least surprised. Without daring to say it, I expected worse. I am supporting my friends who need my help, and I should add that they behave well, except two or three weak souls, who wanted to go to the Left two years ago, and who now would return to the Centre, if they dared. All that is a small matter, the end is all, and the more I think on it, the more convinced I am that an end and aim are worthy of sacrifices and of patience; to give a little foresight to the country, without pushing it into war, to oblige it not to waste its money, and to organize its forces, to prevent it especially from prostituting justice, and to force the administration away from electoral intrigue. . . . I will hold good without anger, without relenting, and I will bring my party through. I have never expected durable success for myself and I do not expect any more for my enemies. All passes, all changes; the world is a movable stage, whose mobility is proportionate to the brevity of our life. With each of us, there is sufficient time for failures and for successes. Some commence well, and finish bad; others commence bad, and finish well. No one dies without having had his portion of good and evil fortune. I cannot tell you how much all this seems to me like a scene at the opera, changing at the sound of the machinist's whistle. In truth, I think, I have not even need to be consoled.

"I continue my book, and, given over to my natural common-sense, confronted with the follies that passion commits, I will have all the severity of judgment that you desire me to have. I only fear one thing: to extinguish the poetry of the subject by the logic of the historian. I will try to substitute a genuine sentiment for enthusiasm; it is the sadness of an enlightened and suffering patriotism. I am going to print.

"There is nothing of interest here. The powers (of the Deputies) are being verified. People malign each other; no one is convinced, but all believe that irregularities have been committed. You cannot imagine what they do. They suspend judgment at trials in order to hold the pleaders in a state of dependence. They pardon the condemned, they exempt from military service . . . they classify and reclassify routes; in a word, there is not a single function attributed to the Government that is not become a source of evil. This sight ends by striking the mind. The *incompatibilités* will not be voted by this Chamber, and electoral reform is inevitable. I have in mind a little reform that will hardly change anything, but that will have infallible results. We will talk of it again." [43]

In such a vein Thiers wrote to Mignet, the man whom he trusted most, and who, in September, 1845, believed that the Dynasty was nearing shipwreck.[44] His reply to Thiers was a warning and a prophecy that finally attained fulfilment. "When you shall have finished your history, you shall not have spoken the last word, for in politics there

LEADER OF DYNASTIC OPPOSITION

is a great and difficult task reserved for you. It must not find you unequal to it in physical force, while you will be equal to it in intelligence and in desire. You shall undertake it, and you shall be just as vigorous and active, but more temperate, I hope. It is gain without loss that you have before you." [45]

When this correspondence ended, a new career was opening for Thiers. The scope of his influence and the quality of his statesmanship was enlarged by changes in the French Chamber and in the English Cabinet.

NOTES TO CHAPTER XIV

[1] Thiers: *Discours*, V. 152, 156 sqq.: November 25, 1840.
[2] *Ibid.*, V. 299–306: December 5, 1840.
[3] *Ibid.*, V. 496: February 25, 1841.
[4] See Thureau-Dangin: *L'Église et l'État Sous la Monarchie de Juillet*.
[5] Duvergier de Hauranne, Herry, June 27, 1841, to Thiers. Bibliothèque Nationale, 20,616, 4.
[6] Thiers: *Discours*, VI. 3: January 20, 1842.
[7] *Ibid.*, VI. 53: January 22, 1842; pp. 81–82.
[8] *Ibid.*, VI. 140: May 10, 1832.
[9] Mignet, Paris, July 14, 1842, to Thiers. Bibliothèque Nationale, 20,616; Série 2, 26.
[10] Merriam, Paris, July 15, 1842, to Thiers. Bibliothèque Nationale, 20,616; Série 2, 25.
[11] Mignet, Paris, July 14, 1842, to Thiers. Bibliothèque Nationale, 20,616; Série 2, 26.
[12] Duc d'Orléans, St. Cloud, Mercredi Soir, 1842, to Thiers: Série 2, 30. Same to same, Villiers, Mardi (probably), 1841: 20. Duchesse d'Orléans, St. Cloud, August 25, 1842: Série 2, 31. Thiers, Paris, Lundi Matin, 1842, to Madame Thiers: Série 2, 38. Bibliothèque Nationale, 20,616.
[13] *Ibid.*, Thiers, Paris, Mardi, 1842, to Madame Dosne. Bibliothèque Nationale: 20,616; Série 2, 39.
[14] Madame Dosne's Notes, July, 1842, p. 217. Bibliothèque Thiers: Fol. in 4°., 32.
[15] Thiers, Paris, Mardi, 1842, to Madame Dosne. Bibliothèque Nationale, 20,616; Série 2, 39.
[16] Félicie Dosne: *Correspondance*, pp. 69–70. Madame Dosne, Vichy, July 17, 1842, to Thiers.
[17] Alexis de Tocqueville, Paris, Lundi Matin, 1842, to his wife. Château Tocqueville.

THIERS AND THE FRENCH MONARCHY

[18] Madame Dosne's Notes, July 1842, p. 220. Bibliothèque Thiers: Fol. in 4°., 32.
[19] Thiers: *Discours*, VI. 206, 209, 250–51 : August 20, 1842.
[20] Guizot: *Mémoires*, VII. 37. Louis Philippe, Neuilly, August 20, 1842, to Thiers: Série 2, 28. Duchesse de Massa, Catenay, August 22, 1842, to Thiers: Série 2, 24. Archbishop of Aix, Aix, January 13, 1843, to Thiers: Série 3, 1. Montalembert, Solesmes, August 22, 1842, to Thiers: Série 2, 29. Piscatory, Château Lavellière, August 22, 1842, to Thiers: Série 2, 32. Madame de Rémusat, Laffitte, Mardi, 1842, to Thiers: Série 2, 35. Gustave de Beaumad, Paris, October 16, 1842, to Thiers: Série 2, 37. Bibliothèque Nationale, 20,616.
[21] Thiers, Paris, Mardi, 1842, to Madame Dosne. Bibliothèque Nationale, 20,616; Série 2, 39.
[22] Thiers, Vienna, September 9, 1841, to Monsieur Martin. Bibliothèque Nationale, 20,616, 22.
[23] Mignet, Aix, October 8, 1842, to Thiers. Bibliothèque Nationale, 20,616; Série 2, 27.
[24] "Of all the faculties that I envy the most at the moment is not that one to which you attach the greatest importance and which gives you so much honour in society. It is frankly the faculty that you have of taking a nap after dinner." Duvergier de Hauranne, Herry, June 27, 1843, to Thiers. Bibliothèque Nationale, 20,616; Série 3, 12.
[25] Viscomte de Launay: *Lettres Parisiennes*, IV. 83 : June 22, 1844.
[26] Duvergier de Hauranne, October 13, 1843, to Thiers. Bibliothèque Nationale, 20,616; Série 3, 13.
[27] Thiers: *Discours*, VI. 253–54 : January 16, 1844.
[28] *Ibid.*, VI. 262–63 : January 16, 1844.
[29] *Ibid.*, VI. 264–65 : January 18, 1844.
[30] *Ibid.*, VI. 285 sqq. : January 22, 1844.
[31] *Ibid.*, VI. 573 : January 27, 1845.
[32] Viscomte de Launay, *Lettres Parisiennes*, III. 215 : March 25, 1845.
[33] Thiers: *Discours*, VI. 449 sqq. : July 13, 1844.
[34] *Ibid.*, VI. 619 : May 2, 1845. *L'Univers*, May 2, 1845.
[35] *La Presse*, May 5, 1845.
[36] Earlier, Thiers wrote : " We are free ! There is no use in deviating, no use in throwing ourselves to the Right after having lived too long with the Left ; we must maintain our equilibrium and keep our position, which, I think, is excellent. The Left Centre has only to wish it to become master of the situation, especially when there is no hurry ; our conduct is easy." Thiers, Lille, October 10, 1844, to Ganneron. Bibliothèque Nationale, 20,616 ; Série 4, 28.
[37] Thiers: *Discours*, VII. 6–33 : January 20, 1846.
[38] Veron: *Mémoires d'un Bourgeois de Paris*, III. 299 (1838).
[39] Protests. Archives Nationales, BB 18, 1436, 1193, 1197, 1437.
[40] Reports. Archives Nationales, BB 18, 1219, 1436.
[41] Reports. Archives Nationales, BB 18, 1900.

LEADER OF DYNASTIC OPPOSITION

[42] Reports. Archives Nationales, BB 18, 1436, 1621, 1435, 839, 807.

[43] Thiers, Paris, August 22, 1846, to Mignet. Bibliothèque Thiers, Fol. 546–7.

[44] Mignet, Aix, September 6, 1846, to Thiers. Bibliothèque Nationale, 20,617; Série 1, 25.

[45] Mignet, Paris, October 8, 1846, to Thiers. Bibliothèque Nationale, 20,617; Série 1, 26.

CHAPTER XV

THIERS, PALMERSTON AND BANQUETS (1846-48)

THE elections of July, 1846, threw Thiers definitely into the arms of the group that followed Barrot and Duvergier de Hauranne, who were demanding reform, and, from the latter part of that year their new ally, convinced by the corruption that he had seen and about which he had written Mignet, became a *Réformiste*. In the eyes of the Barrotists, he was the most important spokesman that they possessed. He alone could vie with Guizot, and of them all, he could point out with more clarity, tact, and precision, the points at issue between the Opposition and the Government. Of these, there were two that were of especial importance: the extension of the suffrage, and the reduction of the number of office-holders who sat in the Chamber of Deputies.

Although the amount of assessment required for the franchise had been reduced in 1831, the arrangement that prevailed continued to exclude many intelligent citizens, especially lawyers and physicians, who were the very flower of the middle class. The Reform Party now demanded that the exercise of one of the liberal professions be recognized as an electoral qualification. Of all people, Guizot opposed this demand, and by supposing a deep gulf that separates intelligence and capacity![1] The second issue was a practice that had become one of the principal props of the Guizot system, the filling of the Chamber of Deputies with men who were in the employ of the Government, and the ministerial manipulation of the elections. In regard to this double abuse, the *Réformistes* did not seek to prevent every office-holder from becoming a Deputy, but they wanted to restrict the number of office-holders who could sit in the Chamber. Only in this way, they asserted, could the independence and authority of the votes of the Deputies be preserved.

This, in general, was the platform of the Reform Party in 1846. It is true that each of the leaders had his own particular ideas, but they agreed in essentials. And when Thiers defined his own opinions in the matter of reform, they were found to fit in with those of Barrot, Rémusat, and Duvergier de Hauranne. His plan called for a general reduction of the tax qualification for franchise, a consequent increase in the number of electoral colleges, and a greater representation of the large towns.[2] In this last demand, one may see the influence of the observations that he made in England during the preceding year.

The possibility of success for such a programme, seemed remote to Guizot when he emerged victorious from the elections of 1846. He regarded the *Réformistes*, or Constitutionalists, as they were often called, as theorists who were dangerous, but who need not be taken too seriously. In this opinion, however, he was mistaken; Guizot failed to take into consideration a change in Ministry that had just taken place in England; he did not perceive that the retreat of the Tories before Palmerston, might have a stimulating effect upon the Opposition in France. It never occurred to him that English Whigs, who mistrusted his foreign policy, and French Constitutionalists, who hated all his policies, might join together against him and try to accomplish his overthrow. Once Palmerston had outwitted Thiers; it was not impossible that he might now be able to outwit Thiers' rival.

Only a little while before the return of the great Whig minister, Anglo-French relations had nearly come to grief over the question of the Spanish marriages. Albert, Prince Consort of England, desired that his nephew Leopold of Saxe-Coburg be married to Isabella, who had just ascended the throne of Spain. For obvious reasons, France had not favoured this scheme, and to save the alliance between the two countries, Aberdeen had

THIERS AND THE FRENCH MONARCHY

promised to abandon the plan, and to allow Louis Philippe to marry his son Montpensier to the younger sister of Isabella, one month after the young Queen had herself been provided with a husband. But, while Guizot trusted Aberdeen and believed that he would keep his promises, he was not sure that Palmerston, his successor, would observe them. Accordingly, in the hope of gaining a march on the new Premier, Guizot instructed Bresson, his minister at Madrid, to arrange for the marriage of Isabella with the Duc de Cadiz, and for that of the Queen's sister with Montpensier. Contrary to the agreement with Aberdeen, these instructions proposed that both marriages should occur simultaneously. When this move became known, England protested. Once again the English alliance was endangered.

This situation was exactly what the Opposition in France desired, and its spokesman lost no time in making the best of it. To the surprise of many, the amusement of some, and the disgust of others, Thiers took the side of Palmerston and the aggrieved English Government! Gone were the memories of the quarrels of 1840, the bitter back-bitings and hatreds. A few short years had healed wounds that had been declared incurable! Palmerston was a Whig; in 1846, Thiers was a Constitutionalist, a *Réformiste* himself. What was more natural than that they should be brought together? Even as early as 1837, the little Frenchman was credited with having declared, " I am a revolutionist in the good sense of the word, and I desire the success of my brethren in any country." [3] Palmerston hated Louis, and Thiers hated Guizotists. Nothing was simpler than to arrange an *entente cordiale* between them. To this *entente*, two things contributed.

Upon his return from Spain in 1845, Thiers had made a visit to England. Although it was unofficial, the journey had a real political significance, for he dined with Whig as well as with Tory. It cannot be definitely established that he saw Palmerston, but it is not at all

THIERS, PALMERSTON AND BANQUETS

unlikely that the two men met. Duvergier de Hauranne, the friend of Thiers, virtually calls the trip a peace move, an effort to dissipate the bad feeling that Thiers had aroused in England at the time of the Mehemet-Ali affair.[4] Another factor contributed to this strange alliance, and this was the fact that Normanby, the friend of Palmerston, was sent to Paris as English Ambassador. Normanby immediately sought out Thiers, and the two became firm friends. At a later time, the Ambassador even supported the Opposition against the very Government to which he was accredited !

Bereft of English sympathy, and confronted with an alliance of English Whig and French Constitutionalist, Guizot had no other alternative than to adopt the principles of Metternich and have his turn " at becoming Holy Alliance." This fact served the interest of the adroit leader of the Opposition. The more reactionary the policy of Guizot became, the more readily Thiers found an increasing support in the Chambers. The game of the Opposition Deputy was clever and was well played, but he did not perceive that he was riding a horse that might run away with him, and carry him farther than he desired to go. Too often, the mud he splashed in Guizot's face, besmirched, also, that of his King. There was a particle of truth in the words that Madame Adelaide is said to have addressed to him, on that fatal day of February 1848, " It is you who have lost us, Monsieur Thiers." [5] It was not a fault of intention but of judgment and of gross miscalculation. When the Chambers opened, he launched his attack against the Ministry. Several events had occurred to give point to his comments.

In Romagna, a new Pope, Pius IX, had proclaimed an amnesty for political offenders. This indication of Liberal sympathies had been followed up by vague promises of reform in the Papal States. Into Cracow Austrians had come, and the city had been annexed. The marriage of Montpensier to the Spanish Princess was a *fait accompli*, and, consequently, English hostility to

THIERS AND THE FRENCH MONARCHY

France had revived. This was the situation when the Parliament opened and Louis Philippe had dared to felicitate himself, Ministry, and Chamber, on the happy and healthy condition of French relations in Europe. But the Opposition did not feel that this was a time for congratulations, and they regarded the King's speech as ridiculous. Consequently, they attempted to force upon the Government a Reply to the Throne that contained a stronger word than *protester* in regard to the Austrian action towards Cracow. It was Thiers, their spokesman, who took this occasion to attack, in general, the foreign policy of the July Monarchy.

" If the Chamber deigns to give a little attention to my actions, I hope that it will bear in mind the great repugnance with which I approach this discussion. It is not because I experience any embarrassment in touching upon the subject with which you are concerned. In fact, how could we, members of the Opposition, who are in no way responsible for the present situation—how could we be embarrassed? You know what the situation is. By the deplorable event at Cracow, France has been separated from the Powers on the Continent. The isolation that we advised several years ago as a temporary attitude, as a more dignified way of entering the concert of Powers, and that the Government then declared was bad and fatal, that isolation is now the policy *forced upon* France. For how long? I do not venture to say.

" That is not all. Within our country, a bad harvest, that is the fault of no one, and a financial policy that is the fault of someone, has made our internal situation as difficult as our external relations. To-day, France has no friends; Austria and the Holy Alliance would force the country to uphold Reaction, and the Liberal movements that are just appearing must gather around England. That country, in turn, has been alienated by our haste to marry off Montpensier and to gain the alliance of Spain. France should not have tried to establish her influence in the Iberian Peninsula by marriage but by supporting the Spanish revolution." [6]

While this speech was undoubtedly the sincere protest of a Liberal against Guizot's policy of non-intervention, it was, as well, a gage of friendship to the Whigs in England. It was a way of telling Palmerston what would happen if the Dynastic Opposition gained control, and it marked the establishment of real understanding between Thiers and the Whig Premier. For the former, it was a brisk about-face, and yet, it was a more fair and a more parliamentary procedure than another method that he might have adopted. Had Thiers been thinking of himself alone he would have taken more of a part in the secret activities of the various sections of the Opposition during the summer and autumn of the year 1847. But he was thinking of France, and so, while he was willing to attack the Government from the Tribune, he refused to be party to conspiracy. And it was conspiracy that developed among the Left in Paris, after the stormy scenes in the Chamber of Deputies during the last year of the July Monarchy.

To meet the situation created by the call for elections in 1846, a temporary alliance of Thiers, Barrot, and Duvergier de Hauranne had taken place. Most of the members of this *entente*, were popularly known as Constitutionalists. They were the advocates of a constitutional and monarchistic system of government. But this union had been followed by one of a more permanent and more inclusive character. Barrot and Duvergier joined with Pagneux, Marrast, and Marie, and this fusion amounted practically to an alliance of the Left Centre with the Left, or Constitutionalist with Republican. Thiers was undoubtedly interested in the movement.

THIERS AND THE FRENCH MONARCHY

He knew Barrot quite well, Duvergier was an intimate friend, and Marrast, as editor of the *National*, had supported him in his campaigns against Guizot between 1840 and 1846. But although the Deputy was personally acquainted with a number of the members of the new combination, he was by no means in favour of all that they did, and of all that they said. The fusion had been made to combat parliamentary corruption and to extend the suffrage. In the eyes of Thiers, that was good, but he did not approve of their methods, and he feared that, with an increase of supporters, their demands would go beyond the limits that he had set. He stood for a moderate extension of the suffrage, and that was all. Furthermore, he disapproved of the methods that they adopted.

To spread their doctrines they proposed, *à la manière d'Angleterre*, to organize petitions and political banquets. It is, indeed, odd that Thiers has been credited with having instigated the Reform banquets, and with then having abstained from them. Even so keen an observer as Alexis de Tocqueville intimates as much, and he adds: " Wherefore, surrounded by his personal friends, he (Thiers) remained mute and motionless, while for three months Barrot travelled all over the country making speeches." [7] But this accusation and others of a like nature, cannot be substantiated. On the contrary, Thiers was worried and annoyed by the banqueters.

The first banquet was held at Château-Rouge, Paris, on July 9, 1847. At this affair, Duvergier and Barrot made toasts in which they inveighed against the Ministry and its practices. Their remarks approached very near to the point of attacking the Monarchy itself. The attitude of their friend, who did not attend, is interesting. On July 14, Thiers wrote to Madame Dosne about the gathering, " The Reform banquet has worried many intelligent people, and it is a very impolitic action on the part of our friends who are in the Opposition."[8] Madame Dosne enjoyed the full confidence of her son-in-law, and politics was their principal topic of conversation.

THIERS, PALMERSTON AND BANQUETS

There would be no reason at all for Thiers to deceive the one whom he trusted above all others, in regard to his attitude to the banquets.

Furthermore, there is additional evidence that he did not countenance the performances of his associates. Madame Dosne was more radical in her opinion than her son-in-law, and, on the very day that he wrote her about Château-Rouge, Madame sent to him a letter in which she tried to win him over to the movement. In this communication she even acknowledged that her own views were quite in accord with those of Duvergier.[9] As to Thiers' attitude, she commented as follows:

> "It is you who should rally these divergent opinions of a very small party. You are disgusted with power, my dear son, and you are tired of the lies of men. But great hearts should rise above these deceptions and should consider only the needs of the country; it is to them that a statesman should devote all his force and courage. Then, too, you should read into the hearts of your political associates, and you should remember that, unlike you, they have not experienced the deceptive satisfactions of power; they aspire to it, need it, and these thoughts and desires motivate them. Do you think that the July Revolution could have been brought about by men without illusions, such as most of you have become? And if you others, young men filled with the desire for good, if you had not joined in, do you believe that the bankers, fathers of families, would have fired the first shot? At that time, they thought that you were too ardent; you were the *avant-garde*, and you were carrying on everything. Now, the situation is less serious, but so disagreeable that you avoid it, delaying your action until the importance of the situation will make you come out of your tent.
>
> "Do not be surprised, therefore, if the soldiers murmur, and if they do little things while they are

waiting for greater ones. Rally them, speak to them the words you can make so seductive and that you have held back too much these past years. *Give absolution to the men of Château-Rouge.*" [10]

But the Deputy did not follow the advice of *Madame-Mère*, and he continued in his attitude of disapproval. In August, Bugeaud wrote to express approval of his stand :

"Whatever these Duvergier de Hauranne and others have to say about the dangers to liberty, that, according to them, are greater now than under the Restoration, we are not on the eve of a Revolution. Nevertheless, as you say, one must admit that these gentlemen present the question in an absurd fashion, and they invent such extravagant necessities, that they cannot help but over-excite and encourage the revolutionaries and that part of the people whose minds are eager for changes. . . . I was very glad to know that you are not mixed up in all this, and that you did not attend the so-called patriotic banquet, which was *au fond*, very revolutionary in spirit, to judge by the toasts that were made." [11]

These letters substantiate a statement that Thiers made in 1851, in regard to the banquets :

"These banquets, conceived at the close of the session of 1847 by the electoral committee of Paris, to demand reforms proposed by Monsieur Duvergier de Hauranne and by Monsieur de Rémusat, were welcomed by all of the Opposition of the Left, but they aroused in me very little enthusiasm and very much alarm. I did not like the rather violent company that one was likely to meet at them, and I feared that the agitation aroused by these *réunions* was not a peaceable one. Furthermore, I knew

THIERS, PALMERSTON AND BANQUETS

that I would have to listen to speeches that were not in keeping with my past or with my opinions. For these reasons I declined to attend them, and for that, I had cause to congratulate myself, for, within a short time they aroused public opinion to a point that was very alarming to those who were trying to take matters quietly. I believed that the new elections would give the Opposition a majority, without having recourse to exciting public sentiment." [12]

Although he was unwilling to attack the Government by these illicit means, he did not refuse to perform his part in the Chamber, as a member of the Opposition, and whenever the Deputies were in session, he did not hesitate to attack the Government. As if to give further proof of his disgust with Guizot's policy and his sympathy with Palmerston, Thiers resumed his interpellations of the Ministry. He tried to arouse among his colleagues an enthusiasm for the noble efforts of Italy. It was, indeed, an odd paradox that he who almost three years earlier had led the attack on the Jesuits, was, now, almost ultra-Catholic in his admiration for the Pope, whom many suspected of Liberal sympathies. From the Tribune, this most recent convert cried out, " Courage, saint père, courage ! " [13] He proclaimed his devotion to brave Swiss democrats, and lauded the wisdom of Frederick William IV, who had dared, in the face of Metternich, to promise his people a Constitution.[14] Like some of his fellows, Thiers failed to perceive that the promised constitution would not be a real charter of liberties, and that this act of the Prussian King was a step towards the consolidation of Prussian influence in North Germany and in the Rhenish States. Strange, indeed, is the contrast that is presented here ; the Deputy who, in 1840, decried Palmerston and British policy, now praised him and lauded the English parliamentary tribune.[15] In 1848, he cried out from the Deputies :

THIERS AND THE FRENCH MONARCHY

" Italiens, soyez unis ! Peuples, princes, soyez unis ! Piémontais, Toscanes, Romans, Néopolitains, soyez unis ! "[16] But ten years later this same Deputy was bitterly opposed to the accomplishment of their designs.

In all of these declarations of Thiers, there is one thing of great significance. No matter how much he inveighed against the policy of the Government, he never made any criticism of Monarchy. It was a principle and not a monarch that he was attacking; the principle happened to be Guizot. *Le roi règne et ne gouverne pas.* Guizot governed; therefore, Guizot was responsible and not the King. To Louis Philippe, his attitude of respect and friendship continued, and it is quite apparent that, until 1848, these sentiments were reciprocated by the royal family. In January 1847, Thiers and his wife attended a function at Neuilly. Madame Adelaide had the Deputy summoned to her side and she recalled to him his first visit to Neuilly in July, 1830 : " I do not forget those things," she said.[17]

But as the Monarchy neared its close, the evidence of friendship for Thiers became less frequent. The increasingly violent attacks made by Thiers on the foreign policy irritated his royal master, but the fact that Louis Philippe was the advocate of policies so despised by Thiers, did not lessen the esteem in which the latter held his King. He understood the reasons for that monarch's fear of war, and at a later time he put them into the following words :

> " Charles X had ever before him the spectacle of the guillotine ; before Louis Philippe there were the memories of the First Empire, and the sight of our burned and ravished provinces. I said one day to some Bonapartists, ' Do you know who is responsible for this peace-at-any-price policy for which you blame Louis Philippe ? It is even yourselves. From your acts, he has retained an impression that will always dominate him.' "

THIERS, PALMERSTON AND BANQUETS

In Thiers' eyes, the King was not a coward. He was a philanthropist who desired to save humanity, but whose head was too much in the clouds. In 1840, when Thiers was carrying France to the verge of war, Louis Philippe remarked to him, at a review of troops : " Look at those poor children. Do you desire to see them all perish before the end of the year ? " And this very humanity of the King made him fear the severity of the man who had so often carried him to the point of hostilities. " I like you better than Guizot," the King said to him, " but with you and Broglie, I am never sure of not awakening and having a war in my nightcap." [18] That Thiers understood his King is clearly shown by a remark that he once addressed to Louis Philippe : " No, I will never be minister unless, being responsible, I am the master." [19] But in 1847, Louis Philippe was the master through Guizot, and on the latter, the Opposition vented all its wrath.

Along with the inauguration of the banquets, came Government scandals and trials of officials, on charges of corruption. These incidents lent only greater *éclat* to the Reform movement, and gave more reason to the vivid remarks of those who proposed the toasts. While the Chamber was in recess, Reform banquets were held all over France. The principal speakers were Barrot, Dupont de l'Eure, Picard, Drouyn de Lhuys, Duvergier de Hauranne, and Garnier-Pagès. To incendiary speeches and Government scandals, were added bad harvests, floods, and failures on the Stock Exchange. When, therefore, the Chamber reconvened, the country was in a mood to demonstrate its hostility to the Ministry.

At this point, Guizot should have resigned. In fact, even some of his intimate friends expressed the hope that he would do so. But to the President, the struggle had become a personal one with Thiers, and even though the welfare of the country was at stake, he was too proud to yield to the little Deputy. Instead, he proposed to silence the Opposition by prohibiting the Reform banquets, and by submitting a scheme for electoral reform. To the first proposal Louis Philippe agreed, but he refused to countenance the second, for he had been hurt by the refusal of some of the Opposition to drink the King's health at the banquets. Accordingly, the Ministry must either resign or go ahead, and the latter plan was adopted by Guizot. When, therefore, the year 1848 opened, the Cabinet was preparing for war to the death with the Opposition.

The occasion for beginning the conflict was the Reply to the Throne. Urged on by Guizot, the ministerial party proposed to insert the following phrase in the Reply: "In the midst of the agitations that are being fomented by hostile and blind passions." In the opinion of Thiers, it was this phrase that provoked all the sinister events that followed.[20] From that hour, Barrot, Dufaure, and Garnier-Pagès never allowed the Ministry a moment's respite from their relentless and cruel attacks. On January 25, Thiers joined them and pounced upon the matter of financial policy. In this speech he excoriated the Cabinet, and almost won the day. This assault was followed by others in which he criticized the diplomacy of the Ministry and succeeded in discrediting it further in the eyes of the Chamber.[21] The Opposition was growing apace, for Thiers' sallies and the fatal phrase used in the Address, had alienated for ever the men of the Left and the Left Centre from the Government. When, therefore, the Ministry refused to allow the electoral committee of the twelfth arrondissement in Paris to hold a banquet, Duvergier de Hauranne defied the Government by announcing that the Left would attend the banquet anyhow. He added, as well, that the banquet would be held.[22] In an effort to conciliate, the Government allowed a measure to be proposed that would suppress the words *passions ennemies ou aveugles*, but the measure was lost.[23] It remained to be seen if the Left would follow Duvergier and disobey the Government by attending the forbidden function.

The days that ensued were tense with uncertainty and excitement. Barrot, de Lasteyrie, and Vavin favoured defiance. Provided that Ledru-Rollin, the most radical, did not attend, and provided that the banquet was held in the Champs-Élysées, far from the quarter of the working people, these three promised to be present. But the Opposition was not a unit on this question. There remained some few Conservatives who cherished a more peaceable method of protest and of bringing Guizot to terms. These advised a general resignation from the Chamber, an act which would necessitate convoking one hundred and fifty electoral colleges. Among the lukewarm advocates of this more sensible plan was Thiers, to whom the proposal of Duvergier was tantamount to beginning a revolution. He said to his hot-headed friends:

"The Government will resist; it could not do otherwise. If you try to brave its resistance, there will be a bloody affair. If, in this fray, the Opposition is vanquished, it will be damned in the eyes of the country. All responsibility for the bloodshed will be placed upon it. If the Opposition is victorious, what will the victory be? The overthrow of the Monarchy perhaps. I do not desire your defeat or your victory. Hence I refuse the fight; I refuse the banquet, and to avoid both, I prefer even the plan of resignation, no matter how bad it may be in many ways." [24]

This was not the advice that the hot-heads desired; Barrot and Duvergier were deaf to his pleas.[25]

As time wore on, Thiers and Rémusat who were, by this time in complete agreement, became more alarmed. Anxiously, they attended the next meeting of the Opposition. It was held on February 13, in the *entresol* of the

Restaurant Durand, 2 Place de la Madeleine. There were gathered an odd assortment; all phases of the Opposition were represented: the Left Centre, the Republican Left, and the Legitimists, Barrot and Berryer, Thiers and Garnier-Pagès, La Rochejaquelein and Duvergier, de Rémusat and Lamartine, even Marrast of the *National*. The meeting was opened by Barrot, who held forth at great length against the plan of resignation. Chambolle replied to him and upheld the scheme. He relates that, after his speech, he was perplexed to discover that of the three former ministers present, two of whom had advocated the plan, not one of them arose to defend it. He approached Thiers, and asked him to explain his silence. The answer that he received mystified him even more, " They asked me not to take part in the debates to-day, and I have given my word not to do so." [26] Chambolle's bewilderment was dissipated later, when he was informed that, on the very day of the meeting, Thiers was still hoping that secret negotiations opened between Rémusat and the Government, would be successful. At that very time, he even had reason to hope for a reconstitution of the Ministry.[27] For this reason, Thiers remained silent and did not speak his approval of any action. It was one more gage of loyalty to Louis Philippe.

But he was destined to disappointment, for the Rémusat negotiations failed. To make matters worse, another move that had been set into motion by hardier spirits, succeeded. Of this second overture to the Monarchy Thiers was aware, but his disapproval was so strong that he hastened to disclose his feelings to Duvergier, who had kept him informed of all the plans of the Opposition. Through Vitet, friend of the Minister of the Interior and of de Morny, the Duvergier–Barrot group finally came to an arrangement with Duchâtel. The minister consented to allow the Opposition to make a test case as to the legality of the banquets. The proposed affair should be held in the Champs-Élysées, whither the Opposition might go accompanied by the National

THIERS, PALMERSTON AND BANQUETS

Guard. The banqueters were to enter the hall, and then, at the first order from a *commissaire de police*, they should retire. The commissaire was then to lodge an order against them, thereby bringing before the proper tribunal, the matter at issue between the Opposition and the Ministry.[28]

This was the ridiculous compromise of February 20, 1848. It was a mistake which both the Government and the Opposition regretted before twenty-four hours had elapsed, for the more extreme of the Left set about to carry the arrangement further than many of the leaders of both sides desired. Without consulting the Deputies most concerned with the plan, Marrast of the *National*, Ledru-Rollin, and Garnier-Pagès drew up an elaborate programme of the event. On the following day, their unauthorized arrangements were printed and issued in what appeared to be an official form. The programme, as published in the *National*, called forth the entire population of Paris, and assigned to the various units of soldiers, National Guardsmen, students, political societies, clubs, Deputies, journalists, and workmen, places where they were to join the mammoth procession to the banquet hall. The announcement was couched in the form of an authoritative order.[29]

In reality, it had not emanated from the Government, nor from the Duvergier–Barrot group. It was the *National* that, after eighteen years, was attempting to dictate to Paris again. The Ministry was alarmed, for it perceived the danger of so large a demonstration as the Radical element of the Left proposed to organize. At Guizot's order, the Prefect of Police announced that the law against unauthorized processions would be enforced in the case of all those who tried to attend the banquet in a body. At the same time, Duchatel appealed indirectly to Rémusat with the request that he attempt to dissuade his more rash friends to abandon the idea.

Upon receiving this request, Rémusat hurried to Thiers with whom he concerted to prevent the disastrous affair. Together they went to the House of Odilon Barrot, where they found Duvergier, de Malleville, and Abbatuci. The situation that they discovered was most alarming; all three of the latter favoured the idea of holding the banquet even in spite of the new restrictions that the Government had placed on the affair. After much argument, however, they finally consented to hold another meeting, where Thiers and Rémusat should have an opportunity of expressing their views.

The second meeting was held at the Restaurant Durant, 2 Place de la Madeleine. "Messieurs," said Thiers, when he addressed the gathering, "I perceive the *bonnet rouge* under the banquet table. As to the battle of which you talk, and which you seem to foresee, I do not desire it. Do you know why? It is because I do not wish to be vanquished, and I desire even less to be the vanquisher."[30] In order not to irritate too much the susceptibilities of his audience, he only touched on the banquet, which, he insisted, they must abandon.[31]

His counsel prevailed, for, while no vote was taken, it appeared to Rémusat and his colleague, that the meeting was almost unanimously in favour of Barrot's announcing from the Tribune of the Chamber, that the demonstration would not take place. Confident of the general sentiment, Thiers approached Barrot, and said:

> "My friend, here is one of those occasions when you must know how to take a decision. Your party does not dare to recede (from its position). Take it out of its embarrassment. Mount the Tribune and say that, in view of the recent unforeseen resolutions of the Government, the proposed manifestation would only be an occasion for bloodshed, and that you are unwilling to take such an extreme measure for the defence of a right, no matter how well founded it is. (Say) that you will continue to demand this right by other methods, and that, in consequence, you call upon all good citizens to

remain at home. You will have all of the Chamber for you; you will prevent the mob from coming to-morrow; you will save order, and you will put the majority under obligations to you. A few of your friends will protest. I offer to share the responsibility with you, and I promise to say whatever you wish."

Thiers relates that Barrot replied to him in the most obscure and vague terms.[32]

Meanwhile, the gathering had broken up to proceed to the Chamber to carry on the interpellation of the Ministry. This was a practice that had become by now a daily occurrence. Thiers and Barrot proceeded to the Deputies. When they reached the Chamber, Barrot took his accustomed place in the Tribune, and began his interpellation. Although he spoke at length of the moderate sentiment of the Opposition, he did not say what Thiers had advised.[33] In spite of this omission, Thiers and his friends were convinced that all but Lamartine and a few *exaltés*, were willing to abandon the plan for the banquet. These last concurred heartily in the dramatic utterance of Monsieur Marie: " Vous avez assigné un rendez-vous à la population de Paris; ce serait une lâcheté d'y manquer; mais le peuple n'est point lâche, lui, et il y sera."[34] The more moderate of the Opposition realized that the Radical Deputy had spoken the truth; Paris would be ready to-morrow. With the fear of this in their hearts, they returned to Barrot's house to discuss the measures that should be taken to calm Paris, and to prevent a rising. Thiers did not join them: " I was resolved to combat with all my power the project of going to the banquet, if it was not abandoned, but to keep quiet, if my intervention was not necessary. The less I meddled in matters, the less the Opposition would be accused of yielding to the paralyzing influence of Monsieur Thiers."[35]

His conversation with Barrot and the behaviour of

the latter had thoroughly alarmed the Deputy, and, when he returned to the Place Saint-Georges, an incident occurred that disquieted him further. At his home, he found a long letter from an unknown person from whom he had been receiving communications for some time. The writer reproached him for his careless confidence and inactivity. It accused Thiers of not taking the situation seriously enough. " We are nearing a great democratic crisis to which you should ally yourself. Commit yourself just a little, if only for the purpose of moderating and guiding the movement, of making it more innocent, and more useful." The writer went on to rebuke him for wasting his time in the gratification of his literary and artistic tastes, and for limiting his political activities to discussions with Rémusat. " Rémusat is an ermine who fears to soil his fine clothes." [36] This letter made quite an impression on Thiers, so much so that he mentioned it to Rémusat that very evening and commented, " It may be that we must resign ourselves every fifteen years, to seeing democracy make some great stride forward." But, even then, he did not join with the *exaltés* in their plans. Instead, he warned them : " Take care, if you miss the chance of making yourselves odious, not to miss the chance of making yourselves ridiculous." [37] But the Left seemed determined to do this very thing. They returned to their senses long enough to abandon the plan for the banquet, but they embarked upon another scheme that was almost as dangerous.

The officers of the National Guard, that was permeated with Republicanism, were angry at the Deputies of the Left for what they termed their desertion. In an effort to appease the wrath of these gentlemen, Barrot, de Malleville, and Duvergier agreed to register an act to impeach the Ministry.[38] To Thiers, this plan was almost as foolish as the earlier banquet proposal, for such action would keep the public in its excited condition ; what Paris needed was time to quiet down. He communicated at once, therefore, with Duvergier, who had always kept him informed as to their plans, and who had always received his advice courteously even though he did not often follow it.[39] The reply that he received did not satisfy him, and so he decided to make another attempt to moderate the sentiment of his too radical friends. On the morning of the 22nd, he set out again with Rémusat to interview Barrot and to bring him to reason. It was at the latter's house, that the accusation against the Government was being drawn up, and the two disciples of moderation hoped to forestall it. But when they arrived, they discovered, to their dismay, that the document had been already approved by Barrot's followers. Much to the disgust of some of those who were present, Thiers began at once to argue the matter.[40] Barrot was not cordial and responded with some heat. During the discussion, reports to the effect that the excitement was spreading throughout Paris, began to pour in, but the Opposition would do nothing to quiet the city. Rémusat and Thiers proposed a petition to the King to enlarge the Ministry. After some reluctance on the part of the gathering, Monsieur Sallandrouze asked that his section of the Opposition be allowed to present the measure that Rémusat and his friend had proposed. To this request, both of them acquiesced in good faith.[41]

Exhausted by the excitement that prevailed at Barrot's house, Thiers left to reconnoitre and to inform himself as to the real condition of Paris. What he discovered appalled him. " I crossed the Place Louis XV, the Place de la Madeleine, to the Ministry of Foreign Affairs, and I returned by the rue Saint-Florentin. Children and workers were tearing up the streets with an unimaginable promptitude ; they were beginning to build barricades three rows deep." [42] Opposite them stood troops, drawn up in order, silent, and obstinate.[43] The memories of June, 1831 and of April, 1834 came up before the little statesman. Those days were but a prelude to a more awful day. In the barricades of that evening of February 22, 1848, he beheld and recognized the possible setting of the sun of the July Monarchy.

NOTES TO CHAPTER XV

[1] *Moniteur*, March 27, 1847.
[2] Duvergier de Hauranne, Herry, July 23, 1847, to Thiers. Bibliothèque Nationale, 20,617; Série 2, 18 *bis*.
[3] Quoted, Bourgeois: *Modern France*, I. 275. Palmerston, London, 22, 25, 29 September, 31 October 1846. P.R.O.F.O. 27, 746, 14, 20, 21, 41; and 781, 25.
[4] Duvergier de Hauranne, Herry, October 17 and 30, 1845, to Thiers. Bibliothèque Nationale, 20,617; Série 5, 16 and 17.
[5] Boughi: *Nuova Antologia*, 2ᵉ VI. 272, 277, 637.
[6] Thiers: *Discours*, VII. 363: February 4, 1847.
[7] de Tocqueville: *Souvenirs*, p. 19.
[8] F. Dosne: *Correspondance*, p. 163. Thiers, Paris, July 14, 1847, to Madame Dosne. See attitude of a Republican to the affair of Château-Rouge. Garnier-Pagès: *Histoire de la Révolution de* 1848, IV. 102.
[9] *Ibid.*, p. 159. Madame Dosne, Vichy, July 14, 1847, to Thiers.
[10] *Ibid.*, pp. 160–61. Same.
[11] Bugeaud, *La Dalmatie*, August 1, 1847, to Thiers. Bibliothèque Nationale, 20,617; Série 2, 29. See also Merriam, Paris, n.d. 1847, to Thiers. Bibliothèque Nationale, 20,617; Série 2, 29. Bugeaud, *La Dalmatie*, July 14, 1847, to Thiers. Bibliothèque Nationale, 20,617; Série 2, 12.
[12] Thiers: *Notes et Souvenirs*, pp. 3–5.
[13] Thiers: *Discours*, VII. 421–22: February 4, 1847.
[14] *Ibid.*, VII. 423, 424: same date.
[15] *Ibid.*, VII. 493: January 31, 1848.
[16] *Ibid.*, VII. 513–14: January 31, 1848.
[17] F. Dosne: *Correspondance*, p. 149. Thiers, Paris, July 8, 1847, to Madame Dosne.
[18] *Le Correspondance*, October 10, 1922, p. 27: Thiers to Lacombe.
[19] *Ibid.*, December 11, 1922, p. 28. Same.
[20] Thiers: *Notes et Souvenirs*, p. 6.
[21] *Ibid.*, p. 8. Thiers: *Discours*, VII. 432, sqq. January 25, 1848.
[22] Thiers: *Notes et Souvenirs*, p. 9.
[23] *Ibid.*, p. 10. See also Thiers: *Discours*, VII. 592–93: February 10, 1848.
[24] Thiers: *Notes et Souvenirs*, p. 12. See also Thiers: *Discours*, VII. 587–95: February 10, 1848. Thureau-Dangin: *Histoire*, Mlle. Dosne's copy, MSS. note, p. 387.
[25] Duvergier de Hauranne, Paris, February 13, 1848, to Thiers.

Bibliothèque Nationale, 20,617; Série 3, 33. Thiers: *Notes et Souvenirs*, p. 12.
[26] Quoted, Chambolle, *Retours sour la vie*, p. 236.
[27] *Ibid.*, p. 237. Thiers: *Notes et Souvenirs*, p. 13.
[28] Duvergier de Hauranne, Paris, February 19, 1848, to Thiers. Bibliothèque Nationale, 20,617; Série 3, 34.
[29] *National*, February 21, 1848.
[30] Quoted, Beaumont Vassy: *Societé sous Louis Philippe*.
[31] Thiers: *Notes et Souvenirs*, p. 18.
[32] *Ibid.*, p. 19.
[33] *Moniteur*, February 21, 1848, p. 448.
[34] Quoted, Chambolle: *Retours sur la vie*, p. 237.
[35] Thiers: *Notes et Souvenirs*, p. 21.
[36] Anonymous; Corbeil, February 20, 1848, to Thiers. Bibliothèque Nationale, 20,617,
[37] Quoted, de Rémusat: *Thiers*, p. 97.
[38] Duvergier de Hauranne, Paris, February 22, 1848, to Thiers. Bibliothèque Nationale, 20,617; Série 3, 35.
[39] Thiers: *Notes et Souvenirs*, p. 23. See also Duvergier de Hauranne, Paris, February 19, 1848, to Thiers. Bibliothèque Nationale, 20,617; Série 3, 34.
[40] Thiers: *Notes et Souvenirs*, p. 23.
[41] *Ibid.*, p. 25.
[42] *Ibid.*, pp. 25–26.
[43] *Ibid.*, p. 1.

CHAPTER XVI

EXEUNT LOUIS PHILIPPE AND THIERS

WHEN Thiers made his exploration of Paris on that last night of the July Monarchy, he was confronted with a situation that was quite different from that which prevailed on the eve of another French Revolution in which he had participated. In 1830, the capitalists had thrown the workers on the streets and thereby begun the movement that culminated in the departure of Charles X and the rise of a Bourgeois Monarchy in its stead. But in 1848, it was the workers who took the initiative and who drove the King of the bourgeois from the capital.

In Paris, during the months that preceded February 1848, a new Opposition, more subtle than that in the Parliament, was preparing. It was this Opposition that Guizot and Thiers failed to consider, on the eve of the crisis in the Chambers. It could be found principally in three sections of the city, the Faubourgs Saint-Antoine and Saint-Martin, the Latin Quarter, and the Boulevards. In the Faubourgs, dwelt the labourers who had experienced two hard winters, frequent clashes with their employers, and who were being worked upon by the various Radical influences in the city. The Latin Quarter, home of the student-youth of Paris, was decidedly touched with Liberal tendencies. This element had been turned against the Government by the silencing of two of their most popular masters and by the compromises in the matter of public instruction that Guizot had recently made to the Catholics. On the Boulevards, were the small shopkeepers and retailers. These were, for the most part, intelligent and able, patriots, members of the National Guard, and, by that very fact, convinced that

EXEUNT LOUIS PHILIPPE AND THIERS

they had played a part in the establishment of the Bourgeois Monarchy and had got nothing out of it. Like their more elegant fellows, the lawyers and doctors, they too were disfranchised.

Here was a mass of discontented citizens who were deprived of the right to exercise their opinions and who were played upon by Flocon, Blanc, Ledru-Rollin, and Marrast, through the *Réforme, National,* and the less pretentious papers of the Latin Quarter. This was the element that had taken heart when the Opposition made its demands for electoral reform and for the resignation of Guizot, whom they hated more than any other man in France. It was among these sections of Paris society that the Reform party had found its greatest support, and it was for them that the Reform banquets had been given. All the oratory of Barrot and Duvergier had been devoted to arousing these classes. But when, on that February day, the Deputies of the Opposition, urged by Thiers, had decided to abandon the proposed banquet, the great mass of Parisians turned against them. It is important to remember that, outside of the Chamber, the Popular Opposition became, after February 21, hostile to the Ministry and to most of the Deputies of the Parliamentary Opposition as well. They soon took matters into their own hands, with the result that on the morning of February 22, they began to make their power felt.

The first evidence of their activity occurred when the students from the Latin Quarter marched to the Chamber with a mammoth petition. About the same time, the labourers quit their work and went to the Champs-Élysées where the banquet was to have been held. By the late forenoon, the latter became so numerous that police reserves were called to drive the mob from the Place de la Concorde. In retaliation, crowds began to pillage gunshops to procure arms. At two o'clock in the afternoon, the troops were called out, but the order was given not to fight. Probably, this was a wise command, for many soldiers were disaffected and could not have been controlled by their officers, many of whom were of mediocre courage and ability. Plans had been laid for more extensive operations on the part of the military on the morrow, but, when the decision of the Opposition Deputies not to participate in a demonstration became known, these orders were cancelled. Evidently, the Government did not grasp the gravity of the situation. When evening came, however, they should have realized the danger, for barricades began to appear in the streets where the workmen dwelt.

The morning of the 23rd brought with it more serious news; the commanders of the National Guard gave notice that the men whom they had summoned were evidently arming, but that they were arming against the Ministry and not on its behalf. More barricades had appeared, especially in the vicinity of the rue Saint-Martin and the rue Saint-Denis. Around the Hôtel de Ville, the workmen had begun their attack, while the students were establishing themselves at the Panthéon. This was the situation when Thiers arrived at the Chamber of Deputies on that fatal morning.

The Deputies had been in session only a short time, when they were informed that a great number of the National Guard was approaching the Chamber. The session was suspended immediately, until the law-makers could ascertain the purpose of this unexpected visit. To this end, Thiers and Barrot went out to meet the Guardsmen. The latter harangued them at great length, exhorting them to order and to loyalty to the King. In the name of his fellows, he received their petition. When this ceremony had been concluded, the Deputies reconvened. It was now about two o'clock in the afternoon. The Opposition had just resumed its interpellation of the Ministry as to what measures it would take to calm Paris, when Guizot received a summons to the Tuileries. The President left the Chamber abruptly and hastened to the Palace, where he informed Louis Philippe that he could not sanction reform or order the

EXEUNT LOUIS PHILIPPE AND THIERS

troops to fire on the National Guard.[1] Thiers remarked later, that, on the afternoon of February 23, Guizot did not appear to realize the gravity of the situation.[2] When the President returned, Vavin took up the interpellation where it had been left off, but he found Guizot stubborn and reticent. Finally, however, the minister admitted that he had agreed to resign, and that the King had sent for Molé.[3] If either the President or the King had thought to placate the Deputies by such an action, they were doomed to disappointment. The Chamber was astonished at this announcement, and no one was more surprised than Thiers, for, in the opinion of most of his colleagues, Molé was almost as impossible as Guizot. The perplexity of the Deputy from Aix, however, was even greater when Duchâtel came to him and when he received a summons from Molé.[4]

Meanwhile, the news of Guizot's retirement had had a beneficial effect on Paris; by five o'clock in the afternoon, it was reported that the city was calmer and that the crowds that thronged the streets were in a more amiable frame of mind. This improvement in the situation, however, was of brief duration, for at ten o'clock, a change occurred and Paris became infuriated. A large crowd had gathered around the *National*, where they were feasting and singing the Marseillaise. The mob was met by the Guard of the Foreign Office, with whom certain individuals began to fraternize. But the officer in command of the troops refused to countenance it. He ordered his troops into line, a musket went off, and firing ensued. A hundred were killed on both sides. This incident set the spark to a conflagration that did not subside until Monarchy had been expelled again from France. Before the incident the only cries were " Vive la Réforme," but, after the fray at the Foreign Office, the more sinister cheer of " Vive la République " was heard.

Shortly after this affair, Molé came to the Place Saint-Georges, and interviewed Thiers. The latter informed the Count that he could not serve with him in a Cabinet, because he knew that Molé would not take Barrot and other men of the Opposition. He added that, if he joined any ministerial combination, he must be the head.[5] Molé then informed him that the King wished to ascertain how he would feel about becoming President of the Council, and what the conditions of his acceptance would be. To this question, Thiers replied that, as far as he himself was concerned, he would accept without making any conditions. But he added that he believed that his friends would make conditions, and, among them, the dissolution of the Chamber.[6] When Molé had gone, Monsieur de Scala arrived from the *bureau* of the *National*, to tell Thiers that the attack of the mob had recommenced and that only the announcement of a Thiers–Barrot ministerial combination could save matters.[7] This news was given to Thiers a little after ten o'clock on the evening of February 23; he did not receive a summons from the Tuileries until two o'clock the following morning. In the opinion of the Deputy, the King paid heavily for the precious time that was lost during the Molé negotiations.[8]

At last, during the earliest hours of the 24th, a message came to the Place Saint-Georges from Louis Philippe. It was delivered by General Berthois, who accompanied Thiers to the Palace. The streets were crowded; in the lower part of the city, the two experienced some difficulty in making their way.[9] When they arrived at the Palace, Thiers was met by the Duc de Montpensier and the Duc de Nemours who ran up to him and said : " Ménagez le Roi." [10] He was conducted immediately to the King's apartment, where, he relates, he was much affected to find himself in the royal presence again.[11]

Louis Philippe was not in the best of humours. He greeted Thiers with a question, " Have you found me a Ministry ? " The Deputy replied that he had just received His Majesty's commands. At this the King flared up, " Ah, you do not wish to serve under my rule ? " The response was angry, " No, Sire." There-

EXEUNT LOUIS PHILIPPE AND THIERS

upon, the King suggested that they both try to be reasonable. He asked for a list of possible ministers.[12] Thiers suggested Rémusat, Duvergier de Hauranne, and Barrot. At the mention of the latter, Louis Philippe was not pleased.[13] He then asked what their platform would be. Thiers replied that it would probably be electoral reform, by the extension of suffrage to fifty or one hundred thousand more voters, and the dissolution of the Chamber.[14] The first stipulation the King accepted, but he objected to the dissolution of the Chamber, for, he said, a new Chamber would give them bad laws.[15] From this topic, the King turned to the more immediate question of controlling and fortifying Paris. *A propos* of this matter, he announced that he had appointed Bugeaud to the chief command. This intelligence alarmed Thiers, for, because of the part that the General had played in suppressing the revolts of 1831 and 1834, old Bugeaud was very unpopular. The King, however, would not heed the protests of the man whom he desired to be his minister, and said, " Go, mon cher, and talk with Bugeaud."[16] To Louis Philippe's mind, only one thing more needed to be done that night and Paris would be quiet; the King must announce to the public the nomination of Thiers and Barrot. To this plan, the former objected, arguing that they had not yet constituted a Ministry. But, at the King's insistence, he finally consented to an announcement to the effect that Thiers and Barrot had been asked to form a Cabinet.[17] As Thiers sat down to draw up the message, Louis Philippe took the paper from him, and said : " No, I will be your secretary."[18]

When the announcement had been written and despatched to the *Moniteur*, King and prospective minister parted. The latter set out to find a Ministry during the early morning hours. As he went on his way, he was not happy, for the interview at the Tuileries had convinced him that his sovereign was not really cognizant of the situation, and that he would never sincerely accept the reforms that were being demanded. With the belief that Louis Philippe would use him and his friends to extricate himself from his difficulty, and, then, once secure, dismiss them, he set about his miserable task of collecting his colleagues.[19]

It was now about three o'clock, when, obedient to the King's wish, he went to the Place du Carrousel to interview Bugeaud.[20] It would be a trying scene, for Bugeaud was eager to become Minister of War, while Thiers was equally persuaded that he could not be appointed. He [21] admired the ability of the old General, but he feared his unpopularity. He found the veteran war-house in a rage, " déclamatoire comme d'habitude." [22] Here he had been appointed as Commander for two hours and he had not received a single order! He had not sixteen thousand men, and those that he had, were weary and demoralized from standing with knapsacks on their backs and in the mud for two days! There was no fodder for the horses. However, " J'aurau plaisir de tuer beaucoup de cette canaille et c'est toujours quelque chose." [23] At Bugeaud's, the news was not encouraging, and from his head-quarters, Thiers went to the house of Barrot. When he had received the latter's promise to accept a ministerial portfolio, he proceeded to his own home.[24]

At six o clock in the morning, the men whom he had summoned as his future colleagues, began to arrive at the Place Saint-Georges. When they entered, Thiers was carefully shaving, as was his habit, and he was as deliberate as usual about his toilet. This irritated Barrot, who said that Thiers and the King wasted time throughout that famous day of February 24.[25] When Monsieur was carefully and neatly arrayed, the informal Council began its deliberations.

Barrot opposed Bugeaud's command. The others regretted it, but they were all in complete agreement in regard to the conditions for their acceptance of the King's commission. These were, the dissolution of the Chamber, the adoption of Rémusat's plan for electoral

EXEUNT LOUIS PHILIPPE AND THIERS

reform, and a complete indifference as to foreign affairs.[26] If these terms were accepted by the King, Thiers would become President of a Ministerial Council that was to include Barrot, Rémusat, Cousin, La Moricière, Duvergier de Hauranne, Billaut, Dufaure, and Passy.[27] This group were so completely in accord, that they might have saved the Monarchy, had it not been for other factors of which they were already cognizant, and over which they were unable to establish their control.

Just as they were setting out for the Tuileries, they learned of the effect of the announcement of Bugeaud's nomination. As they had feared, it had stirred up the more Radical sections of the Left. The *Mairies* of the arrondissements in the labour sections, Latin Quarter, and Boulevards had been seized by the populace. Flocon, Pyat, Louis Blanc, and Ledru-Rollin, who had made an effort to restrain the zeal of their excited followers, had lost control of them. At the same time, Thiers was informed that supplies and ammunition were lacking.[28] It was with heavy hearts, that the candidates for a new Ministry resumed their journey to the Palace at seven o'clock.[29]

Paris presented a very different aspect, and one much more ominous. Barricades were everywhere. The mob, however, seemed to be friendly to the little group of Deputies. The crowds allowed them to pass through, crying, " Vive Barrot," " Vive Thiers," but they also cried " À bas Bugeaud," and at that, Barrot began to weaken. When they arrived at the Louvre, they found steady firing going on between the infantry that was stationed there and the Republicans who had established themselves in the house opposite it. In order to get his party by this barrage, Thiers had to go up to the officers and order them to cease firing. When, finally, they were able to pass and had reached the Tuileries, it was seven o'clock. The Deputies noted that there was hardly a sign of a guard in the courtyard. There, they met the Duc de Nemours and the Duc de Montpensier, who had

THIERS AND THE FRENCH MONARCHY

been talking with Bugeaud about the lack of ammunition. The Princes told Thiers that they had sent to Vincennes, and that the troops would bring it up by the most direct road.[30] At this, Thiers held up his hands in despair, for the road would take the troops through the very heart of the riot, and the people might be able to seize the precious cargo.[31] This is exactly what happened. Had the ammunition been brought up by river, it might have arrived safe and in time.

When they reached the King's Cabinet, there was a delay, for Louis Philippe was not yet up.[32] At last, he came in; he looked hard at Duvergier de Hauranne of Reform banquet fame, and said: " Je les accepte tous. Verrons aux choses." [33] Thiers then informed the King of their terms. To the plan for the dissolution of the Chamber, Louis Philippe replied: " Impossible." To the question of Bugeaud's removal demanded by Barrot, he, at first, demurred, and, finally, consented to a compromise that would associate La Moncière with him. At the same time, he agreed to the suggestion to use the National Guard in Paris, and to concentrate the other troops outside the city, to be used in case of an emergency. The Council urged this policy because they felt that the National Guard was more popular, and its use by the Government would not have quite so much the appearance of an act of hostility against the people.[34] These matters settled, Thiers then brought up the question of reform. The King hedged, half promised, and then, to the consternation of the Council, he arose and turned towards the door leading to his private apartments. Thiers arose, made a few steps forward to follow him. Louis Philippe slammed the door in his face.[35] To add to the perturbation of the gentlemen whom the King had left, two of them announced that they had glimpsed through the half-open door Guizot, who was surrounded by the women of the royal family. Guizot does not tell of his presence, but others relate it, and the evidence is sufficient to establish the fact.[36] Three times, Louis

EXEUNT LOUIS PHILIPPE AND THIERS

Philippe went into that room, and each time he returned from it more irresolute than before.

Had Thiers desired to overthrow the Monarchy, here was the opportunity. He and his colleagues were not even constituted as a Ministry, for all of their terms had not yet been accepted, and the King had left them without a word. They could quite reasonably have put on their hats, and gone home to a breakfast that was long overdue. Instead, after they had recovered from their surprise, they debated what to do to save the Monarchy. The most immediate thing was to quiet the populace; this could only be accomplished by giving to them the proof that the King had consented to make concessions. Of this, the people were ignorant, for the *Moniteur* had been barricaded, and the proclamation that the King had written early in the morning, in the presence of Thiers, had not been circulated widely. As it was necessary to spread the news, Barrot consented to be a " walking placard," and to go out on the Boulevards.[37] The next thing was to give the people a proof of the King's pacific intentions; this was done when Thiers, after deliberation with his friends, sent an order to Bugeaud to cease firing.[38] Had the news of the Thiers–Barrot combination been spread earlier, disaster might have been averted, but it was too late. While Barrot was cordially received, he was not heeded, and, when Bugeaud, in obedience to orders, grumblingly withdrew his troops to the Place du Carrousel, the mob was free. It seized the Hôtel de Ville, and then began its march on the Tuileries.

In the meantime the King had resumed his conversation with Thiers. The latter suggested that the King retire to St. Cloud with the regular troops, leaving the National Guard in Paris. Then, in case the Guard could not settle matters alone, Louis Philippe, with reinforcements from the provinces, could march on Paris on the morrow. The King appeared to consider the matter for a moment; then went again into that fatal room, from which he emerged irresolute.[39] Upon his return, he announced his intention of reviewing the National Guard. Had he reached this decision alone, or had he been advised by the retiring President who sat in the royal apartments? The review was pathetic. With Thiers holding the bridle of his horse, he rode along the ranks of the Guardsmen, crying out that he had granted the reform. Suddenly, he stopped the proceedings and returned to the Palace, discouraged and grey.[40] He sat down at his desk, with Thiers at his side. Monsieur Crémieux broke in upon them. He informed the King that the mob was nearing the Palais Royal, which was quite near the Tuileries, that Thiers' name was not strong enough to stop the mob, and that only Barrot could save him. Louis Philippe looked up at Thiers. The latter assented, and the King wrote out Barrot's nomination.[41]

It was now about eleven o'clock and there was a brief time of suspense while they waited for news of Barrot. Meanwhile, the latter's mission had failed and, fearing to draw the crowd that was following him to the Tuileries, Barrot set out for the Ministry of the Interior. About the same time, news reached the Palace that the insurgents had reached the Palais Royal, and that Arago, Lagrange, and other leaders had conceded to the people. Monsieur de Reims, who then arrived, informed Thiers that his family was safe, and also that the only resource that remained, seemed to be an abdication in favour of the Comte de Paris. The Duc de Nemours who had been watching the conversation, called Thiers over to him. " What is the news, what are you hearing?" he asked. " About the safety of my own family," Thiers replied. But Nemours persisted: "What about the people?" " Nothing good," was the reply. " Can your informant be relied upon?" "Perfectly," responded Thiers. At that, the Prince went to Monsieur de Reims and questioned him. The latter finally told the Prince that he regarded an abdication in favour of the Comte de Paris as the only possible resource left them. At this, Nemours looked at Thiers and said, "What say you, Monsieur Thiers?"

EXEUNT LOUIS PHILIPPE AND THIERS

The reply was decisive : " I cannot venture, I cannot bear to talk on such a matter."[42] Nemours and Montpensier then approached the King to tell him that a terrible sacrifice was necessary. Louis Philippe looked up at Thiers and asked, " Cher ami, que dites-vous ? " Thiers did not speak. After a few minutes' talk with his sons, the King went back into the room where the Queen, the Duchess of Orléans, the ladies of the Court, and Broglie and Guizot were gathered.[43] Finally, he issued from the Chamber, accompanied by Marie-Amélie, the Duchesse d'Orléans, and other members of his family. When he returned to the Cabinet, he could hear the voices outside crying : " L'abdication ! l'abdication ! " The Queen turned and said, " You do not deserve so good a King." [44] Thiers, unable to endure the scene, left the room. He had reached the hall when someone ran after him, calling, " Come back ! Come back ! We want your advice for the King." As he turned, he caught sight of Émile de Girardin crying with the rest : " Abdicate ! Abdicate ! " He saw Louis Philippe sign his abdication. Then he slipped from the room. He stayed in the vicinity of the Palace until the King and his family had escaped by the very route that he had suggested.[45] Then the little man stumbled blindly out of the courtyard. He fell into the hands of a mob that insulted him and threatened him. Later, he found himself at the Chamber in the Salle des Pas Perdus. Some of the Deputies tried to make him go in, but he turned on them and said : " No, I will have nothing to do with you, your venality, your subservience, your selfishness. I will never again enter that den of iniquity." [46] And he left them. He did not know that the Duchesse d'Orléans who had remained behind, was, at that very moment, in the Chamber.[47] Only Barrot, of the two, saw her, and Barrot expected Lamartine to move the Regency. To his surprise, Lamartine did nothing of the sort, but moved for a Provisional Government, declaring the Monarchy dead.[48]

THIERS AND THE FRENCH MONARCHY

In the meantime, Thiers, bewildered, had wandered out to the entrance, and there he met an acquaintance.

" He came up to me, led me aside and told me that he would be murdered by the mob, if I did not assist him to escape. I took him by the arm and begged him to go with me and to fear nothing. Monsieur Thiers wished to avoid the Pont Louis XV, for fear of meeting the crowd. We went to the Pont des Invalides, but when we got there, he thought he saw a gathering on the other side of the river, and refused to cross. We then made for the Pont d'Iéna which was free, and we crossed without any difficulty. When we reached the other side, Monsieur Thiers discovered some street boys shouting on the foundation of what was to have been the palace of the King of Rome, and, forthwith, turned down the rue d'Auteuil, and made for the Bois de Boulogne. There, we had the good fortune to find a cabman who consented to drive along the boulevards, to the neighbourhood of the Boulevard de Clichy, through which we were able to reach his house. During the whole journey, and especially at the start, Monsieur Thiers seemed almost out of his senses, gesticulating, sobbing, uttering incoherent phrases. The catastrophe that he had just beheld, the future of his country, his own personal danger, all contributed to form a chaos amid which his thoughts struggled and strayed increasingly." [49]

" This was the rôle that I played in this terrible catastrophe. Called when all was lost, I came, for my honour's sake, to offer my useless presence to a dynasty whose elevation I had beheld and whose downfall I would have prevented; I came, and I carried away with me only pain and sorrow."—Thiers: *Notes et Souvenirs*, p. 60.

EXEUNT LOUIS PHILIPPE AND THIERS

NOTES TO CHAPTER XVI

[1] Thiers: *Notes et Souvenirs*, p. 32. Rumigny: *Souvenirs*, p. 301.
[2] Senior: *Conversations, Second Empire*, I. 130 (Thiers' account).
[3] Guizot: *Mémoires*, VII, 585.
[4] Molé, Paris, February 23, 1848, to Thiers. Bibliothèque Nationale, 20,617; Sec. 3, 61, 62, 63. Thiers: *Notes et Souvenirs*, p. 33.
[5] Senior: *Conversations, Second Empire*, I. 128 (Thiers' account).
[6] Thiers: *Notes et Souvenirs*, p. 34.
[7] *Ibid.*, p. 36.
[8] Senior: *Conversations, Second Empire*, I. 128 (Thiers' account).
[9] Thiers: *Notes et Souvenirs*, p. 36. Thiers and Duvergier de Hauranne: Statement, 1851. Bibliothèque Nationale, 20,618; Série 2, 28. Tocqueville: *Souvenirs*, Appendix I. 379 (Beaumont's account). Appendix II, 385 (Barrot's account). Senior: *Conversations, Second Empire*, I. 5 (Thiers' account); I. 71 (Duvergier's account).
[10] Thiers: *Notes et Souvenirs*, p. 37. Senior: *Conversations, Second Empire*, I. 5 (Thiers' account).
[11] Thiers: *Notes et Souvenirs*, p. 37.
[12] Senior: *Conversations, Second Empire*, I. 5 (Thiers' account).
[13] Thiers: *Notes et Souvenirs*, p. 37. Senior: *Conversations, Second Empire*, I. 5 (Thiers' account). Tocqueville: *Souvenirs*, Appendix I. 379 (Beaumont's account).
[14] Senior: *Conversations, Second Empire*, I. 6 (Thiers' account).
[15] *Ibid.*, I. 6.
[16] *Ibid.*, I. 6.
[17] *Ibid.*, I. 6.
[18] *Ibid.*, I. 6.
[19] *Ibid.*, I. 7.
[20] Thiers: *Notes et Souvenirs*, p. 40. Senior: *Conversations, Second Empire*, I. 7 (Thiers' account).
[21] Bugeaud, Garde Nationale, Department de la Seine, February 24, 1848, to Thiers. Bibliothèque Nationale, 20,617; Série 3, 11.
[22] Thiers: *Notes et Souvenirs*, p. 40.
[23] Senior: *Conversations, Second Empire*, I. 7 (Thiers' account).
[24] Thiers: *Notes et Souvenirs*, p. 41. Tocqueville: *Souvenirs*, Appendix II. 385 (Barrot's account).
[45] *Ibid.*, Appendix II. 386 (Barrot's account). Senior: *Conversations, Second Empire*, I. 71 (Duvergier's account).
[26] Thiers: *Notes et Souvenirs*, p. 41.
[27] Dufaure and Passy refused because they believed that they were too unpopular. Thiers: *Notes et Souvenirs*, p. 27.
[28] Thiers and Duvergier de Hauranne: Statement, 1851. Bibliothèque Nationale, 20,618, Série 2, 28. Senior: *Conversations, Second Empire*, I. 7 (Thiers' account); I. 71–72 (Duvergier's account). Thiers later declared that Bugeaud's statement was inaccurate. A goodly supply

at Vincennes. Senior: *Conversations, Second Empire*, I. 23 (Thiers' other account).
[29] Thiers: *Notes et Souvenirs*, p. 44. Senior: *Conversations, Second Empire*, I. 8 (Thiers' account).
[30] *Ibid.*
[31] *Ibid.*, I. 9 (Thiers' account).
[32] Thiers: *Notes et Souvenirs*, p. 46. Senior: *Conversations, Second Empire*, I. 72 (Duvergier's account).
[33] *Ibid.*, I. 11 (Thiers' account).
[34] Thiers and Duvergier de Hauranne: Statement, 1851. Bibliothèque Nationale, 20,618; Série 2, 28. Thiers: *Notes et Souvenirs*, p. 46. Senior: *Conversations, Second Empire*, I. 12 (Thiers' account).
[35] *Ibid.*, I. 73 (Duvergier's account). Tocqueville: *Souvenirs*, Appendix II. 386 (Barrot's account).
[36] Senior: *Conversations, Second Empire*, I. 72 (Duvergier's account); I. 13 (Thiers' account).
[37] Thiers and Duvergier de Hauranne: Statement, 1851. Bibliothèque Nationale, 20,618; Série 2, 28. Senior: *Conversations, Second Empire*, I. 13 (Thiers' account). Tocqueville: *Souvenirs*, Appendix II. 387 (Barrot's account).
[38] Thiers: *Notes et Souvenirs*, p. 49.
[39] Senior: *Conversations, Second Empire*, I. 14 (Thiers' account).
[40] *Ibid.*, I. 15 (Thiers' account).
[41] Thiers and Duvergier de Hauranne: Statement, 1851. Bibliothèque Nationale, 20,618; Série 2, 28. Thiers: *Notes et Souvenirs*, p. 55. Senior: *Conversations, Second Empire*, I. 74 (Duvergier's account); I. 16 (Thiers' account).
[42] Thiers and Duvergier de Hauranne: Statement, 1851. Bibliothèque Nationale, 20,618; Série 2, 28. Thiers: *Notes et Souvenirs*, p. 56. Senior: *Conversations, Second Empire*, I. 16 (Thiers' account). Monsieur Reims has been said by some to have been secretary to Thiers. In her copy of Thureau-Dangin, Mademoiselle Dosne has written on Vol. VII. 489: " Monsieur de Reims n'a jamais été le secrétaire de M. Thiers." For a slightly different version see Tocqueville: *Souvenirs*, Appendix I. 383 (Beaumont's account).
[43] Senior: *Conversations, Second Empire*, I. 17 (Thiers' account).
[44] *Ibid.*, I. 17 (Thiers' account). Rumigny: *Souvenirs*, p. 305.
[45] Senior: *Conversations, Second Empire*, I. 18 (Thiers' account).
[46] *Ibid.*, I. 19 (Thiers' account).
[47] *Ibid.*, I. 19 (Thiers' account).
[48] Senior: *Conversations, Second Empire*, I. 9 (Barrot's account).
[49] Tocqueville: *Souvenirs*, pp. 75–76 (account of Monsieur Talabot).

EPILOGUE.

1 March, 1848.

I AM fifty years old, and I have been allowed, or forced, to see three monarchies fall: those of Napoleon, of the old House of Bourbon, and of the younger house.

These events affected profoundly my childhood, my youth, and my maturity.

For what else am I now destined?

I have arrived at the age when life begins to darken, to lose its colour, and, above all else, to restrict itself; shall I be called upon to witness other catastrophes? I fear so; in fact, I believe that I shall; but truly I shall never experience anything more strange, more sad, and more alarming than the collapse of the dynasty of Orléans that I beheld, even as I had beheld its elevation.

ADOLPHE THIERS.

BIBLIOGRAPHY

I. THE principal sources for the study of Adolphe Thiers (1797–1848) are to be found at the Bibliothèque Nationale at Paris, the Bibliothèque Thiers at Paris, and the Musée Arbaud at Aix-en-Provence. At the Bibliothèque Nationale there is a large and important collection of Thiers' papers. These were presented to the Bibliothèque by Mademoiselle Dosne. The collection contains the personal correspondence of Thiers with his friends and associates, and a great many letters addressed to him; but the letters are by no means all of them personal. Evidently Thiers, as President of the Council, was careful to have copies made of his official despatches and of the reports that he received from his envoys and agents. A careful comparison of the papers in the collection at the Bibliothèque Nationale with the official files at the Archives du Ministère des Affaires Étrangères reveals the fact that, with only a very few exceptions, the files of the *Lettres Politiques de Thiers* are practically complete. The period covered by this book is included in volumes 20,601–20,617, Fonds-nouvelles acquisitions françaises, Salle des Manuscrits, Bibliothèque Nationale. It should be noted, however, that the collection at the Nationale is very incomplete as far as the early part of Thiers' life is concerned.

The Bibliothèque Thiers is the famous hôtel de la Place Saint-Georges that was left to the Institute of France upon the death of Mademoiselle Dosne. It contains an invaluable collection of source material relative to the private and personal life of Thiers. Birth certificates, marriage contracts, personal and political correspondence, contracts with editors and publishers, notes for the Histories of the Revolution, Art, Florence,

BIBLIOGRAPHY

and other studies, annotated copies of the *National*, original manuscripts and copies of the earlier essays, and Thiers' own library, that contains many books with marginal notes made in his own hand. In addition, there is a very valuable series of notes prepared by Madame Dosne in anticipation of an autobiography that she had expected him to write. Another curious document is Mademoiselle Dosne's personal copy of Thureau-Dangin's *Histoire de la Monarchie de Juillet*, with corrections and refutations in her own hand. There is also a very complete iconography and complete files of the Archives Parlementaires, *Moniteur*, etc., and pamphlets.

The Musée Arbaud at Aix possesses about eighty letters covering the period 1797–1848, most of them relating to Thiers' youth and experiences at Aix. These, together with a smaller collection at the Musée at Carpentras and certain letters published by F. Benoit in *Le Correspondant* for 1922, have made it possible to reconstruct almost in its entirety the principal facts of his career before he came to Paris.

Additional source material relative to Thiers may be found at the Archives Nationales in the files of the Ministry of the Interior, Police Générale (F7) and in the papers of the Ministère de la Justice, Direction des Affaires Criminelles (BB). These relate principally to the career of Thiers in Paris between his arrival there and the outbreak of the July Revolution, and his activities as Minister of the Interior. The Archives du Ministère des Affaires Étrangères contain files relating to the policies of Thiers in 1836 and in 1840, but most of this material is duplicated in the collection of the Bibliothèque Nationale. At the Château de Tocqueville there are some letters from Thiers that were communicated to me by the late Mr. Paul Lambert White. Corroborative material relative to the attitude of England in 1836 and 1846, may be found in the correspondence of Palmerston and his agents, in the Public Records Office, London (P.R.O.F.O.).

BIBLIOGRAPHY

II. Primary Sources

Published. (In the following list the books principally used are marked with an asterisk.)

1. *Collections of Documents.*
    Anderson, C. H. : *Constitutions and Documents.*
    Bulletin des Lois : 5ᵉ et 7ᵉ Série.
    Cours de Cassation : Réquisitoire, VII.
    De Clerq, A., et De Clerq, J. : *Recueil des Traités de France depuis 1715.* Paris, 1880.
    *Duvergier : *Recueil des lois françaises.*
    *Hélie, F. A. : *Constitutions de la France.* Paris, 1878.
    *Madival et Laurent : *Archives Parlementaires,* 2ᵉ Série.
    Monier, H., et Duguit, L. : *Les Constitutions de la France.* Paris, 1898.
    Paris Révolutionnaire. 4 vols. Paris, 1833-4.
    Pégout, J. : *Documents sur les Mouvements insurrectionels à Paris.* Paris, 1857.
    Publications du Ministère des Affaires Étrangères, 1815-30.
    Taschereau : *Revue Retrospective,* 1849.
    Teissier, Q. : *Documents inédits sur la famille de Monsieur Thiers.* Marseilles, 1877.
2. *Letters and Speeches.*
    *Berryer, A. : *Discours et Correspondances.* 5 vols. Paris, 1870-74.
    Beugnot, J. C. : *Écrits et Discours.* 2 vols. Paris, 1866.
    Cauchois-Lemaire : *Lettre écrite à Monsieur Thiers.* Paris, 1830.
    *Dino, Duchesse de : " Lettres à Monsieur Thiers." *Revue des Deux Mondes,* July 15, 1923, pp. 241-61.
    Doudan, X. : *Mélanges et Lettres.* 4 vols. Paris, 1876.
    *Falloux, Comte de : *Discours et Mélanges Politiques.* 2 vols. Paris, 1882.
    *Guizot, F. P. G. : *Lettres à sa famille et à ses amis.* Paris, 1884.
    Halévy, D. : *Le Courrier de Monsieur Thiers.* Paris, 1924.
    d'Herbelot, A. : *Lettres.* Paris, 1908.
    Talleyrand, Périgord, Ch. M. de : *Correspondance diplomatique.* Paris, 1891.
    *Thiers, L. A. : *Correspondances,* 1845-65. (Monsieur Thiers à Madame Thiers, à Madame Dosne. Madame Dosne à Monsieur Thiers.) Paris, 1904.
    *" Lettres de Monsieur Thiers à ses amis en Italie." *Chroniques* (G. Manguin). January, 1919.
    *" Lettres à Émile et Séverin Benoit." *Le Correspondant* (F. Benoit), June 10, 1922.
    Lettres à Jerome Bonaparte. Paris, 1873.
    Discours Parlementaires. 12 vols. Paris, 1879-93.

BIBLIOGRAPHY

3. *Memoirs and Conversations.*
   *Barante, Baron de : *Souvenirs.* 4 vols. Paris, 1828-1858.
   *Barrot, O. : *Mémoires.* Paris, 1824-29.
   *Beaumont-Vassy, Vicomte de : *Histoire de Mon Temps,* 6 vols. Paris, 1855-65.
   *Berard, A. : *Souvenirs historiques sur la Révolution de* 1830. 3 vols. Paris, 1830-34.
   *Béranger, P. J. : *Ma Biographie.* Paris, 1859.
   *Broglie, Duc de : *Souvenirs.* 4 vols. Paris, 1886.
   Capefigue, R. : *Mémoires tirés des papiers d'un homme d'état.* 4 vols. Paris, 1836.
   Cavaignac, Général : *Souvenirs et Correspondance.* Paris, 1889.
   *Chambolle, A. : *Retours sur la vie.* Paris, 1917.
   *Chateaubriand, R. de : *Mémoires d'Outre Tombe.* 6 vols. Paris.
   *Colmanche, M. : *Reminiscences of Prince de Talleyrand.* 2 vols. London, 1848.
   Décazes, Duchesse de : Journal. *Revue Hebdomadaire,* 1911, Vol. VIII, 443.
   *Dino, Duchesse de : *Chronique de* 1831 à 1862. 2 vols. Paris, 1909.
   *Dupin, A. M. J. J. : *Mémoires.* 4 vols. Paris, 1855-63.
   *Falloux, Comte de : *Études et Souvenirs.* Paris, 1885.
   Mémoires d'un royaliste. 2 vols. 1888.
   Faucher, Léon : *Ma Biographie et Correspondance.* Paris, 1875.
   *Foinville, " Chevalier " de : *Mémoires historiques,* 1824.
   *Guisquet : *Mémoires d'un Préfet de Police.* Paris, 1840.
   *Guizot, F. P. G. : *Mémoires pur servir à l'histoire de mon temps.* Paris, 1867 and 1868.
   d'Haussonville, Comte J. : *Ma Jeunesse.* Paris, 1885.
   Souvenir et Mélanges. Paris, 1878.
   Houssaye, A. : *Souvenirs de ma Jeunesse.* 2 vols. Paris, 1896.
   Joigneaux, P. : *Mémoires d'un représentant du peuple.* 2 vols. Paris, 1890.
   *Joinville, Prince de : *Vieux Souvenirs.* Paris, 1894.
   *Lacombe, H. de: " Conversations avec Monsieur Thiers." *Le Correspondant,* September 28, October 10, October 25, 1922.
   La Fayette, M. S. M. : *Mémoires.* 6 vols. Paris, 1838 and 1858.
   *Lamartine, A. de : *Mémoires inédites.* Paris, 1870.
   Souvenirs et Portraits. 3 vols. Paris, 1871.
   Choix de Discours et Écrits politiques. 2 vols. Paris, 1878.
   Correspondance. 6 vols. Paris, 1873.
   *La Mennais, F. de : *Correspondance,* édition Blaize. Paris, 1866.
   Correspondance, édition Longues. Paris, 1858.
   Ledru-Rollin, A. P. A. : *Discours politiques et écrits divers.* 2 vols. Paris, 1878.
   *Metternich, Prince de : *Nachgelassene Papieren.* 8 vols. Paris, 1884.
   Meunier, E. : *Souvenirs intimes et notes.* Paris, 1896.

BIBLIOGRAPHY

*Neuville, Hyde de : *Mémoires.* Paris, 1889.
Pasquier, E. D. : *Mémoires.* Paris, 1893.
*Périer, Casimir : *Opinions et Discours.* 4 vols. Paris, 1834.
Proudhon, J. : *Confession d'un révolutionnaire.* Paris, 1891.
*Rémusat, Charles de : *Correspondance pendant la Restauration.* 6 vols. Paris, 1883-6.
*Senior, N. W. : Conversations with Monsieur Thiers, Guizot and other distinguished persons during the Second Empire. 2 vols. London, 1878. Journal kept in France and Italy. 2 vols. London, 1875.
Serre, Baron de : *Memoirs.* Paris, 1876.
*Talleyrand, Périgord, Ch. M. de : *Mémoires.* 6 vols. Paris, 1890.
Temonie, E. : *L'Abdication du Roi Louis Philippe raconté par lui-même.* Paris, 1851.
*Thiers, L. A. : *Notes et Souvenirs. La Revolution de* 1848. Paris, 1902.
de Tocqueville, A. : *Souvenirs.* Paris, 1864.
Veuillot, L. : *Correspondance.* 7 vols. Paris, 1883-92.
*Veron, M. : *Mémoires d'un Bourgeois de Paris.* 4 vols. Paris, 1851.
Villèle, Comte de : *Mémoires et Correspondances.* 5 vols. Paris, 1887-90.
*Vitrolles, Baron de : *Mémoires et Relations Poltiques.* Paris, 1884.

4. *Newspapers and Periodicals.*
   *Constitutionnel, 1821-40.
   **Journal des Débats*, 1830-45.
   L'Avenir, 1830-31.
   Le Globe, 1821-40.
   Le Commerce, 1836-48.
   *La Réforme, 1840-48.
   *Le National, 1830-48.
   *London Times, 1830-48.
   Quotidienne, 1832-40.
   *Revue Parisienne, July 25, August 25, 1840 (Balzac).
   **L'Album*, Vol. VI., 1822 (Thiers : " Des Littératures classifiés et antiques ").
   **Tablettes Universelles*, Nos. 36 to 58 (Thiers).

5. *Contemporary Literature, Pamphlets, etc.*
   Anonymous : *Discours politiques—pétitions des Réformistes de 1840.* Paris, 1840.
   De l'avenir des idées impérialistes et les changements à opérer dans un songe législatif. Paris, 1840.
   Barrault, C. : *Guerre ou Paix en Orient.* Paris, 1836.
   *Bresson, E. : *Guizot, Thiers et l'Histoire.* Paris, 1835.
   de Carné : *de l'Avenir de la France.* Paris, 1832.
   *Cauchois-Lemiare : *Sur la Crise actuelle.* Lettre à S. A. R. le Duc D'Orléans. Paris, 1827.

BIBLIOGRAPHY

Celliez, H. : *Devoir des Révolutionnaires.* Paris–Brussels, 1840.
Chasserian, F. : *Armée et Marine,* 1847. Paris, n.d.
Chateaubriand, Ch. de : *De la Restauration et de la Monarchie élective.* Paris, 1831.
Considerant, V. : *De la Souveraineté et de la Régence.* Paris, 1842.
Delbousquet, J. : *De la politique de MM. Molé et Thiers à l'égard d'Espagne.* Paris, 1839.
*Dolle, F. : *Réflexions d'un Royaliste.* Paris, 1835.
*Duvergier de Hauranne, P. : *De la politique extérieure et intérieure de la France.* Paris, 1841.
De la Réforme parlementaire et la Réforme élective. Paris, 1847.
Fauvety, Ch. : *Le Système Guizot, Duchâtel et Cie.* Paris, 1846.
*Foinville, "Chevalier" de : *L'École des Ministres.* 2 vols. Paris, 1836.
Groiselliez, F. de : *L'Art de devenir député et même ministre par un oisif qui n'est ni l'un ni l'autre.* Paris, 1846.
de Jouffroy : *Avertissements aux souverains sur les dangers actuels de l'Europe.* Paris, 1830.
*Hugo, V. : *Le roi s'amuse.* Paris, 1834.
*Launay, Viscomte de : *Lettres Parisiennes.* 4 vols. Paris, 1862.
L'École des Journalistes. Paris, 1839.
de Suleau : *Appel à la France sur les véritables causes de la Révolution de 1830.* Paris, 1831.
Thiers, L. A. :
　Sur l'Éloquence Judiciaire. Académie d'Aix, Séance publique, 1818–28.
　Mémoirs sur le Sieur Erard contre le Sieur Martin. Aix, 1820.
　Notice sur la Mistress Bellamy. Paris, 1822.
　Salon de 1822. Paris, 1822.
　Les Pyrénées ou le Midi de la France. Paris, 1822.
　Réflexions sur la réduction de la rente et sur l'état du crédit. Paris, 1824.
　De La Peinture en France. Paris, 1824.
　Le Salon de 1824. Paris, 1903.
　Histoire de la Révolution et de l'Empire. 10 vols. Paris, 1823–8.
　Law et son système de Finances. Paris, 1826 (1858).
　Sur les Mémoires du Maréchal Gouvion de St. Cyr. Paris, 1829.
　Thiers aux électeurs d'Aix, 1830. Paris, 1830.
　Discours addressé par M. Thiers aux électeurs d'Aix en Provence, 1831.
　Discours relatif aux affaires étrangères, 1831. Paris, 1831.
　Discours sur la proposition du général Lamarque, 1831. Paris, 1831.
　De la Monarchie de 1830. Paris, 1831.
　Réponse a M. Pataille, le 13 Juin, 1831. n.d.
　Discours sur les associations. Paris, 1834.
　Discours sur les troubles de Lyon, de Paris et de Clermont Ferrand. Paris, 1834.

BIBLIOGRAPHY

Discours de réception, 1835. Paris, 1835.
Discours comme député de Bouches-du-Rhône, 6 May, 1837. Paris, 1837.
**Rapport sur le projet de loi, relative aux fortifications de Paris*. Paris, 1841.

III. Secondary Sources

1. *General Histories.*
   Cambridge Modern History. 20 vols.
   Cambridge History of British Foreign Policy, 1783–1919.
   Hanotaux, G.: *Histoire de la Nation Française.* Paris, 1922.
   Lavisse, E.: *Histoire de la France Contemporaine depuis la Révolution jusqu'à la Paix de* 1919. Paris, 1922.
   Lavisse et Rambaud: *Histoire Générale.*
2. *Particular Histories.*
   *Barthelemy, J.: *Introduction du régime parlementaire sous la Restauration.* Paris, 1922.
   *Blanc, L.: *Histoire de dix ans.* 5 vols. Paris.
   Histoire du Travail. Paris.
   *Bourgeois, E.: *Manuel historique de la politique étrangère.* 3 vols. Paris, 1910.
   Modern France. 2 vols. Cambridge, 1919.
   *Calmon-Levy: *Histoire Parlementaire des Finances de France.*
   Challamel, A.: *Histoire de la Liberté en France depuis* 1789. Paris, 1886.
   Cormenin, L.: *Orateurs Parlementaires.* 2 vols. Paris, 1838.
   Dairnwell, G.: *Histoire de MM. Thiers et Guizot.* Paris, 1842.
   Darest, M. C.: *Histoire de la Restauration.* 2 vols. Paris, 1879.
   Daudet, E.: *Histoire de la Restauration.* Paris, 1882.
   Le Procès des Ministres en 1830. Paris, 1881.
   D'Ault-Dumesnil, E.: *Relation de l'expédition d'Afrique et de la conquête d'Alger.* Paris, 1869.
   *Debidour, A.: *Histoire des rapports de l'Église et l'État en France,* 1789–1870. Paris, 1880.
   De Grandmaison: *La Congrégation,* 1801–1830. Paris, 1830.
   *De Riancey, H.: *Histoire Critique de la Liberté de l'Enseignement en France.* 2 vols. Paris, 1844.
   Dickenson, G. L.: *Revolution and Reaction in Modern France.* London. 1892.
   *Du Bled, V.: *Histoire de la Monarchie de Juillet.* 2 vols. Paris, 1877.
   Du Camp, M.: *L'Attentat Fieschi.* Paris, 1877.
   *Dulaure et Augis: *Histoire de la Révolution depuis* 1814 *jusqu'à* 1830. Paris, 1834–8.

BIBLIOGRAPHY

*Duvergier de Hauranne, P. : *Histoire du gouvernment parlementaire en France.* 10 vols. Paris, 1860–72.
Fabre, A. : *La révolution de 1830 et le vrai parti républicain.* 2 vols. Paris, 1833.
*Festy, O. : *Le Mouvement ouvrier au début de la Monarchie de Juillet.* n. d.
*Girandeau, C. : *La Presse Périodique.* Paris, 1868.
Gomard, P. : *Les origines de la Légende Napoléonienne.* Paris, 1906.
Grimaud, A. : *Histoire de la liberté de l'enseignement en France.* Paris, 1898.
Guichen, Vicomte de : *La Révolution de Juillet 1830 et l'Europe.* Paris, 1906.
Hamel, E. : *Histoire de France depuis la Révolution jusqu'à la chute du Seconde Empire.* 7 vols. Paris, 1881–91.
*Hatin : *La Presse.*
*d'Haussonville, Comte J. : *Histoire de la politique extérieure de la Monarchie de Juillet.* Paris, 1850.
*Heine, H. : *Lutèce.* 10 vols. Hamburg, 1875.
d'Hericault, Ch. : *Histoire anecdotique de France.* 6 vols. Paris, 1877–91.
*Hillebrand, K. : *Geschichte Frankreichs.* 2 vols. Leipzig, 1877–9.
Hugo, V. : *Actes et Paroles.* 3 vols. Paris, 1875.
Choses Vues. Paris, 1900.
Jaurez : *Histoire Socialiste.* 18 vols. Paris.
*Juste, Th. : *La Révolution de Juillet, 1830.* Brussels, 1888.
*La Hodde, L. de : *Histoire des Sociétés Secrètes en France de 1830 à 1848.* Paris, 1850.
Leroy-Beaulieu, A. : *Les Catholiques libéraux de 1830 à nos jours.* Paris, 1885.
*Levasseur, C. : *Histoire des classes ouvrierer en France depuis 1789.* 2 vols. 1867.
Malo, H. : *Une Muse et Sa Mère.* Paris, 1924.
Malo, H. : *La Gloire du Viscomte de Launay.* Paris, 1925.
Martin, H. : *Histoire de France de 1789 à nos jours.* Paris, 1879.
*Mazade, Ch. de : *Cinquante Années d'histoire contemporaine.* Paris, 1884.
Nettement, A. : *Histoire de la Restauration.* 8 vols. Paris, 1860–72.
Neuville-Bargemart, B. I. de : *Les journées de Juillet.* n. d.
Petit, Abbé J. A. : *Histoire contemporaine de la France.* 12 vols. Paris, 1881–9.
Pierre, P. : *Histoire des Assemblées Politiques en France.* Paris, 1877.
Rambaud, A. : *Histoire de la Civilization Française.* 2 vols. Paris, 1887.
Histoire contemporaine de la France. Paris, 1898.
Histoire des doctrines économiques. Paris, 1902.

BIBLIOGRAPHY

Saint Simon : *Œuvres*, Vol. I. Paris, 1865–78.
Sainte-Beuve : *Causeries du Lundi*, I. XII. XIV. XV. Paris, 1857–62.
  Nouveaux Lundis, III. Paris, 1863–78.
Sarrans, B. : *Lafayette et la Révolution de 1830*. Paris, 1834.
Scherer, E. : *Études sur la littérature contemporaire*. 9 vols. Paris, 1885.
Seignobos, Ch. : *Political History of Europe since 1814*. New York, 1907.
*Stern, L. : *Geschichte der Socialen Bewegung in Frankreich*. 3 vols. 1850.
*Thureau-Dangin, P. : *Histoire de la Monarchie de Juillet*. 4 vols. Paris, 1887–92.
  L'Église et l'État sous la Monarchie de Juillet. Paris, 1880.
  Le Parti Libéral sous la Restauration. Paris, 1876.
*Tschernoff, I. : *Le parti républicain sous la Monarchie de Juillet*. Paris, 1901.
*Vaulabelle, A. de : *Histoire des deux Restaurations*. 8 vols. Paris, 1857–8.
Viel-Castel, L. de : *Histoire de la Restauration*. 2 vols. Paris, 1860–78.
*Weill, G. : *Histoire du parti républicain en France, 1814–30*. Paris, 1900.
  L'École Saint Simonienne. Paris, 1896.
  La France sous la Monarchie Constitutionelle. Paris, 1902.
  Les élections législatives depuis 1789. Paris, 1895.

3. *Biographies.*

*Arcay, Joseph : *Notes inédites sur Monsieur Thiers*. Paris, 1888.
*Audebrand, Ph : *Nos Révolutionnaires*. Paris, 1886.
*Barante, Baron de : *Vie politique de Royer Collard*. Paris, 1861.
Bardoux, A. : *Chateaubriand*. Paris, 1893.
  Guizot. Paris, 1894.
Bontard, Abbé Ch. : *La Mennais*. 2 vols. Paris, 1908.
*Blanc, L. : *Le Cabinet de Monsieur Thiers*. Paris, 1871.
*Borlay, F. : *Notice Biographique sur Monsieur Thiers*. Paris, 1839.
Castille, H. : *Les Hommes et les Mœurs sous la règne de Louis Philippe*. Paris, 1853.
Chabrier, A. : *Les orateurs politiques de la France*. Paris, 1885.
Charavay, E. : *Le général La Fayette*. Paris, 1898.
*Crozales, J. de : *Guizot*. n. d.
Faguet, E. : *Politiques et Moralistes du XIX siècle*. Paris, 1891.
Flers, Marquis de : *Le roi Louis Philippe*. Paris, 1891.
Foisset, Th. : *Le Comte de Montalembert*. Paris, 1895.
Frank, F. : *Thiers, sa vie*. Paris, 1877.
*Gastaldy, A. : *L'origine d'Adolphe Thiers*. 1878.
*d'Ideville, H. : *Le Maréchal Bugeaud*. Paris, 1881.
*Lacombe, H. de : *Vie de Berryer*. Paris, 1894.

BIBLIOGRAPHY

*Laya, A. : *Études politiques sur Monsieur Thiers*. Paris, 1846.
Histoire populaire de Monsieur Thiers. Paris, 1872.
*Lecaunet, E. : *Berryer, sa vie et ses œuvres*. 3 vols. Paris, 1893.
Montalembert. 3 vols. 1894.
*Le Goff : *Thiers*. London, 1878.
Mazade, Ch. de : *Le Comte de Serre*. Paris, 1879.
Meaux, Vicomte de : *Montalembert*. Paris, 1897.
*Mirabeau, Comtesse de : *Talleyrand et la Monarchie de Juillet*.
*Pellison : *Les orateurs politiques de la France de 1830 à nos jours*. Paris, 1898.
Prokesch-Osten : *Méhémet-Ali*. Vienna, 1877.
Rémusat, Ch. de : *Thiers*. Paris, 1885.
Rouquette, Jules : *Célébrités contemporaines*. Paris, n. d.
Sainte-Beuve, Ch. A. : *Portraits littéraires*. Vol. III. Paris, 1864.
*Simon, J. : *Thiers, Guizot, Rémusat*. Paris, 1885.
Simpson, F. A. : *The Rise of Louis Napoleon*. London, 1909.
*Spuller, E. : *Royer-Collard*. Paris, 1895.
Thirria : *Napoléon III avant l'Empire*. 2 vols. Paris, 1895.
La Duchesse de Berry. Paris, 1900.
Thouvenel, E. : *Épisodes d'histoire contemporaire*. Paris, 1892.
*Thureau-Dangin, P. : *Royalistes et Républicains*. Paris, 1874.
Trognon, A. : *Marie Amélie*. Paris, 1876.
*Tschernoff, I. : *Louis Blanc*. Paris, 1904.
*Veyssiere, A. : *Études sur la vie parlementaire de Monsieur Thiers*. Martel-Valeat, 1884.
*Wallace, Sir R. : *The Englishman in Paris*. London, 1892.
*Zervort, E. : *Thiers*. Paris, 1892.

4. *Magazine Articles, Monographs, etc.*

Anonymous : " Thiers." *Blackwood's Magazine*, XLIII. 311–33. 1835.
Anonymous : " Reminiscences of Thiers." *Fraser's Magazine*, XXVII. 289–301. 1843.
*Benoit, Fernand : *Monsieur Thiers, à la conquête de Paris, avec trente quatre lettres inédites*. Le Correspondant. Paris, 1922.
*Blanc, Ch. : *Le Cabinet de Monsieur Thiers*. Paris, 1871.
*Camino, Princesse de : *Réfutation de Lucien Bonaparte suivant Thiers*. Paris, 1845.
*De Carné : " La Monarchie de 1830." *Revue des Deux Mondes*, May 1853.
*Dolle, F. : *Dubois et Monsieur Thiers*. Paris, 1842.
Facour-Gayette, C. : " L'ambassade de Talleyrand à Londres." *Revue des Études Historiques*, May 1921.
*Faguet, E. : " Thiers." *Revue des Deux Mondes*, November-December, 1920.
*Lanzac, H. : *A. Thiers*. Paris, 1864.
*Loeve-Veymars : " Thiers." *Revue des Deux Mondes*, 1835.

BIBLIOGRAPHY

Malo, H.: " Monsieur Thiers et les Artistes." *Revue de Paris*, July 1, 1924.

*Manguin, G.: " Thiers et son histoire de Florence." *Chroniques des lettres franco-italiens*. Grenoble, January 1918.

*Mantoux: " Talleyrand en 1830." *Revue Historique*, 1902, p. 268.

*Napoléon, Prince: " Une page d'histoire contemporaire—Monsieur Thiers et les Napoléons (Jerome)." *Lettres et documents inédits*. Paris, 1873.

*Pinard, A.: *L'histoire à l'audience*, 1840-48. Paris, 1848.

Salverte: " Histoire de la Révolution française." *Revue encyclopédique*, XLII. 374-95, and XLIV. 630-83.

Semonville, Marquis de: " Mémoires sur la Révolution de Juillet." *Revue de Paris*, Vols. 94-95, pp. 63-101.

Veuillot, Louis: " M. A. Thiers." *Revue des Deux Mondes*, IV. 641-98.

INDEX

A

ABERDEEN, Lord, 325
Address of the 221, 100
Adelaide, Madame, 119-120
Adrianople, Treaty of, 99
Aix-en-Provence, 8, 9
Algiers, 99, 187-188, 221, 275, 308
Alibaud, Louis, 222, 231
Ancona Expedition, 160, 255
Argenson, Voyer d', 136, 181
Argout, Comte d', 169
Arlatan, Lauris d', 12, 13-14
Arnaud, Doctor, 12

B

Balzac, Honoré de, 262
Barante, Baron de, 229
Barrot, Odilon, on July 26, 105; in service of July Monarchy, 130; supporter of Monarchy during August Days, 140; opposition to foreign policy of Périer, 156; protests against *Résistance* Ministry, 163; and Thiers 1836, 218; and the Coalition, 256; supports Thiers' Second Cabinet, 278; opposition to Guizot, 293; demands electoral reform, 317; platform, 325; approaches Extreme Left, 329; and Reform banquets, 335; agrees to test legality of banquets, 338; refuses Thiers' counsel, 341; plan for *acte d'accusation*, 343; harangues National Guard, 348; suggested by Thiers for Cabinet, 351; opposes Bugeaud, 352; futile attempt to calm mob, 355
Beaumont, Gustave de, 309, 311
Belgium, 140, 142, 147, 285-287, 307
Béranger, Pierre, 117
Berry, Duchesse de, 164, 171
Berryer, Antoine, 164, 256-258, 338
Blanc, Louis, 347, 353
Bonaparte, Jerome, 246
Bonaparte, Napoleon, 265, 281, 305
Bonapartists, 264-266
Bonnefoux, Émilie, 17-18

Breton Resistance, League of, 86
Broglie, Duc de : in first Ministry of July Monarchy, 127; and the clubs, 139; attacks of Third Party, 185; retirement, 187; again President of the Council, 190; retirement, 1836, 212; suggested to replace Molé, 254; consulted by Thiers, 272; disapproves Thiers' policy in Egypt, 286
Broglie Cabinet, 139, 190, 212
Bugeaud, General, 169, 174, 183, 220 237-238, 332, 351-352

C

Canestrini, Giuseppe, 249
Carbonari, 86
Carlsbad Conference, 1830, 141
Carrel, Armand, 87, 123, 140, 181
Cavaignac, General, 111, 123
Chambolle, Comte de, 262, 338
Charles of Artois : and the Charter, 22; accession as Charles X, 51; character, 51; coronation, 69; resignation of Martignac, 83; speech from throne, 1830, 99-100; and address of 221, 100; Ordinances of July, 103; stubbornness, 110; concession to Deputies, 115
Charter of 1814 : provisions, 21-22; Article XIV, 104; revised version of 1830, 127
Chateaubriand, François, 69, 251
Chenier, André and Joseph, 1, 5
Church : Law of Sacrilege, 73; attitude to July Monarchy, 131; attitude to Duchesse de Berry, 172; Young Catholics of 1840, 294; Young Catholics' demand for educational reform, 312; anti-Jesuit agitation, 313
Clubs : Society of Order and Progress, 137; *Condamnés Politiques*, 137; *Aide-toi et le ciel t'aidera*, 137; Friends of the People, 137; riot of October, 1830, 142; riot of December, 1830, 146; revival of clubs, 1832, 159; Society of the Rights of Man 181; " The Seasons," 263-264

INDEX

Coalition, the: plans, 256-260; attacks Molé, 260; collapse of Molé Cabinet, 261; effect of, in France, 266
Constant, Benjamin, 71
Constitutionnel, 87, 184, 214, 262, 303, 317
Cottendorf, Baron Cotta de, 40-41
Cousin, Victor, 55, 257, 314, 353
Cracow, 157, 224, 327

D

Decazes, Duc de, 22
Dino, Duchesse de, 211, 212, 239
Doctrinaires: *see* Guizot, Broglie, etc.; also 18, 23, 48, 49, 254
Don Carlos, 233-236
Dosne, Alexis, 200, 247
Dosne, Madame Eurydice: early life, 200; acquaintance with Thiers, 201; character, 200; social qualities, 203; interest in politics, 203; influence with Thiers, 204; described by Duchesse de Dino, 247; and crisis of 1839, 262; and Molé's difficulties, 272; reproves Thiers for attitude to Reform banquets, 331-332
Drouyn de Lhuys, Edouard, 335
Duchâtel, Comte, 213, 254, 339
Dupin, Charles: and Paris journalists, 105; drafts Deputies' proclamation, 111; and the clubs, 139; and Talleyrand, 1832, 163; displeased with Louis Philippe, 165; efforts to become Minister 1832, 165; and Third Party, 184; and Ministerial crisis of 1835, 189; and public education, 314
Dupont de l'Eure, Jacques, 127, 139, 143, 335

E

Education, 312-315
Egypt: plans of Mehemet Ali for, 186; Thiers and Egypt, 226; English interests in, 278; Thiers and Mehemet Ali, 279-287; final settlement, 293
Electoral reform: demands of Barrot, Rémusat, Thiers, 325; *see also* Reform banquets.
England: and Louis Philippe, 141; and Belgium, 142; and French alliance, 214; and Thiers, 233; and Spanish Liberals, 233; Tahiti, 311; Pritchard affair, 312; Spanish marriages, 328; *see also* Palmerston.
English Constitution, 60-63, 91
Étienne, Charles, 58, 184
Exhibition of Industry, 175, 184

F

Fabre, Auguste and Victorin, 134
February Cabinet: composition, 213; cold reception of, 214; declaration of policy, 215; economic plans, 219; Algiers, 221; Alibaud's attempt, 222; foreign policy of reconciliation, 223-232; Cracow, 224; Austrian marriage, 229; Spanish Liberals, 233-238; retirement, 239
February Revolution, 346-358
Fieschi, 192
Flocon, Ferdinand, 137, 347, 353
France: *see* Charter of 1814, Decazes Ministry, Richelieu Ministry, Villèle Ministry, Charles X, Polignac Ministry, July Revolution, Laffitte Cabinet, *Résistance* Cabinet, Thiers' First Cabinet, Molé Cabinet, Soult Cabinet, Thiers' Second Ministry, Guizot, February Revolution.

G

Garnier-Pagès, 136, 163, 181, 335, 338-339
Gay, Sophie, 59
Gerard, François, 29
Gerard, Marshal, 127, 188-189, 233
Girardin, Delphine de, 243, 280-281, 257-258, 273, 295
Girardin, Émile de, 257, 295, 315, 357
Globe, 82, 87, 98
Greece, 75-76
Guizot, F. P. G.: attitude in 1824, 54; in first Cabinet of July Monarchy, 127; and the clubs, 139; speech at Lisieux, 140; and Doctrinaires, 156; Ancona, 160; and Talleyrand, 1832, 164; in Soult Ministry, 168; differences with Thiers, 193; competes with Thiers for Ministry, 1836, 212; in Molé Cabinet, 254; and the Coalition, 256; supports Thiers in attack on Molé, 259; ambassador to England, 1840, 274; deserts Thiers over Egyptian question, 286; Minister of Foreign Affairs, 292; blindness of, 294; parliamentary corruption under, 295; public education, 312; attempts to outwit Palmerston and Spanish marriage question, 326; and Reform banquets, 335; unpopularity of, 346; resignation, 349; errors of judgment during the February Days, 349; presence with Royal Family, February 24, 354

INDEX

H

Harrispe, General, 233
Hauranne, Duvergier de : identified, 258 ; and Thiers, 1841, 296; platform for electoral reforms, 325 ; joins with Barrot in approaching Extreme Left, 1847, 329 ; plan for *acte d'accusation*, 343
Hugo, Victor, 317

I

Ingres, Jean-Auguste, 244
Italy :
  Modena, 147, 181, 247-248
  Naples, 181, 247-248
  Papal States, 147, 160, 181, 247-248, 327
  Piedmont, 181, 247-248

J

Jesuits, 314-315
Joinville, Prince de, 205
July Revolution, 102-120

L

Lacordaire, Père, 294, 312
La Fayette, General : in 1824, 53 ; in 1829, 86; and Constitutionalist Deputies during July Days, 110-111 ; at Hôtel de Ville, 111 ; and Republican sentiments, 113; interview with Louis Philippe, 120; and the clubs, 142 ; reorganization of National Guard, 146; parting shot at Monarchy, 146
Laffitte, Jacques : patron of Young Liberals, 55 ; collaborates with Thiers, 71 ; during the July Days, 110 ; and the clubs, 139, 142 ; protests against *Résistance* Ministry, 163
Laffitte Cabinet : weakness, 143-146; retirement, 148
Lamartine, Alphonse de : remark about Thiers, 93 ; and return of Napoleon's ashes, 281 ; attacks Thiers as President of Council, 277; and Regency Bill, 303 ; advocate of lower classes, 317 ; and Reform banquets, 338
Lamoricière, General, 354
Lasteyrie, Charles de, 337
Launay, Viscomte de : see Delphine de Girardin.
Ledru-Rollin, A. P. A., 303, 312, 337, 339, 347, 353
Legitimists : in August, 133 ; co-operation with clubs, 147 ; attitude to foreign policy, 147 ; Duchesse de Berry, 164 ; in dynastic opposition, *see* Berryer.
Leopold of Belgium, 285, 287
Liberal Catholics, 132
Liéven, Princesse de, 284, 312
Louis XVIII : and the Charter, 21-22; early government, 23 ; fear of White Terror, 23 ; appoints Villèle, 49 ; reactionary, 49 ; death, 51
Louis Philippe d'Orléans : during Restoration, 24 ; indirectly referred to in *National*, 96 ; not a conspirator, 113 ; suggested for throne, 114 ; during early July Days, 118 ; arrival at Paris, 119 ; visits to Hôtel de Ville, 120 ; accepts the crown, 126 ; promises, 126 ; and the clubs, 142 ; personal diplomacy, 1830, 140 ; and European Liberals, 147 ; relations with Laffitte, 148 ; attitude to Périer, 160 ; virtual head of *Résistance* Ministry, 160 ; and the Legitimists, 164 ; abandons personal rule, 1832, 165 ; asks advice of Thiers, 166 ; and Third Party, 187 ; names de Broglie President of Council, 167 ; assumes direction of affairs, 187; attitude to Spanish Liberals, 189 ; Fieschi's bomb, 192 ; personal interests in foreign policy, 1836, 208-210 ; wearies of de Broglie, 211 ; Ministerial crisis 1836, 212; and February Cabinet, 214; attitude to Thiers upon retirement of February Cabinet, 243 ; controls Molé's Cabinet, 254 ; collapse of Molé Cabinet, 261 ; and Thiers' Second Cabinet, 274 ; and European affairs, 1840, 278 ; alarm at Thiers' policy in Egypt, 280 ; sends for Guizot, 286 ; conference at death of heir, 302 ; interview with Thiers, 302 ; determination to keep Guizot, 317 ; relations with Thiers in 1847, 334 ; summons Thiers on February 24, 350; conference with Thiers' friends, 354 ; tragic review of National Guard, 356 ; abdication and departure from Paris, 356-357
Louis, Baron, 64, 71, 127, 131, 144, 149, 317
Lyons, 182-183

M

Madagascar, 308
Manuel, Jacques : relations with the young Thiers, 26 ; expelled from Chamber of Deputies, 53
Marie-Amélie d'Orléans : interview with Thiers, July 1830, 118 ; character, 119 ; and Austrian marriage, 227 ; at close of February Revolution, 357
Marmont, Marshal, 103, 110, 115

INDEX

Marrast, Armand, 137, 317, 338, 339, 347
Martignac Ministry, 81–82, 83
Mazzini, Giuseppe, 181
Mehemet-Ali: *see* Egypt.
Metternich, Prince Clément de: during Restoration, 141 *sqq.*; attitude to July Monarchy, 141; revolts in Europe, 160; Carlsbad Conference, 141; attitude to Duchesse de Berry, 171; opinion of Thiers as President, 215; visit of Duc d'Orléans, 228; Austrian marriage, 230–232; Alibaud affair, 232; interview with Thiers at Como, 251–252
Michelet, Jules, 314
Mignet, François: meeting with Thiers, 9; lawyer at Aix, 15; and Talleyrand, 32; opinion of France in 1823, 48; *History of the French Revolution*, 57; with Thiers on *National*, 87; in service of July Monarchy, 130; recalls Thiers to politics, 305; letter to Thiers in regard to prospects in 1845, 320–321
Molé, Comte, 143, 213, 269, 274, 349, 350
Molé Cabinet, 269, 254–255
Montalembert, Charles de, 294
Montalivet, Comte de, 143, 148, 149, 312
Montebello, Comte de, 226
Mortier, Marshal, 189–190, 192
Mutuallistes, 181

N

National: founding, 88–89; theories, 90; prophesies in January the Revolution of July, 95; possible compliment to Louis Philippe, 97; fined for seditious remarks and Address of 221, 98; on July 26–27, 1830, 105; presses dismantled and repaired, 108; and riots of August, 1830, 139; advocates electoral reform, 317; and Reform banquets, 339; and February Revolution, 347–349
National Guard: abolished 1827, 74; reappearance of, July 1830, 109; reorganization of, 146; attitude on February 23, 1848, 348; King reviews for last time, 356
Nemours, Duc de, 350
Nesselrode, Count, 141

O

Orléans, Duc d': marriage prospects, 227; journey to Prussia and Austria, 229–232; supports Thiers' policy in Egypt, 285; death, 298; character, 298
Ozanam, Frédéric, 294

P

Palmerston, Lord: entente with Louis Philippe in regard to Belgium, 147; Spain, 189, 210; and February Cabinet, 209; and Mehemet-Ali, 1839, 267; the Egyptian question, 1840, 278–287; and Guizot, 326; rapprochement of Palmerston and Thiers, 1846, 326–327
Paris: change in, 1824, 54; at time of July Revolution, 103; riots during July Monarchy, 183; during the February Days, 346–358
Passy, Hippolyte: in Cabinet, 184; Third Party, 184; during the February Days, 353
Périer, Casimir: in 1824, 54; patron of Liberals, 55; during the July Days, 110; member of the Provisional Government, 112; interpretation of July Revolution, 126; Minister without portfolio, 127; and Charter of 1814, 128; Thiers' admiration for, 131; and the clubs, 139; elected President of the Deputies, 143; President of the Council 1831, 148; policies, see *Résistance* Ministry, methods; attitude to Thiers, 151; death, 160; attitude of Louis Philippe to, 160
Place Saint-Georges: acquired by Thiers, 129; the salon, its importance in political life of Paris, 204; art collections, 249; the study of Thiers, 305–306
Poland: after July Revolution, 147, 157; *see also* Cracow.
Polignac, Jules Duc de: Minister, 83; character, 83; and the Press, 98; foreign policy, 99; refusal to heed Deputies' petition, 110
Press: laws of 1824, 55; "Vandal Bill," 74; under Martignac, 82; and Polignac, 87, 98; the July Ordinances, 104–105; a newspaper revolution, 104; Protest of the journalists, 108; the Ministerial crisis of 1839, 262; radical papers in Paris before the February Revolution, 347; see also *National, Constitutionnel, Globe, Tribune*.
Pritchard affair, 312
Prussia: and the Restoration, 50; Treaty of Adrianople, 99; and the July Revolution, 141; the visit of the Duc d'Orléans to Berlin, 230; involved in the Egyptian question, 282; reforms in, 333
Puyraveau, Audrey de, 110

376

INDEX

Q

Quinet, Edgar, 314

R

Raspail, François, 136, 137
Reform banquets: *see* Barrot, de Hauranne, Thiers, de Rémusat, *National*.
Rémusat, Charles de: signs Protest of journalists, 106; in Thiers' Second Cabinet, 274-276; plan for electoral reform, 325; the Reform banquets, 332; effort to forestall test banquet, 339; suggested for Cabinet, 351
Republicans: *see* La Fayette, Constant, Clubs.
Résistance Ministry: composition, 148; policy towards clubs, 160; foreign policy, 148; Ancona, 160; death of Périer, 160; Louis Philippe virtual head of *Résistance*, 163; protest of Deputies against, 163; and labour troubles of 1834, 182; opposition of Third Party, 185
Richelieu Ministry, 23
Risorgimento: *see* Italy.
Romanticism, 23-24
Rossi, Pellegrino, 315
Rouchon-Guiges, 16, 27, 78
Rouen, 317
Royer-Collard, 100, 213
Russia: Treaty of Adrianople, 99; attitude to July Monarchy, 141; Carlsbad Conference, 141; Egyptian question, 186; and French policy of conciliation, 224; Treaty of Unkiar Skelessi, 266; and Mehemet-Ali, 186, 279-287

S

Sainte-Aulaire, Comte de, 285
Salvandy, Achille de, 312
Sand, Georges, 317
Scheffer, André, 118
Sébastiani, Marshal, 118, 143, 149
September Laws, 192-193
Soult, Marshal, 149, 167, 188, 233, 263, 267-269
Spain: revolution of 1820, 33; French expedition to, 50; attitude of France to Spanish Liberals in 1834, 189; and Palmerston in 1835, 210; early attitude of Thiers to Spanish question, 217; relation to French interests in Algiers, 221; reactionaries interfere in Austrian marriage proposal, 228; relations with February Cabinet in 1836, 232-239; Molé's negotiations with, 254; Spanish marriages, 328-329
Switzerland, 225

T

Tahiti, 308, 311-312
Talleyrand-Périgord, Prince Charles de: and Mignet, 32; meeting with Thiers, 39; early relations, 40; Thiers' *History*, 58-63; sent to England 1830, 141; intrigues with King after Périer's death, 163; and Thiers' election to Academy, 179; considered as Ministerial candidate, 188; letter to Thiers, 1835, 193; disgust at Thiers' resignation, 239; a visit from Thiers, 247
Teste, Charles, 136
Thiers, Louis Adolphe: birth, 4; childhood, 6; schooling, 7; meeting with Mignet, 9; earliest works of, 13; and d'Arlatan, 12; and Doctor Arnaud, 12; *Vauvenargues*, 13-14; lawyer at Aix, 15-16; departure from Aix, 18-21; love affair at Aix, 17-18; arrival in Paris, 25; Secretary to La Rochefoucauld, 26; meeting with Manuel, 26; and the *Constitutionnel*, 26, 28; Salon de 1822, 29-30; and Gerard, 29; articles in *L'Album*, 30; *Life of Mistress Bellamy*, 31; *Les Pyrénées*, 33-35; and Restoration Government, 35-36; journey to Spain, 38; visit to Aix, 37-38; presentation to Talleyrand, 39; early relations, 40; stockholder in *Constitutionnel*, 40-41; debut in Parisian society, 41, 42; political theories of, 1828, 43-45; *History of the French Revolution*, 56-67; letter to Étienne about *History*, 57; attitude to English Government, 60-63, 91; defects in *History*, 63; relations with Baron Louis, 64; hero-worshipper, 64; attitude to people, 65; not an apostle of success, 65; contract with publisher, 67; *John Law*, 72; collaborates with Laffitte, 71; letter from Villèle, 72; Salon de 1824, 76-77; writes on style, 79; journey to Provence, 1827, 80; opinion of war, 84; military and political careers, 84; attitude to bourgeoisie, 93; *le roi règne et ne gouverne pas*, 94; and Polignac Ministry, 95; and Address of 221, 100; addresses journalists July 26, 1830, 106; articles in *National*, 106-109; retires to Montmorency, 108; returns to Paris, 113; suggestion of Louis Philippe for throne, 114; drafts Orleanist proclama-

377

INDEX

tion, 115; mission to Neuilly, 118–121; presents friends to Louis Philippe, 123; acquisition of Place Saint-Georges, 129; in service of July Monarchy, 130; admiration for Périer, 131; Under-Secretary of Finances, 131; Secretary-General of Finances, 144; and Laffitte, 143; debut in Chamber of Deputies, 144; poor impression of first speech, 145; relation to Périer, 151; relation to Laffitte, 149; *La Monarchie de Juillet*, 150; improvement as orator, 153; defends Périer's foreign policy successfully, 157; defence of hereditary peerage, 158; attitude to Ancona expedition, 160; and Talleyrand, 1832, 164; interview with Louis Philippe in regard to new Ministry, 166; Minister of the Interior, 168; defence of policy towards Legitimists, 170; attitude to agitators of the Left, 171; pursuit and capture of Duchesse de Berry, 173; Minister of Public Works, 175–176; and public buildings, 176; and fortifications of Paris, 177; and art, 177; the *History of Florence*, 177, 248; election to Academy, 178; returns to Ministry of the Interior, 181; theory of equality, 182; and labour troubles 1834, 182; views on Algiers, 188; and Ministerial crisis, 1835, 190; in second Broglie Cabinet, 1835, 191; attempt on life of King, 1836, 192; and September Laws, 193; differences with Guizot, 193; relations with father and family, 196–198; acquaintance with Madame Dosne, 201; betrothal and marriage, 202; influence of Madame Dosne, 204; his love of ceremony, 205; break with de Broglie, 211; rival with Guizot for Ministry 1836, 212–213; Thiers' Cabinet 1836, *see* February Cabinet; charges of Jaubert, 219; and colonization, 221; after Alibaud's attempt, 222; attitude to Liberal movements on French frontiers, 224–225; Thiers and Austrian marriage of the heir to the French throne, 223–232; comment upon failure of Austrian marriage plans, 232; and Metternich, 1836, 232; attitude to Spain, 232; resignation, 238; attitude to Monarchy upon retirement, 239; Italian interests, 244–246; relations with Jerome Bonaparte, 246; library, 250; *History of the Consulate and the Empire*, 251, 304; interview with Metternich at Como, 251–252; opposed to Molé's policies, 256–257; agreement with Barrot and Guizot, 256–257; leads attack on Molé, 259–261; as orator in 1839, 268–269; Second Ministry, *see* Thiers' Second Ministry; leader of dynastic opposition, 292; attacks Right of Search Treaty, 297; and death of Duc d'Orléans, 299; journey to Germany, 304–305; attacks on Jesuits, 314; first demand for electoral reform, 317; charges Guizot Ministry with electoral corruption, 320; platform for electoral reform, 325; overtures to Palmerston, 1840, 326–327; attitude to Extreme Left, 1847, 330; attitude to Reform banquets, 330–335; sympathy for Italy, 333; and Louis Philippe, 1847, 334; interferes in Reform banquets, 337; efforts to restrain Barrot, 340; efforts to restrain Left, 340; failure, 342; interview with Molé, 350; interview with Louis Philippe, 350; unofficial Cabinet formed, 353; return to Place Saint-Georges, 358

Thiers' Second Ministry: composition, 274; policy of "transaction," 276–277; foreign policy, 278; and Egypt, 278–287; retirement, 287; economic improvement of France in 1840, 289; increases in armament, 290

Thiers, Madame Élise: marriage, 201; beauty and social qualities, 202; described by Duchesse de Dino, 247; referred to by *Viscomte de Launay*, 280

Thiers, Pierre Louis Marie: marriage, 4; reappearances, 196–197

Third Party: beginning, 184, 185; attitude to Laffitte, 185; attacks de Broglie, 185–186; and Ministerial crisis, 1834, 187.

de Tocqueville, Alexis de, 330
Toulouse, 317
Trélat, 136
Tribune, 136, 137, 181

U

Ultras: in 1814, 21; and the "White Terror," 23; upon accession of Charles X, 51; demand for indemnity, 70–71; Law of Sacrilege, 51; Press laws, 55, 74; July Ordinances, 103
United States of America, 187, 316

V

Vauvenargues, 13–14
Vavin, 337, 349
Veron, L., 262

INDEX

Veuillot, Louis, 294

Villèle Ministry: Villèle, 49; policies, 51; gradual reaction, 49; and indemnity for Ultras, 70–71; anonymous letter to Thiers, 72; foreign policy, 75; Ministerial crisis, 81

Villemain, François, 55, 312

Vivien, 257, 274

W

Walewski, Comte Alexandre, 262, 280